# THE NEW
# MARKET
# WIZARDS

# THE NEW MARKET WIZARDS

## CONVERSATIONS WITH
## AMERICA'S TOP TRADERS

## JACK D. SCHWAGER

JOHN WILEY & SONS, INC.

New York  •  Chichester  •  Brisbane  •  Toronto  •  Singapore

This text is printed on acid-free paper.

Copyright © 1992 by Jack D. Schwager
Published by John Wiley & Sons, Inc.
Published by special arrangement with HarperCollins, Inc.

All rights reserved. Published simultaneously in Canada.

*Library of Congress Cataloging-in-Publication Data*:

ISBN 0-471-13236-5

Printed in the United States of America

10  9  8  7  6  5  4  3  2  1

*To my family*
*Jo Ann*
*Daniel*
*Zachary*
*Samantha*
*Who are all very special to me*
*With love*

More is learned from one's errors than from one's successes.

—Primo Levi

I must create a system or be enslaved by another man's.

—William Blake

# Contents

# *Preface*

Here's what I believe:

1. The markets are not random. I don't care if the number of academicians who have argued the efficient market hypothesis would stretch to the moon and back if laid end to end; they are simply wrong.
2. The markets are not random, because they are based on human behavior, and human behavior, especially mass behavior, is not random. It never has been, and it probably never will be.
3. There is no holy grail or grand secret to the markets, but there are many patterns that can lead to profits.
4. There are a million ways to make money in markets. The irony is that they are all very difficult to find.
5. The markets are always changing, and they are always the same.
6. The secret to success in the markets lies not in discovering some incredible indicator or elaborate theory; rather, it lies within each individual.
7. To excel in trading requires a combination of talent and extremely hard work—(surprise!) the same combination required for excellence in any field. Those seeking success by buying the latest $300 or even $3,000 system, or by following the latest hot tip, will never find the answer because they haven't yet understood the question.

8. Success in trading is a worthy goal, but it will be worthless if it is not accompanied by success in your life (and I use the word *success* here without monetary connotation).

In conducting the interviews for this book and its predecessor, *Market Wizards,* I became absolutely convinced that winning in the markets is a matter of skill and discipline, not luck. The magnitude and consistency of the winning track records compiled by many of those I interviewed simply defy chance. I believe the Market Wizards provide role models for what it takes to win in the markets. Those seeking quick fortunes should be discouraged at the onset.

I have strived to reach two audiences: the professionals who have staked careers in the markets or are serious students of the markets, and the lay readers who have a general interest in the financial markets and a curiosity about those who have won dramatically in an arena where the vast majority loses. In order to keep the book accessible to the layperson, I have tried to avoid particularly esoteric topics and have included explanations wherever appropriate. At the same time, I have strived to maintain all core ideas so that there would be no loss of meaningful information to those with a good working knowledge of the markets. I think this book should be as meaningful to the layperson as to the professional simply because the elements that determine success in trading are totally applicable to success in virtually any field or to achieving any meaningful goal.

# *Acknowledgments*

My thanks to those who graciously agreed to be interviewed for this volume, freely sharing their thoughts and experiences while refraining from requests for cosmetic changes when presented with the finished manuscript for review. (Not all those I interviewed proved as accommodating; the exceptions do not appear in this book.) In a number of cases, the traders I interviewed had nothing to gain from participating, at least not monetarily, as they either do not manage any public funds or are not open to further investment. I am particularly appreciative of their cooperation.

I would like to thank my wife, Jo Ann, for reading the original manuscript and providing some well-directed suggestions, all of which were taken. Mostly, I must thank Jo Ann for enduring yet another year as a "book widow," not to mention keeping the kids quiet so that I could sleep in the mornings after those all-night writing sessions. My three wonderful children—Daniel, Zachary, and Samantha—were as understanding as could possibly be expected for any group aged eight, seven, and three in accepting all those hours stolen from our time together and activities foregone as a result of my involvement in this work.

Finally, I would like to thank the following friends for their suggestions and advice regarding potential interview candidates: Norm Zadeh, Audrey Gale, Douglas Makepeace, Stanley Angrist, Tony Saliba, and Jeff Grable.

# *Prologue*

## *The Jademaster*

One cold winter morning a young man walks five miles through the snow. He knocks on the Jademaster's door. The Jademaster answers with a broom in his hand.

"Yes?"

"I want to learn about Jade."

"Very well then, come in out of the cold."

They sit by the fire sipping hot green tea. The Jademaster presses a green stone deeply into the young man's hand and begins to talk about tree frogs. After a few minutes, the young man interrupts.

"Excuse me, I am here to learn about Jade, not tree frogs."

The Jademaster takes the stone and tells the young man to go home and return in a week. The following week the young man returns. The Jademaster presses another green stone into the young man's hand and continues the story. Again, the young man interrupts. Again, the Jademaster sends him home. Weeks pass. The young man interrupts less and less. The young man also learns to brew the hot green tea, clean up the kitchen and sweep the floors. Spring comes.

One day, the young man observes, "The stone I hold is not genuine Jade."

\* \* \*

I lean back in my chair, savoring the story. My student interrupts.

"OK. OK. That's a great story. I don't see what it has to do with making money. I come to you to find out about the markets. I want to learn about the bulls and the bears, commodities, stocks, bonds, calls and options. I want to make big money. You tell me a fable about Jade. What is this? You ..."

"That's all for now. Leave those price charts on the table. Come back next week."

Months pass. My student interrupts less and less as I continue the story of *The Trader's Window*.

—from *The Trader's Window*,
ED SEYKOTA

# PART I

# *Trading Perspectives*

# Misadventures in Trading

O n the lecture tour following the completion of this book's predecessor, *Market Wizards,* certain questions came up with reliable
frequency. One common question was: "Has your own trading
improved dramatically now that you've just finished interviewing some
of the world's best traders?" Although I had the advantage of having
plenty of room for dramatic improvement in my trading, my response
was a bit of a cop-out. "Well," I would answer, "I don't know. You see,
at the moment, I'm not trading."

While it may seem a bit heretical for the author of *Market Wizards*
not to be trading, there was a perfectly good reason for my inaction. One
of the cardinal rules about trading is (or should be): Don't trade when
you can't afford to lose. In fact, there are few more certain ways of guar-
anteeing that you *will* lose than by trading money you can't afford to
lose. If your trading capital is too important, you will be doomed to a
number of fatal errors. You will miss out on some of the best trading
opportunities because these are often the most risky. You will jump out
of perfectly good positions prematurely on the first sign of adverse price
movement only to then see the market go in the anticipated direction.
You will be too quick to take the first bit of profit because of concern
that the market will take it away from you. Ironically, overconcern about
losing may even lead to staying with losing trades as fear triggers indeci-
siveness, much like a deer frozen in the glare of a car's headlights. In
short, trading with "scared money" will lead to a host of negative emo-

tions that will cloud decision making and virtually guarantee failure.

The completion of *Market Wizards* coincided with my having a house built. Perhaps somewhere out in this great country, there is someone who has actually built a house for what they thought it would cost. But I doubt it. When financing the building of a house, you find yourself repeatedly uttering that seemingly innocuous phrase, "Oh, it's only another $2,000." All those $2,000s add up, not to mention the much larger sums. One of our extravagances was an indoor swimming pool, and to help pay for this item I liquidated my commodity account—in the truest sense of the word. It was my sincerest intention not to resume trading until I felt I had adequate risk capital available, and an unending stream of improvements on the house kept pushing that date further into the future. In addition, working at a demanding full-time job and simultaneously writing a book is a draining experience. Trading requires energy, and I felt I needed time to recuperate without any additional strains. In short, I didn't want to trade.

This was the situation one day when, in reviewing my charts in the afternoon, I found myself with the firm conviction that the British pound was about to collapse. In the previous two weeks, the pound had moved straight down without even a hint of a technical rebound. After this sharp break, in the most recent week, the pound had settled into a narrow, sideways pattern. In my experience, this type of combined price action often leads to another price decline. Markets will often do whatever confounds the most traders. In this type of situation, many traders who have been long realize they have been wrong and are reconciled to liquidating a bad position—not right away, of course, but on the first rebound. Other traders who have been waiting to go short realize that the train may have left without them. They too are waiting for any minor rebound as an opportunity to sell. The simple truth is that most traders cannot stand the thought of selling near a recent low, especially soon after a sharp break. Consequently, with everyone waiting to sell the first rally, the market never rallies.

In any case, one look at the chart and I felt convinced this was one of those situations in which the market would never lift its head. Although my strong conviction tempted me to implement a short position, I also felt it was an inappropriate time to resume trading. I looked at my watch. There were exactly ten minutes left to the close. I procrastinated. The market closed.

That night before leaving work, I felt I had made a mistake. If I was so sure the market was going down, I reasoned, I should have gone short, even if I didn't want to trade. So I walked over to the tewnty-four-hour trading desk and placed an order to go short the British pound in the overnight market. The next morning I came in and the pound was down over 200 points on the opening. I placed a token amount of money into the account and entered a stop order to liquidate the trade if the market returned to my entry level. I rationalized that I was only trading with the market's money, and since my plan was to cease trading on a return to breakeven, I was not really violating my beliefs against trading with inadequate capital. Thus, I found myself trading once again, despite a desire not to do so.

This particular trade provides a good illustration of one of the principles that emerged from my interviews for *Market Wizards*. Patience was an element that a number of the supertraders stressed as being critical to success. James Rogers said it perhaps most colorfully, "I just wait until there is money lying in the corner, and all I have to do is go over there and pick it up. I do nothing in the meantime." In essence, by not wanting to trade, I had inadvertently transformed myself into a master of patience. By forcing myself to wait until there was a trade that appeared so compelling that I could not stand the thought of not taking it, I had vastly improved the odds.

During the next few months, I continued to trade and my equity steadily increased, as I seemed to be making mostly correct trading decisions. My account grew from $0 (not counting an initial $4,000 deposit that was quickly withdrawn once profits more than covered margin requirements) to over $25,000. It was at this juncture, while traveling on a business trip, that nearly all my positions turned sour simultaneously. I made some hasty decisions between meetings, virtually all of which proved wrong. Within about a week, I had lost about one-third of my gains. Normally, when I surrender a meaningful percentage of my profits, I put on the brakes, either trading only minimally or ceasing to trade altogether. Instinctively, I seemed to be following the same script on this occasion, as my positions were reduced to minimal levels.

At this time, I received a call from my friend Harvey (not his real name). Harvey is a practitioner of Elliott Wave analysis (a complex theory that attempts to explain all market behavior as part of a grand structure of price waves).* Harvey often calls me for my market opinion and in the process can't resist telling me his. Although I have usually found it to be a mistake to listen to anyone else's opinions on specific trades, in my experience Harvey had made some very good calls. This time he caught my ear.

"Listen, Jack," he said, "you have to sell the British pound!" At the time, the British pound had gone virtually straight up for four months, moving to a one-and-a-half-year high.

"Actually," I replied, "my own projection suggests that we may be only a few cents away from a major top, but I would never sell into a runaway market like this. I'm going to wait until there are some signs of the market topping."

"It will never happen," Harvey shot back. "This is the fifth of a fifth." (This is a rerference to the wave structure of prices that will mean something to Elliotticians, as enthusiasts of this methodology are known. As for other readers, any attempt at an explanation is more likely to confuse than enlighten—take my word for it.) "This is the market's last gasp, it will probably just gap lower on Monday morning and never look back." (This conversation was taking place on a Friday afternoon with the pound near its highs for the week.) "I really feel sure about this one."

I paused, thinking: I've just taken a hit in the markets. Harvey is usually pretty good in his analysis, and this time he seems particularly confident about his call. Maybe I'll coattail him on just this one trade, and if he's right, it will be an easy way for me to get back on a winning track.

So I said (I still cringe at the recollection), "OK Harvey, I'll follow you on this trade. But I must tell you that from past experience I've found listening to other opinions disastrous. If I get in on your opinion, I'll have no basis for deciding when to get out of the trade. So understand that my plan is to follow you all the way. I'll get out when you get out, and you need to let me know when you change your opinion." Har-

*The Elliott Wave Principle, as it is formally called, was originally developed by R. N. Elliott, an accountant turned market student. Elliott's definitive work on the subject was published in 1946, only two years befors his death, under the rather immodest title: *Nature's Law—The Secret of the Universe*. The application of the theory is unavoidably subjective, with numerous interpretations appearing in scores of volumes. (SOURCE: John J. Murphy, *Technical Analysis of the Futures Markets*, New York Institute of Finance, 1986.)

vey readily agreed. I went short at the market about a half-hour before the close and then watched as prices continued to edge higher, with the pound closing near its high for the week.

The following Monday morning, the British pound opened 220 points higher. One of my trading rules is: Never hold a position that gaps sharply against you right after you have put it on. (A gap refers to the market opening sharply higher or lower than the previous close.) The trade seemed wrong. My own instincts were to just get out. However, since I had entered this trade on Harvey's analysis, I thought it was important to remain consistent. So I called Harvey and said, "This short pound trade doesn't look so good to me, but since I don't think it's a good idea to mix analysis on a trade, my plan is to follow you on the exit of the position. So what do you think?"

"It's gone a little higher than I thought. But this is just a wave extension. I think we're very close to the top. I'm staying short."

The market continued to edge higher during the week. On Friday, the release of some negative economic news for the pound caused the currency to trade briefly lower during the morning, but by the afternoon prices were up for the day once again. This contrarian response to the news set off warning bells. Again, my instincts were to get out. But I didn't want to deviate from the game plan at this late juncture, so I called Harvey again. Well, as you might have guessed, the wave was still extending and he was still as bearish as ever. And yes, I stayed short.

On the next Monday morning, it was no great surprise that the market was up another few hundred points. A day later, with the market still edging higher, Harvey called. His confidence unshaken, he triumphantly announced, "Good news, I've redone my analysis and we're very close to the top." I groaned to myself. Somehow this enthusiasm over an event that had not yet occurred seemed ominous. My own confidence in the trade reached a new low.

No need to continue the gruesome details. About one week later, I decided to throw in the towel, Harvey or no Harvey. By the way, the market was still moving higher seven months later.

It is amazing how one trading sin led to a cascade of others. It started out with greed in wanting to find an easy way to recoup some losses—by following someone else's trade. This action also violated my strong belief that it is unwise to be swayed by other people's opinions in trading. These errors were quickly followed by ignoring some screaming market clues to liquidate the position. Finally, by surrendering the decision process of the trade to another party, I had no method for risk control. Let me be absolutely clear that the point is not that I followed bad advice and lost money, but rather that the market is a stern enforcer that unmercifully and unfailingly extracts harsh fines for all (trading) transgressions. The fault for the losses was totally my own, not Harvey's (nor that of the method, Elliott Ware Analysis, which has been wed effectively by many traders).

I traded lightly for another month and then decided to call it quits as my account neared the breakeven point. It had been a quick ride up and down, with little to show for it except some market experience.

Several months later I was a speaker at a seminar at which Ed Seykota had agreed to make a rare appearance. Ed was one of the phenomenal futures traders I interviewed for *Market Wizards*. His views on the markets provide an unusual blend of scientific analysis, psychology, and humor.

Ed began his presentation by asking for a volunteer from the audience to point to the time periods on various charts that coincided with the dates of financial magazine covers he had brought along. He started in the early 1980s. The cover blared: "Are Interest Rates Going to 20%?" Sure enough, the date of the magazine cover was in near-perfect synchrony with the bottom of the bond market. At another point, he pulled out a cover with an ominous picture of farm fields withering away under a blazing sun. The publication date coincided with the price peak of the grain markets during the 1988 drought. Moving ahead to then-current times, he showed a magazine cover that read: "How High Can Oil Prices Go?" This story was written at the time of skyrocketing oil prices in the months following the Iraqi invasion of Kuwait. "My guess is that we've probably seen the top of the oil market," said Ed. He was right.

"Now you understand how to get all the important information about impending market trends from news and financial magazines. Just read the covers and forget about the articles inside." Quintessential Ed Seykota.

I was eager to speak to Ed so that I could relay my trading experiences and glean the benefits of his insights. Unfortunately, at every break during the seminar, each of us was surrounded by attendees asking questions. We were staying at the same small hotel in San Francisco. After we got back, I asked Ed if he cared to go out and find a spot where we could relax and talk. Although he appeared a bit beat, he agreed.

We walked around the area trying to find something that resembled a comfortable local bar or café, but all we managed to find were large hotels. Finally, in desperation we wandered into one. In the lounge, a loud band and a truly bad singer were belting out their version of what else—"New York, New York." (I'm sure if we were in New York, the band would have been playing "I Left My Heart in San Francisco.") This certainly would not do for a quiet conversation with the man I hoped would be my temporary mentor. We sat down in the lobby outside, but the strains of the music were still uncomfortably loud (yes, Virginia, there are sounds worse than Muzak), and the atmosphere was deadly. My hopes for an intimate conversation were quickly fading.

Trying to make the best of a bad situation, I related my recent trading experiences to Ed. I explained how I started trading again despite my reluctance to do so and the incredible string of errors I committed on the one British pound trade—errors that I thought I had vanquished years ago. I told him that, ironically, at one point before I put on the British pound trade, when I was still up about $20,000, I was in the market for a new car that cost exactly that amount. Since my house had virtually drained me of assets, I was tempted to cash in the account and use the proceeds to buy the car. It was a very appealing thought since the car would have provided an immediate tangible reward for a few months of good trading without even having risked any of my own funds.

"So why didn't you close the account?" Ed asked.

"Well," I said, "how could I?" Although I managed to turn a few thousand dollars into $100,000 on a couple of occasions, I had always stalled out. I had never been able to really break through and extend it into some serious money. If I had decided to cash in my chips to make a purchase, I would always have wondered whether this would have been the time that I would have realized my trading goals. Of course, with the benefit of hindsight, I would have been much better off taking my profits, but at the time I couldn't see giving up the opportunity. I rationally explained all this to Ed.

"In other words, the only way you could stop trading was by losing. Is that right?" Ed didn't have to say anything more. I recalled that in my interview of him for *Market Wizards,* his most striking comment was: "Everybody gets what they want out of the market." I had wanted not to be trading, and sure enough that's what I got.

The moral here is: You don't always have to be in the market. Don't trade if you don't feel like it or if trading just doesn't feel right for whatever reason. To win at the markets you need confidence as well as the desire to trade. I believe the exceptional traders have these two traits most of the time; for the rest of us, they may come together only on an occasional basis. In my own case, I had started out with the confidence but without the desire to trade, and I ended up with neither. The next time I start trading, I plan to have both.

# Hussein Makes a Bad Trade

In many ways, the elements of good and bad decision making in trading are very similar to those that apply to decision making in general. The start of my work on this book coincided with the events immediately preceding the Persian Gulf War. I couldn't help but be struck by the similarity between Saddam Hussein's actions (or, more accurately, the lack thereof) and the typical responses of a foundering novice trader.

Hussein's trade was the invasion of Kuwait. Initially, he had solid, fundamental reasons for the trade. (The fundamentalist reasons came later, of course, as Hussein found it convenient to discover religion.) By invading Kuwait, Hussein could drive up oil prices to Iraq's benefit by eliminating one of the countries that consistently exceeded its OPEC quota and by creating turmoil in the world oil markets. He also stood a perceived good chance of permanently annexing part or all of Kuwait's oil fields, as well as gaining direct access to the Persian Gulf. And, last but certainly not least, the invasion provided a wonderful opportunity for Hussein to feed his megalomaniacal ambitions.

In exchange for all this upside potential, the initial risk on the trade seemed limited. Although forgotten by many because of the eventual decisive stance taken by the United States, the State Department's initial response to Iraq's invasion-threatening pronouncements and actions could essentially be paraphrased as "It's not our problem." In dealing with Hussein, such an ambivalent policy was almost tantamount to offering to lay out a red carpet for Iraq's tanks.

So initially, from Hussein's perspective, the invasion of Kuwait was a good trade—large potential and limited risk. However, as so often happens, the market changed. President Bush committed the United States to the defense of Saudi Arabia by sending in troops and spearheaded the passage of UN resolutions aimed at convincing Hussein to leave Kuwait. At this point, Hussein could probably have negotiated a deal in which he would have withdrawn from Kuwait in exchange for some disputed territorial gains and port rights—a quick profit. However, although the trade had started to deteriorate, Hussein decided to stand pat.

Next, Bush sent a stronger signal by doubling U.S. forces to four hundred thousand—an action indicating not only that the United States was ready to defend Saudi Arabia but that it was also establishing the capability for retaking Kuwait by force. Clearly the market had changed. Hussein ignored the market signal and stood back.

President Bush then set a January 15 deadline for Iraq's withdrawal from Kuwait in compliance with the UN resolution—the market moved further against the trade. At this point, the profit potential was probably gone, but Hussein could still have approximated a breakeven trade by offering to withdraw from Kuwait. Once again, he decided to hold the position.

Once the January 15 deadline had passed and the United States and its allies in the Gulf War embarked on the massive bombing of Iraq, the original trade was clearly in losing territory. Moreover, the market was moving down sharply every day, as each day's procrastination resulted in more destruction in Iraq. But how could Hussein give in now when so much had been lost? Much like a bewildered trader caught in a steadily deteriorating position, he pinned his hopes on the long shot: If only he held on long enough, perhaps fear of casualties would prompt the United States to back down.

The trend continued to go against the trade as the United States issued another deadline ultimatum—this time linked to the initiation of a ground war against Iraq. At this juncture, Hussein was readily consenting to conditions contained in the Soviet peace proposal, an agreement that probably would have been perfectly sufficient earlier but was now inadequate. Hussein's behavior was very much like that of a trader holding a long position in a steadily declining market who says, "I'll get out when I'm even," and then, as the situation grows more desperate, "I'll get out at the last relative high," with the relative high moving steadily down with the passage of time.

Ultimately, with the ground war well under way and his army largely decimated, Hussein finally capitulated. He was like a trader who has held on to a losing position until his account has been virtually destroyed, and then, in complete desperation, finally exclaims to his broker, "Get me out of the market. I don't care at what price, just get me out!"

> Moral: If you can't take a small loss, sooner or later you will take the mother of all losses.

# PART II

# *The World's Biggest Market*

# *Bill Lipschutz*

## THE SULTAN OF CURRENCIES

Quick, what is the world's largest financial market? Stocks? No, not even if you aggregate all the world's equity markets. Of course, it must be bonds. Just think of the huge government debt that has been generated worldwide. Good guess, but wrong again, even if you combine all the world's fixed-income markets. The correct answer is currencies. In the scope of all financial trading, stocks and bonds are peanuts compared with currencies.

It is estimated that, on average, $1 trillion is traded *each day* in the world currency markets. The vast majority of this currency trading does not take place on any organized exchange but rather is transacted in the interbank currency market. The interbank currency market is a twenty-four-hour market, which literally follows the sun around the world, moving from banking centers of the United States, to Australia, to the Far East, to Europe, and finally back to the United States. The market exists to fill the needs of companies seeking to hedge exchange risk in a world of rapidly fluctuating currency values, but speculators also participate in the interbank currency market in an effort to profit from their expectations regarding shifts in exchange rates.

Note: For a few sections of this interview, a basic understanding of option terminology would be very helpful. Readers totally unfamiliar with options may wish first to read the primer provided in the Appendix.

In this huge market, there has been only a handful of high-stakes players. Ironically, although these traders sometimes take positions measured in billions of dollars—yes, billions—they are virtually unknown to most of the financial community, let alone the public. Bill Lipschutz is one of these traders.

The interviews I held with Lipschutz were conducted in two marathon sessions at his apartment. Lipschutz has market monitor screens everywhere. Of course, there is the large TV monitor in the living room, receiving a feed of currency quotes. There are also quote screens in his office, the kitchen, and near the side of his bed, so that he can roll over in his sleep and check the quotes—as indeed he does regularly (since some of the most active periods in the market occur during the U.S. nighttime hours). In fact, you can't even take a leak without literally running into a quote screen (there is one conveniently located, somewhat tongue in cheek, at standing height in the bathroom). This fellow obviously takes his trading very seriously.

I had first contacted Bill Lipschutz through a public relations agent, Tom Walek. Yes, a public relations agent for a trader sounds rather odd. In fact, this is particularly true for Lipschutz, who had managed quite deliberately to maintain virtually total public anonymity for his entire career despite his huge trades. However, after having spent eight years as Salomon Brothers' largest and most successful currency trader, Lipschutz had just left the firm to start his own management company to trade currencies (initially as a subsidiary of Merrill Lynch; later, the company evolved into a completely independent venture, Rowayton Capital Management). It was this project that required the public relations support. Anyway, after Walek discussed my interview proposal with Lipschutz, he called to tell me that Bill first wanted an informal meeting so that he could see if it "felt right."

We met at a Soho bar, and after downing several French beers (no joke, the French actually produce some excellent beers) Lipschutz said, "I think you'll find the story of how, in less than a decade, Salomon Brothers grew from a zero presence in currencies to becoming perhaps the world's largest player in the currency market an interesting tale." Besides feeling a sense of relief, since that comment obviously reflected a consent to the interview, his statement certainly whetted my appetite.

In our first meeting at his apartment, with my tape recorders whirring, I said, "OK, tell me the story of Salomon's spectacular growth as a major trading entity in the world currency markets." I sat back, anticipating a lengthy response full of wonderful anecdotes and insights.

Lipschutz answered, "The currency options market, Salomon's currency options department, and I all started at the same time and grew and prospered simultaneously."

"And ...," I said, prompting him to continue. He rephrased the same response he had just given.

"Yes," I said, "that's a very interesting coincidence, but could you fill in the details? How about some specific stories?" He responded again with generalizations. My hopes for the interview went into a rapid nosedive.

I've done interviews that I knew were dead in the water after the first hour and have ended up ditching the results afterwards. However, this interview was different. Although I felt that I was getting very little useful material during the first one or two hours of our conversation, I sensed there was something there. This was not a dry well; I just had to dig deeper.

After the first few hours, we started to connect better and Lipschutz began relating specific stories regarding his trading experiences. These make up the core of the following interview.

As mentioned earlier, the large TV screen in Lipschutz's living room is normally tuned to a currency quote display, with a Reuters news feed running across the bottom. Although Lipschutz seemed to be paying full attention to our conversation, on some level he was obviously watching the screen. At one point, the Australian dollar was in the midst of a precipitous decline following some disastrously negative comments made by the Australian finance minister. Although the market was in a virtual free-fall, Lipschutz felt the sell-off was overdone and interrupted our interview to call in some orders. "Nothing big," he said. "I'm just trying to buy twenty [$20 million Australian, that is]." Immediately afterward, the Australian dollar started to trade higher and continued to move up throughout the rest of the evening. Lipschutz didn't get a fill, however, because he had entered his order at a limit price just a hair below where the market was trading, and the market never traded lower. "Missing an opportunity is as bad as being on the wrong side of a trade," he said.

During our second interview, Lipschutz wanted to short the Deutsche mark and was waiting for a small bounce to sell. When noticing that the mark had started to move lower instead, he said, "It looks like I'm going to miss the trade."

"That sounds just like last week when you missed getting long the Australian dollar by using a limit order," I said. "If you feel that strongly," I asked, "why don't you just sell the Deutsche mark at the market?"

"What! And pay the bid/ask spread?" Bill exclaimed. I wasn't sure whether he was serious or joking—or perhaps some combination of the two. (Incidentally, the Deutsche mark kept going lower.)

Our interviews were conducted after U.S. market hours, but, since the currency markets never close, Lipschutz, apparently, never stops trading. However, despite his admitted obsession with the markets and trading, Lipschutz appeared very relaxed. I wouldn't even have known that he was watching the markets had he not occasionally made references to price movements and placed orders over the phone.

---

**What happened to architecture?**

What happened to *architecture?*

**Well, I had heard that you have a degree in architecture. How is it that you ended up as a trader?**

While I was enrolled in the architectural program at Cornell, my grandmother died and left me a portfolio of a hundred different stocks with a total value of $12,000, which I liquidated at great cost because all the positions were odd lots. The proceeds provided me with risk capital. I found myself using more and more of my time playing around with the stock market. It wasn't that I got less interested in architecture, I just became a lot more interested in trading.

Also, architecture is very much an Old World profession. There is a long apprenticeship—three years in this country—before you can take your licensing exam. Then you spend many more years as a draftsman. It takes a long time before you get to the point where you have control over the design process.

**Did you get your degree eventually?**

Yes, of course. Actually, I got two degrees. The full-time architectural program took five years. It was not unusual for architectural students to also enroll in other courses and take longer to finish their degree. I ended up taking a lot of business courses and also earned an M.B.A.

**What happened after you graduated Cornell? Did you get a job related to architecture?**

No, I never practiced as an architect because of the long apprenticeship process I just explained. I went directly to work for Salomon.

**How did you get that job?**

It's typical for students in the M.B.A. program to get business-related summer jobs. In the summer of 1981 I got a job at Salomon Brothers. By that time, I was trading stock options very actively for my own account.

**Was this the account you started with the $12,000 your grand-mother left you?**

Yes, and by this time I had built it up a bit.

**What did you know about stock options when you started trading?**

I didn't know a whole lot.

**Then on what basis did you make your trading decisions?**

I tried to read everything I could on the subject. I spent a lot of time in the library reading annual company reports. I became an avid reader of the various financial periodicals such as *The Economist, Barron's*, and *Value Line*.

I also began to watch the stock tape on cable. Because Ithaca, New York, is surrounded by mountains, it has particularly poor television reception. As a result, it was one of the first places in the country to get cable TV in the early 1970s. One of the channels had a fifteen-minute delayed stock tape. I spent many hours watching the tape and, over time, I seemed to develop a feel for the price action.

**Was that when you decided to become a trader?**

I can't remember making any conscious decision, "I want to be a trader; I don't want to be an architect." It was a gradual process. Trading literally took over my life.

**Was the Salomon summer job related to trading?**

My wife and I met while I was attending Cornell. She's very aggressive and has a very strong economics background. The previous summer she had managed to get a job working for Dr. Henry Kaufman [a world-renowned economist] in the bond research department. I subsequently met her immediate superior, who also happened to be a Cornell alumnus. He arranged for me to interview with Henry Kaufman for the same position my wife had held (by this time, she had graduated and had a full-time job).

Ironically, around the same time, Salomon Brothers sent a representative to Cornell to do recruiting. I was invited to come to New York to interview for their summer sales and trading intern program. I was interviewed by Sidney Gold, the head of Salomon's proprietary equity options desk. Sidney is a very high-strung guy who speaks very, very fast.

He took me into an office that had a glass wall facing out onto a large trading room, with a view of an electronic tape running across the wall. I sat with my back to the tape, and the whole time he was interviewing me, he was also watching the tape. He started firing questions at me, one after the other. Here I am, a college kid, wearing a suit and tie for the first time in my first formal interview, and I had no idea what to make of all of this. I answered each of his questions slowly and deliberately.

After about ten minutes of this question-and-answer process, he stops abruptly, looks me straight in the eye, and says, "OK, forget all this bullshit. So you want to be a trader. Every fucking guy comes here and tells me he wants to be a trader. You said you're trading your own account. What stocks are you trading?"

"I've been pretty involved in Exxon recently," I reply.

He snaps back, "I don't know that stock. Give me another one."

"I've also been pretty involved in 3M," I answer.

"I don't know that one either," he shoots back. "Give me another one."

I answer, "U.S. Steel."

"U.S. Steel. I know Steel. Where is it trading?"

"It closed last night at 30 1/2."

"It just went across the board at 5/8," he says. "Where did it break out from?" he asks.

"Twenty-eight," I answer.

He fires right back, "And where did it break out from before that?"

"Well, that must have been over three years ago!" I exclaim, somewhat startled at the question. "I believe it broke out from about the 18 level."

At that point, he slows down, stops looking at the tape; and says, "I want you to work for me." That was the end of the interview.

A few weeks later, I received a call from the fellow who ran Salomon's recruiting program. He said, "We have a bit of a problem. Sidney Gold wants to hire you, but Kaufman also wants you to work for him. So we worked out an arrangement where you'll split your time between the two." I ended up working the first half of the summer doing research for Dr. Kaufman and the second half working on the options trading desk.

At the end of the summer, Sidney offered me a job. Since I still had one semester left in business school and also had to finish my thesis for my architectural degree, I arranged to work for Sidney during the fall semester, with the understanding that I would return to school in the spring.

**Did the job working on the equity options desk prove valuable in terms of learning how to trade options?**

The job was certainly helpful in terms of overall trading experience, but you have to understand that, at the time, equity options trading at Salomon was highly nonquantitative. In fact, when I think back on it now, it seems almost amazing, but I don't believe anybody there even knew what the Black-Scholes model was [the standard option pricing model]. Sidney would come in on Monday morning and say, "I went to buy a car this weekend and the Chevrolet showroom was packed. Let's buy GM calls." That type of stuff.

I remember one trader pulling me aside one day and saying, "Look, I don't know what Sidney is teaching you, but let me tell you everything you need to know about options. You like 'em, you buy calls. You don't like 'em, you buy puts."

**In other words, they were basically trading options as a leveraged outright position.**

That's exactly right. But that whole trading approach actually fit very well with my own tape-reading type of experience.

**Did you return to the equity options department when you finished Cornell?**

I worked there at the beginning of the summer, but then I went into the Salomon training program, which is something that every new hire does. The great thing about the Salomon training course is that you get exposed to all the key people in the firm. All the big names at Salomon came in, told their story, and in essence delivered their persona. You were indoctrinated into Salomon Brothers, and the culture was passed on. Having spent my entire career at Salomon, I feel very strongly that it was important for the culture to be passed on.

In the late 1980s, a lot of that culture was lost. The programs got too large. When I started at Salomon, there was one program of 120 people each year; by the late 1980s, there were two programs with 250 people apiece. The trainees also seemed to come from more of the same mold, whereas in the early 1980s there appeared to be a greater willingness to hire a few wild-card candidates.

**What did you get out of the Salomon training course besides being indoctrinated into the culture?**

That was what I got out of it.

**It doesn't sound like very much. Was there more to it?**

No, that was a tremendous amount. Clearly you have never worked for Salomon. The company is all about the culture of Salomon Brothers.

**OK, tell me about the culture of Salomon Brothers.**

Salomon Brothers was a firm that was almost solely involved in proprietary trading and for years was run by a handful of very strong, charismatic individuals. They were street fighters who were betting their own
money and who really understood what it meant to take risk. It was all
about personalities, guts, insight, and honesty and integrity beyond any
shadow of a doubt.* Salomon was an institution. There was virtually no
turnover of key personnel at the firm. The chairman, John Gutfreund,
had a desk on the trading floor that he sat at every day. In my nine years
at Salomon, I never sat more than twenty feet away from him.

I remember my first conversation with John Gutfreund. I had been
with the firm as a full-time employee for less than a year. You have to
picture the scene. It was the early evening of July 3. The Salomon trading floor is a huge, two-story space—at one time it was the largest trading floor in the world. The twilight colors of the fading sunlight were
flooding through the huge glass windows. Because of the approaching
holiday, the entire floor was completely abandoned except for John
Gutfreund and myself.

I heard him call, "Bill, Bill." I had no idea why he would even
know my name, but that was the kind of place Salomon was. I was
wrapped up in what I was doing, and I suddenly realized that he was
calling me. I walked over to his desk and said, "Yes, Sir."

He looked at me and asked, "Where did the franc close?"

Racing through my mind are all the possible reasons he might be
asking me this question in this very scripted scenario. I looked at him
and asked, "Which one, Swiss franc or French franc?"

John Gutfreund is a man who exudes power. He is very charismatic
and you can almost feel the aura around him. He didn't hesitate, and
looked straight at me and said, "Both." So I gave him both quotes in a
voice that was probably one octave higher than normal.

A little over a year later on another summer day, the same scene is

---

*This interview was conducted several months prior to the government bond-buying scandal
that rocked Salomon. Following this development, I asked Lipschutz if he still wished to maintain
the terms *honesty* and *integrity* in his description of Salomon, as the words now had an ironic ring
in light of the latest revelations. Lipschutz, however, felt strongly about maintaining his original
description, as he believed it reflected his true feelings. Queried about how he reconciled this
image of integrity with the apparent ethical lapses in the bidding procedures at several government
bond auctions, he replied, "I believe it was more a matter of ego on the part of a single individual,
which ran counter to the qualities embodied by Gutfreund and the firm."

virtually repeated. The light of the setting sun is streaming into the trading room, and John Gutfreund and I are nearly the only two people left. Again, I hear a voice behind me, "Bill, Bill."

I am struck by the déjà vu quality of the moment. I walk over and say, "Yes, Sir."

"Where did the franc close?" he asks.

"Which one?" I ask. "The Swiss or the French?"

Without missing a beat, and without showing any trace of a smile, he looks straight at me and says, "Belgian."

Here's a guy who is chairman of Salomon Brothers, which in those years was probably the most powerful firm on the street, while I am a nobody trainee. It has been a year since that first encounter, and he has the presence of mind and the interest to set me up like that. As the years went by, and I got to know him better through more contact, I realized that he was fully aware of the impact that conversation would have on me. Here we are talking about it nearly ten years later, and I remember every word of that conversation. He had that effect on people. He would very often have conversations with trainees and support people.

**Was Gutfreund a trader himself?**

John came up through the ranks as a trader. When he was chairman, he spent his day on the trading floor to see what was going on. We always said that John could smell death at a hundred paces. He didn't need to know what your position was to know what your position was, or how it was going. He could tell the state of your equity by the amount of anxiety he saw in your face.

Salomon Brothers was a culture like no other. People often spoke of Salomon's appetite for risk. It wasn't that the company was a risk-seeking firm, but it was certainly a firm that was comfortable with risk or with losing money, as long as the trade idea made sense.

**How was it that you ended up in currencies after the training session was over as opposed to going back to equities?**

Actually, I wanted to go back to equities, but one of the senior people in the department took me aside and said, "You're much too quantitative.

You don't need to be down here in equities." He talked me into going into this new department that was being formed: foreign exchange. I was one of the more highly thought-of trainees, and at the end of the session, I was recruited by several departments, including the currency department, which was just being formed.

**How did you choose the currency department?**

I wanted a trading position, and I got along well with the people. However, I had a lot less choice than I might have been led to believe at the time.

**What do you mean?**

You get recruited, do your lobbying, and pick your choices, but by the end of the day, the powers that be get to move the chess pieces and decide where they want you placed.

**Did you know anything about currencies at the time?**

I didn't even know what a Deutsche mark was. But, then again, no one in the department really knew much about currencies.

**No one?**

Not really. There was one junior person on the desk who had previously worked for a bank.

**Wasn't there anybody else in the firm with expertise in currencies?**

No.

**Why wasn't there any thought given to getting someone from the outside with experience to develop the department?**

That's not how Salomon did things. At Salomon everything was home-grown. You're asking questions like you think there was some sort of written business plan. The reality was that a few senior people got together one day, and one said, "Hey, shouldn't we really start a foreign exchange department?"

"Okay. Who can we get to run it?"

"How about Gil?"

"Okay. Hey, Gil. Do you want to run the department?"

"Sure, I'll do it."

Gil came from bond arbitrage. He had no experience in currencies. His idea was to get a bunch of bright people together, figure out how this foreign exchange stuff worked, let them trade the product around, and see if they could make some money.

**With no one in the department having any real background in currencies, how did you get the experience to know what to do?**

One of the fellows in the department was very extroverted. He had us going out to dinner with international bankers three or four times a week. In those days, I was particularly shy. In fact, I remember one day one of the traders on the desk asked me to call Morgan Guaranty to place a D-mark transaction. I protested, saying, "But I don't know anyone there."

He said, "What do you mean you don't know anybody? Just pick up the Hambros [a book that lists all the international foreign exchange dealers], flip through, find Morgan's D-mark dealer, and call him."

I must have sat there agonizing for over ten minutes, trying to figure out how I could call somebody I didn't know.

**Tell me about your early trading experiences in currencies.**

At around the same time that the Salomon Brothers foreign exchange department was formed, the Philadelphia Stock Exchange introduced a currency option contract. I was the only one at the desk who even knew what a put or call was. Also, the product was being traded on a stock exchange with a specialist system, and I was the only one on the desk with any background in equities. Everyone else in the department came from fixed-incomeland, which is the forty-second floor. Equityland is on the forty-first, where I came from. I don't think anybody else in the department had ever even been on the forty-first. I also knew specialists and market makers on the Philadelphia Stock Exchange floor. No one else in the department even knew what a specialist was. [In a specialist system, a single individual matches buy and sell orders for a security, as opposed to an open outcry system, in which orders are executed by brokers shouting their bids and offers in a trading ring.] The situation was tailor-made for me. Gil said, "You're the only one in the department who knows anything about this, so just do it."

The key point I am trying to make is that Salomon's foreign exchange department, Bill Lipschutz as foreign exchange trader, and currency options all started at the same time, and we grew together. It was a unique, synergistic type of experience.

**How did you become successful as a currency trader without any previous experience?**

Foreign exchange is all about relationships. Your ability to find good liquidity, your ability to be plugged into the information flow—it all depends on relationships. If you call up a bank and say, "I need a price on ten dollar [$10 million] mark," they don't have to do anything. They can tell you, "The mark dealer is in the bathroom; call back later." If I call up at 5 P.M. and say, "Hey, Joe, it's Bill, and I need a price on the mark," the response is going to be entirely different: "I was just on my way out the door, but for you I'll see what I can do."

**As someone brand new in the business, how did you develop these contacts?**

One thing that helped me a great deal was that I had a background in options when it was new to the marketplace. "He knows options," they would say. Hell, I didn't know *that* much about it, but the point was that no one in foreign exchange knew very much about it either. Their perception was: "He can derive the Black-Scholes model; he must be a genius." A lot of senior guys in the currency market wanted to meet me simply because their customers wanted to do options, and they needed to get up to speed on the subject quickly.

Also, I worked for Salomon Brothers, which at that time provided an element of mystique: "We don't know what they do, but they make a lot of money."

Another factor in my favor was that, although I worked for an investment bank, I tried not to act like a pompous investment banker. The typical guys in investment banks who were doing foreign exchange back then were fixed-income types. They were prissy in the eyes of the FX [foreign exchange] guys. They wore suspenders and Hermès ties; they were white-wine-and-arugula-salad type of guys. They were not the go-out-for-pasta-and-dribble-marinara-sauce-all-over-yourself type of guys, which is what the foreign exchange traders basically were. I was really different; my background was different.

I was the first person at Salomon Brothers to have a Telerate at home. They couldn't believe it. "You want a screen at home? Are you out of your mind? Don't you ever turn off?"

I would look at them and say, "Foreign exchange is a twenty-four-hour market. It doesn't go to sleep when you leave at 5 P.M. The market is really there all night, and it moves!"

**Is having contacts important in order to be plugged into the news?**

Absolutely. Those of us who did well were generally the ones who were accepted by the interbank circle. The traders who stayed aloof tended to be the ones who couldn't make any money trading foreign exchange. These traders would end up calling a clerk on the Merc floor [the Chicago Mercantile Exchange, which trades futures on currencies—an active but still far smaller market than the interbank market] and would say, "So, how does the Swissy look?" What is a clerk going to know about what is actually driving the international currency market? I would be talking to bankers throughout the day and night—in Tokyo, London, Frankfurt, and New York.

**Were you trading off of this information flow?**

That's what foreign exchange trading is all about.

**Can you give me a recent example of how information flow helps in trading?**

At the time the Berlin Wall came down, the general market sentiment was that everyone would want to get money into East Germany on the ground floor. The basic assumption was that large capital flows into Eastern Europe would most directly benefit the Deutsche mark. After a while, the realization set in that it was going to take a lot longer to absorb East Germany into a unified Germany.

How does that shift in attitude come about? Kohl makes a statement; Baker makes a comment; statistics reveal very high East German unemployment. The East Germans, who have lived all their life under a socialist system, begin saying, "We don't want to work as hard as those West Germans, and by the way, how come the state is not paying for our medical bills anymore?" The investment community begins to realize that the rebuilding of Eastern Europe is going to be a long haul. As this thinking becomes more prevalent, people start moving capital out of the Deutsche mark.

**You could have made all those same arguments when the wall first came down.**

I don't think many people saw it that way at the time, and even if they did, that's not important. What is important is to assess what the market is focusing on at the given moment.

**And the way you get that information is by talking to lots of participants in the foreign exchange market?**

Yes. Not everyone is going to interpret things in the same way, at the same time, as you do, and it's important to understand that. You need to be plugged into the news and to know what the market is looking at. For example, one day the foreign exchange market may be focusing on interest rate differentials; the next day the market may be looking at the potential for capital appreciation, which is exactly the opposite. [A focus on interest rate differentials implies that investors will shift their money to the industrialized countries with the highest interest rate yields, whereas a focus on capital appreciation implies that investors will place their money in the countries with the strongest economic and political outlooks, which usually happen to be the countries with lower interest rates.]

**Are there any trades that stand out from your early days as a currency trader?**

In 1983, in the very early days of currency options trading on the Philadelphia Stock Exchange, one of the specialists was quoting a particular option at a price that was obviously off by 100 points. I bought fifty. Since this was a deep-in-the-money option, I immediately sold the underlying market and locked in a risk-free profit. [A deep-in-the-money option is just like an outright contract, with the added advantage that if the market has an extreme move the maximum risk is theoretically limited.]

I asked my broker whether the specialist was still offering to sell more options at the same price. "Yes," he replied, "the offer is still there."

"Buy another fifty," I said.

At the time, I was the only currency options trader on the Philadelphia Exchange that regularly traded in fifties. The entire daily volume in the market was only about two or three hundred contracts. I did another fifty, another fifty, and another fifty. Then Goldman Sachs came in and did fifty. All of a sudden, the specialist had sold three to four hundred of these options. He obviously thought he had a locked-in arbitrage profit, but he had done his arithmetic wrong. I knew exactly what was happening. Finally, I said to my broker, "Ask him if he wants to do one thousand."

"Just a second," he answered. The broker came back a half-minute later and said, "He'll do one thousand at this price."

The specialist had backed off his offer, but he was obviously still off by almost 100 points in his quote. Finally I said to my broker, "Tell him to call me on my outside line."

The specialist calls me up and says, "What are you doing?"

I respond, "What are *you* doing?"

He asks, "Do you really want to do one thousand?"

I answer, "Listen, you're off by a big figure on your price."

"What are you talking about?" he exclaims. I start walking him through the numbers. Before I finish he says, "I've got to go," and the phone goes dead.

I got off the phone and thought about it for a few minutes. I realized that holding him to the trade would put him out of business—a development that would be bad for the exchange and terrible for the product [currency options], which we were just beginning to trade in a significant way. I called my broker and said, "Break all the trades after the first fifty."

At about the same time, my outside phone line rang. The specialist was on the other end of the line. "I can't believe it!" he exclaimed, agonizing over the immensity of his error. "This is going to put me out of business."

I said, "Don't worry about it, I'm breaking all the trades, except the first fifty."

(By the way, Goldman refused to break any of the 150 they had done. Years later, after the specialist company had gone out of business, and the individual specialist had become the head trader for the largest market maker on the floor, he always made it very difficult for Goldman on the floor.)

My action of breaking the trades represented a long-term business decision, which I didn't think about a lot at the time, but which I agonized over for years afterward.

**Why is that?**

I have a reputation as being one of the most—if not the most—hard-assed players in the market. I never, ever, ever, *ever,* cut anybody a break, because I figured that at Salomon everybody was trying to knock us off. I was sure that if the tables were reversed, no one would ever give us a break. My view was always that these are the rules of the game. I don't give any quarter, and I don't expect any quarter.

Traders would sometimes call up when they had just missed the expiration of an over-the-counter option that went out in the money. There were a million excuses: "I tried to get through earlier." "I forgot." "I'm only a few minutes late, couldn't you just make an exception?" I always knew that if we called late, no one would let us exercise. The fact is, in all the time I was there, we never missed an expiration. The argument I made was, "Look, we've put a lot of money and thought into our back-office operations. We've instituted numerous fail-safe measures to make sure that we don't make mistakes."

When I was working out the management company details with Merrill, they asked me how much they should budget for back-office errors. I said, "Zero."

They asked in disbelief, "What do you mean by *zero?*"

I said, "Zero. We don't have back-office errors."

They said, "What do you mean—of course you have back-office errors."

I answered, "No, we don't make errors. If you put in enough fail-safes, you don't make errors."

That was my attitude, and that was why I wouldn't break the rules. People who knew me really well would say, "Lipschutz, why do you have to be such a hard-ass about everything?" I would simply say, "Hey, these are the rules; that's the way the game is played." So for me, letting the specialist off the hook was very much out of character.

**Did you decide to give the specialist a break because it was such an obvious mistake? Or because you thought it might threaten the longevity of what was then a fledgling exchange and product?**

It was a long-term business decision based on the opinion that it would have been bad for my business to hold him to the trade.

**Bad for your business in what way?**

My business in trading currency options was exploding, and the Philadelphia Stock Exchange was where they were traded. (The over-the-counter currency options market was only just starting at the time.)

**So you did it more to protect the exchange.**

No, I did it to protect me.

**To protect your marketplace?**

That's exactly right.

**Then, hypothetically, if the exchange had been there for ten years, trading volume was huge, and this trade would not have made any difference to the survival of the exchange, you would have made a different decision.**

That's correct. It wasn't charity.

**So the fact that it was such an obvious error ...**

No, that wasn't the motive, because I said to the broker, "Ask him to check his price." "Ask him if he is sure." "Ask him if he wants to do another fifty."

**In the interbank market, don't the dealers sometimes inadvertently quote a currency off by one big figure—for example, the real price is 1.9140 and they quote 1.9240. Do you hold a dealer to the quote even if it's an obvious mistake?**

The convention is that there has to be an honest attempt. Let's say that some news comes out and the market is moving like crazy. You may not even know what the big figure is. Assume a dealer quotes 1.9140, and you think the price should be 1.9240. The convention is to say, "1.9140. Are you sure? Please check your price." And if the dealer responds, "Yeah, yeah, yeah, I'm sure. Do you want to deal or don't you?" then the price should stand.

**Has this happened to you?**

Yes, and I can tell you that every time that it has happened, the other institution has come back and either wanted to cancel the trade or split the difference.

**And what did you say?**

I refused, because I had asked them to verify the price.

---

There is a break in the formal interview to devour some Chinese food that we have ordered in. During the meal, we continue to discuss markets. One of the subjects discussed is clearly stated to be off the record, because it contains a number of references regarding one of the exchanges. Since I believed that the comments and viewpoints expressed in this discussion would be of interest to many readers, I eventually prevailed on Lipschutz to permit the use of this conversation. In accordance with this agreement, I have edited out all specific references to the exchange, market, and traders.

**In exchange-traded markets, do you believe that stops have a tendency to get picked off?**

As you know, I do very little trading on exchanges with trading pits. The vast majority of my trades are done either in the interbank market or on the Philadelphia Exchange, which uses a specialist system. However, in answer to your question, I can tell you a story about a fellow who was at Salomon in the late 1980s.

He had been trading a market that had gone into a narrow range, and trading activity had dried up. During this period, a lot of stops had built up right above this trading range. One day, this trader's clerk on the floor calls and says, "Listen, the talk is that tomorrow [a day on which the liquidity was expected to be substantially below normal because of a holiday affecting the cash market] they're going to gun for the stops above the market." At that point, the stops were relatively close—about 40 or 50 ticks higher.

The next day, this trader's plan is to sell the market heavily once the stops are hit, because he believes such a rally would be artificial and that the market would be vulnerable to a subsequent sell-off. During the morning, the market trades sideways and nothing happens. Then around 1 P.M., prices start to move—down.

**You did say that the stops were above the market?**

That's right. Anyway, the market moves down 50 points, 100 points, and within a few minutes the market is down over 200 points. What happened was that the floor traders went for the stops below the market, which were 200 points away, instead of the stops above the market, which were only 50 points away. The reason was that everybody was ready for the rally to take out the stops on the upside. Therefore, everyone was long, and the direction of greatest price vulnerability was on the downside.

During the sharp break, my friend realizes that the market is way overextended on the downside. He screams at his clerks, "Buy 'em! Buy any amount they'll sell you. Just buy 'em!" He was bidding for hundreds of contracts between 100 and 200 points lower, and he was only filled on fifty, even though the market traded down over 200 points, with a couple thousand lots trading at those levels.

## What happened to his bid?

You've obviously never traded on the floor of an exchange. In a trading pit, it's possible for the market to trade at several different prices at the same moment during periods of rapid movement. They were looking right past my friend's floor brokers, who were bidding higher. It was a fast market. [When an exchange designates "fast market" conditions, floor brokers can't be held for failing to fill orders that were within the day's traded price range.] A fast market gives the floor brokers a special license to steal, above and beyond their normal license to steal.

I'm not making any allegations, because I can't prove that any of this happens. It's just my opinion that situations like this sometimes occur in some open outcry markets.

---

Dinner is over, and we return to the living room for a continuation of the interview "on the record."

---

## Do you remember your first major trade and the thinking behind it?

The trade involved a bond issue that allowed for redemption in either sterling [another name for British pounds] or U.S. dollars. The issue was grossly underpriced—the problem was that it was mispriced by Salomon Brothers, one of the lead underwriters. When I first heard the details, I couldn't believe how mispriced it was. I actually wanted to buy the whole issue.

## What was the essence of the mispricing?

At the time, U.K. interest rates were a lot lower than U.S. rates. Consequently, forward sterling was trading at a huge premium to the spot rate. [If two countries have different interest rates, forward months of the currency with lower rates will invariably trade at a premium to the spot currency rate. If such a premium did not exist, it would be possible to borrow funds in the country with lower rates, convert and invest the proceeds in the country with higher rates, and buy forward currency positions in the currency with lower interest rates to hedge against the currency risk. The participation of interest rate arbitrageurs assures that the forward premiums for the currency with lower interest rates will be exactly large enough to offset the interest rate differential between the two countries.]

The way the bond issue was priced, the sterling redemption option essentially assumed no premium over the spot rate, despite the huge premium for the currency in the forward market. Therefore, you could buy the bond and sell the sterling forward at a huge premium, which over the life of the bond would converge to the spot rate.

**What was the term of the bond?**

The bond matured in four tranches: five, seven, nine, and twelve years.

**I don't understand. Is it possible to hedge a currency that far forward?**

Of course it is. Even if you can't do the hedge in the forward market, you can create the position through an interest rate swap. However, in the case of sterling/dollar, which has a very liquid term forward market, there was certainly a market for at least ten years out.

**How big was the issue?**

There were two tranches: the first for $100 million and the second for $50 million.

**What happened when you pointed out that the issue was grossly mispriced?**

The initial response was that I must be wrong somehow. They spent nine hours that day running it past every quant jock in the house until they were convinced I was right.

**Did they let you buy the issue?**

Yes, but by the time I got the approval, $50 million of the first tranche had already been sold. For the next year or two, I tried to acquire the rest of the issue in the secondary market. I always had a bid in for those bonds. Largely with the help of one salesperson who knew where the original issue was placed, over the next two years, I was able to acquire $135 million of the total outstanding issue of $150 million.

Once I bought the issue, I immediately sold an equivalent of 50 percent of the total amount in the forward sterling market. Remember that the forward pound was at a large premium. For example, the spot rate (and the rate at which the bonds were redeemable in sterling) was $1.3470, while seven-year forward sterling was trading at approximately $1.47 and twelve-year forward sterling at approximately $1.60. [The sale of half the total amount in the forward market effectively converted half the position into a proxy put on the British pound, while the original issue was, in effect, a call position. Thus, half the position was a call and half a put, the key point being that the put was established at a much higher price than the call. This gap essentially represented a locked-in profit, with the potential for an even greater profit if the forward pound moved below $1.3470 or above, say, $1.47 in the case of the seven-year tranche.]

Anyway, what ultimately happened is that U.K. interest rates eventually reversed from below to above U.S. rates, thereby causing the British pound forward rates to invert from a premium to a discount to the spot rate. I covered the whole position at a huge profit.

**Are there any other trades in your career that stand out as particularly memorable?**

One that comes to mind occurred at the time of the G-7 meeting in September 1985, which involved major structural changes that set the tone in the currency markets for the next five years. [This was the meeting at which the major industrialized nations agreed to a coordinated policy aimed at lowering the value of the dollar.]

**You were obviously very closely tied into the currency markets. Did you have any idea that such a major policy change was at hand?**

No. There were some people who had an inkling that there was going to be a meeting at which the Western governments were going to drive the dollar down, but nobody understood the magnitude of what that meant. Even after the results of the meeting were reported, the dollar traded down, but nothing compared to the decline that occurred in the ensuing months. In fact, after an initial sell-off in New Zealand and Australia, the dollar actually rebounded modestly in Tokyo.

**How do you explain that?**

People didn't really understand what was happening. The general attitude was: "Oh, another central bank intervention." Remember that this meeting took place after years of ineffective central bank intervention.

**What was different this time?**

This was the first time that we saw a coordinated policy statement from the seven industrialized nations. Anyway, I was out of the country at the time of the G-7 meeting. I don't take vacations very often, but I had had a very good year, and I was in Sardinia at the time. Sardinia is fairly isolated, and it takes something like two hours to make an overseas call.

**Were you aware of the situation?**

I didn't even know what the G-7 was. The meeting didn't have any significant implication at the time; it was just a bunch of bureaucrats getting together to talk down the value of the dollar.

**There was never any G-7 meeting before that time that had any significant impact on the dollar?**

Absolutely not. Anyway, I'm lying on the beach, totally oblivious to the ongoing bedlam in the world currency markets. For whatever reason— probably because it was close to the end of my vacation and I was starting to think about getting back into the markets—I decided to call my office early Monday morning, New York time, and check whether everything was running smoothly in my absence. With great difficulty, I finally got a line through to New York, but there was no answer in my office. The failure to get an answer was very unusual because my assistant, Andy [Andrew Krieger], always came in very early. I was a little concerned. I then called our London office to check on the currency markets.

"Dennis, what's going on in the currency market?" I asked.

"You know about the G-7 meeting, of course, don't you?" he asked.

"No," I answered. "What are you talking about?"

"Well, they've come up with this manifesto to bring down the value of the dollar, and the dollar is going to hell."

"Do you know where Andy is?" I asked.

"Oh, Andy is out sick today," he answered.

This was odd, because neither one of us was ever out sick. After a great deal of effort, I finally got through to Andy at home. He was in bed with the flu and running a high fever.

**Did you have any position going into the G-7 meeting?**

Yes, we had a small short dollar position, but nothing significant.

**Did Andy have the authority to trade?**

Yes, of course. He was not only monitoring my positions but was responsible for trading rather significant ones himself. The interesting thing was that as soon as Andy read the news, he went into the New Zealand market, which is the first of the world's currency markets to trade after the weekend. Not many people traded in that time zone, and it was a very thin market. I think he was only able to get price quotes at all because we (Salomon Brothers) frequently traded $20 million to $50 million on Monday mornings in New Zealand. Therefore, it was not abnormal for Andy or myself to call. We had established relationships in that trading center when very few others—New Yorkers or Europeans—had.

On very wide price quotes—literally two big figures wide because everyone was confused—he sold $60 million in New Zealand, which was a tremendous amount back then.

[At this point, Bill re-created Andy's conversation with the New Zealand Bank:]

"What's your price for twenty [million] dollars?"

"Two eighty bid, two eighty-two offered."

"Sold. How do you remain?"

"Two seventy-nine, two eighty-one."

"Yours twenty. How do you remain?"

"Two seventy-eight, two eighty."

"Yours twenty."

Andy was hitting bids six big figures below Friday's close. I was really impressed that he had that type of insight. I wouldn't have done that.

To make a long story short, for six hours I had an open line from my hotel room in Sardinia to Andy, who was out sick, flat on his back, in Englewood, New Jersey. It was so difficult getting an overseas phone connection that we just left the line open all day. Andy had the line to me and an open line to the floor on the Philadelphia Stock Exchange, where we were trading currency options. In addition, he had his wife run out to Radio Shack as soon as they opened to purchase one of those extra-long telephone cord extensions. He then brought in a third line from the neighbor's house to allow him to establish an open phone to our spot dollar/mark broker so that we could trade the cash market. We traded that way for six hours. We made $6 million that day, which at that time was probably more than 25 percent of our total annual profits.

We were staying at this luxurious resort that was largely frequented by wealthy Europeans. One humorous sidelight was that, while all that was going on, these two industrial magnate types—older German men, impeccably groomed, with perfect tans and accompanied by women who were obviously their daughters—kept coming by my room every ten minutes to ask in German what was happening. My wife did the translating. They knew that something important was going on in the foreign exchange market, but no one knew anything specific. Sardinia is so isolated that all the available newspapers are at least two days old. But I was right there.

**Were there any other trades that were particularly unusual for one reason or another?**

One trade that was interesting because it turned into a virtual poker game occurred in 1987. I had put on a huge option spread position: long twenty-three thousand Japanese yen 54 calls and short twenty-three thousand 55 calls. If the calls expired in the money, each side of the spread would represent nearly $800 million—an enormous position at the time. When I put on the position, the calls were well out of the money.

[The position Lipschutz is describing is a bull call spread. In order for the trade to be profitable, the price of the yen must rise above 54 by an amount sufficient to at least offset the cost of the spread. Unlike a straight call position, however, the profit potential is limited to one full point per contract, since the long 54 call position is offset by the sale of an equal size 55 position. Although the sale of the 55 call limits the profit potential, it also substantially reduces the cost of the trade, as the income generated by selling the 55 call partially offsets the cost of buying the 54 call. The maximum profit would be realized at any price above 55, in which case each spread position would generate one full point profit ($625) minus the price difference between the 54 and 55 calls at the time of the position implementation. Given the numbers described by Lipschutz, the maximum profit potential on the entire spread, which again would occur at a price above 55, would approximate $13 million.]

The risk of doing this type of trade is that if the front strike is in the money but the back strike is not [i.e., a price between 54 and 55], you could end up exercising the long 54 call and not getting called away on your short 55 call. While this would imply a profit at expiration, it would also mean that you would be left net long a near $800 million position, which would have to be carried over the weekend until the Tokyo market opened on Sunday night. In other words, you would be left with a tremendous risk exposure to an adverse price move over the weekend.

## Couldn't you hedge the position near expiration?

You could if you were sure about whether the market was going to settle significantly above or below the 55 strike level. But what if the market is trading near the strike price as expiration approaches? In that case, you're not sure whether you're going to be assigned on the contracts or not. You certainly don't want to try to liquidate the entire twenty-three thousand contract spread position in the final hours of trading, since you would have to pay away a tremendous amount in the bid/offer spread to get out of a trade that size at that point. If you don't hedge the long 54 call position because of the assumption that the market will expire above 55 [an event that would cause the short 55 call to get exercised], but instead the market closes below 55, you can end up carrying a net huge long position over the weekend. If, on the other hand, you hedge your long 54 call position on the assumption that the market is going to close below 55, but instead it closes above 55 and the short 55 call is exercised, then you can end up net short the entire face amount over the weekend. It's the uncertainty about whether the market will close above or below 55 (or, equivalently, whether or not your short 55 call position will be exercised) that makes it impossible to effectively hedge the position.

One particularly interesting element of the trade was that one market maker was on the opposite side of about twenty thousand lots of the spread position. When you deal with positions of that size on an exchange, you generally know who is on the other side.

The expiration day arrives, and as the market is in its final hours of trading, guess what? The price is right near 55. The market-making firm doesn't know whether I have hedged my long 54 call or not, and I don't know whether they have hedged their short 54 call or plan to exercise their long 55 call to offset the position. Neither one of us will know the other's position until Sunday morning, which is when you get notified of any option exercises.

On Sunday evening we get to play the same poker game all over again in the Tokyo market. If they have exercised their long 55 call (making me short that position), they won't know if I'm short yen or not, depending on whether or not I've hedged. If they haven't exercised their call, they won't know if I'm net long yen or neutral, again depending on whether or not I'm hedged. For my part, I also won't know whether they are net long, short, or neutral, since I don't know whether or not they have hedged. Consequently, going into the early New Zealand and Australian market openings, either I'm going to be long nearly $800 million worth of yen and they are going to be short the same position, or they are going to be long that amount and I'm going to be short, or one of us is going to have a net long or short position while the other is hedged, or we could both be hedged. Neither one of us will be able to figure out the other's position with any certainty, and given our size at that time of the day in those trading centers, we're the only game in town.

On Friday afternoon (the expiration day), I heard that the firm on the other side of the trade was buying yen in the cash market. They had tipped their hand. I knew then that they had not already hedged their short 54 call position and had no intention of exercising their long 55 calls.

At 5 P.M., the yen closed within one tick of the 55 strike level. Because of the other firm's actions in the cash market, I thought they probably wouldn't exercise their long 55 calls, but I couldn't be certain.

On Saturday, the phone rang and it was the other firm's trader. "How are you doing?" I asked.

"Very good. How are you doing?" he asked in return.

"I don't know, you tell me," I answered. Remember, you don't get your notices until Sunday, and this conversation was taking place on Saturday. "What did you do?" I asked.

He said, "What do you think I did? You'll never guess."

"Well, I think you kind of tipped your hand on Friday afternoon," I answered.

"Yeah, that was the stupidest thing," he said. The purchase of yen in the interbank market hadn't been his decision; it was a committee decision at his company. He finally told me, "We're not going to exercise."

**Did he just call to let you know that they weren't going to exercise and let you off the hook?**

I would have had that information prior to the New Zealand opening anyway. He was probably trying to sniff out my position—that is, whether I had hedged or not. If he could figure out what I had done, there would be a potential play for him in the marketplace. As it turns out, I had not hedged, and I was net long the yen position. If he knew that, he could have gone into New Zealand, which is the first interbank market to open, and pushed the market against me. By telling him that they had tipped their hand by selling the yen on Friday afternoon, I let him believe that I had figured out their position—which I had—and hedged—which I had not. In any event, there was some news over the weekend, and the dollar opened up sharply lower against the yen. I actually ended up substantially increasing my profit on the trade.

**How much did you end up making on that trade?**

A totally ridiculous amount—something like $20 million. However, the thing that was so great about the trade was not the money but the mental chess game that Friday afternoon—all the back-and-forth bluffing. People were calling my desk all Friday afternoon to ask us what was going on between us and the other firm. There was nothing else going on in the market. These were the biggest positions in the market by a hundredfold that day.

**Are there any other trades you can think of that were particularly memorable?**

I can tell you about the one time since I first started trading that I was really scared. In fall 1988, there wasn't much going on in the currency markets. The D-mark had been in a very tight trading range. As was very typical in those types of low-volatility periods, our position size tended to grow as we tried to capture smaller and smaller price moves and still produce the same results. As a result, our position size at the time was larger than normal.

We knew that Gorbachev was going to make a speech at the UN, but we didn't know what he was going to say. At the time, I was short about $3 billion against the D-mark.

**Three billion! Was that the largest position size you ever traded?**

I've been bigger, but that was a very large position. The market had been trading in a narrow 1–2 percent range, and I had expected that sideways price action to continue. Then Gorbachev made a speech about troop reductions, which was interpreted by the market as meaning that the United States could also cut its armed force commitment—a development that would be beneficial for the budget deficit. All of this was considered very bullish for the dollar. The dollar started moving up in New York, and there was no liquidity. Very quickly, it was up 1 percent, and I knew that I was in trouble.

**One percent of a $3 billion position is $30 million! Did this loss transpire in just one afternoon?**

It transpired in just eight minutes. All I wanted to do was to make it through to the Tokyo opening at 7 P.M. for the liquidity. If you really have to buy $3 billion, you can do it in Tokyo; you can't do it in the afternoon market in New York—you can't even do it on a normal day, let alone on a day when major news is out. My strategy was to try to cap the dollar in New York. Normally, if you sell several hundred million dollars in the afternoon New York market, you can pretty much take the starch out of the market. I sold $300 million, and the market went right through it.

The people on my desk didn't really know the size of our position, with the exception of Robert, who was my number two man. I looked at Robert and said, "That didn't slow the market down too much, did it?" He grimaced and shook his head slowly from side to side. I realized that I couldn't cover these positions. I was really scared. I remember thinking: This is the bullet that finally catches me in the back of the head.

Tom Strauss, the president of the company, sat about fifteen feet away from me. (Gutfreund was not there that day.) I got up and walked over to Strauss and said, "Tommy, we have a problem."

He looked at me and calmly said, "What is it?"

I answered, "I'm short the dollar and I've misjudged my liquidity in the market. I've tried to hold the market down, but it's not going to work. And I can't buy them back."

He very calmly asked, "Where do we stand?"

"We're down somewhere between seventy and ninety million."

"What do we want to do about this?" he asked. I distinctly remember being struck by the fact that he used the word *we,* not *you.*

I said, "If I try to buy some back, I may get a little here and a little there, but it won't amount to very much, and we'll just end up pushing the market further against us. The first liquidity is Tokyo."

"What's the plan?" he asked.

I answered, "When Tokyo opens, I have to see where it's trading. My intention now is to cover half the position at that time, and go from there.

He said, "We've had a good run on this. Do what you need to do." That was the entire conversation. It was over in two minutes.

In discussing this episode several days later, Robert said, "I never saw you look like that." I asked him what he meant. He answered, "You were as white as a sheet." My perception of what was going on around me at the time was, of course, quite distorted because I was so focused on that situation. I was later told that, for the entire afternoon, there was virtually not a word spoken on the desk and that Robert didn't let anybody come near me. I was oblivious to all this at the time.

Continuing our conversation, Robert said, "I don't know how you went over to Strauss."

"Why?" I asked. "What would you have done? It was the only thing I could do; I had to inform Strauss about what was going on."

Robert responded, "Ninety million. You were down $90 million! Do you understand what that means?"

I asked, "What would you have done?"

He answered, "I would have put my coat on and walked out of here. I would have figured that was it, it's over, I'm fired."

Now, I don't know if that's what he really would have done, but it never occurred to me to walk out. The idea that I had possibly just lost my job never entered my mind. This was a firm that bore me and nurtured me; it was just inconceivable that that could happen. The first thing I thought about was the position. The second thing I thought about was making sure that management knew about it. In absolute consistency with the firm's approach, as exemplified by Tom Strauss's response, there wasn't going to be any negativity in our conversation. It was a measured discussion, but if there was going to be any analysis of what went wrong, it would be after the situation was resolved.

**What eventually happened to the position?**

By the time Tokyo opened, the dollar was moving down, so I held off covering half the position as I had previously planned to do. The dollar kept on collapsing, and I covered the position in Europe. I ended up with an $18 million loss for the day, which at the time seemed like a major victory.

**Most people in your situation would have been so relieved to get out that they would have dumped the position on the Tokyo opening. Apparently, you deferred to your market judgment and avoided that emotional temptation.**

The reason that I didn't get out on the Tokyo opening was that it was the wrong trading decision. Actually, I'm a much better trader from a bad position than from a good position.

**What did you learn from the entire experience?**

Mostly I learned a lot about the firm and myself. I have a lot of respect for Salomon's willingness to understand what happens in the markets. If you want to play the game, sometimes somebody is going to get assassinated, sometimes someone is going to make a speech at the UN, and you're going to be on the wrong side of the trade—it's just the way it is. Exogenous events are exogenous events. They really understood that.

**You said that you also learned about yourself. What did you learn?**

That was the first time it hit home that, in regards to trading, I was really very different from most people around me. Although I was frightened at the time, it wasn't a fear of losing my job or concern about what other people would think of me. It was a fear that I had pushed the envelope too far—to a risk level that was unacceptable. There was never any question in my mind about what steps needed to be taken or how I should go about it. The decision process was not something that was cloudy or murky in my vision. My fear was related to my judgment being so incorrect—not in terms of market direction (you can get that wrong all the time), but in terms of drastically misjudging the liquidity. I had let myself get into a situation in which I had no control. That had never happened to me before.

**Any other traumatic trading experiences?**

You never asked me about what happened to my own account.

**All right, what happened? As I remember, you started out with about $12,000.**

That's right, and the peak was about $250,000.

**Really? You had built it up that much!**

Well, this was over a period of about four to five years.

**Still ...**

Yes, I had a lot of success. Anyway, I ended up blowing out virtually the entire account in a few days.

**What happened?**

On September 23, 1982, the Dow went from down 30 points to closing up 20. This was the famous Granville reversal, which was the bottom of the bear market.

**Does "Granville reversal" refer to the rally occurring just after Joe Granville [an extraordinarily popular market advisor at the time] had put out a sell recommendation?**

Exactly. I was very bearish and heavily long puts. I kept pyramiding all the way down. I was really pressing. I lost most of the money that Monday, and by Wednesday the account was virtually all gone.

**You took over four years to turn $12,000 into $250,000 and lost it all in a matter of days. Did you have a moment of self-questioning?**

No, I just saw it as one major mistake. I've always had a lot of confidence as a trader. My feeling was that I had developed and practiced the basic trading skills that had landed me at Salomon Brothers and that I had a tremendous amount of fun in the process. I was devastated by the way I had traded, but the money never had a major effect on me.

**Did you change anything because of this experience?**

I decided that since I was going to work for Salomon Brothers, all my attention should go into doing that very well, not trading my own account. After that point, I never again traded my own account—not because I had lost money but because I didn't want to split my focus, as I saw some other people do over the years. I basically took my paycheck every two weeks and put it in a money market account—a government-securities-only money market account because I wanted the extra protection.

**How did the sudden demise of your personal account change you as a trader?**

I probably became more risk-control oriented. I was never particularly risk averse.

**What do you mean by "risk control"?**

There are a lot of elements to risk control: Always know exactly where you stand. Don't concentrate too much of your money on one big trade or group of highly correlated trades. Always understand the risk/reward of the trade as it *now* stands, not as it existed when you put the position on. Some people say, "I was only playing with the market's money." That's the most ridiculous thing I ever heard. I'm not saying that all these concepts crystallized in one day, but I think that experience with my own account set me off on the track of considering these aspects much more seriously.

**On the subject of risk control, how do you handle a losing streak?**

When you're in a losing streak, your ability to properly assimilate and analyze information starts to become distorted because of the impairment of the confidence factor, which is a by-product of a losing streak. You have to work very hard to restore that confidence, and cutting back trading size helps achieve that goal.

**With all the loyalty you had to Salomon, why did you eventually leave?**

Gil, who started the department, left in 1988, and I ended up running the department for a year and a half. I would find myself talking on the phone a lot—not about trading, but rather about a lot of personnel problems. I was also not crazy about traveling all over. I didn't like managing people in Tokyo, London, and New York.

I wanted to bring someone in as a comanager for the department. I wanted to run trading and let someone else run the administrative side. That's not the style of Salomon Brothers, however. Instead they brought in someone from above me. Initially, I thought that it might work out, but the person they picked had no foreign exchange background at all. He came from the fixed-income department and saw everything in the eyes of the bond world. He would frequently ask, "Gee, isn't that just like the government bond market?" The answer in my mind was, "No, it's nothing like the government bond market. Forget the government bond market."

**How does your current trading for your own management firm differ from your trading at Salomon?**

At the moment, I'm trading a lot smaller than at Salomon, which is a disadvantage.

**How is large size an advantage?**

You're kidding.

**No, I'm serious.**

If a big buyer comes in and pushes the market 4 percent, that's an advantage.

**He still has to get out of that position. Unless he's right about the market, it doesn't seem like large size would be an advantage.**

He doesn't have to get out of the position all at once. Foreign exchange is a very psychological market. You're assuming that the market is going to move back to equilibrium very quickly—more quickly than he can cover his position. That's not necessarily the case. If you move the market 4 percent, for example, you're probably going to change the market psychology for the next few days.

**So you're saying size is an advantage?**

It's a huge advantage in foreign exchange.

**How large an account were you trading at Salomon?**

That question really has no direct meaning. For a company like Salomon, there are no assets directly underlying the trading activity. Rather, over time, the traders and treasurer built up greater and greater amounts of credit facilities at the banks. The banks were eager to extend these credit lines because we were Salomon Brothers. This is an example of another way in which size was an advantage. By 1990, our department probably had $80 billion in credit lines. However, no specific assets were segregated or pledged to the foreign exchange activities.

**I would like to get some feeling for how you reach your price directional decisions. Strictly for purposes of illustration, let's use the current outlook for the Deutsche mark. I know that you expect the dollar to gain on the Deutsche mark. What is your reasoning behind the trade?**

First of all, I'm very concerned about the effects of unification on the German economy. There are tremendous infrastructure problems in East Germany that may take a decade or longer to solve. Also, the plans to restructure the Bundesbank [the German central bank] to include representatives of the former East German central bank create a lot of uncertainty. Finally, Kohl's government currently appears to be on a much weaker footing. All of these factors should operate to provide disincentives for capital flowing into Germany.

At the same time, a combination of low U.S. interest rates, an apparent desire by the Federal Reserve to continue to stimulate the economy, and preliminary signs of favorable economic data suggest that the United States may be coming out of its recession. Therefore, people are starting to think that the United States may not be a bad place in which to invest their money.

**Having established a long-term philosophy about which way the**

**currency is going—in this case, the dollar going higher against the
D-mark—how would you then recognize if that analysis were
wrong?**

Events that would change my mind would include evidence that the
German government was dealing effectively with some of the problems
I listed before and economic statistics suggesting that my assumption of
an end to the U.S. recession was premature—essentially, the converse
of the situation I described for making me bullish on the dollar.

**For argument's sake, let's say that the fundamentals ostensibly
don't change but the dollar starts going down. How would you
decide that you're wrong? What would prevent you from taking an
open-ended loss?**

I believe in this scenario very strongly—but if the price action fails to
confirm my expectations, will I be hugely long? No, I'm going to be
flat and buying a little bit on the dips. You have to trade at a size such
that if you're not exactly right in your timing, you won't be blown out
of your position. My approach is to build to a larger size as the market
is going my way. I don't put on a trade by saying, "My God, this is the
level; the market is taking off right from here." I am definitely a scale-
in type of trader.

I do the same thing getting out of positions. I don't say, "Fine, I've
made enough money. This is it. I'm out." Instead, I start to lighten up as
I see the fundamentals or price action changing."

**Do you believe your scaling type of approach in entering and exit-
ing positions is an essential element in your overall trading success?**

I think it has enabled me to stay with long-term winners much longer
than I've seen most traders stay with their positions. I don't have a
problem letting my profits run, which many traders do. You have to be
able to let your profits run. I don't think you can consistently be a winning trader if you're banking on being right more than 50 percent of the
time. You have to figure out how to make money being right only 20 to
30 percent of the time.

**Let me ask you the converse of the question I asked you before: Let's say that the dollar started to go up—that is, in favor of the direction of your trade—but the fundamentals that provided your original premise for the trade had changed. Do you still hold the position because the market is moving in your favor, or do you get out because your fundamental analysis has changed?**

I would definitely get out. If my perception that the fundamentals have changed is not the market's perception, then there's something going on that I don't understand. You don't want to hold a position when you don't understand what's going on. That doesn't make any sense.

**I've always been puzzled by the multitude of banks in the United States and worldwide that have large rooms filled with traders. How can all these trading operations make money? Trading is just not that easy. I've been involved in the markets for nearly twenty years and know that the vast majority of traders lose money. How are the banks able to find all these young trainees who make money as traders?**

Actually, some of the large banks have as many as seventy trading rooms worldwide. First of all, not all banks are profitable in their trading every year.

**Still, I assume that the majority are profitable for most years. Is this profitability due to the advantage of earning the bid/ask spread on customer transactions, or is it primarily due to successful directional trading?**

There have been a lot of studies done on that question. A couple of years ago, I read a study on the trading operations of Citibank, which is the largest and probably the most profitable currency trading bank in the world. They usually make about $300 million to $400 million a year in their trading operations. There is always some debate as to how they make that kind of money. Some people argue that Citibank has such a franchise in currency trading that many of the marginal traders and hedgers in the currency market immediately think of Citibank when they need to do a transaction—and Citibank can earn a wide spread on those unsophisticated trades. Also, Citibank has operations in many countries that don't have their own central bank. In these countries, much or even all of the foreign currency transactions go through Citibank. The study concluded that if Citibank traded only for the bid/ask spread and never took any position trades, they probably would make $600 million a year.

**That would imply that they probably lose a couple of hundred million dollars a year on their actual directional trading. Of course, that would help explain the apparent paradox posed by my question—that is, how can all those traders make money? Am I interpreting you correctly?**

Personally, that's what I believe. However, the argument within Citibank would probably be: "We doubt that's true, but even if it were, if we weren't in the market doing all that proprietary trading and developing information, we wouldn't be able to service our customers in the same way."

**That sounds like rationalization.**

Assume you're a trader for a bank and you're expected to make $2.5 million a year in revenues. If you break that down into approximately 250 trading days, that means you have to make an average of $10,000 a day. Let's say an unsophisticated customer who trades once a year and doesn't have a screen comes in to do a hedge. You do the trade at a wide spread, and right off the bat you're up $110,000. You know what you do? You spec your buns off for the rest of the day. That's what almost every currency trader in New York does, and it's virtually impossible to change that mentality. Because if you are lucky, you'll make $300,000 that day, and you'll be a fucking hero at the bar that night. And if you give it all back—"Ah, the market screwed me today."

**Bottom line: If it weren't for the bid/ask spread, would the banks make money on their trading operations?**

Probably not in conventional position trading in the way you think of it. However, there is another aspect of directional trading that's very profitable. Take Joe Trader. Day in, day out, he quotes bid/ask spreads and makes a small average profit per transaction. One day a customer comes in and has to sell $2 billion. The trader sells $2.1 billion, and the market breaks 1 percent. He's just made $1 million on that one trade.

**In a lot of markets that's illegal. It's called frontrunning.**

It's not illegal in the interbank market. He's not putting his order in front of the customer's; he's basically riding his coattails.

**So he does the whole order at the same price?**

Generally, the first $100 million would be the bank's. That's just the way the market is.

**Is there any difference between that transaction and what is normally referred to as frontrunning?**

Yes, it's legal in one market and illegal in the other.

**That's the answer from a regulatory viewpoint. I'm asking the question from a mechanical perspective: Is there an actual difference in the transaction?**

The real answer is no, but I'll give you the answer from a bank's perspective. When I allow you to come in and sell $2 billion in the foreign exchange market, I'm accepting the credit risk and providing the liquidity and facility to make that trade. In exchange, you're providing me with the information that you're about to sell $2 billion. That is not a totally unreasonable rationalization.

**How do you move a large order like $2 billion? How do you even get a bid/ask quote for that amount?**

I'll tell you what happens. Let's say an order comes in for $500 million or more. The dealer stands up and shouts, "I need calls!" Immediately, among the dealers, junior dealers, clerks, and even the telex operators, you have forty people making calls. Everyone has their own call lists so they don't call the same banks. They probably make an average of about three rounds of calls; so there are 120 calls in all. All of this is done in the space of a few minutes. The dealer acts as a coordinator—the bank staff shouts out bids to him and he calls back, "Yours! Yours! Yours!" all the time, keeping track of the total amount sold. A large bank can move an amazing amount of money in a few minutes.

**When you get right down to it, virtually all the trading profits seem to come from profit margins on the bid/ask spread and coattailing of large orders. That makes a lot more sense to me, because I couldn't figure out how the banks could hire all those kids right out of school who could make money as traders. I don't think trading is that easily learned.**

You know my pet peeve? Is *that* trading? Even at Salomon Brothers, where there's a perception that everyone is a trader, it came down to only about a half-dozen people who took real risk. The rest were essentially just making markets. That nuance is lost on most people.

**Getting back to the credit risk associated with the interbank market that you mentioned earlier, when you do a trade, are you completely dependent on the creditworthiness of the other party? If they go down, are you out the money?**

You got it.

**Has that ever happened to you?**

No.

**How often does it happen?**

If a trade involves anyone who is even in question, you can ask them to put up margin.

**Isn't it possible for a bank with a good credit rating to suddenly go under?**

Suddenly? No. What is the worst case you can think of? Drexel? Salomon stopped doing currency transactions with Drexel a year and a half before they went under.

**Are you saying that there's not much of a credit risk involved?**

There is some risk, but does a Conti fail overnight? We stopped trading with Conti five months before the Fed bailed them out.

**But someone was trading with Conti in those last few months. Were they just less well informed?**

Not necessarily. They were just willing to take the risk. You can be sure that in those final months, Conti was not dealing at the market. At a certain interest rate level, you would lend any bank money. The reason why surprises don't happen is because it's in everyone's interest to know when there is a problem. Therefore, credit officers are very quick to share information whenever they think a problem exists.

**Do you ever have dreams about trades?**

On one particular occasion, I had a very specific dream the night before a balance-of-trade number was to be released. I dreamt that the trade figure would be a specific number; the revision would be a specific number; the dollar would move up to a certain level, and I would buy dollars; the dollar would move up to a second level, and I would buy more dollars; the dollar would move up to a third level, and I would buy yet again; the dollar would move up to a fourth level, and I would want to sell but would buy again.

The next day, the trade number came out, and it was exactly the same number as in my dream. The revision was also exactly the same number. Even the price sequence was exactly the same as in my dream. The only difference was that [he pauses] I didn't trade at all.

**Why not?**

Because I don't trade on dreams or rumors. I'm a fundamental trader. I try to assemble facts and decide what kind of scenario I think will unfold. To walk in and trade on a dream is absurd. I told my assistant about my dream, and we laughed about it. He said, "The day you start trading on dreams is the day we might as well pack it up."

As I watched the price action unfold, the market looked good at each of the price levels. Ironically, if I had never had the dream, I might very well have bought dollars.

**In your conscious state, you agreed with the basic trade. Right?**

Absolutely.

**Was it a matter of not taking the trade because you didn't want to appear to be trading on a dream?**

Very much so. Within myself, I was very confused as to what was happening. It was a very odd experience.

**Was it sort of shades of the Twilight Zone?**

Just like it. I couldn't believe it. My assistant and I just kept looking at each other. When the trade numbers came out exactly as I had dreamt, he said, "Billy, come on, where did you get those numbers?"

**Has this type of experience happened to you at any other time?**

That was the time that I remember the best. I had similar experiences on other occasions, but I don't remember the specifics as clearly.

**Do you want my theory on a logical explanation?**

I'd love to hear it. How do you explain picking the exact number?

**You work, relax, eat, and literally sleep with the markets. You have a storehouse of fundamental and technical information embedded in your mind. Let's say that because of some unconscious clues you picked up—maybe something somebody said, or some positions**

you saw certain people take, or whatever—you thought that the trade numbers would be out of line with expectations. But for some reason, you didn't want to trade on this expectation. Maybe, in this case, the expectation seemed irrational and you would have felt stupid trading on it. Maybe you don't like trading in front of the release of government numbers because of some past negative experiences. The reason is not important. I'm just making up examples. The point is that it's easy to envision how you might correctly anticipate an unreleased statistic and why such a projection might occur on a subconscious level.

Your projection of the market moving in a certain direction is even easier to explain. Given your vast experience, once you were right about the trade numbers, it would hardly be surprising that you would get the direction of the market right. Even dreaming about the exact price levels is not so absurd, because you have an exceptional feel for market swings. In fact, just the other day, I saw you pause in midconversation to place a buy order in a plummeting Australian dollar market at what proved to be the exact turning point.

All I'm saying is that all this information is in your mind, and it may come out in a dream because, for whatever reason, you haven't translated it into action. There is nothing particularly mysterious about it. You don't have to believe in precognition to explain it.

You can even argue further that playing out scenarios is something that I do all the time. That is a process a fundamental trader goes through constantly. What if this happens? What if this doesn't happen? How will the market respond? What levels will the market move to?

So you think that not backing up an expected scenario by taking a position will tend to force it out in the subconscious mind as a dream?

Sometimes—sure. I'm not speaking as an expert. I'm not a psychologist, but it seems logical to me. I'll give you a personal example. Several years ago, I had a strong feeling that the Canadian dollar was in the early stages of a multiyear bull market. The market had a good upmove and then went into a narrow consolidation. I felt it was going to go higher, but I was already long four contracts, which was a relatively large position for a single market, given my account size.

That night I had a dream that the Canadian dollar just went straight up. The next morning I came in and, right off the bat, I doubled my position from four to eight contracts. The market went straight up. I believe the reason this projection came out in a dream was that my logical mind couldn't accept taking the trading action dictated by my market experience. My logical side said, "How can I double my position when the market has gone straight up without even a slight reaction?" Of course, as we both know, trades that are the most difficult to take are often the successful ones.

**On a somewhat related topic, do you believe that exceptional traders are aided by accurate gut feelings about the markets?**

Generally speaking, I don't think good traders make gut or snap decisions—certainly not traders who last very long. For myself, any trade idea must be well thought out and grounded in reason before I take the position. There are a host of reasons that preclude a trader from making a trade on a gut decision. For example, before I put on a trade, I always ask myself, "If this trade goes wrong, how do I get out?" That type of question becomes much more germane when you're trading large position sizes. Another important consideration is the evaluation of the best way to express a trade idea. Since I usually tend not to put on a straight long or short position, I have to give a lot of thought as to what particular option combination will provide the most attractive return/risk profile, given my market expectations. All of these considerations, by definition, preclude gut decisions. Having said this, there are instances when, despite all my planning, trading decisions are made that might best be described as instinctive.

For example, consider the situation when I attempted to buy the Australian dollar the last time you were here. In that particular instance, the Australian finance minister had made a statement to the effect that he didn't care if the currency lost 10 percent of its value overnight. How do you react? Those types of panic situations are the instances when gut feeling comes into play. During the market turmoil that followed his statement, I felt that there was no way the currency could adjust even remotely close to 10 percent before large buyers would come in and push it the other way.

**How far was it down at the time you entered your buy order?**

About 5 percent. Even though I was already long a long-term position that was adversely affected by the news, I just felt that, over the short term, the market was bound to rebound.

**How do you gauge when a panic has run its course?**

I think it's a combination of market experience and innate feel. Many currency traders operate under rules that if they lose a certain amount of money, they must liquidate the position. Those are not the type of decisions that are made rationally given the specific situation at a given moment; rather, they are general rules that have been established previously. How do you decide when that type of last-ditch selling is nearly exhausted? It's probably largely a matter of past experience that has suffused your subconscious. In this sense, what people describe as gut feel is probably better described as subconscious market experience.

**What do you believe are the characteristics of the truly superior traders?**

Let me start with an analogy. When I was in college, my impression was that people who were really smart could do very well, even if they didn't work that hard, and people who really worked hard could also do very well, even if they weren't outstandingly bright. In contrast, in trading, I think you need both elements. The best traders I know are really quite brilliant, and they all work very hard—much harder than anyone else.

By the way, when I talk about working hard, I mean commitment and focus; it has nothing to do with how many hours you spend in the office. These traders have tremendous commitment to the markets—to their craft, so to speak. They develop scenarios, reevaluate scenarios, collect information, and reevaluate that information. They constantly ask themselves: What am I doing right? What am I doing wrong? How can I do what I am doing better? How can I get more information? It's obsessive.

**Is this type of analysis something that's ongoing during all your waking hours?**

Absolutely. Some professional traders may claim that they separate their personal life from their business life and are able to completely turn off on the weekends. I don't believe that for a second. I think that when they're relaxing in their sailboats, at some level they're still focused on the market.

**I know you like to play golf. When you're out on the course, are you still thinking about the markets?**

Probably so. The really best traders around don't think twice about how many hours they're working or whether they come in on a weekend. There's no substitute for that level of commitment.

**When you're interviewing someone for a job as a trader, how do you determine whether they have that type of commitment?**

Sometimes it's obvious. For example, in an interview someone might ask you, "What time do I have to come to work in the morning?" In my opinion that's a very bizarre question. Come in whatever time you believe is appropriate. "How late do I have to stay in the afternoon?" Leave whenever you want. I'm not going to tell someone when to come in and when to leave.

**Besides intelligence and extreme commitment, are there any other qualities that you believe are important to excel as a trader?**

Courage. It's not enough to simply have the insight to see something apart from the rest of the crowd, you also need to have the courage to act on it and to stay with it. It's very difficult to be different from the rest of the crowd the majority of the time, which by definition is what you're doing if you're a successful trader.

Many people think that trading can be reduced to a few rules. Always do this or always do that. To me, trading isn't about *always* at all; it is about each situation.

So many people want the positive rewards of being a successful trader without being willing to go through the commitment and pain. And there's a lot of pain.

## The pain being what?

You give up a lot of things. It's all tradeoffs. It's the middle of the night, everyone else is asleep, and you're sitting in front of a machine with glowing green numbers, with a pain in your psyche because the market is going against you and you don't know whether the fundamentals have changed or whether it's just a meaningless short-term move. Those are very trying times.

## Trading is such a pervasive element in your life, including being up half the night on a regular basis. Does this obsession, as you yourself termed it a little earlier, create a source of friction in your married life?

Not at all. My wife was a bond salesman at Goldman Sachs for many years. Personally, I think she would make a very good trader—she has many of the right qualities—but she doesn't want to trade. I wouldn't lessen it by saying simply that she is understanding, because that sounds so docile. She's more than understanding; she's fully cognizant, supportive, and I think she gets a big thrill out of what I do.

## Why do you trade?

I like the game. I think it's a great challenge. It's also an easy game to keep score of.

## With trading consuming most of your day, not to mention night, is it still fun?

It's tremendous fun! It's fascinating as hell because it's different every day.

## Would you still trade if there were no monetary remuneration?

Absolutely. Without question, I would do this for free. I'm thirty-six years old, and I almost feel like I have never worked. I sometimes can't believe I'm making all this money to essentially play an elaborate game. On the other hand, when you look at all the money I've produced over the years, I've been vastly underpaid.

---

The more supertraders I interview, the more convinced I become that, at least to some degree, their success can be attributed to an innate talent. Bill Lipschutz provides an excellent example. His first encounter with trading actually involved paper trading in a college investment course. Lipschutz ended up running a hypothetical $100,000 into an incredible $29 million by the end of the course. Although this accomplishment has to be taken with a grain of salt because it didn't involve real money and the rules of the experiment were flawed by the lack of realistic limitations on leverage, the results were striking nonetheless.

Lipschutz's first experience in actual trading was prompted by a $12,000 inheritance that he steadily built up to $250,000 over a four-year period. Although he ended up blowing the entire account because of one drastic mistake of wildly overleveraging his position, that does not take away from the skill that was needed to produce the steady equity growth in the first place.

Finally, and most important, despite having had no previous experience whatsoever in the currency markets, Lipschutz was significantly profitable in his very first year of trading these markets and extraordinarily profitable over the next seven years. Although he declines to quote any specific figures, it has been estimated that his trading alone accounted for an excess of one-half billion dollars in profits for Salomon Brothers over his eight-year stay with the firm.

Lipschutz himself cites hard work and an all-consuming commitment to the markets as the principal ingredients for his success. Although hard work by itself is not sufficient to make one a great trader, it does appear to be an important ingredient in the success of many of the world's best traders. Lipschutz also believes that superior intelligence is an important ingredient to trading success. However, it should be noted that others whom I have interviewed (e.g., Victor Sperandeo) do not share this view.

One theme that seems to recur in many of my conversations with the world's top traders is their view of the markets as a wonderful game rather than as work. Lipschutz emphatically claims that, for him, trading is such an engaging game that he would do it for free if he had to.

One lesson that could be drawn from Lipschutz's trading style is that you don't have to get in or out of a position all at once. Lipschutz scales in and out of virtually all his trades. One sensible piece of advice for most traders is this: Avoid the temptation of wanting to be completely right. For example, let's say you become convinced that a market should be bought, but prices have already had a sizable run-up. In many instances, if the trade is really good, by waiting for a significant reaction before putting on the entire position you are apt to miss the move completely. However, by adopting a scale-in plan—putting on part of the intended total position at the market and the remainder on a scale-down basis—you assure that you will at least have a partial position if the market keeps on going, without the excessive risk that would be implied by putting on the entire position after a large, uninterrupted advance.

As another example, assume that you are long with a large profit and are concerned about a market top. If you get out of the entire position and the market advance continues, you can miss a large part of the total move. On the other hand, if you keep the entire position and the market does indeed top, you can end up giving back a very large portion of the gain. By using a scale-out approach, you may never get the best outcome, but at the same time you will never get the worst outcome either. Also, by using a scale-in and scale-out approach, you can restrict full positions to those instances in which your confidence in a trade is greatest.

Another lesson to be learned from this interview is that if you have a strong conviction about a trade and the market has a large move because of a news event, the best decision may well be to bite the bullet and buy on extreme strength (or sell on extreme weakness). A perfect example of this concept was provided by the way the trader in Lipschutz's group handled trading the market following the G-7 meeting.

In *Market Wizards*, Marty Schwartz made the observation that if a trade that you are very worried about does not turn out as badly as feared, don't get out. The rationale is that if there is no follow-through in a direction adverse to your position, then there must be some very strong underlying forces in favor of the direction of the original position (since the reasons—fundamental or technical—for your own fears are probably shared by many others in the marketplace). A prime example of this rule in action was provided by the one trade that Bill Lipschutz admitted scared him. In that instance, he was short a very large dollar position against the D-mark in the midst of a sharp dollar rally and had to wait for the Tokyo opening to find sufficient liquidity to exit the position. However, by the time Tokyo opened, the dollar was weaker, letting him off the hook easily and therefore implying that he shouldn't get out. Lipschutz, being a highly skilled trader, responded exactly right and delayed liquidating his position, thereby recouping most of his loss.

One item I found particularly curious was that, after more than four years of steady trading gains in his stock option account, Lipschutz lost virtually the entire amount in a few days' time. Ironically, this loss coincided with his start of full employment at Salomon Brothers. Interestingly, as expressed in the interview, he had strong feelings against simultaneously trading personal and company accounts. The demise of his own account, therefore, played neatly into avoiding any potential source of conflict. In our conversation, Lipschutz insisted that the loss was probably coincidental since he was only in the training class and not yet aware of any potential conflict.

Despite Lipschutz's denial, I couldn't help but be reminded of the provocative aphorism: "Everybody gets what they want out of the market."* I wondered whether Lipschutz's subconscious was perhaps a bit more foresightful than he realized. In any case, the timing of this large loss and its relative uniqueness in Lipschutz's trading career does seem somewhat ironic. Whether this interpretation is strained conjecture or fact, one thing is certain: Lipschutz did indeed get what he wanted—a perfect job, huge trading profits, and an absence of conflict between his personal and company trading.

---

*As proposed by Ed Seykota in *Market Wizards*.

# PART III

# *Futures—The Variety-Pack Market*

# Futures—Understanding the Basics

Today's futures markets encompass all the world's major market groups: interest rates (e.g., T-bonds), stock indexes (e.g., the S&P 500), currencies (e.g., Japanese yen), precious metals (e.g., gold), energy (e.g., crude oil), and agricultural commodities (e.g., corn). Although the futures markets had their origins in agricultural commodities, this sector now accounts for only about one-fifth of total futures trading. During the past two decades, the introduction and spectacular growth of many new contracts have resulted in the financial markets (currencies, interest rate instruments, and stock indexes) accounting for approximately 60 percent of all futures trading. (Energy and metal markets account for nearly half of the remaining 40 percent.) Thus, while the term *commodities* is often used to refer to the futures markets, it has increasingly become a misnomer. Many of the most actively traded futures markets, such as those in the financial instruments, are not true commodities, and many commodity markets have no corresponding futures markets.

Trading volume in futures has expanded tremendously during the past generation. In 1991 total volume of all futures traded in the United States alone exceeded 263,000,000. Conservatively assuming an aver-

Note: This chapter was adapted from Jack Schwager, *Market Wizards* (New York: New York Institute of Finance, 1989).

71

age contact value of at least $40,000, the total dollar value of these contracts exceeded $10 trillion! (Yes, trillion, not billion.)

The essence of a futures market is in its name. Trading involves a standardized contract for a commodity, such as gold, or a financial instrument, such as T-bonds, for a future delivery date, as opposed to the present time. For example, if an automobile manufacturer needs copper for current operations, it will buy its materials directly from a producer. If, however, the same manufacturer were concerned that copper prices would be much higher in six months, it could approximately lock in its costs at that time by buying copper futures now. (This offset of future price risk is called a hedge.) If copper prices climbed during the interim, the profit on the futures hedge would approximately offset the higher cost of copper at the time of actual purchase. Of course, if copper prices declined instead, the futures hedge would result in a loss, but the manufacturer would end up buying its copper at lower levels than it was willing to lock in.

While hedgers, such as the above automobile manufacturer, participate in futures markets to reduce the risk of an adverse price move, traders participate in an effort to profit from anticipated price changes. In fact, many traders will prefer the futures markets over their cash counterparts as trading vehicles for a variety of reasons:

1. *Standardized contracts*—Futures contracts are standardized (in terms of quantity and quality); thus, the trader does not have to find a specific buyer or seller in order to initiate or liquidate a position.

2. *Liquidity*—All of the major markets provide excellent liquidity.

3. *Ease of going short*—The futures markets allow equal ease of going short as well as long. For example, the short seller in the stock market (who is actually borrowing stock to sell) must wait for an uptick before initiating a position; no such restriction exits in the futures markets.

4. *Leverage*—The futures markets offer tremendous leverage. Roughly speaking, initial margin requirements are usually equal to 5 to 10 percent of the contract value. (The use of the term *margin* in the futures market is unfortunate because it leads to tremendous confusion with the concept of margins in stocks. In the futures markets, margins do not imply partial payments, since no actual physical transaction occurs until the expiration date; rather, margins are basically good-faith

deposits.) Although high leverage is one of the attributes of futures markets for traders, it should be emphasized that leverage is a two-edged sword. The undisciplined use of leverage is the single most important reason why most traders lose money in the futures markets. In general, futures prices are no more volatile than the underlying cash prices or, for that matter, many stocks. The high-risk reputation of futures is largely a consequence of the leverage factor.

5. *Low transaction costs*—Futures markets provide very low transaction costs. For example, it is far less expensive for a stock portfolio manager to reduce market exposure by selling the equivalent dollar amount of stock index futures contracts than by selling individual stocks.

6. *Ease of offset*—A futures position can be offset at any time during market hours, providing prices are not locked at limit-up or limit-down. (Some futures markets specify daily maximum price changes. In cases in which free market forces would normally seek an equilibrium price outside the range of boundaries implied by price limits, the market will simply move to the limit and virtually cease to trade.)

7. *Guaranteed by exchange*—The futures trader does not have to be concerned about the financial stability of the person on the other side of the trade. All futures transactions are guaranteed by the clearinghouse of the exchange.

Since, by their very structure, futures are closely tied to their underlying markets (the activity of arbitrageurs assures that deviations are relatively minor and short-lived), price moves in futures will very closely parallel those in the corresponding cash markets. Keeping in mind that the majority of futures trading activity is concentrated in financial instruments, many futures traders are, in reality, traders in stocks, bonds, and currencies. In this context, the comments of futures traders interviewed in the following chapters have direct relevance even to investors who have never ventured beyond stocks and bonds.

# *Randy McKay*

## VETERAN TRADER

There are few futures traders who have gone from a starting account of several thousand dollars to double-digit million-dollar gains. Those who have kept their winnings are even fewer. If we now add the stipulation of holding a twenty-year record of highly consistent profitability, we are down to about the same number as there are Republican supporters of Teddy Kennedy. Randy McKay is one of those individuals (a consistent trader, that is—I don't know what his political leanings are).

The start of McKay's trading career coincided with the birth of currency futures trading. Although currencies have become among the most actively traded futures markets, at their inception they were moribund. In those days, the currency trading ring was so quiet that in the list of daily activities conducted in the pit, trading was probably a distant third to newspaper reading and board games. Yet, although the currency futures market's survival was initially in question, McKay's success as a trader was never in doubt. Despite the lack of activity, McKay was able to parlay an initial $2,000 stake into $70,000 in his first calendar year in the business (actually, a seven-month time span).

McKay continued his success, making more money each year than in the previous year. This pattern of steadily increasing annual gains was broken when McKay decided to switch from trading on the floor to trading at home. He quickly made the necessary adjustments, however, and by his second year of trading from home, he registered his first million-dollar gain. McKay continued to increase his winnings each successive year until 1986, when he suffered his first trading loss. Prior to that point, he had strung together seven consecutive million-dollar-plus years in his own account.

Over his entire trading career, McKay has been profitable for his own account in eighteen out of twenty years. A conservative estimate would place his cumulative earnings in the tens of millions. McKay has also managed a handful of accounts for family and friends. The two oldest accounts, which were initiated in 1982 with a starting equity of $10,000, have each generated cumulative earnings in excess of $1 million.

Despite his great success in the markets, McKay has maintained a very low profile. Until recently, even within the industry, few people had heard of him, myself included. McKay, however, has decided to enter the world of money management, a transition that requires at least a modestly higher public profile.

The interview was conducted in McKay's office during trading hours. Although McKay traded intermittently throughout the interview, he seemed totally focused on our conversation, with the exception of when he made actual trading decisions. I found McKay refreshingly open about his personal experiences and his thinking process in regards to the markets.

---

**How did you first get involved in this business?**

In 1970, I returned from a tour of duty in Vietnam ...

**Before you continue, I'm curious, were you drafted or did you volunteer?**

I was drafted. In my second year of college, I learned to play bridge and became addicted to the game. I played day and night and skipped all my classes. My lack of attendance led to six Fs. I flunked out and was immediately drafted by the marines.

**I didn't know that the marines drafted recruits.**

They normally don't. However, there were two months in 1968—April and May—in which they were allowed to take eight thousand draftees.

**Did you try to avoid getting drafted?**

I didn't have to be drafted. My father was a colonel in the reserves and he could easily have gotten me a cushy job in the reserves.

**How come you didn't take that option?**

At the time, I felt it was my obligation to serve. I guess I was a conservative kid. I felt that if I accepted the privileges of being a U.S. citizen, I also had to accept the responsibilities.

**Did you have any personal opinions about the war at the time?**

I thought it was a stupid war, but I felt that we elected leaders and they made the decisions.

**You make it sound like it was a matter of civic responsibility.**

That's exactly the way I felt about it *before* Vietnam. During and after the war, my feelings changed drastically.

**In what way?**

One of the experiences that will always be with me is standing guard duty, which is something everyone did regardless of his job. I would hear a noise in the bushes and think, "What is that?" Of course, the worst possibility was that it was one of the enemy sneaking up to try to shoot me. I would think to myself, "This is the enemy; I really want to kill him." Then I thought about who was really out there. It was probably a young kid just like me. He didn't hate me; he was just doing what his superiors told him to do—just like me. I remember thinking, "What's going on here? Here's a kid who's as scared as I am, trying to kill me, and I'm trying to kill him."

I started to realize that war is insanity. It doesn't make the slightest bit of sense for countries to try to settle their political differences by sending their children out to kill each other and whoever kills the most people gets the piece of land. The longer I was in Vietnam, and the more personal my experiences became, the more intently I felt that war was insanity.

**It almost sounds as if the war made you a pacifist.**

Very much so.

**What about the rest of the unit? Was there any prevailing sentiment about the war?**

There was a pretty wide range of feelings, but most of the unit leaned to the hawkish side. Most of them thought that we were doing the right thing; that we were there to help free these people from communism. I don't know if they were, as we say in the markets, "talking their position," or whether they really believed it.

**Did you get into arguments because your beliefs were different?**

I tried to avoid it. You have to remember that the marines were almost all volunteer. Therefore, the people who were there believed in what they were doing. Their backgrounds were very different from mine. Few of them were college educated. A number of them came from street gangs. Some were even there because the judge had given them a choice between jail and probation on condition of joining the service.

**Did you feel out of place?**

I felt very much out of place. I was in an artillery unit. Each hour we received weather reports, which we were supposed to use to derive a composite adjustment factor. We filled out a form specifying the wind direction and velocity, air density, temperature, rotation of the earth, and other factors and performed a mathematical process to derive a net factor. Every time the weather report came in, it became a game to see who could derive this factor most quickly. Before I was there, the speed record was nineteen seconds. On my second day there, I broke the record, and I eventually got the time down to nine seconds. I thought this was great fun. Little did I realize that I was making enemies by the truckload.

The people who were there preferred the new guys being ignorant so that they could have the feeling of helping to bring them along. Here I was, a new guy, a college kid, doing things better and faster than they were. I also got three promotions in my first four months, which was unheard of in the marines. All of this didn't go over too well. It took me a while, but I finally realized that being a college hotshot was doing me a lot more harm than good. I made an effort to blend in better, with modest success.

**Were you in situations in which your unit was in direct line of fire?**

Oh sure. We were bombarded by mortars and rockets nearly every other day, and there were about a dozen times when we were in face-to-face combat with troops trying to overrun our position. However, for the most part, the greatest danger was that artillery pieces were primary targets for the North Vietnamese troops and Vietcong.

**What was the emotional response to going from civilization into a situation where your life was being threatened almost daily?**

There are two responses one has. The first is fear. I remember getting off the plane in Da Nang, with gunfire all around, and being rushed into the back of a jeep. There were repeated bursts of gunfire throughout our ride to the base camp. We had our weapons with us, but we had no experience in shooting at people. I was absolutely terrified.

After a few months, the primary feeling changed from fear to boredom. Once you get used to the idea that you might die, you're faced with a sixteen-hour workday in absolutely horrible conditions. Either it was 110 degrees with dust blowing in your face, or during the monsoon season you were knee-deep in mud and freezing, even though the temperature was about 50 or 60 degrees.

**Did the fear dissipate after a while?**

There is always fear, but you get used to it. There were even times when an attack was almost welcome because it helped break up the boredom. I don't mean that to sound flip—some of my friends were killed or lost their arms and legs in these attacks—but after a few months, the boredom became a bigger problem than the fear.

**Did you have any experiences in hand-to-hand combat in which you know that you killed somebody?**

Yes and no. I know that I personally killed people, but there were no specific instances in which I fired and saw someone drop. Firefights are different in reality than they are on TV. You don't fire single shots at specific targets. Instead, you put your rifle on automatic and put out as much lead as you can. I know that I killed people with my rifle and certainly with the artillery shells that I was directing, but fortunately I never had the experience of seeing a person bleed to death by my bullet. I'm very thankful for that. I have nightmares to this day, but I'm sure my nightmares would be much worse if I had that experience.

**Nightmares because you were the instrument of death? Or because you were exposed to death?**

Nightmares from being exposed to death. The one nightmare I still have to this day is being chased by people with rifles. My feet get bogged down; I can't run fast enough; and they're gaining on me.

**While you were in Vietnam, did you feel that you were going to come out of it alive?**

I guess you're always an optimist in that type of situation. I thought I would, but I certainly had plenty of friends who didn't. I knew that was a possibility. But you can't have an anxiety attack every thirty seconds for a year. Eventually, your mind forces you to get used to the idea that you might die or lose a leg, and you go on.

**How did the Vietnam experience change you?**

The major change was that I went from being a rule follower to thinking for myself. When I realized that the leaders in the country didn't necessarily know what they were doing, I became much more independent.

**Given that you came out of Vietnam in one piece, in retrospect do you consider it a beneficial experience?**

The discipline of boot camp and learning that war is insanity were beneficial experiences. Outside of that, it was largely a waste of two years. I used to have philosophical arguments with one of the other members of the fire direction control unit. I would argue that I would prefer to be put to sleep for two years and then be awakened rather than to go through the actual experience. He argued that any experience was worthwhile.

**How do you feel now?**

The same way. I feel that it was two years stolen out of my life. When I was in Vietnam, the term for everywhere else was "the world." "What's happening in *the world?*" "I want to get back into *the world.*" We felt as if we had not only been removed from our home and friends but from the entire world as well. It was as if we were in another dimension.

**I guess the day you left must have been one of the best days of your life.**

Absolutely! I'll never forget the feeling. I had a window seat. When I saw that runway in Da Nang getting farther and farther away, I felt as if I were on my way up to heaven.

**I'm afraid we got off on a bit of a tangent. Before I interrupted you, I had asked how you became a trader.**

Since I didn't finish college before I left for Vietnam, I needed a job that would allow me to go to school at the same time. My brother, Terry, was a floor broker on the Chicago Mercantile Exchange [CME]. He got me a job as a runner on the floor, which allowed me to work in the morning, attend school in the afternoon, and study in the evening. I worked as a runner for a couple of years with absolutely no intention of getting into this business, or for that matter any other business. I was studying to be a clinical psychologist.

**Obviously you changed your mind at some point. What happened?**

Just at the time I was finishing college, in 1972, the CME launched a subdivision, the International Monetary Market [IMM], to trade currencies. At the time, CME seats were selling for $100,000, which is equivalent to nearly $500,000 today. The seat price was such an astronomical amount to me that becoming a floor trader didn't even appear to be a remote possibility. When the exchange started the IMM division, they sold seats for only $10,000 in an effort to try to get bodies into these new trading pits. They also gave away free IMM seats to all existing members. As a member, my brother received one of these seats. He had no particular need for this seat at the time, and he asked me if I'd like to use it in the interim.

While working on the floor, I had become interested in the mechanics of the market. I had always liked juggling numbers and playing strategy games, such as bridge and chess. I enjoyed watching prices fluctuate and trying to outguess the market. I thought that trading might be an interesting thing to do.

**You said that your studies were directed toward a career goal of being a clinical psychologist. Did you see a connection between psychology and the markets?**

As a matter of fact, I did. While I was on the floor during those two years, I realized that prices moved based on the psychology of the people who were trading. You could actually see anxiety, greed, and fear in the markets. I found it very interesting to follow the customers' moods and to see how these emotions translated into orders and ultimately into market price movements. I was fascinated by the process.

I decided to accept my brother's offer. He gave me the use of the seat and lent me $5,000. I put $3,000 in the bank to pay my living expenses, and I used the $2,000 for my trading account.

**As I recall, currency futures didn't trade very much in the first couple of years.**

That's right. There was a bit of activity in the first few weeks the contracts traded, but once the novelty wore off, the market liquidity completely dried up. In an effort to keep the market alive, each day the president of the exchange, Leo Melamed, who had conceived and spearheaded currency futures, would collar traders in the livestock pits once those markets had closed and cajole them into trading in the currency pit. Thus, the currency futures markets were dead all day long, but then there was a small flurry of activity after the livestock markets closed. For most of the day, though, we just sat around playing chess and backgammon.

**How did you manage to trade the markets during those years of minimal liquidity?**

A few limit orders [buy or sell orders indicating a specific execution price] would come in from the brokerage houses. In those days, the prices were still posted on a chalkboard. If I saw someone buying up all the offers in the Swiss franc, I would buy the offers in the Deutsche mark. I had no idea, however, as to the probable direction of the overall price move. On average, I made about two trades per day.

**That doesn't sound like very much. Given the market's very limited liquidity, how much were you making off your trading?**

Currency trading began in May 1972. By the end of that calendar year, I had made $70,000, which was a sum beyond my wildest dreams.

**It's amazing that you could have made so much in such an inactive market.**

It is. Part of the explanation is that the price inefficiencies were very great in those days because of the tremendous amount of ignorance about the currency markets. For example, we didn't even realize that the banks were trading forward currency markets, which were exactly equivalent to futures.

**Did you continue to meet success after your initial year? Were there any pivotal trades in those first years?**

I read your other book [*Market Wizards*]. There are traders you interviewed whom I respect tremendously. Many of them talked about their early experiences of going broke two or three times before they made it. I didn't have that experience. I don't want to sound arrogant, but I was successful at trading right from the start. The trade that was a turning point for me was the one that took me from being a twenty-to-forty-lot trader to trading hundreds of contracts.

In 1976, the British government announced that they weren't going to allow the pound to trade above $1.72. They were concerned that the pound's strength would lead to increased imports. At the time, the pound was trading in the mid-160s. To my surprise, the market responded to the announcement by immediately going to $1.72. The pound then fell back to $1.68 and rebounded again up to $1.72. Every time it reached $1.72, it fell back, but by smaller and smaller amounts each time. The price range steadily converged until the pound was trading narrowly just below the $1.72 level.

Most of the people I knew said, "They're not going to let it go above $1.72. We might as well sell it. It's a no-risk trade." I saw it differently. To me, the market looked like it was locked limit-up. [In many futures markets, the maximum daily price change is restricted by a specified limit. "Limit-up" refers to a price rise of this magnitude. When the market's natural equilibrium price lies above this limit price, the market will *lock* at the limit—that is, trading will virtually cease. The reason for this is that there will be an abundance of buyers but almost no sellers at the restricted limit-up price.]

I felt that if the government announced that they weren't going to let the price go above a certain level and the market didn't break, it indicated that there must be tremendous underlying demand. I thought to myself, "This could be the opportunity of a lifetime." Up to that point in time, the largest position I had ever taken was thirty or forty contracts. I went long two hundred British pound contracts.

Although intellectually I was convinced that I was right, I was scared to death because the position was so much larger than what I had been trading. In those days, there was no Reuters or similar service providing cash market quotes in the currencies. I was so nervous about my position that I woke up at five o'clock each morning and called the Bank of England to get a quote. I would mutter something about being a trader from CitiBank or Harris Trust and needing a quote quickly. I would normally talk to some clerk who thought I was a big shot, and he would give me the quotes.

One morning, I made the call from my kitchen, and when I asked the clerk for the quote, he answered, "The pound is at $1.7250."

I said, "What!? You mean $1.7150, don't you?"

"No," he replied. "It's $1.7250."

I realized that was it. By that time, I had gotten my brother and a number of my friends into the trade, and I was so excited that I called all of them with the news. I was so confident that I even bought some more contracts for myself. I then just sat back and watched the market ride all the way up to the $1.90 level.

**How long did it take for the market to get up that high?**

About three or four months.

**Weren't you tempted to take profits in the interim?**

Once the market pushed past the $1.72 level, it was like water breaking through a dam. I knew there was going to be a big move.

**How did you decide on $1.90 as the level for getting out?**

I thought that, as a round number, it would be a psychologically critical area. Also, I think $1.90 had been an important chart point on the way down.

The day that I got out was one of the most exciting days of my life. I had a total of fourteen hundred contracts to sell, because I had talked everyone that I knew into the position. That morning, it seemed like everyone in the world was buying, arbitrageurs included. I went into the pit and started hitting all the bids. It lasted for about forty-five minutes. I was so excited that I actually ended up selling four hundred contracts more than I was supposed to. When the impact of my selling finally hit the bank market, the pound fell about a hundred points, and I actually ended up making money on those four hundred contracts as well.

**What part of the fourteen hundred contracts represented your own position?**

About four hundred contracts.

**How much did you end up clearing on the trade?**

About $1.3 million.

**I assume that up to that point your maximum profit had been under $100,000.**

Correct. But the most important thing about that trade was that it propelled me into being a hundred-lot trader. One of my goals at the time was to become a larger trader as quickly as possible, because I felt the business was just too damn easy and that it couldn't possibly last forever. Fortunately I had that insight, because trading is much more difficult now than it was then.

**The insight being that those were really good days to be involved in the market?**

Right. Many of the people I knew were spending money as fast as they were making it, assuming that they would be able to continue making the same rate of return ad infinitum. In contrast, I thought that some day the opportunity wouldn't be there.

**When did things change?**

The markets started getting more difficult during the 1980s. The high inflation of the 1970s led to many large price moves and heavy public participation in the markets. The declining inflation trend in the eighties meant there were fewer large moves, and those price moves that did occur tended to be choppier. Also, more often than not, the price moves were on the downside, which led to reduced public activity, because the public always likes to be long. Therefore, you ended up with more professionals trading against each other.

**What about today [1991], when the professionals account for an even larger portion of total trading activity, while inflation rates have remained low? Has trading become even more difficult?**

Trading has not only become much harder, but it has also changed. In the 1970s, the price moves were so large that all you had to do was jump on the bandwagon. Timing was not that critical. Now it's no longer sufficient to assume that because you trade with the trend, you'll make money. Of course, you still need to be with the trend, because it puts the percentages in your favor, but you also have to pay a lot more attention to where you're getting in and out. I would say that in the 1970s prognostication was 90 percent and execution 10 percent, whereas today prognostication is 25 percent and execution 75 percent.

**You provided a good example of prognostication in the British pound trade you talked about earlier. However, can you generalize your approach in forecasting prices?**

I watch the market action, using fundamentals as a backdrop. I don't use fundamentals in the conventional sense. That is, I don't think, "Supply is too large and the market is going down." Rather, I watch how the market responds to fundamental information.

**Give me a specific example.**

Over the past year or two, we've had a severe recession—probably worse than the government is admitting—the worst real estate bust since the depression, and a war. Moreover, the market should have been particularly vulnerable after a nine-year advance. In the midst of all this negative news, the stock market has hardly budged, and we're still trading just below all-time highs. The fact that the stock market has been a lot stronger than it should have been tells me that it's likely to go higher.

**Can you give me another example?**

On the eve of the U.S. air war against Iraq, gold was trading near the crucial $400 level. The night our planes started the attack, gold went from $397 to $410 in the Far East markets and closed the evening at about $390. Thus, gold had broken through the critical $400 level, starting the rally that everyone expected, but it finished the evening significantly lower, despite the fact that the United States had just entered the war. The next morning, the market opened very sharply lower and it continued to move down in the following months.

**I'll keep pumping you for examples, as long as you can think of them. Any others?**

During the past summer, soybean prices were trading at relatively low levels just under $6.00. In close proximity, we witnessed a dry spell as the critical phase of the growing season approached, and we saw dramatically improved relations with the Soviet Union, which enhanced the chances of increased grain sales to that country. Export sales and the threat of drought have always been the two primary price-boosting factors. Here we had both these factors occurring at the same time, with prices at relatively low levels. Not only did soybeans fail to manage more than a short-lived, moderate rally, but on balance prices actually moved lower. In this context, the more recent price break down to the $5.30 level was almost inevitable. If prices couldn't sustain an advance with large exports expected to the Soviet Union and the threat of a drought, what could possibly rally the market?

**Besides the British pound trade we discussed earlier, what other trades stand out as particularly prominent in your twenty-year career?**

One of my favorite trades was being short the Canadian dollar from about 85 cents down to under 70 cents during the early 1980s. Up until about five years ago, the Canadian government had a policy of not intervening aggressively to support its currency. It would intervene halfheartedly at obvious points (for example, 120 to the U.S. dollar, 130, 140) for a few days and then let the Canadian dollar go. It was a very easy move. I was able to hold between one thousand and fifteen hundred contracts for virtually the entire decline, which spanned five years.

**Was the fact that the government was intervening to support the Canadian dollar, albeit inefficiently, a reinforcement for being in the trade? In fact, is that one of the things you look for in a currency trade—being on the opposite side of the intervention trend?**

Exactly. Of course, you have to be careful in situations where intervention might be forceful. But as I mentioned, at the time, intervention in the Canadian dollar was never forceful. That government policy, however, changed in the course of the price move I'm talking about.

The Canadian dollar eventually declined to 67 cents. Then, one day, it opened 120 points higher. The next day it opened 120 points higher again. My profits declined by over $1 million on each of these two successive days, which helped wake me up a little bit. On the third day, there was a story on Reuters quoting Prime Minister Mulroney, and I'm paraphrasing here, "We will not allow Chicago speculators to determine the value of our currency. Our currency is solid and we will not permit it to fall apart because of a bunch of gamblers." Touché.

**I take it that you got out at that point.**

Right, that was the end of it. When the trade was easy, I wanted to be in, and when it wasn't, I wanted to be out. In fact, that is part of my general philosophy on trading: I want to catch the easy part.

**How do you define the "easy part"?**

It's the meat of the move. The beginning of a price move is usually hard to trade because you're not sure whether you're right about the direction of the trend. The end is hard because people start taking profits and the market gets very choppy. The middle of the move is what I call the easy part.

**In other words, the markets you're least interested in are the tops and bottoms.**

Right. I never try to buy a bottom or sell a top. Even if you manage to pick the bottom, the market can end up sitting there for years and tying up your capital. You don't want to have a position before a move has started. You want to wait until the move is already under way before you get into the market.

**Do you see that as a mistake that many traders make, spending too much effort trying to pick tops and bottoms?**

Absolutely. They try to put their own opinion of what will happen before the market action.

**You talked earlier about the general desirability of being on the opposite side of central bank intervention. Let's talk about situations in which such intervention is very forceful. To take a specific case, in November 1978 the Carter dollar rescue plan, which was announced over a weekend, caused a huge overnight price break in foreign currencies. I assume that, being a trend trader, you must have been long going into that announcement.**

I was extremely long, but I had liquidated over half my position a week earlier.

**I don't understand. What was your motivation for liquidating part of the position? As I recall, there was no evidence of any weakness before the actual announcement.**

The upmove was decelerating instead of accelerating. It's possible to see market weakness even when prices are still going up and setting new all-time highs. I had been long both the Deutsche mark and British pound. I sold my Deutsche mark position and kept the British pound.

**Can you describe what your response was on Monday morning when the market opened drastically lower?**

I knew the market was going to open sharply lower well before the opening. I was very lucky in being able to get a couple hundred contracts sold in the futures markets, which was locked limit-down. [Since the cash currency market was trading far below the permissible daily limit decline in futures, there was a plethora of sellers at the limit-down price, but virtually no buyers; hence, the market was locked limit-down. Presumably, there were some naive buy orders on the opening from traders who didn't realize that the cash market was discounting an additional two limit-down days in futures, and these were the orders that partially offset McKay's sell order.]

I liquidated the rest of the position in the bank market, which was down about 1,800 points [equivalent to approximately three limit-down moves in futures].

**You just took the 1,800 point loss on the first day?**

Of course.

**Would the loss have been greater if you waited until the futures market traded freely?**

It would have been a little worse.

**In catastrophic situations, when a surprise news event causes futures to lock at the daily limit and the cash market to immediately move the equivalent of several limit days in futures, do you find that you're generally better off getting out right away, as opposed to taking your chances by waiting until the futures market trades freely?**

There's a principle I follow that never allows me to even make that decision. When I get hurt in the market, I get the hell out. It doesn't matter at all where the market is trading. I just get out, because I believe that once you're hurt in the market, your decisions are going to be far less objective than they are when you're doing well. And if the market had rallied 1,800 points that day to close higher, I couldn't have cared less. If you stick around when the market is severely against you, sooner or later they're going to carry you out.

**How much did you end up losing in that overnight break?**

About $1.5 million.

**I assume that was your worst loss up to that point.**

It was.

**Can you describe what your emotions were at the time?**

As long as you're in the position, there's tremendous anxiety. Once you get out, you begin to forget about it. If you can't put it out of your mind, you can't trade.

**What other trades in your career stand out for one reason or another?**

Are we talking both winners and losers?

**Sure.**

[*He laughs.*] I missed the giant gold rally in 1979, which culminated in early 1980. I had tremendous anxiety attacks about missing that move.

**Can you tell me why you missed it?**

The market simply ran away from me. Every day I thought, "If only I had bought it yesterday, I would have been OK." But I had a twofold problem. First, here was one of the greatest price moves in the history of commodities, and I was missing it. Second, the cash I had in the bank was steadily losing value because of the inflationary environment. I felt really horrible about the situation. I finally ended up buying gold on the exact day it made its high. I bought fifty contracts. The next day, the market opened $150 lower. I was out $750,000, but I was so relieved that the torture was finally over that I couldn't have cared less about the money I lost. In fact, I was actually praying for the market to open lower.

**In essence, then, you just went long to stop the pain.**

That's right.

**It sounds like you found that the pain of missing a move was actu-**

**ally far worse than being on the wrong side of the market.**

It was—at least in my first ten or twelve years in the markets. I hope that I've become somewhat more mature now and no longer feel that way.

**What did you learn from that experience?**

I learned that you have to be more concerned about the moves you're in than the moves you're not in. I didn't always realize that. In those days, if I had a small position instead of a big one, I would actually hope that the market would open against me.

**Are there any other trades that stand out on the losing side? For example, what was your worst loss ever?**

My worst loss ever. [*He laughs as he slowly repeats the phrase, mulling it over in his mind.*] In 1988, I became very bullish on the Canadian dollar once it broke through the 80-cent level. I started steadily building a large position until I was long a total of two thousand contracts.

**What made you so bullish?**

I had always been very good with the Canadian dollar. The market was in an extreme bull move and it had just broken through the psychologically critical 80-cent level. I just felt very strongly that the market was going to move much higher.

Anyway, this was going to be my second-to-last play. Ever since my early years in this business, my goal has been to take $50 million out of the market. I wanted $25 million in a bank account so that I could live as high as I wanted off the interest, and another $25 million to play with—to buy a newspaper or a baseball team. (In those days, you could buy a baseball team for that amount of money.)

I had planned from very early on that my last trade was going to be five thousand contracts and my second-to-last trade approximately twenty-five hundred contracts. This was that trade. My plan was to hold the position until the Canadian dollar reached the 87–88-cent area, a price move that would net me about $15 million on the trade. My next play would be to make $30 million, and then I would be done.

That was the plan, but it didn't work out that way. At the time, I was having a house built in Jamaica, and I had to go back every few weeks to supervise the construction. One Sunday evening, as I was leaving to catch a connecting flight to Miami, I stopped to check my screen for the currency quotes in the Far East. The Canadian dollar rarely moves much in the Far East market. I was startled to see that the price was 100 points lower. I literally had the bag in my hand, and the limo was waiting. I said to myself, "The Canadian dollar never moves 100 points in the Far East. It doesn't even move 20 points. That quote must be a mistake. It's probably just off by 100 points." With that thought in mind, I walked out the door.

It wasn't a mistake. The market opened more than 150 points lower on the IMM the next morning. To make matters worse, I had no phone in the house. The best I could do was to go to a nearby hotel and wait on line to use the public phones. By the time I got my call through, I was down over $3 million on the position.

**What caused that sudden collapse in the Canadian dollar?**

At the time, the Canadian election was about a month away. The prime minister, Mulroney, had an enormous lead in the polls over his opponent, Turner, who espoused extremely liberal views, including his support for an independent Quebec. There was a debate that Sunday evening and Turner destroyed Mulroney. The next morning, the polls showed that Mulroney's overwhelming 24 percent lead had shrunk to a mere 8 percent margin overnight. All of a sudden, the outcome of the election, which had been a foregone conclusion the day before, appeared to be a toss-up. To make matters worse, at the time, Canada and the United States were in the midst of delicate negotiations on a trade agreement, and a Turner victory would also have placed that agreement in jeopardy. This sudden uncertainty on the political front threw the market into complete turmoil.

**Did you get out of your position?**

I got out of about four hundred contracts, but the market was down so much that I couldn't see it going down much further. The next two or three days, however, it broke even more. By that time, I was out $7 million. Once I realized I was down that much, I told my clerk, "Get me out of everything."

**Was that the bottom of the market?**

It was the exact bottom. Within a month, the price was back to where it had been before the debate.

**Did you miss the rest of the move?**

I missed the entire move, and the market eventually surpassed my original target. I had made $2 million on the rally and lost $7 million on the break, because I had been adding all the way up. Instead of earning the $15 million I had planned to make on the trade, I ended up losing about $5 million.

**Was it during that period down in Jamaica that you suffered the most anxiety you ever had in the markets?**

No. It was the most I ever lost, but it wasn't the most anxiety.

**Which trade caused the most anxiety?**

The British pound trade in November 1978 that we talked about earlier, because it was my first big loss.

**Any other memorable trades?**

In 1982, I began to notice on the evening news that the Dow was up almost every day. I started getting very strong bullish feelings about the stock market. This was the first time I had ever had any market feel based on something other than watching futures. I was reluctant to start picking stocks, because that was someone else's game.

I opened an account with a friend of mine who was a stockbroker, instructing him to buy a cross section of stocks because I felt the market in general was going higher. At the time, I didn't know that his method of picking stocks was exactly opposite to my approach in the futures market. His theory was to buy the weakest stocks on the premise that they could go up the most. Well, that certainly wasn't my theory. He ended up buying me only three stocks, his favorites, which he had been in love with for the past ten years.

After watching the Dow go up for about three months while my account went down at the same time, I asked him to send me charts on the stocks I owned. I discovered that he was steering me into stocks that were near their lows, while my natural inclination was to buy stocks that were moving higher. I decided the arrangement wasn't working out, and I closed the account.

I pulled out the phone book and found that there was a Merrill Lynch office nearby at the corner of Michigan and Wacker [in Chicago]. One summer afternoon after the market had closed, I walked over to the bank and withdrew a cashier's check for $1 million. I then went to the Merrill Lynch office, walked through the door and asked, "Who's in charge here?" The branch manager came over, and I told him, "I want to talk to your *least* experienced broker." That's the honest truth. I wanted somebody without any opinions.

He turned me over to a broker who was about twenty-three years old. I put the check down in front of him and said, "I want to open an account, and here's what I want you to do. I want you to start out by investing three-quarters of this money in a wide variety of stocks, all of which are at or near all-time highs. After that, each week, I want you to send me a list of stocks broken down by market sector, ranking the stocks in each sector by how close they are to their all-time highs.

He followed my instructions exactly, and I did very well in that account. However, that same year, the Chicago Mercantile Exchange began trading the S&P 500 futures contract, which solved my problems on how to trade the general stock market. I thanked my broker for his efforts, closed the account, and switched into buying S&P futures. I felt bad about closing the account because he had done exactly what I had wanted him to do. He broke the market down into different sectors and bought the strongest stock in each sector.

**Don't feel bad; you probably taught him a lot about the markets. How did you fare once you switched to stock index futures?**

Very well. I was fortunate to catch most of the move in the S&P from 120 to 300.

**Could you tell me more about what made you so bullish on the stock market?**

Part of it was just seeing the market up almost every day without any particular supporting news. In fact, the news was actually quite negative: inflation, interest rates, and unemployment were all still very high. Another important factor was that the stock market was virtually unchanged from its level twenty years earlier, while inflation had skyrocketed in the interim. Therefore, in real dollar terms, stock prices were extremely low. Also, I liked the fact that most of the experts weren't particularly bullish. One popular analyst at the time whose comments I found particularly amusing was Joe Granville. Each time the market made a new high, he got more bearish than ever—and he was supposed to be a technician!

**Are there any specific trading mistakes you made that provided valuable lessons?**

In my first significant loss, I was short the Deutsche mark when the market went limit-up. I could still have gotten out limit-up, but I didn't. The next day, the market went limit-up again. I ended up not only doubling my loss, but it also took me two months to recover to my account size before that trade. I basically learned that you must get out of your losses immediately. It's not merely a matter of how much you can afford to risk on a given trade, but you also have to consider how many potential future winners you might miss because of the effect of the larger loss on your mental attitude and trading size.

**How has the tremendous increase in professional trading that we discussed earlier changed market behavior during the past decade?**

The big picture is probably the same, but the nature of the short-term price action is almost diametrically opposite to what it used to be. In order to get a rally, you need people on the sidelines who want to buy. When most market participants were unsophisticated, traders tended to wait until the market was in the headlines and making new highs before they started to buy. In contrast, professional traders, who dominate the markets today, will only be on the sidelines when there's a large move in the opposite direction. As a result, the price moves that precede major trends today are very different from what they used to be because the behavior of professional traders is very different from that of naive traders.

**How have these considerations changed the way you trade?**

I used to like buying or selling on breakouts [price moves outside of a previous range—a development frequently interpreted by technicians as signaling an impending price extension in the same direction]. However, nowadays the breakouts that work look similar to the breakouts that are sucker plays. In fact, the false breakouts probably outnumber the valid signals. Consequently, trading on breakouts is a strategy that I no longer employ. I find that major trends are now frequently preceded by a sharp price change in the opposite direction. I still make my judgments as to probable price trends based on overall market action, as I always did. However, with a few exceptions, I now buy on breaks and sell on rallies.

**If you're always waiting for a reaction before entering the market, don't you take a chance of missing major moves?**

Certainly, but so what? I've got thirty-eight markets on my screen. If I miss moves in ten of them, there will be ten others that have a price move. The worst thing that can happen to you in the markets is being right and still losing money. That's the danger in buying on rallies and selling on breaks these days.

**You make it sound like a chess game. When your opponent is a farmer or a dentist, you play one way, and when your opponent is a professional, you play another.**

No doubt about it. That's exactly right. You have to keep adapting to changes.

**What was your motivation for coming off the floor?**

I stopped trading on the floor when my first child was born, because I wanted to be home with her. I was determined not to be one of those fathers that spends an hour with his kids before bedtime and that's it. I was going to use the advantage of being self-employed to not only get wealthy but also to better enjoy my life.

**How did you find the transition from trading on the floor to trading at home?**

At first I found it very tough. During the first twelve or thirteen years I traded, the only time I made less money than the previous year was the year I started trading at home. In the pit, you can make quick hits by taking advantage of prices being out of line. In trading off the floor, however, you have to be willing to trade longer term, because you have an execution disadvantage. I think part of my problem that first year off the floor was that I just assumed I would keep on making more money year after year and didn't have to worry about it. Once I had a mediocre year, I realized I had to put much more energy and focus into my trading. The next year I came back with a lot more determination, and I had my first million-dollar year.

**You said earlier that you were a winning trader right from the start. Is there anything specific you did that helps explain that early success?**

One of the things I did that worked in those early years was analyzing every single trade I made. Every day, I made copies of my cards and reviewed them at home. Every trader is going to have tons of winners and losers. You need to determine why the winners are winners and the losers are losers. Once you can figure that out, you can become more selective in your trading and avoid those trades that are more likely to be losers.

**What other advice would you have for traders?**

The most important advice is to never let a loser get out of hand. You want to be sure that you can be wrong twenty or thirty times in a row and still have money in your account. When I trade, I'll risk perhaps 5 to 10 percent of the money in my account. If I lose on that trade, no matter how strongly I feel, on my next trade I'll risk no more than about 4 percent of my account. If I lose again, I'll drop the trading size down to about 2 percent. I'll keep on reducing my trading size as long as I'm losing. I've gone from trading as many as three thousand contracts per trade to as few as ten when I was cold, and then back again.

**Is this drastic variation in your trading size a key element to your success?**

Absolutely, because every trader will go through cold spells.

**In essence, then, you treat McKay as a trend as well.**

Definitely, and there's a logical reason for that. When you're trading well, you have a better mental attitude. When you're trading poorly, you start wishing and hoping. Instead of getting into trades you think will work, you end up getting into trades you hope will work.

**In other words, you want to wait until you get back into the proper frame of mind, but the only way you can do that is by winning, and you don't want to bet large in the meantime.**

That's right.

**You've seen lots of traders in your day both on and off the floor. Do the winners and losers separate into any distinct profiles?**

One very interesting thing I've found is that virtually every successful trader I know ultimately ended up with a trading style suited to his personality. For example, my brother is a very hardworking, meticulous type of person. When April 15 comes around, he loves to sit down, sharpen his pencils, and do his income tax. In fact, he probably gets all his pencils sharpened in March.

**He must be a population of one.**

Right. Anyway, he became a spreader, which suited his personality perfectly. [A spreader seeks to take advantage of discrepancies between related contracts by simultaneously implementing both long and short offsetting positions, as opposed to being net long or short the market.]

And he was great at it. You could go into the pit and ask him for a quote on any spread combination, and he would be able to give you the price in an instant. He would never step out and take a risk like I would, but he traded the way he wanted to trade. On the other hand, my friends who are speculators are the type of people who will fly off to Las Vegas at a moment's notice or climb a mountain in Africa. The bottom line is that the trading styles of successful traders tend to match their personalities.

**How about your own personality—how does that match your trading style?**

It matches it very well, I think. I grew up being very conservative. I was raised as a Catholic, and I was actually in a seminary for four years because I wanted to be a priest. As we discussed earlier, I deliberately allowed myself to get drafted. I was a straight-down-the-line kid. In adulthood, once I got the freedom that came with making money, I became much more of a risk taker. I went to Africa fifteen years ago, before it became a popular thing to do. I've taken lots of personal chances as an adult, because I believe life is short and you should live and enjoy it while it's here.

My trading style blends both of these opposing personality traits. I take the risk-oriented part of my personality and put it where it belongs: trading. And, I take the conservative part of my personality and put it where it belongs: money management. My money management techniques are extremely conservative. I never risk anything approaching the total amount of money in my account, let alone my total funds.

**You're implying that it doesn't make any difference what one's personality is, as long as there's no conflict between personality and trading style.**

That's right, it doesn't make any difference because there are so many different trading styles that you can always find one that will suit your personality.

**Any specific advice for a losing trader?**

Sometimes the reason people lose is that they're not sufficiently selective. Upon analysis, a trader may find that if he only concentrates on the trades that do well and lets go of the other types of trades, he might actually be successful. However, if a trader analyzes his trades and still can't make money, then he probably should try another endeavor.

---

What is the first rule of trading? I would argue that before anything else, the prospective trader must find the approach that he or she is comfortable with—that is, the approach that suits the trader's personality. McKay cites this quality as the single most important element separating winners from losers. Each trader must select the appropriate market arena, choose between system trading and discretionary trading, fundamental and technical methods, position trading and spread trading, short-term and long-term horizons, aggressive and conservative approaches, and so on. For all of these opposing choices, one alternative will suit the trader's personality, while the other will lead to internal conflict.

At this point, you might be thinking that the concept of selecting a trading methodology in sync with one's personality doesn't sound like much of an insight. "After all," you might ask, "doesn't every trader choose a method compatible with his or her personality?" Absolutely not! My own experience in this regard is detailed in the final section of this book.

In a more general sense, it is remarkably common for traders to adopt methods entirely unsuited to their personalities. There are traders who are good at system development but end up consistently overriding and interfering with their own systems, with disastrous results. There are traders who are naturally inclined toward developing long-term strategies but end up instead trading short term because of impatience or a compulsion to "do something." There are naturally born floor traders with great intuitive skills who abandon their environment of expertise and become mediocre portfolio managers. And there are theoretically oriented individuals who develop intricate, low-risk arbitrage strategies but then decide to become position traders—an approach that may require a degree of risk acceptance far beyond their comfort levels in order to be applied successfully.

In all the above cases, individuals with a natural bent for one style of trading end up utilizing a diametrically opposite style, usually to fulfill some emotional need. In other words, the need to match personality and trading style may be a matter of common sense, but it is certainly not common. The importance of this concept, however, is highlighted by McKay's assertion that virtually every successful trader he knew ended up with a trading style suited to his personality.

An essential element in McKay's own trading approach is the drastic variation in position size. When he is doing well and therefore assumes his chances for success are greatest, McKay will trade very large. On the other hand, when he is doing poorly, he will shrink his trading size to minuscule levels. It is not uncommon for McKay to vary his trade size by more than a factor of 100:1. This approach serves not only to reduce risk during the losing periods but also to enhance profits during the winning periods. A trader who utilizes a constant-position-size approach gives up an important edge in much the same way as does a blackjack player who always bets the same amount regardless of the cards that have been previously dealt.

Risk control is another essential element in McKay's approach, as indeed it is for most of the great traders. In addition to sharply reducing position size during losing streaks, as just discussed above, McKay also believes in immediately getting out of a position that has gone sour. In one of the few instances when he deviated from this self-proclaimed critical principle (the long Canadian dollar position discussed in the interview), an uncharacteristic two-day procrastination turned a $3.5 million loss into a $7 million loss.

Although McKay is predominantly a technical trader, fundamental analysis plays a critical role in defining his major trade strategies. His use of fundamentals, however, is somewhat unconventional. McKay doesn't try to gauge whether the fundamentals are bullish or bearish, nor does he place any direct weight on whether the fundamental news is bullish or bearish. Rather, he focuses on the market's response to fundamental news. For example, if the market is shrugging off a barrage of bearish news, McKay would view that as evidence of an impending bull move.

# William Eckhardt

## THE MATHEMATICIAN

W illiam Eckhardt is one of the key figures in a famous financial tale, yet he is virtually unknown to the public. If elite traders were as familiar as leading individuals in other fields, one could picture Eckhardt appearing in one of those old American Express ads (which featured famous yet obscure names such as Barry Goldwater's vice presidential running mate): "Do you know me? I was the partner of perhaps the best-known futures speculator of our time, Richard Dennis. I was the one who bet Dennis that trading skill could not be taught. The trading group known in the industry as the Turtles was an outgrowth of an experiment to resolve this wager." At this point, the name WILLIAM ECKHARDT might be printed across the screen.

So *who is* William Eckhardt? He is a mathematician who just short of earning his Ph.D. took a detour into trading and never returned to academics (at least not officially). Eckhardt spent his early trading years on the floor. Not surprisingly, he eventually abandoned this reflexive trading arena for the more analytical approach of systems-based trading. For a decade, Eckhardt did very well with his own account, primarily based on the signals generated by the systems he developed but supplemented by his own market judgment. During the past five years, Eckhardt has also managed a handful of other accounts, his average return during this period has been 62 percent, ranging from a 7 percent loss in 1989 to a 234 percent gain in 1987. Since 1978, he has averaged better than 60 percent per year in his own trading, with 1989 the only losing year.

At the time of our interview, after a career of anonymity, Eckhardt was poised to expand his involvement in managed money to a broader audience. Why was Eckhardt now willing to emerge into the limelight by actively seeking public funds for management? Why not simply continue to trade his own account and those of a few friends and associates, as he had done all along? In an obvious reference to the Turtles [see next chapter], Eckhardt candidly admitted, "I got tired of seeing my students managing hundreds of millions while I was managing comparatively paltry amounts." Obviously, Eckhardt felt it was time to collect the dues he had earned.

Trading system research is obviously something Eckhardt enjoys, and, of course, it is the way he earns his living, but his true passion may be scientific inquiry. Indeed, in a sense, trading and trading-related research is the means by which Eckhardt generates his own personal grants for the scientific projects that intrigue him. He is drawn to exploring some of the great paradoxes that continue to baffle scientists. Quantum mechanics has captured his interest because of the common-sense-defying Bell's theorem, which demonstrates that measurements on distantly separated particle systems can determine one another in situations in which no possible influence can pass between the systems. Evolution is another area he studies, trying to find an answer to the riddle of sexual reproduction: Why did nature evolve sexual reproduction, wherein an organism passes on only half of its genes, whereas in asexual reproduction 100 percent of the genes are passed on? Perhaps his most intensive study is directed at understanding the concept of time. When I interviewed Eckhardt, he was working on a book about the nature of time (his basic premise is that the passage of time is an illusion).

Eckhardt brings many strengths to the art of trading system design: years of experience as a trader both on and off the floor, an obviously keen analytical mind, and rigorous mathematical training. This combination gives Eckhardt an edge over most other trading system designers.

---

**How did you become partners with Richard Dennis?**

Rich and I were friends in high school. We probably met because of a mutual interest in the markets, but the friendship was never about trading. Rich began trading when he was in college. I stayed in school, working toward a doctoral dissertation in mathematical logic. In 1974 I got bogged down for political reasons.

**What do you mean by "bogged down"?**

I was writing a doctoral dissertation on mathematical logic at the University of Chicago under a world-famous mathematician. Everything was going along fine until a new faculty member whose specialization happened to be mathematical logic joined the staff. Theoretically, I was his only student. Consequently, the supervisory role on my thesis was shifted from my existing advisor to this new faculty member, who then decided that he really wanted me to do a different thesis. As a result, after I had done all my course work, taken my exams, and finished three-quarters of my dissertation, my progress was stymied.

At the time, Rich suggested that I take a sabbatical to try trading on the floor. I did, and I never returned to school.

**The shift from being a graduate student of mathematics to a floor trader sounds like a radical transition.**

Yes, it was. Although I had maintained an interest in the nature of speculative prices, I have to admit that mathematical logic is a far cry from floor trading. If anything, I went into the pit with too many preconceptions of how markets work.

**What kind of preconceptions?**

I went in with the idea that I could apply the analytical techniques that I had picked up as a mathematician to the markets in a straightforward manner. I was wrong about that.

**Did you try doing that?**

Off-the-floor traders live or die by their ideas about the market or their systems. That's not true of floor traders. As a pit trader, you only need to be able to gauge when a market is out of line by a tick, or a few ticks. Once you master that skill, you tend to survive, whether your underlying theory is sound or not. In fact, I know a lot of pit traders who subscribe to various bogus systems: moving averages, lunar cycles, and god only knows what. When they get signals from these systems, they essentially buy on the bid or sell on the offer. At the end of the month, they have a profit, which they always attribute to their system. Yet some of these systems are completely vacuous. Perhaps I did a variation of the same theme. I had ideas about speculating and trading, and I did well in the pit. But I'm not sure that I made any money from my ideas about the market.

**What was the basis of your buying and selling decisions on the floor?**

Basically, I would buy when weak hands were selling and sell when they were buying. In retrospect, I'm not sure that my strategy had anything to do with my success. If you assume that the true theoretical price is somewhere between the bid and the offer, then if you buy on the bid, you're buying the market for a little less than it's worth. Similarly, if you sell on the offer, you're selling it for a little more than it's worth. Consequently, on balance, my trades had a positive expected return, regardless of my strategy. That fact alone could very well have represented 100 percent of my success.

**Is that, in fact, what you think?**

I think that the execution edge was probably the primary reason for my success as a floor trader. The major factor that whittles down small customer accounts is not that the small traders are so inevitably wrong, but simply that they can't beat their own transaction costs. By transaction costs I mean not only commissions but also the skid in placing an order. As a pit trader, I was on the other side of that skid.

**As a former Ph.D. candidate in mathematics, did you miss the intellectual challenge in what you were doing?**

Initially, yes. But I eventually got into serious research on prices, and that was as tough a problem as anything I ever came across in academia.

**Were any of the areas you studied in mathematics applicable to developing trading systems?**

Certainly—statistics. The analysis of commodity markets is prone to pitfalls in classical statistical inference, and if one uses these tools without having a good foundational understanding, it's easy to get into trouble.

Most classical applications of statistics are based on the key assumption that the data distribution is normal, or some other known form. Classical statistics work well and allow you to draw precise conclusions if you're correct in your assumption of the data distribution. However, if your distribution assumptions are even a little bit off, the error is enough to derail the delicate statistical estimators, and cruder, robust estimators will yield more accurate results. In general, the delicate tests that statisticians use to squeeze significance out of marginal data have no place in trading. We need blunt statistical instruments, robust techniques.

**Could you define what you mean by "robust"?**

A robust statistical estimator is one that is not perturbed much by mistaken assumptions about the nature of the distribution.

**Why do you feel such techniques are more appropriate for trading system analysis?**

Because I believe that price distributions are pathological.

**In what way?**

As one example, price distributions have more variance [a statistical measure of the variability in the data] than one would expect on the basis of normal distribution theory. Benoit Mandelbrot, the originator of the concept of fractional dimension, has conjectured that price change distributions actually have infinite variance. The sample variance [i.e., the implied variability in prices] just gets larger and larger as you add more data. If this is true, then most standard statistical techniques are invalid for price data applications.

**I don't understand. How can the variance be infinite?**

A simple example can illustrate how a distribution can have an infinite mean. (By the way, a variance is a mean—it's the mean of the squares of the deviations from another mean.) Consider a simple, one-dimensional random walk generated, say, by the tosses of a fair coin. We are interested in the average waiting time between successive equalizations of heads and tails—that is, the average number of tosses between successive ties in the totals for heads and tails. Typically, if we sample this process, we find that the waiting time between ties tends to be short. This is hardly surprising. Since we always start from a tie situation in measuring the waiting time, another tie is usually not far away. However, sometimes, either heads or tails gets far ahead, albeit rarely, and then we may have to wait an enormous amount of time for another tie, especially since additional tosses are just as likely to increase this discrepancy as to lessen it. Thus, our sample will tend to consist of a lot of relatively short waiting times and a few disquietingly large outliers.

What's the average? Remarkably, this distribution has no average, or you can say the average is infinite. At any given stage, your sample average will be finite, of course, but as you gather more sample data, the average will creep up inexorably. If you draw enough sample data, you can make the average in your sample as large as you want.

**In the coin toss example you just provided, computer simulations make it possible to generate huge data samples that allow you to conclude that the mean has no limit. But how can you definitively state that the variances of commodity price distributions are not finite? Isn't the available data far too limited to draw such a conclusion?**

There are statistical problems in determining whether the variance of price change is infinite. In some ways, these difficulties are similar to the problems in ascertaining whether we're experiencing global warming. There are suggestive indications that we are, but it is difficult to distinguish the recent rise in temperature from random variation. Getting enough data to assure that price change variance is infinite could take a century.

**What are the practical implications of the variance not being finite?**

If the variance is not finite, it means that lurking somewhere out there are more extreme scenarios than you might imagine, certainly more extreme than would be implied by the assumption that prices conform to a normal distribution—an assumption that underlies most statistical applications. We witnessed one example in the one-day, 8,000-point drop in the S&P on October 19, 1987. Normal estimation theory would tell you that a one-day price move this large might happen a few times in a millennium. Here we saw it happen within a decade of the inauguration of the S&P contract. This example provides a perfect illustration of the fact that if market prices don't have a finite variance, any classically derived estimate of risk will be significantly understated.

**Besides implying that traders need to be more conservative in risk control than might be implied from straightforward statistical interpretations, are there other practical implications of using what you term a *robust* approach as opposed to methods that assume a normal probability distribution?**

One important application concerns a situation in which you have several indicators for a certain market. The question is: How do you most effectively combine multiple indicators? Based on certain delicate statistical measures, one could assign weights to the various indicators. But this approach tends to be assumption-laden regarding the relationship among the various indicators.

In the literature on robust statistics you find that, in most circumstances, the best strategy is not some optimized weighting scheme, but rather weighting each indicator by 1 or 0. In other words, accept or reject. If the indicator is good enough to be used at all, it's good enough to be weighted equally with the other ones. If it can't meet that standard, don't bother with it.

The same principle applies to trade selection. How should you apportion your assets among different trades? Again, I would argue that the division should be equal. Either a trade is good enough to take, in which case it should be implemented at full size, or it's not worth bothering with at all.

**You talked earlier about the pitfalls in market analysis. Can you provide some other examples?**

Any meaningful approach must be invariant to the choice of units. An egregious violation of this rule occurs in a certain class of bar chart techniques. Some of these are simple (45-degree angles), and some are harebrained (drawing regular pentagons on the chart), but what they all have in common is the use of angles on a bar chart. Many of the trading technique compendia, even some that claim sophistication, treat such ideas.

There's a simple consideration that absolutely invalidates all such angles-of-certain-size methods in a single swipe: The size of an angle on a bar chart is *not* invariant to changes of scale. For instance, consider the technique of drawing a line from the low of a move at a 45-degree angle. If you do this on two charts of the same contract but with different time and price scales, say from two different services, the 45-degree lines will be different. They will subsequently intersect the price series in different places. In fact, the angle of a line joining two prices on a bar chart is not a property of the price series at all. It depends completely on what units you use for price and time and how you space them on the chart, all of which are quite arbitrary. There are good methods and bad methods, but these angle techniques are no method.

As an aside, note that trend lines that involve connecting two or more points on the price series are invariant under changes of scale and, hence, make sense in a way that lines determined by slopes do not. On differently scaled charts, a given trend line has different slopes, but it intersects the price series in precisely the same places.

The lack of intrinsic meaning of angles on a bar chart has significance even for chart-oriented traders who do not employ angles. How sharply a trend slopes on a chart is often a psychological consideration in making a trade. If you fall prey to this influence, you're letting the chart maker's practical and aesthetic considerations impinge on your trading. Any trend can be made to look either gentle or steep by adjusting the price scale.

This example also highlights one of the advantages of computerized trading. A computer ignores all but what it is instructed not to ignore. If you wanted your computer system to be cognizant of slope, you would have to program this feature into it. At that point, it would become abundantly clear that the slope value depends directly on the choice of units and scales for the time and price axes.

I've always been amazed by how many people are either oblivious to the scale-dependent nature of chart angles or unconcerned about its ramifications. My realization of the inherent arbitrariness of slope-of-line methods is precisely why I've never been willing to spend even five minutes on Gann angles or works by the proponents of this methodology.

**What are some of the analytical pitfalls in trading system design?**

There are a lot of pitfalls in designing systems. First of all, it's very easy to make postdictive errors.

**Define "postdictive."**

Using information that can be available only after the fact. Sometimes the postdictiveness is blatant—a programming error. For example, you use the closing price in a computation to decide whether to initiate a trade before the close. This kind of problem, not at all uncommon, usually betrays its presence when you generate unrealistically good performance statistics. But there are subtler kinds of postdictive errors. The highest prices in your data are followed by lower prices, nearly by definition. If you incorporated these highest prices into a trading rule, or sneaked them in via seasonal considerations, the rule would work on your data, but only postdictively.

**Any other pitfalls?**

One that has been mentioned a lot is the problem of overfitting. The more degrees of freedom you have, the more your system is able to fit itself to the price series.

**Please define "degrees of freedom" for the nonmathematical reader.**

In its clearest form, a degree of freedom is a number, a so-called parameter, that yields a different system for every allowed value. For example, a moving average system varies depending on how many days one chooses to average. This is a degree of freedom, and its allowed values are positive integers. But there can also be hidden degrees of freedom. One can have structures within the system that can take on various alternative forms. If various alternatives are tested, it gives the system another chance to conform to past idiosyncrasies in the data.

Not only is it perilous to have too many degrees of freedom in your system, there are also "bad" degrees of freedom. Suppose a certain degree of freedom in your system impinges only on a very few oversized trends in the data and otherwise does not affect how the system trades. By affixing to accidental features of the small sample of large trends, such a degree of freedom can substantially contribute to overfitting, even though the overall number of degrees of freedom is manageable.

**How do you determine to what extent the performance of a system is affected by overfitting past data as opposed to capturing truths about market behavior?**

The best way is to look at hundreds of examples. Add degrees of freedom to a system and see how much you can get out of them. Add bogus ones and see what you can get. I know of no substitute for experience in this matter. Try a lot of systems. Try systems that make sense to you and ones that don't. Try systems that have very few parameters and ones that are profligate with them. After a while, you develop an intuition about the trade-off between degrees of freedom and the reliability of past performance as an indicator of future performance.

**Do you have a limit to how many degrees of freedom you would put into a system?**

Seven or eight is probably too many. Three or four is fine.

**What is your opinion about optimization? [Optimization refers to the process of testing many variations of a system for the past and then selecting the best-performing version for actual trading.]**

It's a valid part of the mechanical trader's repertoire, but if you don't use methodological care in optimization, you'll get results that are not reproducible.

## How do you avoid that pitfall?

You really are caught between conflicting objectives. If you avoid optimization altogether, you're going to end up with a system that is vastly inferior to what it could be. If you optimize too much, however, you'll end up with a system that tells you more about the past than the future. Somehow, you have to mediate between these two extremes.

## Other than the things we have already talked about, what advice do you have for people who are involved in system development?

If the performance results of the system don't sock you in the eye, then it's probably not worth pursuing. It has to be an outstanding result. Also, if you need delicate, assumption-laden statistical techniques to get superior performance results, then you should be very suspicious of the system's validity.

As a general rule, be very skeptical of your results. The better a system looks, the more adamant you should be in trying to disprove it. This idea goes very much against human nature, which wants to make the historical performance of a system look as good as possible.

Karl Popper has championed the idea that all progress in knowledge results from efforts to falsify, not to confirm, our theories. Whether or not this hypothesis is true in general, it's certainly the right attitude to bring to trading research. You have to try your best to disprove your results. You have to try to kill your little creation. Try to think of everything that could be wrong with your system, and everything that's suspicious about it. If you challenge your system by sincerely trying to disprove it, then maybe, just maybe, it's valid.

## Do you use chart patterns in your systems?

Most things that look good on a chart—say, 98 percent—don't work.

## Why is that?

The human mind was made to create patterns. It will see patterns in random data. A turn-of-the-century statistics book put it this way: "Too fine an eye for pattern will find it anywhere." In other words, you're going to see more on the chart than is truly there.

Also, we don't look at data neutrally—that is, when the human eye scans a chart, it doesn't give all data points equal weight. Instead, it will tend to focus on certain outstanding cases, and we tend to form our opinions on the basis of these special cases. It's human nature to pick out the stunning successes of a method and to overlook the day-in, day-out losses that grind you down to the bone. Thus, even a fairly careful perusal of the charts is prone to leave the researcher with the idea that the system is a lot better than it really is. Even if you carry it a step further by doing careful hand research, there is still a strong tendency to bias the results. In fact, this bias exists in all scientific research, which is why they have persnickety double-blind tests. Even the most honest researcher will tend to bias data toward his or her hypothesis. It can't be helped. When I did research by hand, I took the attitude that I had to discount my results by 20 to 50 percent.

**I remember one time when I was on a flight from San Francisco to New York, I had a new system idea that I was excited about and wanted to test preliminarily off the charts. The system involved using a conventional indicator (stochastics, I believe) in an unconventional way. I tried the system on several different markets, and it seemed to do terrifically. When I eventually had the system computer tested, I discovered that it actually lost money. What happened was that my alignment between the indicator on the bottom of the chart and the price on top was off by a day or so. Since the signals tended to come during periods of rapid price movement, being off by one day could mean the difference between being on the wrong side of the market for a 500-point move (say, in a market such as the S&P) instead of on the right side—a 1,000-point ($5,000 in the S&P) difference altogether. So what had actually looked like a great system proved to be totally worthless. Ever since then, I've been very cautious about drawing any conclusions from hand testing. I now wait until the computer results are in.**

The desire to find patterns is the same human quirk that convinces people that there is validity in superstitions, or astrology, or fortune tellers. The successes are much more startling than the failures. You remember the times when the oracle really hit the nail on the head, and you tend to forget the cases in which the prediction was ambiguous or wrong.

**Your comments basically seem to imply that chart reading is just laden with pitfalls and unfounded assumptions.**

Yes, it is. There may be people out there who can do it, but I certainly can't. Every pattern recognition chart trader I know makes the trades he really likes larger than the trades he doesn't like as much. In general, that's not a good idea. You shouldn't be investing yourself in the individual trades at all. And it's certainly wrong to invest yourself more in some trades than others. Also, if you think you're creating the profitable situation by having an eye for charts, it's very difficult not to feel excessively responsible if the trade doesn't work.

**Which, I assume, is bad.**

Yes, it's very destabilizing.

**Whereas if you have a mechanical system, that's not a problem.**

That's right. Your job is to follow the system. If the system does something that results in losses, that's just an expected part of the system. Your judgment might be on the line over the entire performance of your system, but there's no sense in which your judgment is on the line on any single trade.

**I fully understand the psychological advantages of a mechanical approach (assuming, of course, that it's effective), but are you also saying that you're skeptical of chart reading as a general approach to trading?**

When I have an idea based on a chart pattern, I try to reduce it to an algorithm that I can test on a computer. If a method is truly valid, you should be able to explain it to a computer. Even if you can't define it precisely, you should still be able to concoct an algorithm that approximately describes the pattern. If your algorithm gives you an expected gain near zero—as is typically the case—then don't delude yourself into believing that the pattern has validity that depends on some indescribable interpretation you bring to it.

**In other words, the computer doesn't lie; believe it rather than your intuitive notions of a pattern's reliability.**

Yes, because, as I mentioned before, the human mind will tend to find patterns where none exist.

**Do you follow your systems absolutely, or do you sometimes intervene?**

At this stage of the game, computer trading systems are rote algorithms. They may be complex, but they are still simpleminded. Any system that I know of, if traded at a level that is large enough, will occasionally stray into overly risky terrain. Of course, this vulnerability can be avoided by trading too small—that is, scaling to the worst cases—but that is a costly solution in terms of overall performance. It's better to trade at a reasonable level, and when you find yourself with too much exposure, override your system and cut back. Also, a good system will occasionally direct you to do something stupid. In such cases, your own judgment is vital.

Generally speaking, however, if your system is any good, don't override it, except when it's clearly violating the intentions of its design. Don't get into the habit of finagling the system day in and day out. Save your ingenuity and creativity for research.

**Can you give me an example of a system violating the intentions of its design?**

On the day of the stock market crash [October 19, 1987], I was short S&Ps, and I was also short Eurodollars. At the close, the S&Ps were down 8,000 points, but the Eurodollars were down only 5 points. My trader mentality told me that the Eurodollars should have been down at least 40 or 50 points in sympathy with the S&P collapse. Even though my system was still short Eurodollars, I covered my position because I didn't like the market action.

**Was that the right thing to do?**

Yes. The market opened nearly 300 points higher the next day.

**When you discover that your system does something that is not optimal for reasons you can verbalize, as in the Eurodollar example you just cited, do you then modify your system to incorporate a new rule to address such situations?**

If you find yourself repeatedly running into a certain kind of problem, or if you find a structural flaw in the system, then it's time to change the system. But you shouldn't change it every time it does something you don't like. No system of reasonable algorithmic complexity is going to behave according to the intentions of the designer under all constellations of circumstances. A designer cannot anticipate all possible situations. Even if he could, it would be unwise to add a degree of freedom to the system for something that happens less than once a year.

**Any other examples of overriding your system that stick in your mind?**

Yes, around the time of the Gulf War. This was a completely unprecedented situation. We had never before had a war by deadline. My instinct was to not trade, but I had other concerns. I take the point of view that missing an important trade is a much more serious error than making a bad trade. In any worthwhile system, you have all kinds of backups to protect you (that is, to assure that you get out) when you take a bad trade. On the other hand, typically, if you miss a good trade, you have nothing to protect you—that is, nothing in the system will assure that you eventually get in. Also, missing a good trade can be demoralizing and destabilizing, especially if you've been in the midst of a losing period. And like so many bad trading decisions, it ends up costing you more than just the money lost or not made on the trade. Missing a major trade tends to have a reverberating effect throughout your whole trading strategy. Sometimes it can be weeks before you get back on track. For all these reasons, I felt that it was inappropriate to not trade.

**But I thought you said this was an instance when you overrode the system?**

I took the trades, but I cut my normal position size in half.

**What happened?**

I got clobbered, or, more accurately, half-clobbered.

**So, once again, your intervention seemed to help your performance. Were there situations when overriding the system blew up in your face?**

Many. One that stands out occurred several years ago after I had suffered a longer-than-usual string of losses. At the time, I happened to be long currencies. Some international situation developed over the weekend that caused the currencies to move sharply higher. By Monday morning I had what appeared to be a windfall profit. On the alleged basis that I was reducing my exposure because of the increased volatility, I took profits on half of my position. In fact, my exposure across all markets at that time was light, and I could easily have afforded the extra risk in the currency position. It was simply that coming after a period of much losing, I couldn't stand the idea of giving back all that profit. In effect, I reasoned that the currencies had gone up enough—the call of the countertrend. Shortly thereafter, the currencies underwent another upside explosion that exceeded the first. Such willfully missed opportunities hurt more than losses.

**On balance, have you found that your intervention has helped or hindered your performance?**

I had the experience of simultaneously trading for myself, which is what I've done for most of my career, and also managing an account for an associate, which I traded exclusively on a mechanical system. Although the performance in my account was good, the account trading entirely on the mechanical system definitely did better.

I had known that a good system would outperform me in a windfall year, but I thought I could outperform the system in a mediocre year.

(Maybe I could have once, but my systems have improved over the years.) This experience indicated otherwise.

**Yet, I take it that until this unintentional experiment, you must have thought that your overrides were helping performance.**

That's because the times when you do something that appears to out-smart the system are the ones that stay with you. The day-in, day-out slippage is the sort of thing you forget. Clearly, my overriding was cost-ing me money, even though I thought otherwise.

**Have you then changed your viewpoints on overriding?**

Certainly, I now feel that it should be a far more selective process than I did years ago. You should try to express your enthusiasm and ingenuity by doing research at night, not by overriding your system during the day. Overriding is something that you should do only in unexpected cir-cumstances—and then only with great forethought. If you find yourself overriding routinely, it's a sure sign that there's something that you want in the system that hasn't been included.

**Is there anything that you can say about how you pick your trades other than off the system?**

I don't like to buy retracements. If the market is going up and I think I should be long, I'd rather buy when the market is strong than wait for a retracement. Buying on a retracement is psychologically seductive because you feel you're getting a bargain versus the price you saw a while ago. However, I feel that approach contains more than a drop of poison. If the market has retraced enough to make a significant differ-ence to your purchase price, then the trade is not nearly as good as it once was. Although the trade may still work, there's an enhanced chance that the trend is turning. Perhaps even more critical, a strategy of trying to buy on retracements will often result in your missing the trade entirely or being forced to buy at an even higher price. Buying on retracements is one of those ploys that gives psychological satisfaction rather than pro-viding any benefits in terms of increased profits. As a general rule, avoid those things that give you comfort; it's usually false comfort.

**Do you have any rational explanation for why trend-following systems work?**

People tend to focus on the few broad outcomes that appear most probable and ignore the low-probability scenarios. As various possible outcomes become less and more likely, certain neglected ones of small probability pop into view—a threshold phenomenon. The market has to discount these "new" possibilities somewhat discontinuously. Evidently, the success of trend-following means that moves of a characteristic size are more than randomly likely to be the beginnings of such discontinuous adjustments. Of course, the inference problem facing the trend follower is to distinguish the initial parts of such adjustments from random swings.

**Do you have any familiarity with the systems that are sold to the public?**

I used to try to keep abreast of them, but, given the preponderance of garbage out there, I found it an exasperating experience. You have to sift through so much that's both complicated and worthless that I think time is better spent brainstorming.

**Why do you categorize these systems as "worthless"?**

Because they tend to overfit the past data.

**Do you think the overfitting is a consequence of naïveté? Or an unbridled desire to sell more systems?**

At this late date, it's probably predominantly disingenuous.

**Have you looked at a lot of outside systems?**

I've looked at about fifty.

**Out of those fifty, how many had value?**

One. And I don't think it had a value as a system, but it had an element that I was able to use later.

**Do you then feel that purchasing systems is a waste of money?**

For the most part, I feel that's true. I would hate to think how much money a person would have to spend to chance on something good. If you have the resources to evaluate systems, your time is better spent developing your own ideas. I wouldn't recommend buying systems.

**Is the idea that if a system really worked—by that I mean a combination of good profitability, low volatility, and durability—it wouldn't make any monetary sense for someone to sell it?**

Occasionally, it might happen that somebody comes up with something really good and sells it because he needs the money. But in my experience, something good isn't discovered on a Greyhound bus while leafing through the charts; it's something developed over a period of years. Typically, if a person has invested sufficient time and money into developing a system, he or she will want to use the system, not sell it.

**What is your opinion about contrary opinion?**

Contrary opinion attempts to push the idea of trading against the majority in individual trades. Although theoretically this approach might work given the right kind of information about market composition, in practice the information available to contrary opinion traders is of questionable significance.

For instance, consider the consensus numbers. These are based on recommendations from market newsletters, advisory services, and so on. Therefore, these numbers model a very nonrepresentative group of traders—those who trade on market-letter advice. I don't know even one. In any case, this is an empirical question: Do the consensus figures work? Our research indicates that it's marginally profitable to buy—not to sell—a market with an extremely high bullish consensus.

**Do you have any opinion about popular technical overbought/oversold-type indicators, such as RSI and stochastics?**

I think these indicators are nearly worthless. I'm not implying that you shouldn't do research on these approaches—you can be very promiscuous in your research, but not in your trading.

**Having done the research, would you term these approaches "bogus indicators"?**

Yes, they're close to zero in terms of their profit expectations. What these patterns make during market consolidations, they lose during trends.

**Why do you believe these approaches are so popular if they're ineffective for trading purposes?**

For one thing, when you look at these indicators superimposed on a price chart, they look much better than they really are. The human eye tends to pick up the times these indicators accurately called minor tops and bottoms, but it misses all the false signals and the extent to which they were wrong during trends.

Formally, the mistake is the confusion between prior and posterior probabilities. For example, it's true that a lot of extremes have reversal days. [A reversal day is one in which the market reaches a new high (low) and then reverses direction, closing below (above) one or more immediately preceding daily closes.] All that's telling you is the probability of having a reversal day given a price extreme. What you really want to know is what the probability is of having an extreme—that is, a sustained change in market trend—given that you have a reversal day. That is a very different probability. Just because one probability is high, it in no way implies that the other one is high as well. If 85 percent of all tops and bottoms have property X, but property X also occurs often enough in other places, using that indicator as a signal will rip you to shreds.

Also, these approaches are appealing because they play into powerful human tendencies that induce one to trade countertrend or to abbreviate trend-following trades. It's always tempting to liquidate a good trade on flimsy evidence.

**What about cyclical analysis, which is another technique traders use to try to pick tops and bottoms?**

There are very powerful scientific methods of cyclical analysis, particularly Fourier analysis, which was invented in the nineteenth century, essentially to understand heat transfer. Fourier analysis has been tried again and again on market prices, starting in the late nineteenth century with the work of the French mathematician Louis Bachelier. All this scientific research has failed to uncover any systematic cyclic components in price data. This failure argues strongly against the validity of various trading systems based on cycles. And, I want to stress that the techniques for finding cycles are much stronger than the techniques for finding trends. Finding cycles is a classic scientific problem.

**What about all the various studies that purport to find cycles in price data?**

The markets go up and down. So in some loose sense of the word there are cycles. The problem is that you can fit sine waves pretty closely even to purely random patterns. If you allow cycle periods to shrink and expand, skip beats, and even invert—as many of these cycle theorists (or, perhaps more accurately, cycle cranks) do—then you can fit cycles onto any data series that fluctuates. The bottom line is that rigorous statistical techniques, such as Fourier analysis, demonstrate that these alleged cycles are practically random.

**Do you believe that attempts to apply artificial intelligence to trading can succeed?**

I think that eventually cybernetic devices will be able to outperform humans at every task, including trading. I can't believe that just because we're made of carbon and phosphorus there are things we can do that silicon and copper can't. And since cybernetic devices lack many of our human limitations, someday they'll be able to do it better. I have no doubt that eventually the world's best trader will be an automaton. I'm not saying this will happen soon, but probably within the next few generations.

**A good part of the academic community insists that the random nature of price behavior means that it's impossible to develop trading systems that can beat the market over the long run. What's your response?**

The evidence against the random walk theory of market action is staggering. Hundreds of traders and managers have profited from price-based mechanical systems.

**What about the argument that if you have enough people trading, some of them are going to do well, even if just because of chance?**

That may be true, but the probability of experiencing the kind of success that we have had and continue to have by chance alone has to be near zero. The systems worked for us year after year. We taught some of these systems to others, and it worked for them. They then managed other people's money, and it worked again. There's always the possibility that it all could have happened by luck, but the probability would be infinitesimally small.

There has actually been a dramatic shift in the academic view on this subject. When I first started in this business, mechanical trading was considered crackpot stuff. Since then, there has been a steadily increasing number of papers providing evidence that the random walk theory is false. System trading has gone from a fringe idea to being a new kind of orthodoxy. I don't think this could have happened if there weren't something to it. However, I have to admit that I find it unsettling that what began as a renegade idea has become an element of the conventional wisdom.

**Of course, you can't actually prove that price behavior is random.**

That's right. You're up against the problem of trying to prove a negative proposition. Although the contention that the markets are random is an affirmative proposition, in fact you're trying to prove a negative. You're trying to prove that there's no systematic component in the price. Any negative proposition is very difficult to confirm because you're trying to prove that something doesn't exist. For example, consider the negative proposition that there are no chocolate cakes orbiting Jupiter. That may be true, but it's very hard to prove.

The random walk theory has the disadvantage of being a negative proposition. Nevertheless, in the absence of any evidence to the contrary, it might be a plausible theory to maintain. At this point, however, I think there is enough contrary evidence so that any academic who still espouses the idea that the markets are random is not looking at the realities.

**In recent years, there has been a tremendous increase in the amount of money being managed by professional traders using computerized, trend-following strategies. Will this proliferation eventually kill the proverbial goose that lays the golden egg?**

The question of whether the preponderance of system traders, especially the group of large managers, is spoiling systems trading is difficult to answer because there are two very different kinds of evidence that yield opposite conclusions. First there is the quantitative statistical evidence that systems continue to work. Then there is the qualitative argument that a preponderance of system traders has to change the market in such a way that profit can no longer be extracted in this manner. In other words, the random walk theorists may still have the last laugh. It's difficult to treat such heterogeneous evidence in a common framework so that one kind of evidence can be weighed against the other.

**Well, both arguments can't be right. Which do you believe?**

System traders still have an important old ally: human nature. Human nature has not changed. Fortunately, there are still a lot of people trading on their instincts. But there's no question that the game has become much more difficult.

In evolutionary biology, one of the proposed solutions to the question of why sexual (as opposed to asexual) reproduction is so abundant is the Red Queen Hypothesis, based on the character in *Alice in Wonderland* in whose country you had to run as fast as you could just to stay in place. The idea is that competition is so severe that a species has to evolve as fast as it can just to stay where it is; sexual reproduction provides a kind of evolutionary overdrive. Similarly, there is such strong competition in the systems trading niche that the trader has to develop systems as fast as he or she can to merely stay in place.

**Is the implication that the increasing proportion of professionals in the total trading universe will change the nature of the markets in such a way that previously valid systems may no longer work?**

I think that's true. That's why I'm willing to accept systems with somewhat lower theoretical performance if I think they have the property of being different from what I believe most other system traders are using.

When I raise the point with would-be system designers that much historical research may be invalidated by the changing nature of futures markets, they invariably reply that the solution is to develop systems based on recent data—as if it were that easy. There's a serious problem with this approach. Recent data has to be less statistically significant than long-term historical data simply because there is a lot less of it. Systems developed solely on recent data are flimsily supported. There's no way around this basic fact.

**If you were starting out again, what would you do differently?**

I would concentrate more on money management. To my regret, it was something that I ignored in my early years. Ironically, even though money management is more important than the price model, mathematically, it's the more tractable problem.

**Is there anything unique about your approach to money management?**

One drawback to many money management schemes is that they are wedded to the assumption of a logarithmic utility function. Essentially, this model assumes that the increase in people's utility for additional wealth remains constant for equal percentage increases in wealth. The problem with this model is that it is unbounded; eventually it will tell you to bet the ranch.

There is a technical objection to unbounded utility functions, which is known as the St. Petersburg Paradox. I can give the thrust of it with a simplified example. Suppose you have a billion dollars. If your utility function is unbounded, there has to be an amount of money that would have such large utility that you'd be willing to flip a coin for it against your entire billion-dollar net worth. There's no amount of money—although there may be nonmonetary considerations (perhaps an extra hundred years of life)—for which a sane person would gamble away a billion-dollar net worth on the flip of a coin. Therefore, there must be something wrong with unbounded utility functions.

We use only bounded utility functions in our work on risk manage-ment. The particular utility functions we use also have the desirable technical characteristic of optimal investment fractions being indepen-dent of absolute wealth level.

**How much do you risk on a single trade? Do you have a formula you go by?**

You shouldn't plan to risk more than 2 percent on a trade. Although, of course, you could still lose more if the market gaps beyond your intended exit point.

On the subject of bet size, if you plot performance against position size, you get a graph that resembles one of those rightward-facing, high-foreheaded cartoon whales. The left side of the graph, correspond-ing to relatively small position size, is nearly linear; in this range an increase in trading size yields a proportionate increase in performance. But as you increase size beyond this range, the upward slope flattens out; this is because increasingly large drawdowns, which force you to trade smaller, inhibit your ability to come back after strings of losses. The theoretical optimum is reached right about where the whale's blow-hole would be. To the right of this optimum, the graph plummets; an average position size only modestly larger than the theoretical optimum gives a negative performance.

Trading size is one aspect you don't want to optimize. The opti-mum comes just before the precipice. Instead, your trading size should lie at the high end of the range in which the graph is still nearly straight.

**How important is intelligence in trading?**

I haven't seen much correlation between good trading and intelligence. Some outstanding traders are quite intelligent, but a few aren't. Many outstandingly intelligent people are horrible traders. Average intelli-gence is enough. Beyond that, emotional makeup is more important

**I assume you were probably involved in developing the systems that were taught to the Turtles. [See next chapter for background details.]**

Yes, I was.

**As I understand it, the catalyst for the Turtle training program was a disagreement between you and Richard Dennis as to whether successful trading could be taught.**

Yes. I took the point of view that it simply couldn't be taught. I argued that just because we could do it didn't necessarily mean that we could teach it. I assumed that a trader added something that couldn't be encapsulated in a mechanical program. I was proven wrong. The Turtle program proved to be an outstanding success. By and large, they learned to trade exceedingly well. The answer to the question of whether trading can be taught has to be an unqualified yes.

**Do you believe that the systems that Dennis and you presented to the Turtles have degraded because there are now twenty new disciples using the same approaches?**

With hundreds of millions under management, if they were still trading the same way it's hard to see how that could fail to be true. However, it's difficult to say to what extent the Turtles are still trading the same system. I would assume many of them are doing things differently now.

**If trading can be taught, can it be taught to anyone with reasonable intelligence?**

Anyone with average intelligence can learn to trade. This is not rocket science. However, it's much easier to learn what you should do in trading than to do it. Good systems tend to violate normal human tendencies. Of the people who can learn the basics, only a small percentage will be successful traders.

If a betting game among a certain number of participants is played long enough, eventually one player will have all the money. If there is any skill involved, it will accelerate the process of concentrating all the stakes in a few hands. Something like this happens in the market. There is a persistent overall tendency for equity to flow from the many to the few. In the long run, the majority loses. The implication for the trader is that to win you have to act like the minority. If you bring normal human habits and tendencies to trading, you'll gravitate toward the majority and inevitably lose.

**Can you expand on what you consider the normal human habits that lead to losing?**

Decision theorists have performed experiments in which people are given various choices between sure things (amounts of money) and simple lotteries in order to see if the subjects' preferences are rationally ordered. They find that people will generally choose a sure gain over a lottery with a higher expected gain but that they will shun a sure loss in favor of an even worse lottery (as long as the lottery gives them a chance of coming out ahead). These evidently instinctive human tendencies spell doom for the trader—take your profits, but play with your losses.

This attitude is also culturally reinforced, as exemplified by the advice: Seize opportunities, but hold your ground in adversity. Better advice to the trader would be: Watch idly while profit-taking opportunities arise, but in adversity run like a jackrabbit.

One common adage on this subject that is completely wrongheaded is: You can't go broke taking profits. That's precisely how many traders *do* go broke. While amateurs go broke by taking large losses, professionals go broke by taking small profits. The problem in a nutshell is that human nature does not operate to maximize gain but rather to maximize the chance of a gain. The desire to maximize the number of winning trades (or minimize the number of losing trades) works against the trader. The success rate of trades is the least important performance statistic and may even be inversely related to performance.

**Are there any other natural human tendencies that you think tend to sabotage success in trading?**

There is what I refer to as "the call of the countertrend." There's a constellation of cognitive and emotional factors that makes people automatically countertrend in their approach. People want to buy cheap and sell dear; this by itself makes them countertrend. But the notion of cheapness or dearness must be anchored to something. People tend to view the prices they're used to as normal and prices removed from these levels as aberrant. This perspective leads people to trade counter to an emerging trend on the assumption that prices will eventually return to "normal." Therein lies the path to disaster.

**What other aspects of human nature impede trading success?**

What really matters is the long-run distribution of outcomes from your trading techniques, systems, and procedures. But, psychologically, what seems of paramount importance is whether the positions that you have *right now* are going to work. Current positions seem to be crucial beyond any statistical justification. It's quite tempting to bend your rules to make your current trades work, assuming that the favorability of your long-term statistics will take care of future profitability. Two of the cardinal sins of trading—giving losses too much rope and taking profits prematurely—are both attempts to make *current* positions more likely to succeed, to the severe detriment of long-term performance.

**Having seen people who have survived as traders and those who haven't, what do you think are the characteristics that differentiate these two groups?**

The people who survive avoid snowball scenarios in which bad trades cause them to become emotionally destabilized and make more bad trades. They are also able to feel the pain of losing. If you don't feel the pain of a loss, then you're in the same position as those unfortunate people who have no pain sensors. If they leave their hand on a hot stove, it will burn off. There is no way to survive in this world without pain. Similarly, in the markets, if the losses don't hurt, your financial survival is tenuous.

I know of a few multimillionaires who started trading with inherited wealth. In each case, they lost it all because they didn't feel the pain when they were losing. In those formative first few years of trading, they felt they could afford to lose. You're much better off going into the market on a shoestring, feeling that you can't afford to lose. I'd rather bet on somebody starting out with a few thousand dollars than on somebody who came in with millions.

**What can a losing trader do to transform himself?**

I can address two situations. If a trader doesn't know why he's losing, then it's hopeless unless he can find out what he's doing wrong. In the case of the trader who knows what he's doing wrong, my advice is deceptively simple: He should stop doing what he is doing wrong. If he can't change his behavior, this type of person should consider becoming a dogmatic system trader.

**Were there any trades in your experience that proved especially difficult on an emotional level?**

One day in my first year of trading, I went long soybeans just a few cents from limit-up. The market proceeded to go from limit-up to limit-down without an uptick. It took about three minutes. This display convinced me to get short at limit-down. Two minutes later, the market was limit-up again.

**What did that experience teach you?**

It was my first lesson in risk management. I lost more than half my equity on those two trades in five minutes.

**How did you recover from that loss?**

Trading small, making a lot of little decisions rather than trying to make a few blockbuster trades.

**Do you find it difficult to deal with the emotional impact of large losses?**

In many ways, large profits are even more insidious than large losses in terms of emotional destabilization. I think it's important not to be emotionally attached to large profits. I've certainly made some of my worst trades after long periods of winning. When you're on a big winning streak, there's a temptation to think that you're doing something special, which will allow you to continue to propel yourself upward. You start to think that you can afford to make shoddy decisions. You can imagine what happens next. As a general rule, losses make you strong and profits make you weak.

**Allow me to broaden my question then. Do you find it difficult to deal with the emotionality of trading—whether due to large losses or large profits?**

Trading can be a positive game monetarily, but it's a negative game emotionally. On a few occasions, I've had the following experience: A group of markets to which I'm heavily committed open sharply against me, almost at my loss cutoff point. The loss seems crushing; I may even be wondering if my risk hasn't been set too high. Then, miraculously, I'm not stopped out, and by midday these markets have gone roughly as much with me as they were against me earlier. How does this feel? There's nothing in the elation that would approach compensating for the morning's distress. The profit seems large, of course, but it doesn't seem to help nearly as much as the earlier loss hurt.

To some extent, the foregoing example may simply be emotional exaggeration, but asymmetrical responses are perfectly valid. For example, if a price move brings the market to your stop point, you shouldn't be thinking in terms of retracements. This is the kind of hopeful thinking that makes a trader keep giving a loss a little more room. Of course, the market may be retracing (as opposed to having reversed trend), but that's not what you should be thinking about when it's time to get out. Now consider the case where the market is sharply with you, rather than against you. Here it is quite appropriate to think about retracements. The sharpness of the move indicates that volatility has just increased; hence, even a windfall profit might dissipate rapidly. The situation is asymmetrical. When you're losing and the thought that the market is retracing might be comforting, the concept is off limits for consideration. On the other hand, when you have a large profit and the idea of a retracement is a discomforting thought, it should be in the forefront of consideration. Trading is full of such asymmetries that make it an emotionally negative-sum proposition.

**If trading is so emotionally unsatisfying, is the only rationale for doing it financial?**

I can't imagine why anyone would do it if it weren't financially positive. This is one of the few industries where you can still engineer a rags-to-riches story. Richard Dennis started out with only hundreds of dollars and ended up making hundreds of millions in less than two decades—that's quite motivating.

If you're playing for the emotional satisfaction, you're bound to lose, because what feels good is often the wrong thing to do. Richard

Dennis used to say, somewhat facetiously, "If it feels good, don't do it." In fact, one rule we taught the Turtles was: When all the criteria are in balance, do the thing you least want to do. You have to decide early on whether you're playing for the fun or for the success. Whether you measure it in money or in some other way, to win at trading you have to be playing for the success.

Trading is also highly addictive. When behavioral psychologists have compared the relative addictiveness of various reinforcement schedules, they found that intermittent reinforcement—positive and negative dispensed randomly (for example, the rat doesn't know whether it will get pleasure or pain when it hits the bar)—is the most addictive alternative of all, more addictive than positive reinforcement only. Intermittent reinforcement describes the experience of the compulsive gambler as well as the futures trader. The difference is that, just perhaps, the trader can make money. However, as with most of the "affective" aspects of commodity trading, its addictiveness constantly threatens ruin. Addictiveness is the reason why so many players who make fortunes leave the game broke.

## What advice do you have for dealing with the emotional pitfalls inherent in trading?

Some people are good at not expending emotional energy on situations over which they have no control. (I am not one of them.) An old trader once told me: "Don't think about what the market's going to do; you have absolutely no control over that. Think about what you're going to do if it gets there."

In particular, you should spend no time at all thinking about those roseate scenarios in which the market goes your way, since in those situations, there's nothing more for you to do. Focus instead on those things you want least to happen and on what your response should be.

## Any advice about handling the losing periods?

It helps not to be preoccupied with your losses. If you're worried, channel that energy into research. Over the years at C&D [the company at which Dennis and Eckhardt were partners], we made our best research breakthroughs when we were losing.

**Do you think that's because those are the times you have the greatest motivation to improve your approach?**

That's probably true.

**Among the observations you have made about markets and trading over the years, do any stand out as being particularly surprising or counterintuitive?**

Some years back, a company ran an annual charting contest. The contestants had to predict the settlement prices of several futures for a certain date by a given deadline. Someone in our office [Dale Dellutri] decided, I believe prankishly, to use the random walk model. In other words, he simply used the settlement prices of the deadline as his prediction. He fell just short of becoming a prizewinner with this procedure. His name was among the first five of a list of fifty or so close runners-up.

This contest had hundreds of entrants. Therefore, more than 95 percent, and probably more than 99 percent, of the contestants scored worse than blind randomness. This is no mean feat.

The extremeness of the outcome in this story seems to support an apparent phenomenon that I've observed many times over the years, but for which I have no hard evidence: The majority of people trade worse than a purely random trader would.

**Your hypothesis implies that most traders would be better off throwing darts than using their existing method—a provocative thought. How do you explain this phenomenon?**

The market behaves much like an opponent who is trying to teach you to trade poorly. I don't want to suggest that the market actually has intentions, because it doesn't. An appropriate analogy is evolutionary theory, in which you can talk as though evolution has a purpose. For example, birds evolved wings in order to fly. Technically, that's wrong. Birds aren't Darwinians, and you can be sure no bird or protobird ever intended to evolve a wing. Nevertheless, natural selection acts very much like it intends for species to evolve things that are beneficial.

You can talk about the markets in a similar fashion. Anybody who has traded for a while begins to feel that the markets have certain personal characteristics. Very often the feeling you get is that "they are out to get you," which is simply a personalization of the process. This illusion is well founded. The market does behave very much like a tutor who is trying to instill poor trading techniques. Most people learn this lesson only too well.

**Please elaborate. What kind of lessons is the tutor teaching?**

Since most small to moderate profits tend to vanish, the market teaches you to cash them in before they get away. Since the market spends more time in consolidations than in trends, it teaches you to buy dips and sell rallies. Since the market trades through the same prices again and again and seems, if only you wait long enough, to return to prices it has visited before, it teaches you to hold on to bad trades. The market likes to lull you into the false security of high success rate techniques, which often lose disastrously in the long run. The general idea is that what works most of the time is nearly the opposite of what works in the long run.

A basic theme that runs through Eckhardt's comments is that what feels good is usually the wrong thing to do. As one example, decision theorists have demonstrated that people consistently prefer to lock in a sure win rather than accept a gamble with a higher expected payoff. They also prefer to gamble with a loss, even when the bet has a worse expected outcome than a sure loss alternative. These instinctive preferences run counter to perhaps the most fundamental principle of successful trading: Cut your losses short and let your profits run. Just because this aphorism has become a cliché makes it no less valid.

Another example of counterproductive instincts is what Eckhardt terms "the call of the countertrend." Selling on strength and buying on weakness appeals to people's desire to buy cheap and sell dear. While such trades may feel better at the moment of implementation, following a countertrend strategy is almost inevitably doomed to failure. (This contention does not, however, imply that the reverse strategy—trend following—is assured success, since both approaches incur transaction costs.)

Traders' excessive concern regarding their current positions involves yet another example of the detrimental impact of gravitating toward comfortable actions. Taking profits before intended objectives are reached so that the market won't take away the gains, holding positions beyond intended loss liquidation points in the hopes that the market is only witnessing a retracement, and liquidating positions before stop-loss points are reached because of the fear of losing are all examples of actions intended to make current positions feel better. However, all of these actions are likely to negatively impact long-term performance.

People's natural inclinations also lead them astray in systems trading. The more closely a system is fit to past price behavior, the more impressive the historical simulations will appear and the better the trader will feel about using the system. Yet, ironically, beyond a very limited point, the more effort expended to make a system fit past price behavior more closely, the worse actual future performance is likely to be. The desire to design a system that looks great also leads people to accept favorable simulated results without sufficient scrutiny. Very often, great results are simply the consequence of error or naive methodology. Eckhardt's advice is that system designers should believe their results only after they have done everything possible to disprove them.

Eckhardt proposes that the tendency to do what is comfortable will actually lead most people to experience even worse than random results in the markets. In effect, he is saying that most people don't lose simply because they lack the skill to do better than random but also because natural human traits entice them into behavioral patterns that will actually lead to worse than random results—a particularly compelling observation. If Eckhardt is right—and I believe he is—the critical implication is that our natural instincts will mislead us in trading. Therefore, the first step in succeeding as a trader is reprogramming behavior to do what is correct rather than what feels comfortable.

# *The Silence of the Turtles*

Picture an oak-paneled English drawing room. Two obviously wealthy gentlemen sit in their armchairs facing a roaring fire, puffing on their pipes and discussing their philosophy of trading.

"It is my proposition, Colin, that anyone can be taught to be a superior trader. There is nothing magical about it. There is no rare talent involved. It is simply a matter of being taught the appropriate rules and following those rules. There is no question in my mind that I could train virtually anyone to make a fortune trading."

"That is nonsense, Duncan. You just think your trading success is due to your system. What you do not realize is that you have a special talent. You could print out your rules in twelve-inch-high letters and have people read them every day for a year, and they still would not be able to do what you do in the markets. Your success is a function of your talent. It cannot be taught!"

"Well, Colin, this must be the hundredth time we've had this discussion. Let's settle it once and for all. Why don't we just pick ten people, teach them my system, give them each £1 million to trade and see what happens."

"That's an excellent idea, Duncan. Pick your ten people, train them, and if by the end of one year they are not ahead, on average, by at least 25 percent—a modest figure considering that you normally make two to three times that per year—you pay me £1 million. If they are up by more than 25 percent, I will pay you the same amount."

Duncan and Colin then proceed to the window, watching the passersby for potential candidates for their experiment. Each time they agree on an individual, they send their butler out to summon the person.

The above may sound like a fanciful plot for a story or movie. (Actually, it is a very loose adaptation inspired by the delightful Mark Twain story, "The £1,000,000 Bank-Note. ") However, change the setting from London to Chicago, eliminate the monetary element of the bet, and substitute a more sophisticated method for screening candidates, and you actually have a true story. The legendary trader Richard Dennis, who reputedly transformed an initial stake of several thousand dollars into a fortune estimated at $200 million, essentially had the same argument with his partner, William Eckhardt (interviewed in the previous chapter). It was Dennis's contention that trading success could be taught, while Eckhardt scoffed at the idea.

To settle their ongoing argument, Dennis and Eckhardt decided to run a version of the above experiment. They placed an ad in the *Wall Street Journal* seeking persons interested in being trained as traders. Through a process of reviewing written applications, evaluating the results of an exam, and interviewing selected finalists, approximately one thousand respondents were eventually whittled down to a group of thirteen. Over a period of about two weeks, Dennis and Eckhardt taught this fortunate group some of their systems. No holds barred, they gave the group all the specifics. After the training, Dennis then funded this group and sent them off to trade on their own.

The first group performed so well during the initial year that Dennis repeated the experiment the following year with a second group of ten. These two groups of traders collectively became known in the industry as the Turtles. This rather curious name had its origins in a trip Richard Dennis took to the Orient during this period of time. At one point, he visited a turtle farm, in which turtles were raised in huge vats. In Dennis's mind, the image of growing thousands of squirming turtles in a huge vat was a perfect analogy for training traders. The name stuck.

Was Richard Dennis right? Could people actually be trained to be exceptionally successful traders? To answer this question, let's pick up the scene six years later, when I am preparing to do this book. My first job is to research possible candidates to be interviewed. In the area of futures traders, one reference source I used was the quarterly summary provided by *Managed Accounts Reports*. This report summarizes the performance of a large number of commodity trading advisors (CTAs), providing a single synopsis sheet for each advisor. At the bottom of each sheet is a summary table with key statistics, such as average annual percentage return, largest drawdown, Sharpe ratio (a return/risk measure), percentage of winning months, and the probabilities of witnessing a 50 percent, 30 percent, and 20 percent loss with the given CTA. To be objective, I flipped through the pages, glancing only at the tables (not the names at the top of the sheets) and checking off the names of those advisors whose exceptional performance seemed to jump off the page. By the end of this process, I had checked off eighteen of the more than one hundred CTAs surveyed. Eight of these eighteen names (44 percent) turned out to be Turtles. Absolutely astounding! Richard Dennis was obviously right. (Admittedly, the results would have been less dramatic a year later, as 1991 proved to be a tough year for many of the Turtles.)

It seemed clear to me that if I were going to pursue the quest for the ingredients in trading success, I should be talking to the Turtles. The uniqueness of Dennis's experiment seemed to provide an unusual opportunity to see how different individuals exposed to the same training differed in the way they approached the markets.

Although the idea looked good on paper, the execution proved to be very difficult. First of all, I found that a number of the Turtles simply refused to talk. "Look," I would say, "I understand your reticence. However, I assure you that I will not print anything until you have seen it, and if you feel that you have inadvertently divulged any trade secrets, I promise not to use that material. The risk is all mine. I can go through the entire interview and editing process, only in the end to have you refuse to grant me permission to use the copy. What do you have to lose?" Despite these assurances, a number of the Turtles simply refused even to consider participating.

Those who refused to talk at all were only part of the problem. The major problem was that the remainder of the group was largely tight-lipped about anything of interest. I was well aware that the group had signed agreements not to divulge any parts of the system, and I hardly expected them to share these secrets with the world, let alone betray a trust. Therefore, in the interviews, I avoided any specific questions regarding the system. Unfortunately, the Turtles' caution was so extreme that they avoided talking about anything even remotely connected with the system. (I couldn't help but be reminded of the World War II movies where the downed American pilot responds to all the interrogator's questions by repeating his rank, file, and serial number.) The following is a representative segment intended to provide a flavor of the typical interview.

---

**How do you pick your trades?**

I basically use the system, but I can't say much more than that.

**I know we can't discuss the specifics of the system, but can you just tell me in general terms why this system tends to do so much better than the vast majority of trend-following systems that are out there?**

I really don't know the other systems.

**Well, for purposes of comparison, let's just use the typical moving average system, which is essentially a trend-following approach. Without divulging any specific trade secrets, in a general conceptual sense, how do the systems that Dennis taught you differ from these more standard approaches?**

I'd rather not answer that.

**What are the trading rules you live by?**

The same general rules I'm sure you've heard everywhere. I don't think there's anything new I could add.

**Let's talk about a specific trading situation. The recent start of the U.S. air war against Iraq resulted in a number of huge overnight price moves. Were you in any of those markets? Were you watching those markets during the nighttime session?**

I was lucky—I was out of the crude oil market at the time.

**How about a market like gold, which also had a huge price reversal at the time?**

Yes, I had a position in gold.

**It's no secret that Dennis's approach was trend-following in nature. Obviously then, since the market had been rising for a while prior to the outbreak of the air war, you must have been long at the time. The war started at night, and although gold prices initially rose, by the next morning they were down over $30. Were you watching the market during the night session? And if so, how did you react?**

I got out.

**Was this because the market received news that should have been bullish—that is, the outbreak of war—moved slightly higher, and then started trading lower?**

I can't say.

**I'm hardly talking trade secrets here. The concept that a market's failure to respond appropriately to important news is a significant price action clue is something that I put in a book six years ago. And I'm sure I was not the first or last person to talk about this idea. All I'm asking is whether this was the reasoning behind taking the loss quickly or whether there was more to it.**

There was more, but I can't talk about it.

**Is there anything that we haven't discussed concerning the concepts and philosophy of successful trading that you would care to comment on?**

[Long pause.] No, not really. I can't think of anything.

OK, you get the idea. Applying the appropriate trading principle, I decided to cut my losses short and stop requesting additional Turtle interviews after the first few. Obviously, the extraordinary sensitivity of the Turtles to the possibility of revealing anything about what Richard Dennis had taught them, even inadvertently, provided a seemingly insurmountable impediment to achieving the type of relatively open discussions I had enjoyed with other traders.

I have, however, selected short excerpts from two of the Turtle interviews I conducted. The following material offers some feel for the Turtle experience and provides a few insights in terms of useful trading lessons or advice.

## MICHAEL CARR

After the near paranoia, and even rudeness, I encountered in some of my preliminary interview requests among the Turtles, Michael Carr's attitude came as a pleasant relief. (He not only graciously accepted the interview request but, upon learning that I was a hiking enthusiast, was thoughtful enough to send me a brochure on the Ice Age Trail, which passes near his house.)

Carr was in the first group of Turtles trained by Richard Dennis. He began trading in 1984, and in his four years of trading for Dennis, Carr averaged 57 percent annually (he was down moderately for the first third of 1988, when Dennis terminated the program). Carr did not begin trading again until August 1989, when he launched his own CTA company. As of late 1991, Carr was up 89 percent from that starting point.

I interviewed Carr at his Wisconsin home, which virtually sits in a lake and is connected to the mainland by a very long driveway. I arrived just as it began to storm. Carr's office, which has windows all around, offers views of the water in every direction. The combination of the all-encompassing water views and the storm provided a spectacular backdrop. Unfortunately, the setting was far more dramatic than our conversation. Although Carr was quite friendly, our interchange was stymied by the same cautiousness that characterized all the Turtle interviews.

**How did you become a Turtle?**

I was on the creative management staff of TSR, the game company of Dungeons and Dragons fame. I started with TSR when there were only a few employees. In the ensuing years, the company went through a spectacular growth phase, which culminated with over three hundred people on the payroll. The company then hit hard times and made drastic cutbacks in order to survive. I lost my job along with two hundred other workers. It was around this time that I picked up a copy of the *Wall Street Journal.* Ironically, that was the same day that Richard Dennis ran his ad seeking trading trainees.

**Did you have any prior experience in the commodity markets at the time?**

Certainly no trading experience. However, while I was working for TSR, I came up with the idea of creating a commodity game. I thought that the commodity markets had all the necessary ingredients for making a successful game. To get the background information, I had sent away for lots of exchange publications. I also took an extension course, which involved six evening sessions taught by a commodity broker. So I had a rudimentary understanding of the commodity markets, but nothing more.

**As I understand it, there were over a thousand applicants and only thirteen candidates were selected. Why do you believe you were chosen?**

To my knowledge, I was the only candidate that had worked for a game company. I believe the fact that my background was different from the others helped me get noticed. Also, a lot of commodity trading is based on game theory and probability. Therefore, it's not much of a jump to believe that someone with experience in that area might bring something to the table.

**Who interviewed you?**

Richard Dennis and a couple of his associates.

**Can you recall any of your responses during the interview that might have helped you get the job?**

Nothing in particular. I think, however, despite my having had no background in the business, I was able to ask intelligent questions and respond appropriately. However, there was one exception. [*He laughs at the recollection.*] I was probably one of the only candidates who knew virtually nothing about Richard Dennis. Although I didn't know it, Richard Dennis was famous for being one of the world's great technical traders. During the interview I asked, "Do you trade the markets fundamentally or technically?"

That got a good chuckle. He answered, "We trade technically."

I responded by asking, "Is fundamental analysis dead?"

Dennis answered, with a smile, "We certainly hope not."

**Obviously your lack of experience didn't hurt you.**

As it turned out, of the thirteen people selected, one-third had no experience, one-third had significant experience, and the remaining one-third had a little bit of experience.

**I know you can't divulge any of the specifics about the training course. However, are there any general lessons that came out of those sessions that you could talk about?**

One nugget of advice that I believe is valuable to anyone trading the markets is: Don't worry about what the markets are going to do, worry about what you are going to do in response to the markets.

**Any other advice regarding psychology or attitude?**

In my opinion, a large segment of the population should never trade the markets. Although I hesitate to use gambling as an example, I believe it provides a close analogy. Those people who are wise and prudent gamblers would probably also be wise and prudent investors, because they have a somewhat detached view of the value of money. On the other hand, those people who get caught up in the excitement of the amount of the wager, whether it's gambling or investment, are likely to be destabilized by losses.

**Why do you trade?**

Part of it, of course, is to make a living. However, trading has many of the elements of a game. For someone like me who has always been interested in games, I don't think there could be a better job.

# HOWARD SEIDLER

Howard Seidler was certainly the most ebullient of the Turtles I interviewed. He exuded a general sense of enjoyment in trading, in emotion as well as in word. During our interview, his attitude toward trading was so upbeat that I naturally assumed he must have been enjoying a profitable streak in the markets. To my surprise, I later discovered that the half-year period preceding our interview was actually his second worst six-month performance ever (he was down 16 percent). Seidler certainly wins my award for the most happy Turtle. As to performance, he has averaged 34 percent (on an annual compounded basis) since he began trading in 1984.

---

**When did you first become involved in the markets?**

My first exposure was actually as a child, since my father dabbled in the markets. When I was in high school, I became aware of the futures markets. Futures fascinated me because of the symmetry of being able to go short as well as long. I was also attracted by the potential for leverage. As I began to read about the futures markets, the general description seemed to be: "Here's this game, and by the way, hardly anyone ever succeeds at it." To me, that was like throwing down the gauntlet.

**When did you first actually begin to trade the markets?**

In high school. Of course, I was too young to open my own account, so I opened an account under my father's name.

**How large was the account?**

One thousand dollars. I had saved up that money by doing chores, such as shoveling snow and mowing lawns. It took me a little over a year before I lost it all.

**That's actually a pretty long ride considering the minuscule size of the account and the fact that you were a complete novice.**

Of course, I wasn't too thrilled about it at the time. However, as I got older, I realized that I had really done pretty well considering the circumstances. I certainly did get my money's worth in terms of experience.

**Do any trades from that time stand out as a learning experience?**

One trade that I think was quite fortunate was actually a missed profit opportunity. Based on some trading ideas I had developed, I thought that the potato market was going to break sharply. I went short one contract, and the market started going in my direction. Once I had a small profit, I decided to double my position. Now, my account was so tiny that even a one-contract position was pushing it. I really had no business adding to this position.

Shortly after I had sold the second contract, the market started to go up. I became concerned about losing my equity, and I liquidated the contract that I had added, taking the loss on the trade. However, because of that loss, I also ended up getting out of my original contract way before the market reached my objective. Two days after I liquidated my position, the market began a steep collapse, just as I had originally anticipated.

**I don't understand why you termed that trade "fortunate."**

If I had stayed with the entire position and ended up making several hundred percent on the trade, I would have thought that I knew it all. There are certain lessons that you absolutely have to learn to be a successful trader. One of those lessons is that you can't win if you're trading at a leverage size that makes you fearful of the market. If I hadn't learned that concept then, I would have at some later point when I was trading more money, and the lesson would have been far more expensive.

**Did you eventually return to trading before you became a Turtle?**

Shortly before I saw Richard Dennis's ad in the *Wall Street Journal,* I had left my job as an economic consultant to become a full-time trader.

**Only about one out of a hundred respondents to the ad were ultimately chosen for the training program. Do you have any idea why you made the final selection cut?**

Although they weren't looking for people with trading experience, by the same token, being a trader didn't rule you out either. I think that insofar as I did have the trading background, the fact that my philosophy about the markets was similar to Dennis's probably helped out. Also, and I'm just speculating, I think that Dennis might have been curious to see how somebody with my academic background—an MIT engineering degree—would work out.

**What advice would you give someone in regards to being successful in the markets?**

I think the single most important element is having a plan. First, a plan forces discipline, which is an essential ingredient to successful trading. Second, a plan gives you a benchmark against which you can measure your performance.

**Doesn't your bottom line equity give you that information?**

Over the long run, sure. However, you can be following your rules exactly and still lose money. In that situation, you certainly haven't performed poorly as a trader. The basic idea is that if you follow your rules over the long run, the probabilities will be in your favor, and you'll come out ahead. In the short run, however, conformance to a trading plan is more significant than short-term equity fluctuations.

**What else is important to succeed as a trader?**

You need to have the persistence to stay with your ideas day after day, month after month, year after year, which is hard work.

**Why would that be difficult? Why would you want to stray from a winning approach?**

Because human beings are human beings. If you get enough negative feedback over the short run, you're going to be tempted to respond to it.

**Any other trading advice?**

It's important to distinguish between respect for the market and fear of the market. While it's essential to respect the market to assure preservation of capital, you can't win if you're fearful of losing. Fear will keep you from making correct decisions.

---

I realize that this chapter has not provided any definitive answers as to what made the Turtles such a successful trading group. Nevertheless, it does offer an incredibly important message to those interested in trading: It is possible to develop a system that can significantly beat the market. Moreover, if you can discover such a system and exercise the discipline to follow it, you can succeed in the markets without being a born trader.

# *Monroe Trout*

## THE BEST RETURN THAT
## LOW RISK CAN BUY

I first met Monroe Trout several years ago, when a broker in my firm, who was trying to land Trout's account, brought him by as part of the company tour. I knew that Trout was a commodity trading advisor (CTA) new to the business, but I didn't know much else. Subsequently, I often heard Trout's name mentioned as one of the younger CTAs who was doing very well. I didn't realize how well until I started to work on this book.

In consulting the quarterly issue of *Managed Accounts Reports* while doing research for this book, I found that in terms of return/risk measurements, Trout's performance was the best of the more than one hundred managers covered. There were a few who exhibited a larger average annual return, and fewer still with smaller drawdowns (although these CTAs had dramatically lower returns), but no one came close to matching his combination of return to risk. Over the five-year period surveyed, his average return was 67 percent but, astoundingly, his largest drawdown during that entire period was just over 8 percent. As another demonstration of his consistency, he had been profitable in 87 percent of all months. I was particularly surprised to discover that for the period in which Trout has been trading (he became a public money manager in 1986), even such legendary and extraordinary traders as Paul Tudor Jones did not approach his return/risk performance figures.

One of the things I like about Trout is that he does not trumpet his successes. For example, he was already doing quite well as a trader when I first met him several years ago, but, as I recall, he made no mention of his performance.

Trout sees himself as a businessman whose job it is to make money for his customers. As he expresses it, "Some people make shoes. Some people make houses. We make money, and people are willing to pay us a lot to make money for them."

---

**When did you first get interested in the markets?**

When I was seventeen years old, I got a job for a futures trader named Vilar Kelly who lived in my hometown of New Canaan, Connecticut. He had an Apple computer, and at the time (1978), you couldn't buy data on diskette—or at least he didn't know where to buy it if it was available. He had reams of price data that he had collected from newspapers and wanted typed into his computer. He hired me and paid me a couple of bucks an hour to type in this data.

**That sounds like real grunt work.**

Yes, it was. But he also taught me a few things about the futures markets and computer programming. The computer experience was particularly valuable because, at the time, PCs were sort of novel.

That summer job sparked my interest in the markets. By my sophomore year at Harvard, I knew that I wanted to be a trader. I took whatever courses they had on the markets. I did my senior thesis on the stock index futures market.

**What was the conclusion of your thesis?**

The most important conclusion was that the probability of very large price changes, while still small, was much greater than might be assumed based on standard statistical assumptions. Therefore, a risk control methodology must be prepared to deal with situations that statistically might seem nearly impossible, because they're not.

**I assume the stock market on the high-volatility days in October 1987 and October 1989 is a perfect example.**

Absolutely. If you assume that price changes are normally distributed, the probability of daily price moves of that magnitude would be virtually zero, which, of course, it was not.

**I assume that theoretical realization made you trade smaller than you might have been inclined to otherwise.**

Yes. I don't use that much leverage.

**Did your thesis reach any other significant conclusions?**

I found that prices were not independent. That is, there were some statistically significant patterns.

**Did you go on to graduate school?**

No.

**You graduated with honors from Harvard. I assume that you probably could have had your pick of any graduate school in the country. Didn't you hesitate giving up that opportunity?**

Not at all. I knew what I wanted to do—trade. Graduate school would only have delayed that goal. I never considered it.

**How did you break into the business?**

The athletic director at Harvard, Jack Reardon, knew Victor Niederhoffer, who headed NCZ Commodities, a New York trading firm. Victor had graduated from Harvard in 1964 and was a great squash player. (In fact, at one time he was the world's best.) Jack knew I was interested in trading and suggested that I talk to Victor. We hit it off, and he offered me a job. It was a great job because I got a lot of responsibility very quickly.

**Doing what?**

Within two weeks I was trading on the floor of the New York Futures Exchange [trading the stock index]. Victor owned seats all over the place and needed people to trade on the floor for him.

**Executing his orders?**

A little. But mostly I just scalped for myself. I had a profit-sharing type of deal. [Scalping refers to floor brokers trading the market for very quick, small profits. There are two principal methods: (1) capturing the bid/ask spread by taking the opposite side of customer orders; (2) taking advantage of temporary, small price discrepancies between related positions (e.g., the March stock index contract being out of line with the June contract).]

**You were fresh out of school. How did you learn to become a scalper overnight?**

You ask a lot of questions. You stand in the pit and talk to the people around you. It's actually a great place to learn quickly. At some point, you hit a plateau. But when you first get into the business, it's a great place to start, because there are hundreds of traders. If you find the ones who know something about the markets and are willing to talk to you about it, you can learn quickly.

**Do you remember what you learned in those early days?**

I learned how quickly you can lose money if you don't know what you're doing.

**Did you see that happen to some people?**

Sure. One day somebody will be standing next to you in the pit, the next day they're gone. It happens all the time. I also learned a lot about transaction costs. I'm able to estimate transaction costs fairly accurately on various types of trades. This information is essential in evaluating the potential performance of any trading model I might develop.

**Give me a practical example.**

Let's take bonds. The average person off the floor might assume that the transaction costs beyond commissions is at least equal to the bid/ask spread, which in the bond market is one tick [$31.25]. In reality, if you have a good broker, it's only about half a tick, because if he's patient, most of the time he can get filled at the bid. If you have a bad broker, maybe it's one tick. So the transaction cost in that case isn't as high as you might think. Therefore, a T-bond trading system that you might discard because it has a small expected gain might actually be viable— assuming, of course, that you have good execution capabilities, as we do. The S&P market, on the other hand, is just the opposite. You might assume a bid/ask spread of 1 tick [5 points = $25], but very often it's higher, because when you try to buy at the offer, it disappears.

**What else did you learn on the floor?**

I learned about where people like to put stops.

**Where do they like to put stops?**

Right above the high and below the low of the previous day.

**One tick above the high and one tick below the low?**

Sometimes it might be a couple of ticks, but in that general area.

**Basically, is it fair to say that markets often get drawn to these points? Is a concentration of stops at a certain area like waving a red flag in front of the floor brokers?**

Right. That's the way a lot of locals make their money. They try to figure out where the stops are, which is perfectly fine as long as they don't do it in an illegal way.

**Given that experience, now that you trade off the floor, do you avoid using stops?**

I don't place very many actual stops. However, I use mental stops. We set beepers so that when we start losing money, a warning will go off, alerting us to begin liquidating the position.

**What lesson should the average trader draw from knowing that locals will tend to move markets toward stop areas?**

Traders should avoid putting stops in the obvious places. For example, rather than placing a stop 1 tick above yesterday's high, put it either 10 ticks below the high so you're out before all that action happens, or 10 ticks above the high because maybe the stops won't bring the market up that far. If you're going to use stops, it's probably best not to put them at the typical spots. Nothing is going to be 100 percent foolproof, but that's a generally wise concept.

**Do you believe your floor experience helps explain your superior performance?**

I believe so. For example, I have a pretty good eye for picking out where stops are going to be, even from off the floor. I try to get in the market a bit before that point is reached, sometimes even trying to set the stops off myself—and then the market will be off to the races.

**The example of a common stop point you mentioned earlier—the area right beyond a prior high or low—is kind of obvious. Are there any other less obvious examples of popular stop points?**

Round numbers. For instance, when the Dow Jones starts creeping up toward 3,000, I'll start buying some in anticipation of it going through 3,000. The 3,000 level acts like a magnet.

**So the markets are drawn to round numbers. Do markets usually reach the round number, or do they often stop just short of it?**

I believe markets almost always get to the round number. Therefore, the best place to get in is before that number is reached and play what I call the "magnet effect." For example, I might buy the stock index markets when the Dow is at 2,950, looking for it to go to 3,000. When the market gets close to 3,000, things get more difficult. When that happens, I like to have everybody in the trading room get on the phone with a different broker and listen to the noise level on the floor. How excited does it sound down there? What size trades are hitting the market? If it doesn't sound that loud and order sizes are small, then I'll start dumping our position because the market is probably going to fall off. On the other hand, if it sounds crazy and there are large orders being transacted, I'll tend to hold the position.

**Give me a recent example of the noise level on the floor being a good indicator.**

When crude oil reached $20 [during the Persian Gulf crisis], there was a lot of noise on the floor and the market continued to move higher.

**What else did you learn from your floor trading experience?**

I learned what are the most liquid time periods of the day. When you're trading one contract, that's not important. But when you're trading thousands of contracts, it can be critical.

**What are the most liquid times of the day?**

The most liquid period is the opening. Liquidity starts falling off pretty quickly after the opening. The second most liquid time of day is the close. Trading volume typically forms a U-shaped curve throughout the day. There's a lot of liquidity right at the opening, it then falls off, reaching a nadir at midday, and then it starts to climb back up, reaching a secondary peak on the close. Generally speaking, this pattern holds in almost every market. It's actually pretty amazing.

It's also important to know when the illiquid periods occur, because that's a good time to support your position. For example, if I'm long one thousand S&P contracts and it's 11:30 Chicago time, I'm probably going to want to put in some sort of scale-down buy orders, like buying ten lots every tick down, to hold the market in my direction. It doesn't cost me that many contracts at that time of day to support the market, because there are not a lot of contracts trading. The longer you can keep the market up, the better off you're going to be.

**Isn't supporting the market a futile effort? In other words, isn't the market ultimately going to go where it wants to go, whether you support it or not?**

Over the long run, sure. But for the short term, single traders can definitely move the market. There's no doubt about it. I move the market every single day. The idea is to do it in a smart way. For example, if the S&P is near yesterday's high and I'm long a lot of contracts and want to get out, I may try to push prices through yesterday's high to generate excitement and boost the trading volume. The increased volume will make it a lot easier for me to dump my position.

**Why did you leave the floor?**

I found that what I did best on the floor was position trading. I had experience developing computer models in college. Each day when I finished on the floor, I would go back to the office and develop trading models. Victor was kind enough to let me trade off some of these models, and I started making fairly consistent money. Since on the floor I could only directly trade one market, it was more efficient for me to trade off the floor.

**What is the typical length of a trade generated by your models?**

A holding period of about a day to a week.

**My experience with trading models is that the ones that generate very short-term signals—for example, average trade lengths of one week or less—don't beat transaction costs. I see you nodding your head, so you obviously know what I'm talking about. What is it about your models that's different?**

First, our models tend to be more statistically oriented. Second, we have lower transaction costs than virtually anyone in the business. Our round-trip commission is probably lower than 99 percent of the funds.

**Why is that?**

Because the combination of several hundred million dollars under man-agement and frequent turnover means that we generate more trades than virtually anyone else. This large trading volume makes it possible for us to negotiate pretty low commission rates. Also, I believe we get some of the best executions of any off-the-floor trader. We use many different brokers in each pit, and there's a constant selection process going on. If a broker isn't good, we get rid of him. Conversely, if a bro-ker does a good job for us, we give him more business. I have the man-power to call around. We can get ten people on the phone calling a given pit if we need to. We also carefully monitor our slippage [the dif-ference between an estimated fair execution price and the actual execu-tion price]. At the end of every single day, my staff gives me a sum-mary sheet listing the slippage in each market.

**How do you determine what the execution price should be when you're entering an order?**

Every time an order leaves a trader's mouth, he looks at the last price on the screen. Say the price for bonds on the screen is 17 and a buy order is filled at 18, we record the slippage as -1

**How do you know if it's slippage or if the market really moved since the last screen print?**

We make the simplifying assumption that over the long run it will work both ways—that is, the market will trade in the direction of your order as well as away from it. Therefore, sometimes the market will give you a more negative fill than it probably should, but at other times you'll get a more positive one. After you've done thousands of trades, you get a pretty good idea of who the good brokers providing the best fills are, as well as what is a reasonable slippage factor in each trading pit.

**Basically then, since your transaction costs [commissions as well as slippage] are very low, some marginal systems that wouldn't work for a typical trader might be profitable for you.**

Right. For example, if the average profit on a bond trading system is $40 per lot and I'm trading under $10 commission with a slippage factor of half a tick [$16], I'm going to be able to trade that system for a consistent profit. On the other hand, for someone paying $30 a round turn and averaging a slippage factor of one tick, that same system would be a money drain.

## What portion of your profits would you estimate is a function of your control of transaction costs?

I would guess that we save about 6 percent per year in reduced slippage by carefully selecting and monitoring our brokers and another 6 percent by paying $10 per round turn instead of, say, $20.

## Why did you eventually leave Victor's organization?

Two reasons. First, I wanted to avoid the daily commute of one hour and forty-five minutes one way. Second, I felt that, over the long run, I could probably make more money on my own—although that certainly wasn't true over the short run.

## How do you define success in trading?

I sincerely believe that the person who has the best daily Sharpe ratio at the end of the year is the best trader. [The Sharpe ratio is a statistical performance measure that normalizes return by risk, with the variability of returns being used to measure risk. Thus, for example, assume Trader A and Trader B managed identical-sized funds and made all the same trades, but Trader A always entered orders for double the number of contracts as Trader B. In this case, Trader A would realize double the percentage return, but because risk would also double, the Sharpe ratio would be the same for both traders.* Normally, the Sharpe ratio is measured using monthly data. Thus, only equity variability that occurs on a month-to-month basis would be considered. Trout is going a large step further by saying that, by his definition, trading performance should not only incorporate risk but should do so down to day-to-day variations of equity.]

---

*Technically speaking, there would be a slight variation because the risk-free return (e.g., T-bill rate) would also enter into the calculation.

**How do you explain your success as a trader?**

(A) We do good research, so we have an edge. (B) We have a rational, practical approach to money management. (C) We pay very low commissions. (D) Our executions are among the best in the business. (E) Most of the people who work here keep a large portion of their net worth in the fund we manage. Personally, I have over 95 percent of my net worth in the fund.

**I take it that you're not pulling out very much money.**

I don't pull out any money. I rent my condo and I drive a cheap car.

**Is the money you're making then more a matter of keeping score, or do you have some sort of ultimate goal?**

At this point, it's more a matter of keeping score, because I can retire today and live very comfortably off the interest for the rest of my life. The fact is that I like to trade. When I was a kid, I loved to play games. Now I get to play a very fun game, and I'm paid handsomely for it. I can honestly say that there isn't anything else I would rather be doing. The minute I don't have fun trading, or I don't think I can make a profit, I'm going to quit.

**Have the markets changed since you started in the business?**

Volume has gone up dramatically, which is great. The markets also appear to have become more efficient. Some of the patterns I used to trade off are starting to get eliminated as other people start picking up on them.

**Can you give me an example of a pattern that has become obsolete?**

I used to like to put on positions in the stock market in the same direction as the price movement two days earlier. For example, if the market was up on Monday, I would be prone to be a buyer on Wednesday. This is an example of a pattern that I don't believe in much anymore.

**Your type of system development seems to be heavily based on past patterns. If you test enough patterns, aren't some of them going to be profitable a large percentage of the time just based on normal probability? Just like if you had ten thousand people toss a coin ten times, some of them are going to get ten heads in a row. It doesn't mean that those coins have any better chance of landing on heads on the next toss. How do you distinguish between patterns that reflect real inefficiencies in the market and those that are merely coincidental, an inevitable consequence of looking at so many patterns?**

A pattern has to make sense. For example, if I find that the price change of the British pound forty days ago is statistically significant in predicting today's price in the S&P, I wouldn't put any faith in it. Why would the British pound price forty days ago affect the S&P? So we toss out a lot of these types of patterns even if they have a high percentage of success.

**Why would you even bother testing patterns like that?**

It's actually easier to set up giant computer runs to test every combination of market and interval relationships, and then consider the relationships that appear statistically significant, than to decide which individual combinations to test.

**Is a statistical emphasis one of the keys to your trading approach?**

Yes, because it keeps us rational. We like to see that something has worked in the past before we use real money on it.

**How many different models or patterns are you using at any given time to trade the markets?**

Dozens.

**For diversification reasons?**

Yes. We try to diversify everything we possibly can. We like to diversify over both trading strategies and time.

**By time diversification, do you mean you use the same pattern for hourly data, daily data, and weekly data?**

Right. It also means simply following the markets throughout the entire trading session and being ready to trade if something happens at any time in the day.

**What percentage of your trading is automatically determined by specific patterns or systems you use?**

Roughly 50 percent. It's hard to gauge because our systems may tell us to buy one thousand contracts on a given day but it's my discretion as to when to buy them.

**So your skills in entering and exiting positions are an important element in your trading performance?**

Absolutely.

**If you just followed the systems blindly by placing orders using some automatic entry rule—for example, buying on the opening, or on the close, or at some fixed intervals through the day—instead of timing the entry of the trade, what would you guess would be the degradation of results per month?**

It's very hard to say, but if we blindly followed the systems we might make half of what we do now. Maybe even less. I could give ten CTAs the exact systems we use, and some of them still wouldn't make any money.

**You said that roughly 50 percent of your trades are not system determined. Give me an example of that type of trade.**

My favorite is the magnet effect, which we spoke about earlier. When the market approaches a round number or a critical point, I like to play for the market to get to that price.

**Have you ever tried systematizing that concept?**

No, because I don't think it can be systematized. I may suddenly realize that a certain level is a key point, or the information may come from one of our floor contacts. We're always asking our floor people, "What numbers are people looking for?"

**Any other examples of a discretionary [i.e., nonsystem] type of trade?**

We get constant information from the floor. We probably get a call a minute from our clerks.

**Telling you who is doing what?**

Right.

**Is that helpful?**

If, for instance, a lot of players whom we respect seem to be doing the same thing, it might prompt us to take a similar position or increase our position if we're already on the same side.

**Any other examples of nonsystem trades?**

Another trade I like to do is to find out when a price move has been caused primarily by locals—we have very good floor contacts, so we get that type of information—and then go in the opposite direction. The reasoning is that the locals are going to want to cover their position before the end of the day, which is going to bring the market back from whence it came. [Most locals go home flat.]

**I noticed that you have a whole crew of traders working for you. Yet, it's my impression that you are the only one here who makes discretionary trading calls. How do you utilize those people? Couldn't you just watch the markets on your own and use some clerical staff to help you enter the orders?**

There's so much information flowing in here that I can't possibly follow and analyze it all. My traders are under instructions to alert me anytime something important happens. They also keep me posted as to when markets are likely to be particularly volatile based on fundamentals or news announcements. A recent example of that type of an announcement was Jim Baker's statement to the press on January 9. We were set up for a more peaceful type of an announcement. [January 9, 1991, was the day that Secretary of State James Baker met with the Iraqi ambassador in an effort to avert a war. At the time, there was a reasonable degree of optimism going into the meeting because a continued hard-line stance seemed such folly for Iraq. Addressing the press after the meeting, Baker began his statement, "Regrettably...." Traders didn't wait to hear the second word, and a wave of selling hit the stock and bond markets.]

**Did you sell as soon as you heard the word "Regrettably"?**

It was too late for us. With the type of size we trade, it was all over. For example, we lost 1,200 points in the S&P in a half-hour, and most of that was in the first ten seconds. We were long about seven hundred contracts. If we had tried to sell into that type of market, we would have amplified the decline and probably would have ended up selling at the low of the day.

**When some sudden news comes out, how do you decide when you should just get out immediately and when you should wait for the initial selling panic to subside?**

There's a big difference between small size and big size. If I were trading small size—for example, ten lots in the S&P—then I probably would have gotten out right away. That is, I would have sold as soon as I heard the word "Regrettably."

**But obviously you're not in that position anymore. Now that you're always trading larger size, do you just have to grit your teeth and wait when a surprise hits the market?**

I wait until the market stabilizes a bit and then I start getting out—particularly if it's past my pain threshold in terms of dollar loss.

**What eventually happened on that day? Did you get out of your entire S&P position?**

Yes. We basically phased out of the position over the rest of the day. There was no question about what to do because one of my risk management rules is that if we lose more than 1.5 percent of our total equity on a given trade we get out.

**What are your other risk management rules?**

If we're down 4 percent on a single day, we close out all positions and wait until the next day to get into anything again. This rule has been activated only twice in the last two years, one of those days being January 9. I dumped my whole portfolio because I was down 4 percent.

**What was your dollar loss that day?**

About $9.5 million.

**And you lost that amount in a very short period of time?**

From all practical standpoints, I lost most of it in about ten seconds.

**Talk about your emotions when you're losing a million dollars a second.**

In this instance, it happened so quickly that I was a bit speechless. Normally when I lose money, I get angry. That's usually the first emotion that comes into play.

**Angry at the market, or angry at yourself?**

I guess more at the market, but, of course, that's not really rational because the market is not a personal thing; it is not trying to get me. I try to keep my anger in check as much as possible because I believe that to be a good trader it's very important to be rational and have your emotions under control. I've been trying for years to get rid of anger completely when I lose money, and I've come to the conclusion that it is impossible. I can work toward that goal, but until the day I die, I don't think I'm ever going to be able to look a big loss in the face and not get angry.

**Does anger affect your trading?**

No. I'd say that I'm pretty good about that.

**Going back to January 9, after you got past your speechless reaction, what did you do?**

Once I realized that we were down over 4 percent, I devised an orderly plan to exit all markets by the close. In that type of situation I try to devise an exit plan and then get out of the trading room because I want the liquidation done in a rational manner. I leave it to my traders to handle the execution.

**Did the loss keep you awake that night or did you sleep well?**

In general, I don't sleep well at any time. Unfortunately, that's one of the prices you have to pay for being a trader. I wish I didn't have to, but that's the way it is.

**Do you sleep better on days when you win than on days when you lose?**

Not necessarily. In fact, I probably sleep worse when I'm doing well, because I get too excited.

**How long was it until you fully absorbed the impact of that day and were on to the next thing?**

I started forgetting a bit about it the next day. It took me a few days.

**When a loss like this happens, do you think it's going to bother you for a while? Are you surprised that you're completely over it a week later?**

I guess I know that I'm going to be over it in a week. I never want to get into a situation where it's so bad that I can't get over it. That's one of the reasons I try to be conservative in my risk management. I want to make sure I'll be around to play tomorrow.

**Once you get out, even though you've taken a loss, do you feel better because you're out?**

Yes, because the pain is over, and I know exactly what I've lost. There's a bit of a feeling of relief.

**Is it meaningfully tougher to lose 4 percent when you're trading $100 million than when you're trading $1 million?**

It is tougher. Dollars have a lot to do with it, too. There are plenty of traders I know who show track records with an amazing cumulative winning percentage. I've seen situations where they might be up 1,000 percent over a five-year period, but if you examine their track record in terms of net dollars made or lost, you discover they are actually down.

**Because they made the large percentage returns with small capital and then lost money when they were managing large sums?**

Exactly. I'm not in the business of picking CTAs. But if I were, one of the first screens I would use would be a person's total dollar profit— how many dollars did the CTA pull out of the market. If that number were negative, I would eliminate the CTA from consideration, regardless of the percentage return.

**Did your 4 percent maximum daily loss rule help you on January 9?**

On that particular occasion, no. We actually would have been better off gritting our teeth and holding on for a while longer.

**But doesn't that change your faith in the rule?**

No, because if you don't have that type of rule, you can end up being long the S&P on a day like October 19, 1987, when procrastinating in getting out would have been a disaster.

**So far you've mentioned a 1.5 percent maximum loss limit on a single position and 4 percent on the entire portfolio for any given day. Are there any other risk management rules you use?**

We have a maximum loss point of 10 percent per month. If we ever lost that amount, we'd exit all our positions and wait until the start of the next month to begin trading again. Thankfully, that has never happened.

We also have a fourth risk management rule: At the beginning of each month, I determine the maximum position size that I'm willing to take in each market, and I don't exceed that limit, regardless of how bullish or bearish I get. This rule keeps me in check.

**Do you use charts?**

I look at charts primarily to figure out where traders are going to get interested in a market. I know the types of patterns they like to look at.

**You use both discretionary and system trading. Do you have anything to say about the merits or drawbacks of each approach?**

The bottom line is that you need an edge. One of the ways you can get an edge is to find a successful system. However, if you're just a pure systems player and you start managing large amounts of money, you're going to find that your transaction costs start to eliminate a good deal of your profits. In general, it's probably best to be somewhere between a pure discretionary trader and a pure system trader. As I mentioned before, you can help your systems by using some discretion in the entry and exit of positions.

**Have you looked at commercial systems at all?**

Sure, we've bought lots of them. I used to evaluate the systems myself, but now I have other people in the office do it. We have never used any of these systems as is; we use them to give us ideas in constructing our own systems.

**Do you have any advice for the public about systems offered for sale?**

Join Club 3000. [This organization issues a newsletter composed of members' letters that discuss systems and other aspects of trading. The name derives from its origins. Club 3000 was formed in frustration by members who had paid approximately $3,000 for a system they felt was essentially worthless and decided to get together to share information about various systems.] I would also subscribe to such publications as *Futures, Technical Analysis of Stocks and Commodities,* and *Commodity Traders Consumers Report* for their reviews on systems. Also, once you buy a system, make sure you test it on your own data.

**In other words, don't take the vendor's word for it. Do you think that many of the claims for systems are overblown?**

Yes.

**Is that because of deliberate misrepresentation or are most of the vendors actually fooling themselves?**

Some of the system claims may actually be partially legitimate. However, I usually find these systems don't have enough observations to be statistically significant. Also, frequently, the systems base their percentage return claims on the minimum exchange margin requirements.

**I understand. Doing that gives the systems extraordinary leverage and the ads only talk about the return side; they don't discuss the risk side.**

Right. I made the same mistake in my senior thesis. I based my percentage returns on the assumption of an account size equal to double the exchange minimum margin requirement, which was a grossly inadequate sum. In reality, if you ever tried to trade that way, you would go broke, because the drawdowns are too big.

**Do you basically believe that if somebody developed a really good system they wouldn't be selling it?**

To some degree, I believe that. Sure, it's possible that a system developer may not have any money, but if the system is that good, he should be able to convince friends, family, anybody to put some money into the system and trade it.

**Are there any technical indicators in the public domain that you find useful?**

Moving averages are useful. They'll work if you watch your risk management. I believe you can make an above-average return by using moving averages, if you're smart about it.

**Any indicators that you consider overrated?**

Most of the common ones: Fibonacci retracements, Gann angles, RSI, and stochastics. I haven't found anything there for any of these indicators.

**If you have a streak when you're doing very well, day after day, do you get to the point where you say, "This just can't keep on"? And do you start reducing your position because of that?**

Actually, the better I'm doing, the bigger I play, and the worse I'm doing, the smaller I play.

**So you believe in streaks?**

Yes, not just in trading, but in most things in life. If a team has won eight games in a row, you don't bet against them winning their ninth game.

**Are there trading errors that you've learned to avoid?**

In general, I don't like placing stops. If you're a big player, you really have to be careful about putting stops into the market.

**Did you learn that by getting burned in placing stops?**

I never placed a lot of stops throughout my entire career, but I used to place more than I do now.

**If you did place the stop, did you find there was a higher tendency of getting hit?**

If I put a large stop order in the market, not only is it going to have a tendency to get hit, but when it does get activated, prices are likely to run. So I will not only get stopped out, but I will get filled at an average price significantly worse than my stop.

**At your current trading size, I would assume that you probably avoid entering explicit stop orders altogether.**

Right. Sometimes, if I want the price to move toward a certain level, I may put in a stop and then cancel the order once the market gets close. I do stuff like that frequently. Actually, I did it today. It worked today, but sometimes it backfires, and you find yourself the proud owner of some bonds you don't want.

**You seem very confident about your ability to trade the markets profitably. Have you always had that confidence in trading?**

Probably for about four years.

**Not speaking about yourself now, but in general, would you say there is a strong correlation between the degree of confidence and success in trading?**

There is some correlation, but it's nowhere near 100 percent. Some people are just confident, but if they don't have an edge in the market, it doesn't matter; they're still going to lose money.

**What you're saying is that not all confident people are going to be good traders. However, are nearly all good traders confident?**

Yes, I would think that virtually all good traders are probably confident in their trading ability.

**Do you remember when you really became confident as a trader? Is there some transition point that you can recall?**

I guess by the time I decided to go off on my own I was fairly confident. I knew I had to make money just to pay my rent.

**Was that confidence derived from the consistency of your returns?**

Yes, I knew I was getting statistically significant results.

**You come from an academic background and even did your thesis on a subject related to the markets. I'm sure you're quite aware that most of the academic community still holds to the efficient market hypothesis. Obviously, what you're doing couldn't be done if that theory were right.**

The markets are clearly not a random walk. The markets are not even efficient because that assumption implies you can't make an above-average return. Since some people can do that, I disagree with the assumption.

**But still, I'm sure a lot of your professors believe in the efficient market hypothesis.**

Right, and that's probably why they're professors and why I'm making money doing what I'm doing. Also, I think it's amazing what you can do when you have real money on the line. A person in an academic setting might think that they have tested all possible types of systems. However, when you have real money on the line, you can start to think pretty creatively. There is always something else to test. I think that the academic community just hasn't tested many of the approaches that are viable. Certainly, if you just spend a short time doing an academic study, you're not going to find anything significant. It can't be any other way. If it were, everyone would be rich. But if you spend every day of your life researching the markets and have adequate computer support, you can find stuff that works.

**What are the traits of a successful trader?**

A successful trader is rational, analytical, able to control emotions, practical, and profit oriented.

**What advice would you give to a friend who wants to be a trader?**

Learn a lot of statistics. Learn how to use a computer. Find some systems that work. Develop some simple risk management rules.

**Are there any books on the markets that you would recommend to other people?**

We give our new traders three books when they start: your first book, *The Complete Guide to the Futures Markets* [Jack D. Schwager, John Wiley & Sons, 1984], *The Handbook of Futures Markets,* by Perry Kaufman [John Wiley & Sons, 1984], and *The Commodity Futures Game: Who Wins? Who Loses? Why?* by Richard J. Tewles and Frank J. Jones [McGraw-Hill, 1987]. Then there are some fun books I recommend, like your *Market Wizards,* which is a good motivational work. We also have loads of other books in our library, and we let traders choose which other ones they wish to read.

**What kinds of misconceptions do people have about the markets?**

They believe you can make tons of money with little work. They think you can make 100 percent a year doing a little bit of research on the weekends. That's ridiculous.

**They underestimate the difficulty of the game and overestimate the payoff?**

Exactly. Also, some people blame everyone except themselves when they lose money. It galled me to read in a recent *Wall Street Journal* article that some guy actually won a lawsuit against his brokerage firm because he lost all the money in his account. The point is that it wasn't even a matter of his broker giving him bad advice; he was calling his own trades! He sued the brokerage firm, saying that they shouldn't have allowed him to trade his account the way he did. I believe it's a free country, and if you want to trade, you should have every right to do so, but if you lose money, it's your own responsibility.

**What mistakes do most people make in the markets? I'm talking about actual trading mistakes rather than misconceptions.**

First, many people get involved in the markets without any edge. They get in the market because their broker told them that the market is bullish. That is not an edge. However, to tell the truth, most small speculators will never be around long enough to find out whether their system could have worked, because they bet too much on their trades, or their account is too small to start.

**So there are people out there who actually might have a good idea that could make money, but they'll never find out because when they first try to do it, they bet too much and they're knocked out of the game.**

Exactly.

**Do you trade overnight sometimes?**

We have a twenty-four-hour operation. I also have a hand-held quotation device that I use to check the markets when I'm home.

**Isn't that kind of overbearing?**

Yes, it is. Although I check the quotes every night, I try not to overdo it, because I do have a tendency to become compulsive.

**Are your night people under instructions to call and wake you in the middle of the night if something important happens?**

Yes.

**How often does that happen?**

Not that often. Maybe four times a year.

**What do you do for recreation?**

I go to a lot of sporting events, and I do a fair amount of reading. I'm interested in psychology and philosophy. I also read lots of self-improvement books. I probably overdo it, though. I notice that the more memory books I read, the worse my memory becomes.

**Do you still play basketball yourself? [Trout was captain of his college team.] Don't you miss it? I mean, at one time it was obviously pretty important in your life.**

No, because I'm on to the next big thing: trading.

**Did you ever entertain the possibility of making the pros?**

Coming out of my senior year in high school, I had hoped to play for the pros, and I thought that maybe I could. However, after playing my first year in college, I realized that the people were too good. I could have played in Europe. In fact, a lot of my former teammates are playing professionally in Europe, but some of them make just $10,000 a year. I didn't want to do that.

**Do you take any vacation time?**

I have only had three days off in a year and a half.

**Is that because when you go on vacation you're thinking that every day you are away is costing you X amount of dollars?**

To some degree I do that. Also, I feel I need to be around to supervise my staff and make sure that the trading is going properly.

**Do you sometimes feel that you've become a captive to your own creation? Wouldn't you like to be able to just go away for a few weeks somewhere and forget everything?**

I would, but to trade successfully you have to do it full-time. I allot myself ten vacation days a year, but I never take them. I firmly believe that for every good thing in life, there's a price you have to pay.

**What are the trading rules you live by?**

Make sure you have the edge. Know what your edge is. Have rigid risk control rules like the ones we talked about earlier. Basically, when you get down to it, to make money, you need to have an edge and employ good money management. Good money management alone isn't going to increase your edge at all. If your system isn't any good, you're still going to lose money, no matter how effective your money management rules are. But if you have an approach that makes money, then money management can make the difference between success and failure.

**What are your current goals?**

To make a 30 percent return each year, with no peak-to-valley drawdown greater than 10 percent.

**Any other final words?**

Just that I'm excited and confident about the future. If I ever don't feel that way, I will stop trading.

---

I had found Trout's track record—a combination of very high annualized returns and extremely low drawdowns—almost mystifying. Of course, although a combination of high return and low risk is rare, it is not unique; in fact, a number of the other traders I interviewed in this book (and in *Market Wizards*) also exhibited this profile. Why then do I say "mystifying"? Because from what I had heard about Trout, I knew that his trades were based largely on signals generated by computerized technical trading systems.

I have spent many years developing and evaluating technical trading systems. Although I have found systems that make nearly as much as Trout does (based on average annualized return), these systems invariably exhibit much greater volatility. Drawdowns of 25 percent in these systems are commonplace, with worst-case drawdowns even exceeding 50 percent. Certainly, the volatility of these systems could be reduced by cutting back the leverage (i.e., the number of contracts traded per $100,000). Doing so, however, would lower the returns down to mediocre levels.

I have never found any systems that could even remotely approach Trout's performance in terms of return/risk measurements. In fact, every trader I interviewed who displayed a combination of high return and very low risk invariably proved to be a discretionary trader (i.e., a trader who relies on his own internal synthesis of market information to make trading decisions, as opposed to using computer-generated trading signals). How, then, does Trout do it?

I got the answer to that question in this interview. Part of it has to do with his reliance on systems that are based primarily on statistical analysis as opposed to more standard, trend-following approaches. However, perhaps the major factor is that Trout's exceptional skill in timing the entry and exit of his positions, by his own estimate, accounts for fully half of his return. "I could give ten CTAs the exact systems we use, and some of them still wouldn't make any money," he says. Thus, once again, we're talking about synthesis of information that can't be computerized (e.g., the noise level on the floors) accounting for the superior performance. In other words, Trout may reach his trading decisions in a similar fashion to that of system traders, but he executes these decisions like a discretionary trader.

Trout's basic message is twofold. First, you have to have an edge to beat the markets. Everything else is secondary. You can have great money management, but if you don't have an approach that gives you an edge, then you can't win. This may seem obvious, but many traders enter the markets without any evidence that they have an edge.

Second, assuming you have an edge, you must exercise rigid risk control to protect against those infrequent events that cause enormous, abrupt price moves that can quickly decimate overleveraged accounts. And, as demonstrated in Trout's own thesis, the probability of sharp price moves is far greater than suggested by standard statistical assumptions. Hence, risk control is essential. The trader who gets wiped out by a sudden, large, adverse price move is not simply unlucky, since such events occur often enough that they must be planned for.

It is instructive to compare Monroe Trout's message with that of Blair Hull (see Part VI). Although their trading methods are completely different—Trout is a directional trader, whereas Hull is an arbitrageur—their assessments of the key to successful trading are virtually identical: a combination of having an edge and using rigid money management controls.

# *Al Weiss*

## THE HUMAN CHART ENCYCLOPEDIA

In terms of return/risk ratio, Al Weiss may well have the single best long-term track record for a commodity trading advisor. Since he began trading in 1982 as AZF Commodity Management, Weiss has averaged 52 percent annually. One thousand dollars invested with Weiss in 1982 would have been worth almost $53,000 at the end of 1991. However, returns are only half the story. The truly impressive element in Weiss's track record is that these high gains were achieved with extremely small equity drawdowns. During this entire period, the largest single equity drawdown witnessed by Weiss was 17 percent in 1986. In the past four years (1988–91), Weiss has honed his risk control to truly astounding standards: during this period, his worst annual drawdown averaged under 5 percent, while his average annual return exceeded 29 percent.

Despite his exemplary track record, Weiss has kept a very low profile. Until 1991, Weiss repeatedly refused to grant any interviews. He explains this by saying, "I didn't feel my methods were proven until I had realized at least a decade of superior performance." He also felt that interviews would attract the wrong type of investors. At this point, that consideration is no longer a concern, as Weiss is handling as much money as he feels he can manage without negatively affecting his performance (approximately $100 million).

Although Weiss now regularly turns away new investors, he will occasionally make an exception. As he explains, "Sometimes I take on a small account [$100,000] if I feel the person is truly sincere. I still get a kick out of taking on a small account and making it compound. Just recently, I accepted a new investor because I was impressed that he had gone through the track records of five hundred CTAs before making a selection. Ironically, at the same time I was talking to this person, I also received a call from a French bank that wanted to invest $30 million. I turned down the bank, but I accepted the small account's $100,000 investment."

Weiss has also shunned publicity because he is naturally reclusive. He admits that, during the decade he has been managing investor funds, he has met only five of his clients. Although Weiss comes across as an extrovert over the phone, in person his shy side dominates.

One of Weiss's hobbies is investing with other traders. He devotes one or two days per month to this endeavor. He estimates that, over the years, he has reviewed the track records of approximately eight hundred traders. Out of this large group, he has selected about twenty traders for personal investment. His goal is not to pick any individual supertraders but rather to blend traders together in a group whose composite performance reflects both good returns and very low equity drawdowns. Interestingly, the performance characteristics of this group of traders as a whole has the appearance of a Weiss clone. During the period 1988–91, the group realized an average annual return of 19 percent, with an extraordinarily low average maximum annual drawdown under 3 percent. The ratio of these two numbers (19/3 = 6.3) is nearly identical to the ratio of Weiss's corresponding figures for the same period (29/5 = 5.8).

My interview of Weiss proved to be one of the most difficult I have conducted. Quite frankly, had I been less impressed with his track record, I would have given up on this chapter. After virtually every question I posed, Weiss would go off on elaborate tangents and ultimately catch himself, stop talking, and glance at me with a look that seemed to say, "stop me before I digress any further." The interview was such an obvious flop to both of us that we decided to break and go for dinner. In other interviews, I have taken my tape recorder along in such situations, and sections of past interviews have, in fact, transpired over meals. However, in this instance, the prospects seemed so unencouraging that I deliberately left the recorder in my room. I also felt that some casual conversation might help break the ice.

After dinner, we decided to give it another shot by trying to continue the interview on an evening walk. The atmosphere was conducive to conversation, as we strolled along the quiet streets of a small island just off the coast of Florida, on a mild, winter evening. Nevertheless, the interview still proceeded in very jagged fashion. I found myself constantly turning the tape recorder on and off.

Following are excerpts gleaned from our conversations and some additional material from follow-up correspondence.

---

**How did you end up becoming a trader?**

It was not an overnight process. I spent four years of solid research before doing any serious trading. After literally thousands of hours of poring over charts, going back as far in history as I could, I began to recognize certain patterns that became the basis of my trading approach.

**You spent four years doing research before you even started trading?**

Yes. I'm a risk-averse person. I wanted to have confidence in my approach before I started.

**Precisely how far back did you go in your chart studies?**

It varied with the individual market and the available charts. In the case of the grain markets, I was able to go back as far as the 1840s.

**Was it really necessary to go back that far?**

Absolutely. One of the keys in long-term chart analysis is realizing that markets behave differently in different economic cycles. Recognizing these repeating and shifting long-term patterns requires lots of history. Identifying where you are in an economic cycle—say, an inflationary phase versus a deflationary phase—is critical to interpreting the chart patterns evolving at that time.

**How did you support yourself during the four years you devoted to researching the markets?**

In my early twenties, I had pioneered the development of the urethane skateboard wheel, which was a great financial success. I invested the money I made on this venture into the real estate market, which also proved to be very profitable. As a result, I had all the money I needed and was able to devote my full time to research.

**I understand that you're basically a technical systems trader. Why do you believe your track record is so much better than those of other commodity trading advisors using similar methods? In particular, I'm interested in how you have managed to avoid the large drawdowns that seem to be almost intrinsic to this approach.**

Although I employ technical analysis to make my trading decisions, there are a few important differences between my method and the approaches of most other traders in this group. First, I think very few other technical traders have gone back more than thirty years in their chart studies, let alone more than a hundred years. Second, I don't always interpret the same pattern in the same way. I also factor in where I believe we are at in terms of long-term economic cycles. This factor alone can lead to very substantial differences between the conclusions I might draw from the charts versus those reached by traders not incorporating such a perspective. Finally, I don't simply look at the classical chart patterns (head and shoulders, triangle, and so on) as independent formations. Rather, I tend to look for certain combinations of patterns or, in other words, patterns within patterns within patterns. These more complex, multiple-pattern combinations can signal much higher probability trades.

**What popular chart patterns are accurate only 50 percent of the time?**

Most of them. But that's not a drawback. A pattern that works 50 percent of the time can be quite profitable if you employ it with a good risk control plan.

**Is technical analysis an art or a science?**

It's both an art and a science. It's an art in the sense that if you asked ten different traders to define a head-and-shoulders pattern, you'd come up with ten different answers. However, for any individual trader, the definition can be made mathematically precise. In other words, chart traders are artists until they mathematically define their patterns—say, as part of a system structure—at which time they become scientists.

**Why have you chosen a purely technical approach in favor of one that also employs fundamentals?**

Many economists have tried to trade the commodity markets fundamentally and have usually ended up losing. The problem is that the markets operate more on psychology than on fundamentals. For example, you may determine that silver should be priced at, say, $8, and that may well be an accurate evaluation. However, under certain conditions—for example, a major inflationary environment—the price could temporarily go much higher. In the commodity inflation boom that peaked in 1980, silver reached a high of $50—a price level that was out of all proportion to any true fundamental value. Of course, eventually the market returned to its base value—in fact, in the history of markets, I can't think of a single commodity that didn't eventually move back to its base value—but in the interim, anyone trading purely on the fundamentals would have been wiped out.

**Do any particularly memorable trades come to mind?**

Whenever I'm on vacation, I continue to chart the markets. In the summer of 1990, while on vacation in the Bahamas, I was updating my charts on a picnic table beneath the palm trees. I noticed patterns that indicated buy signals in all the energy markets. These signals seemed particularly odd because it's very unusual to get a buy signal in heating oil during the summer. However, I didn't question the trade and simply phoned in the orders. Three days later, Iraq invaded Kuwait and oil prices exploded.

**Do you follow your system absolutely, or do you sometimes override the trading signals?**

I follow the system well over 90 percent of the time, but occasionally I try to do better than the system. Since I employ such deviations from the pure system very selectively, they have improved performance overall.

**Give me an example of a situation in which you overrode the system.**

In October 1987 when the stock market was in the midst of its crash, I started receiving anxious calls from my clients who wanted to know if they had suffered a large loss. I calmly explained that we were still up 37 percent for the year and that the total risk on all our open positions was only 4 percent. I had a feeling that people would be very insecure in the markets and that there would be a resulting flight to T-bills. I decided to take off my entire short position in T-bills, even though my system had not yet provided any reversal signal. That proved to be the right action, as the T-bill market took off on the upside almost immediately afterwards.

**It's obvious from your earlier comments that you consider cycles important. Could you please elaborate?**

There are cycles in everything—the weather, ocean waves, and the markets. One of the most important long-term cycles is the cycle from inflation to deflation. About every two generations—roughly every forty-seven to sixty years—there's a deflationary market. For example, in respect to the commodity markets, we're currently in a deflationary phase that began in 1980. Over the past two hundred years, these deflationary phases have typically lasted between eight and twelve years. Since we're currently in the twelfth year of commodity price deflation, I think we're very close to a major bottom in commodity prices.

Another important consideration in regard to cycles is that their lengths vary greatly from market to market. For example, in the grain markets, which are heavily weather dependent, you may get major bull markets about five times every twenty years. In the gold market, however, a major bull cycle may occur only three to five times in a century. This consideration could make a market such as gold very frustrating for traders trying to play for the next bullish wave.

**What is the single most important statement you could make about the markets?**

The essential element is that the markets are ultimately based on human psychology, and by charting the markets you're merely converting human psychology into graphic representations. I believe that the human mind is more powerful than any computer in analyzing the implications of these price graphs.

---

Weiss's highly individualistic approach doesn't lend itself readily to generalizations. Certainly his comments should inspire those inclined to cyclical analysis, but I would add that other expert traders, such as Eckhardt, argue the opposite viewpoint rather persuasively. Perhaps his most significant input is that the reliability of chart analysis can be greatly enhanced by viewing classic chart patterns as parts of more complex combinations, rather than in isolation, as is typically done. Weiss also emphasizes that students of chart analysis need to conduct their research much further back in history than is usually the case. In markets in which he was able to obtain the data, Weiss has extended his chart studies as far back as 150 years ago.

In essence, I think Weiss is successful because of the combination of a vast amount of research in analyzing charts and a knack for seeing relatively complex patterns. Ultimately, that line of reasoning leads to the conclusion that you, too, can be successful if you can read a chart with the same skill as Weiss. Not very helpful information, is it? However, Weiss's consistent streak of high annual returns and low maximum drawdowns provides compelling proof that pure chart analysis can yield an extraordinarily effective trading approach.

# PART IV

# *Fund Managers and Timers*

# Stanley Druckenmiller

## THE ART OF TOP-DOWN INVESTING

Stanley Druckenmiller belongs to the rarefied world of managers who control multibillion-dollar portfolios. Achieving a near 40 percent return on a $100 million portfolio is impressive, but realizing that performance level on a multibillion-dollar fund is incredible. In the three years since he assumed active management control of the Quantum Fund from his mentor and idol, George Soros, Druckenmiller has realized an average annual return of over 38 percent on assets ranging between $2.0 billion and $3.5 billion.

Druckenmiller has been on a fast track ever since he decided to forsake graduate school for the real world. After less than one year as a stock analyst for the Pittsburgh National Bank, Druckenmiller was promoted to the position of director of equity research. Druckenmiller dismisses his sudden promotion as the act of an eccentric, albeit brilliant, division manager. However, one suspects there was more to it, particularly in light of Druckenmiller's subsequent achievements. Less than one year later, when the division head who had hired Druckenmiller left the bank, Druckenmiller was promoted to assume his slot, once again leapfrogging a host of senior managers maneuvering for the same position. Two years later, in 1980, at the young age of twenty-eight, Druckenmiller left the bank to launch his own money management firm, Duquesne Capital Management.

In 1986, Druckenmiller was recruited by Dreyfus as a fund manager. As part of the agreement, Dreyfus permitted Druckenmiller to continue managing his own Duquesne Fund. By the time Druckenmiller joined Dreyfus, his management style had been transformed from a conventional approach of holding a portfolio of stocks into an eclectic strategy incorporating bonds, currencies, and stocks, with the flexibility of trading any of these markets from both the short side and the long side. Dreyfus was so enamored with Druckenmiller's innate market approach that the company developed a few funds around him, the most popular being the Strategic Aggressive Investing Fund, which was the best-performing fund in the industry from its date of inception (March 1987) until Druckenmiller left Dreyfus in August 1988.

Druckenmiller's popularity at Dreyfus proved to be too much of a good thing. Eventually, he found himself managing seven funds at Dreyfus, in addition to his own Duquesne Fund. The strain of all this activity and his desire to work with Soros, who Druckenmiller considers the greatest investor of our time, prompted him to leave Dreyfus for Soros Management. Shortly thereafter, Soros turned over the management of his fund to Druckenmiller, as Soros left to pursue his goal of helping to transform the closed economies of Eastern Europe and the former Soviet Union.

The longest-running measure of Druckenmiller's performance in the markets is his own Duquesne fund. Since its inception in 1980, the fund has averaged 37 percent annually. Druckenmiller stresses that the early years of Duquesne's performance are not directly relevant since the fund's structure changed completely in mid-1986 to accommodate the flexible trading approach he now uses. Measured from this later starting point, Druckenmiller's average annual return has been 45 percent.

I interviewed Druckenmiller at his co-op apartment on a weekend day. I was surprised by his youth; I had hardly expected someone who had been managing one of the world's largest funds for several years to still be in his thirties. As we relaxed in the living room, our conversation began with Druckenmiller's story of how he got started in the business.

---

I had enrolled in graduate school to study for an economics degree. However, I found the program overly quantitative and theoretical, with little emphasis on real-life applications. I was very disappointed and dropped out in the second semester. I took a job as a management trainee at the Pittsburgh National Bank, with the idea that the program would provide me with a broad overview that would help me to decide on an area of focus.

I had been at the bank for several months when I received a call from the manager in the trust department. "I hear you attended the University of Michigan," he said. When I confirmed his statement, he said, "Great." He asked whether I had an M.B.A. I told him that I did not. He said, "That's even better. Come on up; you're hired."

**What job did he give you?**

I was hired as a bank and chemical stock analyst.

**Was that the type of position you perceived yourself heading toward?**

I really had no idea what kind of job I would end up with. Most of the people who entered the management training program at the bank had an immediate goal of becoming a loan officer. I thought that I had been doing pretty well when the head of the loan department informed me that I would make a terrible loan officer. He said that I was too interested in the actual functioning of the companies, whereas a loan officer's job was essentially a sales position. He thought my personality was too abrupt and generally unsuitable for sales. I remember feeling quite let down by being told that I was going to be a failure, when all along I had thought that I was doing quite well in the program.

**Tell me about your early experiences as a stock analyst.**

The director of investments was Speros Drelles, the person who had hired me. He was brilliant, with a great aptitude for teaching, but he was also quite eccentric. When I was twenty-five and had been in the department for only about a year, he summoned me into his office and announced that he was going to make me the director of equity research. This was quite a bizarre move, since my boss was about fifty years old and had been with the bank for over twenty-five years. More-

over, all the other analysts had M.B.A.'s and had been in the department longer than I had.

"You know why I'm doing this, don't you?" he asked.

"No," I replied.

"For the same reason they send eighteen-year-olds into war."

"Why is that?" I asked.

"Because they're too dumb to know not to charge." Drelles continued, "The small cap [capitalization] stocks have been in a bear market
for ten years [this conversation transpired in 1978], and I think there's
going to be a huge, liquidity-driven bull market sometime in the next
decade. Frankly, I have a lot of scars from the past ten years, while you
don't. I think we'll make a great team because you'll be too stupid and
inexperienced to know not to try to buy everything. That other guy out
there," he said, referring to my boss, the exiting director of equity
research, "is just as stale as I am."

**So, essentially, you leapfrogged your boss. Was there any resent-
ment?**

Very much so, and it was quite unpleasant. Although I now realize that
my boss handled himself very well given the circumstances. He was
very bitter, but I certainly understand his sense of resentment much better now than I did then. I couldn't envision myself responding any better twelve years from now if someone replaced me with a twenty-five-
year-old.

**Obviously, Drelles didn't just make you head of research because of
your youth. There must have been more to it.**

I had a natural aptitude for the business, and I think he was impressed
with the job I did analyzing the banking industry. For example, at the
time, Citicorp was going crazy with international loans, and I had done
a major bearish piece, which proved to be correct. Although I hadn't
taken a business course, I was fairly lucid in economics and probably
made a good impression with my grasp of international money flows.

**What was done with the research that you generated?**

The analysts presented their ideas to a stock selection committee, which consisted of seven members. After the presentation, there was an intense question-and-answer period in which the analysts defended their recommendations.

**What happened to the recommendations after the presentation?**

If a majority of the committee approved the idea, it would be placed on the stock selection list. Once a stock was placed on the list, the portfolio managers at the bank were permitted to buy that stock. They were not allowed to purchase any stocks that were not on the list.

**What happened if you were bearish on a stock?**

If the recommendation was accepted, the stock would be deleted from the approved list.

**Did you like being an analyst?**

I loved it. I came in at six in the morning and stayed until eight at night. Remember, this was a bank, not a brokerage firm at which such hours represent normal behavior. Interestingly, even though Drelles had been at the bank for thirty years, he kept similar hours.

**What kind of analytical approach did you use in evaluating stocks?**

When I first started out, I did very thorough papers covering every aspect of a stock or industry. Before I could make the presentation to the stock selection committee, I first had to submit the paper to the research director. I particularly remember the time I gave him my paper on the banking industry. I felt very proud of my work. However, he read through it and said, "This is useless. What makes the stock go up and down?" That comment acted as a spur. Thereafter, I focused my analysis on seeking to identify the factors that were strongly correlated to a stock's price movement as opposed to looking at all the fundamentals. Frankly, even today, many analysts still don't know what makes their particular stocks go up and down.

**What did you find was the answer?**

Very often the key factor is related to earnings. This is particularly true of the bank stocks. Chemical stocks, however, behave quite differently. In this industry, the key factor seems to be capacity. The ideal time to buy the chemical stocks is after a lot of capacity has left the industry and there's a catalyst that you believe will trigger an increase in demand. Conversely, the ideal time to sell these stocks is when there are lots of announcements for new plants, not when the earnings turn down. The reason for this behavioral pattern is that expansion plans mean that earnings will go down in two to three years, and the stock market tends to anticipate such developments.

Another discipline I learned that helped me determine whether a stock would go up or down is technical analysis. Drelles was very technically oriented, and I was probably more receptive to technical analysis than anyone else in the department. Even though Drelles was the boss, a lot of people thought he was a kook because of all the chart books he kept. However, I found that technical analysis could be very effective.

**Did the rest of the analysts accept you as the research director, even though you were much younger and less experienced?**

Once they realized that Drelles had made a decision and was going to stick with it, they accepted the situation. However, later that same year, Drelles left the bank, and I suddenly found myself unprotected. I was only twenty-five years old, while all the other department heads were in their forties and fifties. As soon as the news broke that Drelles was leaving, a power struggle ensued among the department heads vying for his position.

Every Monday morning, I and the other department heads would present our views to the head of the trust department, a lawyer without any investment background. It was understood that he would use these presentations as input in making an eventual decision on Drelles's replacement. Clearly, everyone assumed that I was out of the running. The general belief was that I would be lucky to simply hold onto my job as research director, let alone inherit Drelles's position.

As it turned out, shortly after Drelles left, the Shah of Iran was overthrown. Here's where my inexperience really paid off. When the shah was deposed, I decided that we should put 70 percent of our money in oil stocks and the rest in defense stocks. This course of action seemed so logical to me that I didn't consider doing anything else. At the time, I didn't yet understand diversification. As research director, I had the authority to allow only those recommendations I favored to be presented to the stock selection committee, and I used this control to restrict the presentations largely to oil and defense stocks.

I presented the same strategy to the head of the trust department each Monday morning. Not surprisingly, the other department heads argued against my position just for the sake of taking the opposite view. They would try to put down anything I said. However, there are times in your career when everything that you do is right—and this was one of those times. Of course, now I would never even dream of putting 70 percent of a portfolio in oil stocks, but at the time I didn't know better. Fortunately, it was the ideal position to have, and our stock selection list outperformed the S&P 500 by multiples. After about nine months, to everyone's complete amazement, I was named to assume Drelles's former position as the director of investments.

**When did you leave the bank?**

In 1980 I went to make a presentation in New York. After the talk, one of the audience members approached me and exclaimed, "You're at a bank! What the hell are you doing at a bank?"

I said, "What else am I going to do? Frankly, I think I'm lucky to be there, given the level of my experience."

After about two minutes of talking, he asked, "Why don't you start your own firm?"

"How can I possibly do that?" I asked. "I don't have any money."

"If you start your own firm," he replied, "I'll pay you $10,000 a month just to speak to you. You don't even have to write any reports."

To put this in perspective, when I started at the bank in 1977, I was making $900 a month. When I was promoted to the research director position, my annual salary was still only $23,000, and all the analysts who reported to me were making more than I was. Even after my promotion to Drelles's position, I was still earning only $48,000 a year. In this context, the offer of $10,000 a month, not counting the money I could potentially earn on managing funds, seemed extremely attractive. I figured that even if I fell completely on my face, I could still get another job that would pay more than I was making at the bank.

In February 1981, with one other analyst and a secretary, I launched Duquesne Capital Management. We began with $1 million under management, which generated $10,000 per year in fees. Most of our income came from the $10,000 per month consulting fee arrangement. We started off extremely well, catching the sharp upmove in low cap stocks. By mid-1981, stocks were up to the top of their valuation range, while at the same time, interest rates had soared to 19 percent. It was one of the more obvious sell situations in the history of the market. We went into a 50 percent cash position, which, at the time, I thought represented a really dramatic step. Then we got obliterated in the third quarter of 1981.

**I don't understand. How did you get obliterated if you went into a 50 percent cash position?**

Well, we got obliterated on the 50 percent position we still held.

**Yes, but you would have lost only half as much as everyone else.**

At the bank, the standard procedure had been to always be nearly fully invested. Although I wasn't working for a bank anymore, I had obviously still maintained some of this same mentality. You have to understand that I was unbelievably bearish in June 1981. I was absolutely right in that opinion, but we still ended up losing 12 percent during the third quarter. I said to my partner, "This is criminal. We have never felt more strongly about anything than the bear side of this market and yet we ended up down for the quarter." Right then and there, we changed our investment philosophy so that if we ever felt that bearish about the market again we would go to a 100 percent cash position.

During the fourth quarter of 1981, the stock market partially rebounded. We were still extremely bearish at that point, and we dumped our entire stock position. We placed 50 percent in cash and 50 percent in long bonds. We loved the long bond position because it was yielding 15 percent, the Fed was extremely tight, and inflation was already coming down sharply. It seemed like a gift.

We did very well, and by May 1982 our assets under management had grown to $7 million. One morning, I came into work and discovered that Drysdale Securities—our consulting client—had gone belly-up. I immediately called my contact at the firm, but he was no longer there.

I realized that I had an immediate problem. My overhead was $180,000 per year and my new revenue base was only $70,000 (1 percent on the $7 million we managed). I had no idea how we could possibly survive. At the time, our firm had assets of just under $50,000, and I was absolutely convinced that interest rates were coming down. I took all of the firm's capital and put it into T-bill futures. In four days, I lost everything. The irony is that less than a week after we went bust, interest rates hit their high for the entire cycle. They've never been that high since. That was when I learned that you could be right on a market and still end up losing if you use excessive leverage.

At the time, I had a client who had sold out a software company at a very young age. He had given the proceeds from this sale, which were quite substantial, to a broker who lost half the amount in the options market. In desperation, this broker had brought him to me, and I ended up doing extremely well for the account. Since it was an individual account, whereas all my other accounts were pensions, I was actually able to go short in the stock market. I was also long bonds. Both positions did very well, and his account went up dramatically.

As a last resort, I went to see this client to ask him if he might be interested in funding us in exchange for a percentage of the company. At the time, it probably looked like one of the dumbest purchases anybody could ever make. Here was a firm with a $40,000 negative net worth and a built-in deficit of $110,000 per year, run by a twenty-eight-year-old with only a one-year track record and no particular reputation. I sold him 25 percent of the company for $150,000, which I figured would be enough to keep us going for another twelve months.

One month later, the bull market began, and within about a year, our assets under management climbed to $40 million. I think 1983 was the first year I had a quarter in which I actually made more than my secretary. We had a bit of a setback during the mid-1983 to mid-1984 period, but the company continued to do well thereafter, particularly once the bull market took off in 1985.

**Given the success of your own trading company, why did you leave to join Dreyfus as a fund manager?**

In 1985 I met Howard Stein, who offered me a consulting agreement with Dreyfus. He eventually convinced me to officially join Dreyfus as a manager of a couple of their funds. They even tailored new Dreyfus funds around my particular style of investment. As part of the agreement, I was allowed to continue to manage the Duquesne Fund. In fact, I'm still managing Duquesne today.

**What were your personal experiences preceding, during, and after the 1987 stock market crash?**

The first half of the year was great because I was bullish on the market, and prices went straight up. In June I changed my stripes and actually went net short. The next two months were very rough because I was fighting the market, and prices were still going up.

**What determined the timing of your shift from bullish to bearish?**

It was a combination of a number of factors. Valuations had gotten extremely overdone: The dividend yield was down to 2.6 percent and the price/book value ratio was at an all-time high. Also, the Fed had been tightening for a period of time. Finally, my technical analysis showed that the breadth wasn't there—that is, the market's strength was primarily concentrated in the high capitalization stocks, with the broad spectrum of issues lagging well behind. This factor made the rally look like a blow-off.

**How can you use valuation for timing? Hadn't the market been overdone in terms of valuation for some time before you reversed from short to long?**

I never use valuation to time the market. I use liquidity considerations and technical analysis for timing. Valuation only tells me how far the market can go once a catalyst enters the picture to change the market direction.

**The catalyst being what?**

The catalyst is liquidity, and hopefully my technical analysis will pick it up.

**What was happening in terms of liquidity in 1987?**

The Fed had been tightening since January 1987, and the dollar was tanking, which suggested that the Fed was going to tighten some more.

**How much were you up during the first half of 1987 before you switched from long to short?**

The results varied depending on the fund. I was managing five different hedge funds at the time, each using a different type of strategy. The funds were up roughly between 40 percent and 85 percent at the time I decided to switch to a bearish posture. Perhaps the strongest performer was the Dreyfus Strategic Aggressive Investing Fund, which was up about 40 percent during the second quarter (the first quarter of the fund's operation). It had certainly been an excellent year up to that point.

Many managers will book their profits when they're up a lot early in the year. It's my philosophy, which has been reinforced by Mr. Soros, that when you earn the right to be aggressive, you should be aggressive. The years that you start off with a large gain are the times that you should go for it. Since I was well ahead for the year, I felt that I could afford to fight the market for a while. I knew the bull market had to end, I just didn't know when. Also, because of the market's severe overvaluation, I thought that when the bull market did end, it was going to be dramatic.

**Then I assume that you held on to your short position until the market actually topped a couple of months later.**

That's right. By October 16, 1987, the Dow had come down to near the 2,200 level, after having topped at over 2,700. I had more than recouped my earlier losses on the short position and was back on track with a very profitable year. That's when I made one of the most tragic mistakes of my entire trading career.

The chart suggested that there was tremendous support near 2,200 based on a trading range that had been built up during most of 1986. I was sure that the market would hold at that level. I was also playing from a position of strength, because I had profits from my long positions earlier in the year, and I was now ahead on my short positions as well. I went from net short to a 130 percent long. [A percentage greater than 100 percent implies the use of leverage.]

**When did you make this transition?**

On Friday afternoon, October 16, 1987.

**You reversed from short to a leveraged long position on the day before the crash? You're kidding!**

That's right, and there was plenty of liquidity for me to switch my position on that day.

**I'm not surprised, but I'm somewhat puzzled. You've repeatedly indicated that you give a great deal of weight to technical input. With the market in a virtual free-fall at the time, didn't the technical perspective make you apprehensive about the trade?**

A number of technical indicators suggested that the market was oversold at that juncture. Moreover, I thought that the huge price base near the 2,200 level would provide extremely strong support—at least temporarily. I figured that even if I were dead wrong, the market would not go below the 2,200 level on Monday morning. My plan was to give the long position a half-hour on Monday morning and to get out if the market failed to bounce.

**When did you realize that you were wrong?**

That Friday afternoon after the close, I happened to speak to Soros. He said that he had a study done by Paul Tudor Jones that he wanted to show me. I went over to his office, and he pulled out this analysis that

Paul had done about a month or two earlier. The study demonstrated the historical tendency for the stock market to accelerate on the downside whenever an upward-sloping parabolic curve had been broken—as had recently occurred. The analysis also illustrated the extremely close correlation in the price action between the 1987 stock market and the 1929 stock market, with the implicit conclusion that we were now at the brink of a collapse.

I was sick to my stomach when I went home that evening. I realized that I had blown it and that the market was about to crash.

**Was it just the Paul Tudor Jones study that made you realize that you were wrong?**

Actually, there's a second important element to the story. In early August of that year, I had received a call from a woman who was about to leave for a vacation to France. She said, "My brother says that the market is getting out of hand. I have to go away for three weeks. Do you think the market will be all right until I get back?"

I tried to be reassuring, telling her, "The market will probably go down, but I don't think it will happen that quickly. You can go on your vacation without worry."

"Do you know who my brother is?" she asked.

"I have no idea," I answered.

"He's Jack Dreyfus," she informed me.

As far as I knew, Dreyfus was busy running a medical foundation and hadn't paid much attention to the market for the past fifteen or twenty years. The following week, Howard Stein brought a visitor to my office. "This is Jack Dreyfus," he announced.

Dreyfus was wearing a cardigan sweater and was very polite in his conversation. "I would like to know about the S&P futures contract," he said. "As you know, I haven't looked at the market for twenty years. However, I've been very concerned about the conversations I've been hearing lately when I play bridge. Everyone seems to be bragging about all the money he's making in the market. It reminds me of everything I read about the 1929 market."

Dreyfus was looking for evidence of margin buying to confirm his conjecture that the market was poised for a 1929-type crash. The statistics on stocks didn't reveal any abnormally high level of margin buying. However, he had read that people were using S&P futures to take long positions in the stock market at 10 percent margin. His hypothesis was that the margin-type buying activity was now going into futures. To check out this theory, he wanted me to do a study to see if there had been any unusually heavy speculative buying of S&P futures.

Since we didn't have the data readily available, it took us a while to complete the study. Ironically, we finished the analysis on Friday afternoon, October 16, 1987. Basically, the data showed that speculators had been consistently short until July 1987 and after that point had switched to an increasingly heavy long position.

I went to see Jack Dreyfus on Saturday, October 17, to show him the results of the analysis. Remember, he had expressed all his concerns about the market in August. At this point, I was already very upset because Soros had shown me Paul Tudor Jones's study.

Dreyfus looked at my study and said, "I guess we're a bit too late to capitalize on my fears." That was the clincher. I was absolutely convinced that I was on the wrong side of the market. I decided that if the market opened above the support level on Monday morning, which was about 30 Dow points lower, and didn't immediately rally, I would sell my entire position. As it turned out, the market opened over 200 points lower. I knew I had to get out. Fortunately, there was a brief bounce shortly after the opening, and I was able to sell my entire long position and actually go net short.

That same afternoon, five minutes to four, Dreyfus came by. He said, "Forgive me for not telling you before, but I had already sold S&P futures to hedge my exposure in the stock market."

"How much did you sell?" I asked.

"Enough," he answered.

"When did you go short?" I asked.

"Oh, about two months ago." In other words, he had gone short at exactly the top, right around the time I had told his sister not to worry about an imminent top in the stock market. He asked, "Do you think I should cover my short position here?"

At that point, even though the Dow had already fallen 500 points to near 1,700, the futures were trading at a level that was equivalent to a Dow of 1,300. I said, "Jack, you have to cover the position here. The S&P futures are trading at a 4,500-point discount based on the Dow!"

He looked at me and asked, "What's a discount?"

**So did he cover his position at that point?**

He sure did—right at the absolute low.

**Getting back to your career path, why did you leave Dreyfus?**

I felt that I was managing too many funds (seven at the time I left). In addition to the actual management, each fund also required speaking engagements and other activities. For example, each fund held four board meetings per year.

**How could you possibly find the time to do all that?**

I couldn't; that's why I left. During this entire time period, I had been talking to Soros on an ongoing basis. The more I talked to him, the more I began to realize that everything people had told me about him was wrong.

**What had they told you?**

There were all these stories about turnover at the firm. George had a reputation for paying people well but then firing them. Whenever I mentioned that Soros had tried to hire me, my mentors in the business adamantly advised me not to go.

Soros had actually started referring to me as his "successor" before I ever joined the firm. When I went to Soros's home to be interviewed, his son informed me that I was his tenth "successor." None of the others had lasted too long. He thought it was hysterical. And when I arrived at Soros's office the next day, the staff all referred to me as "the successor." They also thought it was very funny.

**Did you consider simply going back and managing your Duquesne Fund full-time after you left Dreyfus?**

That was certainly an option. In fact, Duquesne's assets under management had grown tremendously without any marketing at all simply because of all the publicity I had received from the strong performance of the Dreyfus funds.

**Why didn't you go that route?**

Quite simply, because George Soros had become my idol. He seemed to be about twenty years ahead of me in implementing the trading philosophy I had adopted: holding a core group of stocks long and a core group of stocks short and then using leverage to trade S&P futures, bonds, and currencies. I had learned a tremendous amount just in my conversations with Soros. I thought it was a no-lose situation. The worst thing that could happen was that I would join Soros and he would fire me in a year—in which case I would have received the last chapter of my education and still have had the option of managing Duquesne. In the best case, it would all work out.

**Did your relationship with Soros change once you started working for him?**

The first six months of the relationship were fairly rocky. While we had similar trading philosophies, our strategies never meshed. When I started out, he was going to be the coach—and he was an aggressive coach. In my opinion, George Soros is the greatest investor that ever lived. But even being coached by the world's greatest investor is a hindrance rather than a help if he's engaging you actively enough to break your trading rhythm. You just can't have two cooks in the kitchen; it doesn't work. Part of it was my fault because he would make recommendations and I would be intimidated. After all, how do you disagree with a man with a track record like his?

Events came to a head in August 1989 when Soros sold out a bond position that I had put on. He had never done that before. To make matters worse, I really had a strong conviction on the trade. Needless to say, I was fairly upset. At that point, we had our first let-it-all-out discussion.

Basically, Soros decided that he was going to stay out of my hair for six months. Frankly, I wasn't too optimistic about the arrangement because I thought that he had been trying to do that all along but was simply incapable of it. The situation was saved, however, by events heating up in Eastern Europe in late 1989. As you may know, transforming Eastern Europe and the Soviet Union from communist to capitalist systems has been Soros's main endeavor in recent years. He has set up foundations in eleven countries to help achieve this goal. With George off in Eastern Europe, he couldn't meddle even if he wanted to.

Everything started to come together at that time. Not only was I trading on my own without any interference, but that same Eastern European situation led to my first truly major trade for Soros's Quantum Fund. I never had more conviction about any trade than I did about the long side of the Deutsche mark when the Berlin Wall came down. One of the reasons I was so bullish on the Deutsche mark was a radical currency theory proposed by George Soros in his book, *The Alchemy of Finance.* His theory was that if a huge deficit were accompanied by an expansionary fiscal policy and tight monetary policy, the country's currency would actually rise. The dollar provided a perfect test case in the 1981–84 period. At the time, the general consensus was that the dollar would decline because of the huge budget deficit. However, because money was attracted into the country by a tight monetary policy, the dollar actually went sharply higher.

When the Berlin Wall came down, it was one of those situations that I could see as clear as day. West Germany was about to run up a huge budget deficit to finance the rebuilding of East Germany. At the same time, the Bundesbank was not going to tolerate any inflation. I went headlong into the Deutsche mark. It turned out to be a terrific trade.

**How large a position did you put on?**

About $2 billion.

**Did you have any difficulty putting on a position that size?**

No, I did it over a few days' time. Also, putting on the position was made easier by the generally bearish sentiment at the time. The Deutsche mark actually fell during the first two days after the wall came down because people thought that the outlook for a growing deficit would be negative for the currency.

**Any other major trades come to mind? I'm particularly interested in your reasoning for putting on a trade.**

In late 1989 I became extremely bearish on the Japanese stock market for a variety of reasons. First, on a multiyear chart, the Nikkei index had reached a point of overextension, which in all previous instances had led to sell-offs or, in the worst case, a sideways consolidation. Second, the market appeared to be in a huge speculative blow-off phase. Finally, and most important—three times as important as everything I just said—the Bank of Japan had started to dramatically tighten monetary policy. Here's what the Japanese bond market was doing at the same time. [Druckenmiller shows me a chart depicting that at the same time the Nikkei index was soaring to record highs, the Japanese bond market was plummeting.] Shorting the Japanese stock market at that time was just about the best risk/reward trade I had ever seen.

**How did you fare at the start of the air war against Iraq when the U.S. stock market abruptly took off on the upside and never looked back? Were you short because the market had been in a primary downtrend before that point? If so, how did you handle the situation?**

I came into 1991 with positions that couldn't have been more poorly suited to the market price moves that unfolded in the ensuing months. I was short approximately $3 billion in the U.S. and Japanese stock markets, and I was also heavily short in the U.S. and world bond markets.

I started to change my market opinion during the first two weeks of 1991. On the way down, the pessimism regarding the U.S. stock market had become extreme. Everybody was talking about how the market would crater if the United States went to war against Iraq. Also, the breadth was not there. Even though the Dow Jones index had fallen to a new recent low, only about eighty of the seventeen hundred New York Stock Exchange stocks had made new lows.

By January 13, I had covered my short S&P futures position, but I was still short stock. On that day, I spoke to Paul Tudor Jones, who had just returned from participating in a roundtable discussion sponsored by Barron's. He told me that eight out of the eight participating money managers had said they were holding their highest cash position in ten years. I'll never forget that the S&P was near 310 and Paul said, "340 is a chip shot." I was already turning bullish, but that conversation gave me an extra push in that direction. I was convinced that once the war started, the market had to go up, because everyone had already sold.

**Why didn't you wait until the war had actually started before you began buying?**

Because everybody was waiting to buy after the war started. I thought it was necessary to start buying before the January 15 deadline set by the United States.

**Had you switched completely from short to long before the huge rally on the morning following the start of the air war?**

I had in the Duquesne Fund because it was more flexible. In Soros's Quantum Fund, we had switched our S&P futures position from short to long, but we still had a huge short position in actual stocks. A large portion of this position was in the bank and real estate stocks, which were difficult to cover. We were fully long within a few days after the start of the war.

**How did you fare after the smoke cleared?**

As incredible as it may seem, we ended up having an up January after going into the month with a $3 billion short position in equities world-wide, a $3 billion short position in the dollar versus the Deutsche mark, and a large short position in U.S. and Japanese bonds—all of which proved to be the exact wrong positions to hold.

**Why did you have such a large short position in the dollar versus the Deutsche mark?**

This was the same position we had held on and off for over a year since the Berlin Wall had come down. The basic premise of the trade was that the Germans would adhere to a combined expansionary fiscal policy and tight monetary policy—a bullish combination for their currency.

**What caused you to abandon that position?**

There were two factors. First, the dollar had been supported by safe-haven buying during the U.S. war with Iraq. One morning, there was a news story that Hussein was going to capitulate before the start of the ground war. The dollar should have sold off sharply against the Deutsche mark on the news, but it declined only slightly. I smelled a rat. A second factor was the talk that Germany was going to raise taxes. In other words, they were going to reverse their expansionary fiscal policy, which would eliminate one of the primary reasons for our being long the Deutsche mark in the first place. In one morning, we bought about $3.5 billion against the Deutsche mark.

**The United States is experiencing a protracted recession and extremely negative consumer sentiment [at the time of this interview, December 1991]. Do you have any thoughts about the long-term economic prospects for the country?**

In my view, the 1980s were a ridiculous repeat of the 1920s. We had built up the debt-to-GNP ratio to unsustainable levels. I became more convinced about the seriousness of the problem with all the leveraged buyouts of the late 1980s, which made the overall debt situation get worse and worse. I have never believed that the current economic downturn was a recession; I have always viewed it as a debt liquidation, which some people call a depression. It's not simply a matter of a two-quarter recession. It's a problem where you build up years of debt, which will act as a depressant on the economy until it gets worked off over a long period of time. A debt liquidation tends to last for years.

**Given your very negative long-term view of the U.S. economy, are you holding a major long position in bonds?**

I was long until late 1991. However, an attractive yield should be the last reason for buying bonds. In 1981 the public sold bonds heavily, giving up a 15 percent return for thirty years because they couldn't resist 21 percent short-term yields. They weren't thinking about the long term. Now, because money market rates are only 4.5 percent, the same poor public is back buying bonds, effectively lending money at 7.5 percent for thirty years to a government that's running $400 billion deficits.

The current situation is just the inverse of 1981. In 1981 the public should have seen Volcker's jacking up of short-term rates to 21 percent as a very positive move, which would bring down long-term inflation and push up bond and stock prices. Instead, they were lured by the high short-term yields. In contrast, now with the economy in decline, the deficit ballooning, and the administration and the Fed in a state of panic, the public should be wary about the risk in holding long-term bonds. Instead, the same people who sold their bonds in 1981 at 15 percent rates are now buying them back at 7.5 percent because they don't have anything better to do with their money. Once again, they're not focusing on the long term.

**Your long-term performance has far surpassed the industry average. To what do you attribute your superior track record?**

George Soros has a philosophy that I have also adopted: The way to build long-term returns is through preservation of capital and home runs. You can be far more aggressive when you're making good profits. Many managers, once they're up 30 or 40 percent, will book their year [i.e., trade very cautiously for the remainder of the year so as not to jeopardize the very good return that has already been realized]. The way to attain truly superior long-term returns is to grind it out until you're up 30 or 40 percent, and then if you have the convictions, go for a 100 percent year. If you can put together a few near-100 percent years and avoid down years, then you can achieve really outstanding long-term returns.

**What else have you learned from Soros?**

I've learned many things from him, but perhaps the most significant is that it's not whether you're right or wrong that's important, but how much money you make when you're right and how much you lose when you're wrong. The few times that Soros has ever criticized me was when I was really right on a market and didn't maximize the opportunity.

As an example, shortly after I had started working for Soros, I was very bearish on the dollar and put on a large short position against the Deutsche mark. The position had started going in my favor, and I felt rather proud of myself. Soros came into my office, and we talked about the trade.

"How big a position do you have?" he asked.

"One billion dollars," I answered.

"You call that a position?" he said dismissively. He encouraged me to double my position. I did, and the trade went dramatically further in our favor.

Soros has taught me that when you have tremendous conviction on a trade, you have to go for the jugular. It takes courage to be a pig. It takes courage to ride a profit with huge leverage. As far as Soros is concerned, when you're right on something, you can't own enough.

Although I was not at Soros Management at the time, I've heard that prior to the Plaza Accord meeting in the fall of 1985, other traders in the office had been piggybacking George and hence were long the yen going into the meeting. When the yen opened 800 points higher on Monday morning, these traders couldn't believe the size of their gains and anxiously started taking profits. Supposedly, George came bolting out of the door, directing the other traders to stop selling the yen, telling them that he would assume their position. While these other traders were congratulating themselves for having taken the biggest profit in their lives, Soros was looking at the big picture: The government had just told him that the dollar was going to go down for the next year, so why shouldn't he be a pig and buy more [yen]?

Soros is also the best loss taker I've ever seen. He doesn't care whether he wins or loses on a trade. If a trade doesn't work, he's confident enough about his ability to win on other trades that he can easily walk away from the position. There are a lot of shoes on the shelf; wear only the ones that fit. If you're extremely confident, taking a loss doesn't bother you.

**How do you handle the pressure of managing a multi*billion* dollar portfolio?**

I'm a lot less nervous about it now than I was a few years ago. The wonderful thing about our business is that it's liquid, and you can wipe the slate clean on any day. As long as I'm in control of the situation—that is, as long as I can cover my positions—there's no reason to be nervous.

According to Druckenmiller, superior performance requires two key elements: preservation of capital and home runs. The first principle has been quite well publicized, but the second is far less appreciated. From a portfolio perspective, Druckenmiller is saying that in order to really excel, you must take full advantage of the situations when you are well ahead and running a hot hand. Those are the times to really press, not rest on your laurels. Great track records are made by avoiding losing years and managing to score a few high-double-digit- or triple-digit-gain years. On an individual trade basis, going for home runs means really applying leverage in those infrequent circumstances when you have tremendous confidence. As Druckenmiller puts it, "It takes courage to be a pig."

Another important lesson to be drawn from this interview is that if you make a mistake, respond immediately! Druckenmiller made the incredible error of shifting from short to 130 percent long on the very day before the massive October 19, 1987, stock crash, yet he finished the month with a net gain. How? When he realized he was dead wrong, he liquidated his entire long position during the first hour of trading on October 19 and actually went short. Had he been less open-minded, defending his original position when confronted with contrary evidence, or had he procrastinated to see if the market would recover, he would have suffered a tremendous loss. Instead, he actually made a small profit. The ability to accept unpleasant truths (i.e., market action or events counter to one's position) and respond decisively and without hesitation is the mark of a great trader.

Although Druckenmiller employs valuation analysis and believes it is important in gauging the extent of a potential future price move once the current market trend reverses, he emphasizes that this approach cannot be used for timing. The key tools Druckenmiller applies to timing the broad market are liquidity analysis and technical analysis.

In evaluating individual stocks, Druckenmiller recalls the advice of his first boss, who made him realize that the initial step in any analysis is determining the factors that make a particular stock go up or down. The specifics will vary for each market sector, and sometimes even within each sector.

Druckenmiller's entire trading style runs counter to the orthodoxy of fund management. There is no logical reason why an investor (or fund manager) should be nearly fully invested in equities at all times. If an investor's analysis points to the probability of an impending bear market, he or she should move entirely to cash and possibly even a net short position. Recall Druckenmiller's frustration at being extremely bearish in mid-1981, absolutely correct in his forecast, and still losing money, because at the time, he was still wedded to the idea that a stock manager had to be net long at all times. There is little question that Druckenmiller's long-term gains would have been dramatically lower and his equity drawdowns significantly wider if he restricted himself to the long side of the stock market. The flexibility of Druckenmiller's style—going short as well as long and also diversifying into other major global markets (e.g., bonds and currencies)—is obviously a key element of his success. The queen in chess, which can move in all directions, is a far more powerful piece than the pawn, which can only move forward.

One basic market truth (or, perhaps more accurately, one basic truth about human nature) is that you can't win if you have to win. Druckenmiller's plunge into T-bill futures in a desperate attempt to save his firm from financial ruin provides a classic example. Even though he bought T-bill futures within one week of their all-time low (you can't pick a trade much better than that), he lost all his money. The very need to win poisoned the trade—in this instance, through grossly excessive leverage and a lack of planning. The market is a stern master that seldom tolerates the carelessness associated with trades born of desperation.

# Richard Driehaus

## THE ART OF BOTTOM-UP INVESTING

Richard H. Driehaus got hooked on the stock market as a kid, and his enthusiasm for the market has never flagged since. While still in his early teens, Driehaus discovered the folly of following the recommendations of financial columnists. As a result, he decided to educate himself by devouring all the stock newsletters and financial magazines he could find at the local branch library. It was during those childhood years that he began to develop the basic market philosophy that would serve as the core of his approach in his later years as a securities analyst and portfolio manager.

Upon college graduation, Driehaus set out to find a market-related job and landed a slot as a research analyst. Although he liked the job, he was frustrated by seeing his best recommendations ignored by the sales force. Driehaus got his first chance to manage money in 1970 while working in the institutional trading department at A. G. Becker. To his pleasant surprise, Driehaus discovered that his trading ideas were even better in practice than he dared to believe. In his three years as a manager at A. G. Becker, he was rated in the top 1 percent of all portfolio managers surveyed by Becker's Fund Evaluation Service, the largest fund rating service at the time.

After leaving A. G. Becker, Driehaus worked as a director of research for Mullaney, Wells and Company, and then Jessup and Lamount, before starting his own firm in 1980. For the twelve-year period since 1980, Driehaus averaged an annual return in excess of 30 percent (net of brokerage and management fees), nearly double the S&P 500 return of 16.7 percent during the same period. The S&P 500, however, is not the appropriate benchmark, as Driehaus focuses on small cap (capitalization) stocks. In case you think that Driehaus's superior performance is related to the better performance of the low cap stocks, note that the Russell 2000 index, which tracks the performance of the 1,001st through 3,000th largest U.S. companies (a group representative of the stocks in Driehaus's portfolio), was up only 13.5 percent, compounded annually, during the same twelve-year period. One dollar invested in the Russell index in 1980 would have been worth $4.56 at the end of 1991; one dollar invested in Driehaus's Small Cap Fund would have grown to $24.65 during the same time frame.

Although Driehaus's flagship investment vehicle has been small cap stocks, he has broadened his scope to include other types of funds as well. He is particularly fond of the concept that underlies his Bull and Bear Partnership Fund. This fund seeks to remove the impact of the general stock market trend by approximately balancing long and short positions on an ongoing basis. In other words, the fund's market directional exposure is near zero at all times, with performance entirely dependent on individual stock selection. In its first two years of operation, 1990 and 1991, this fund realized back-to-back annual returns of 67 percent and 62 percent (before a 20 percent profit incentive fee payout), with only three out of twenty-four months registering a loss (the largest being a mere 4 percent).

Over the years, philanthropy has become an increasingly important force in Driehaus's life. In 1984, he started the Richard H. Driehaus Foundation with a $1 million contribution of TCBY (The Country's Best Yogurt, originally This Can't Be Yogurt) stock. He manages the foundation's funds, distributing 5 percent of the total equity annually to a variety of charities. By the end of 1991, the foundation's capitalization had grown to approximately $20 million.

I met Driehaus on one of his periodic jaunts to New York City for an art auction. The interview was conducted over a leisurely breakfast (apparently far too leisurely as far as the staff was concerned) in the cavernous dining room of a midtown hotel. Eventually, we moved on to continue the interview at a quiet lounge at a nearby hotel, where the dark, floor-to-ceiling wood-paneled walls and antique fixtures provided a century-old atmosphere.

---

### When did you first become interested in the stock market?

When I was thirteen years old I decided to invest $1,000 saved up from my newspaper route in the stock market. My early investments, which were guided by financial columnist and broker recommendations, fared poorly. I had thought that if I followed the advice of professionals, I would make money. I found the experience very disheartening.

I decided to try to figure out what made stock prices move. I started going down to the local library on a regular basis and reading a variety of financial periodicals and newsletters. One letter that had a particularly strong impact on me was John Herold's *America's Fastest Growing Companies*.

### What appealed to you about that letter?

It was my favorite letter for two reasons. First, it showed me the success that could be achieved by buying growth stocks. Herold had stocks in his newsletter that he had recommended ten years earlier that were up tenfold and twentyfold. These were incredible moves to me. Second, Herold's approach of focusing on earnings growth made a lot of sense to me. It seemed logical that if a company's earnings were growing over a long period of time, its stock price had to go in the same direction. In his newsletter, Herold displayed charts that superimposed a stock's price and its earnings over a ten-year period, with both graphs showing dramatic growth. These charts, which basically demonstrated that a stock's price was in harmony with its long-term earnings growth, became a very powerful image to me.

### Was your first job market related?

Yes. After college, I landed a job as a securities analyst for a small Midwestern brokerage firm. To my dismay, I discovered that many of my recommendations were never implemented in the customers' portfolios.

**Why was that?**

Because the P/E multiples [the ratios of prices to earnings] were too high. Many of the best growth stocks have high multiples and are psychologically difficult to buy. If the brokers weren't turned off by the high P/Es, their clients were. Also, I realized that many brokers weren't portfolio managers but were primarily sales oriented. I found it very discouraging that many of my best recommendations were not being utilized.

After about two years, I left this company to join the institutional trading department of A. G. Becker, which at the time was a very strong force in the Midwestern brokerage business. I published my own in-house recommendation letter for the customers of that department. The company management began to notice that my recommendations were significantly outperforming the stocks in their other portfolios, as well as their own research recommendations. At the beginning of 1970, they gave me approximately $400,000 of the A. G. Becker Profit-Sharing Fund to personally manage. This was my first opportunity to implement my investment philosophy. I was elated.

**Did you find that there were differences between actually managing money and simply making recommendations?**

No, not really. However, the period when I started managing this account coincided with a bear market in stocks. Consequently, I had to suffer through some early, large losses. This is a good example of why you have to have faith in your approach in order to succeed. For example, one of the first stocks I bought was Bandag, which I purchased at $37. The stock first went down to $22, but then in the ensuing 1971–72 bull market, it went up tenfold.

**Did you hold on to the stock for that entire move?**

No, unfortunately, I didn't. About a year later, I was on a business trip and I called my office to check on my stocks. I found out that Bandag was up $5 that day, reaching a new high of $47. I decided to take my profits, with the idea of buying the stock back later. Bandag then proceeded to continue to go straight up to a high of $240 over the next year. That experience taught me that it's not that easy to buy back a good stock once you've sold it. It reinforced the idea that there's great advantage and comfort to being a long-term investor.

**Yet I understand that your average holding period tends to be significantly shorter than that of most other money managers. Why is that?**

Although many of the equities in our portfolios are held for a very long period if they're doing well, you have to be willing to turn over your portfolio more frequently than the conventional norm to get superior performance. I always look for the best potential performance at the *current* time. Even if I think that a stock I hold will go higher, if I believe another stock will do significantly better in the interim, I'll switch.

**In other words, you want the fastest horse, even if your first horse is still trotting in the right direction.**

Yes, but even more importantly, I want to make sure I get off the horse if it starts heading in the wrong direction. Most people believe high turnover is risky, but I think just the opposite. High turnover reduces risk when it's the result of taking a series of small losses in order to avoid larger losses. I don't hold on to stocks with deteriorating fundamentals or price patterns. For me, this kind of turnover makes sense. It reduces risk; it doesn't increase it.

**How long did you stay with A. G. Becker?**

I left in the fall of 1973 to become the research director for Mullaney, Wells and Company, a small regional brokerage firm.

**Did they give you money to manage?**

No, but A. G. Becker let me continue to manage the account I had traded for them. In addition to that, the woman who reconciled the trades in the A. G. Becker office had seen that I was good at picking stocks. She gave me $104,000 of her own money to manage, which constituted most of her liquid assets.

**As I recall, late 1973 would have been a particularly poor time to start a stock account.**

That's right. The 1973–74 bear market was the worst decline since the 1930s.

**Were you fully invested?**

Yes.

**Then I assume the account must have taken a fairly large hit.**

At the worst point, I believe the $104,000 went down to under $60,000.

**Did your client's confidence ever flag?**

That's the beauty of it. Her confidence never wavered. She had the strength to stay in. In fact, she's still with me today. I'll always be grateful to her for sticking with me when I was young and unproven.

**What is her account worth today?**

The account is now up to $5.8 million—and that's after taxes. This stuff really works!

**Any trades stand out in your long trading history?**

My largest position ever was Home Shopping Network [HSN], which I purchased in 1986. I heard about the stock from one of my analysts whom I had sent to a cable television conference several weeks before the company went public. As you probably know, Home Shopping Network sells low-priced merchandise—clothes, jewelry, and so on—over cable television. They had started this venture about a year before the offering, and in their first six months they had sold $64 million in merchandise and earned $7 million fully taxed. These were about the best results I had ever seen for a new company. Even better, the company still had incredible potential. At the time of the offering, they were reaching only a limited number of subscribers but were adding new subscribers very quickly. The cable systems liked the service because they got part of the profits, so it was easy for HSN to get picked up by new cable networks.

**Did you buy the stock on the initial offering?**

I wish I could have, but it was very hard to get stock on the deal. I believe we got only one hundred shares. The offering price was $18 per share and the first trade was in the low $40s. I bought most of my position in a range between the low $40s and low $50s.

**Wasn't it hard to buy the stock when it was up so much?**

No, because the growth was tremendous, the company was making lots of money, and the potential at the time seemed open-ended. I actually felt very good buying stock at those levels. Within five months, the stock was at $100. During this time, the company continued to build its subscriber base and even purchased television stations to reach more viewers. The revenues and earnings remained very strong.

**How long did you hold the stock?**

By early 1987, the stock had reached $200. I sent my analyst down to Florida to an investor meeting hosted by the company. Although the management was very optimistic, at the meeting they admitted that almost all the growth was coming from new subscribers and that the growth in order rates from customers on existing cable systems was not that great. About this time, the stock had also started to break down technically. That was all I needed. I sold the stock aggressively and eliminated my entire position over the next few weeks.

**Any other examples of stock picks that exemplify your investment style?**

A recent example is U.S. Surgical [USS]. Although by now USS has become an institutional favorite, I was fortunate to uncover this story in late 1989, before it really took off. At that time, USS didn't yet have the great stock characteristics that it later showed in 1990 and 1991—accelerating sales and earnings, high relative strength, and institutional sponsorship. But it did have a very powerful, fundamental story. It had developed the best pipeline of noninvasive surgical products—an innovative sector that I thought would become the fastest growing medical market of the nineties. USS is probably a good example of what I try to do because the key to buying this stock was early recognition of the noninvasive surgery market. This new procedure was not heavily covered by Wall Street back in 1989. It didn't have that much to do with what I call "left brain" (micro) factors, which would be growth rates, multiples, margins, and so on. This stock was a "right brain" (macro) story. You had to appreciate the potential of this market *before* the numbers came through so powerfully.

Danek Group [DNKG], a manufacturer of spinal implants, is another good example. I started buying DNKG as soon as it went public in May 1991. It had everything I look for in a growth stock: accelerating revenues and earnings and proprietary products in a rapidly expanding market. Even better, from a trading point of view, DNKG was a strong medical products company at a time when the market couldn't wait to buy such issues. Anything healthcare-related was moving in 1991, and DNKG forcefully participated in this move, exploding from $19 to $43 during its first three months after going public. But then a rumor began circulating that DNKG was going to run into some trouble at the FDA. Although this news was unsubstantiated, the stock cracked from $43 to $34 in just a couple of days. This was my second largest position. Usually, I sell a portion of my position when there's a problem—and trouble at the FDA certainly qualifies as a big problem. But in this case, I just didn't believe the rumors, and medical stocks were in strong demand in the marketplace, so I stayed with my full position. This proved to be the right decision, as DNKG not only recovered but went on to hit new highs, exceeding $60 by the end of 1991.

In this instance, the key to making money in the stock was trading the position properly. Some portfolio management decisions are investment oriented and some are trading oriented. This was a trading decision. Also, I might have made a different decision if other factors were different. For example, if the market weren't strong, or if the medical products group had been weakening, then I might have sold the entire position. There are a lot of different inputs that can affect a decision, and there are no universal decision rules.

**Any other illustrative case histories?**

Another interesting company was Blockbuster Entertainment [BV], which operates and franchises video rental stores. This is a franchise expansion story. I first learned of this company from a very bullish research report issued by a Texas brokerage firm. The estimated revenues and earnings growth rates left me a little skeptical at first, but the technical indicators were improving and the concept was unbelievable. The story had good credibility because the company was being launched by Wayne Huizenga, who was already a successful businessman. He was one of the founders and former chairman of Waste Management, another company in which I was an early investor after the company went public in the early 1970s.

The Blockbuster story started to appeal to me even more when the company made its next quarterly earnings announcement. The growth rates were impressive and made me believe that the street estimate I had frowned upon earlier was not only achievable but maybe even conservative. I instructed one of my analysts to increase his research efforts. Huizenga planned to continue opening company-owned and franchised video rental stores under the Blockbuster name. I learned that these were superstores that stocked thousands of videocassettes. I felt the concept would work because VCR sales were still growing quite substantially and Blockbuster's main competition came from mom-and-pop video retailers that had a much smaller selection of videocassettes. We continued to increase our position in the stock over the next few months and made a lot of money, as the stock more than doubled.

**In all these examples, it sounds like you bought the stock and the stock took off. Can you think of a major winner that first headed south after you bought it?**

In the summer of 1984, a broker friend called me and said, "I have a good stock for you."

"Okay, what is it?" I asked.

"This Can't Be Yogurt [TCBY]," he answered.

"I don't know," I said. "I don't really like yogurt."

"No," he said, "this yogurt really tastes good. Let me send you a prospectus."

He sent over not only a prospectus but a sample of the product as well. The prospectus looked very interesting, showing about 70 to 80 percent growth in earnings, but perhaps even more importantly, I thought the product tasted great—just like ice cream. When the company went public, I bought a large amount of stock at the initial offering price of $7. After I bought it, the stock went down to $4[fr1/4]. At that point, I got a call from one of my clients, questioning the advisability of maintaining our large holding in the stock. The company's earnings growth was so spectacular that I told him I thought the stock was still a buy.

**Did you buy more?**

As a matter of fact, I did, but I waited until the stock started to uptick.

**Did you have any idea why the stock was going down?**

I couldn't figure it out. My best guess was that the market was so negative for small cap stocks that TCBY was probably just getting dragged down with the rest of the group.

**What ultimately happened to the stock?**

Eventually it went up to $200.

**What was the catalyst that turned it around?**

The environment changed. The market began to appreciate growth stocks. It was partly the company and partly the environment. There's a saying, "You can't make a harvest in the wintertime." That was the situation initially. It was wintertime for small cap, high growth stocks. The market just wasn't interested. Once this general attitude changed, the market focused on the company's excellent earnings, and the stock took off.

**Were there any situations in which you bought a stock very heavily because of good earnings growth and prices went down and never recovered?**

Sure, that happens a lot. We probably have more losers than winners, but we cut our losses.

**How do you decide where to cut your losses?**

It could be a change in the fundamentals, such as a disappointing turn in earnings, or it could be due to the price action.

**Wouldn't negative price action have gotten you out of a stock like TCBY? Where do you draw the line?**

It's not purely deterministic; there's an element of art involved. Ultimately, you have to balance your underlying faith in the company with the price action.

**Was it then a matter of your confidence in the fundamentals for TCBY being so strong that it overrode everything else?**

Exactly. It was a matter of my conviction on the stock.

**What do you look for in terms of the price action?**

I look at the total image. It's more the visual impression than whether the stock breaks a particular point.

**I take that to mean that you use charts.**

Absolutely. Technical analysis is vital for success.

**How long have you been using charts?**

About twenty-five years. That probably says as much as anything about how helpful and reliable I have found them. They give you a very unemotional insight into a stock in an otherwise emotional market.

**Do you always check the chart before you buy a stock?**

Absolutely. I won't buy a stock when it's dropping even if I like the fundamentals. I have to see some stability in the price action before I buy the stock. Conversely, I might also use a stock's chart to trigger the sale of a current holding. Again, the charts are a very unemotional way to view a stock's behavior and potential.

**Is it fair to say that you determine your trading ideas based on fundamental analysis but that you time your trade entry using technical analysis?**

Generally speaking, that's probably true. However, often the trigger for buying a stock is fundamental news. For example, recently I purchased a stock called Dataram Corporation following the release of a very positive earnings report. The company, which makes memory products for personal computers and workstations, reported quarterly earnings up from $.32 to $.75 and revenues up from $7 million to $11 million. The stock, which had closed at $26 3/8 on the previous day, shot up $4 on the news. We purchased twenty-five thousand shares at an average cost of $30 1/4.

**Do you put a limit on the order in that type of situation?**

Oh no! We would never have gotten filled. I felt very comfortable buying the stock, even after its large price move that day, because the numbers were very strong and the market was moving toward technology stocks anyway. We ultimately ended up purchasing almost 4 percent of this company at an average cost of $31 1/2. The stock now sells at $58.

**Is it generally true that stocks that witness a huge, one-day move tend to keep going in the same direction over the near term?**

That has been my observation over the years. If there's a large move on significant news, either favorable or unfavorable, the stock will usually continue to move in that direction.

**So you basically have to bite the bullet and buy the stock.**

Yes, but it's hard to do.

**Were you always able to do that?**

It's taken time to get good at it.

**Does a stock have to be stronger than the overall market in order for you to buy it?**

Generally speaking, yes. I like to see the stock's relative strength in the top 10 percent of the market, or at least the top 20 percent.

**You implied earlier that you'll often buy stocks with high P/E ratios. Does this imply that you believe P/E ratios are irrelevant?**

The P/E ratio might show statistical significance for broad stock groups, but for the type of stocks we buy, it's usually not a key variable. Stocks with long-term, high-growth potential often sell at higher multiples, particularly if they're newer companies. The P/E ratio really measures investors' emotions, which swing wildly from fear to greed, and is only significant at extremes.

**Do you feel there's an advantage to buying stocks that are not too heavily covered by the street?**

Absolutely! There's a definite market inefficiency there. Typically, the more the street covers a stock, the less opportunity there is.

**What are the major misconceptions people have about the stock market?**

They tend to confuse short-term volatility with long-term risk. The longer the time period, the lower the risk of holding equities. People focus too much on the short term—week-to-week and month-to-month price changes—and don't pay enough attention to the long-term potential. They look at all movement as negative, whereas I look at movement as a constructive element. For many investors, the lack of sufficient exposure to high-returning, more volatile assets is their greatest risk. In my opinion, investment vehicles that provide the least short-term volatility often embody the greatest long-term risk. Without significant price movement, you can't achieve superior gains.

One market paradigm that I take exception to is: Buy low and sell high. I believe that far more money is made buying high and selling at even higher prices. That means buying stocks that have already had good moves and have high relative strength—that is, stocks in demand by other investors. I would much rather invest in a stock that's increasing in price and take the risk that it may begin to decline than invest in a stock that's already in a decline and try to guess when it will turn around.

Finally, another major trap people fall into is trying to time the market. Since January 1980, the market has realized an average annual compounded return of 17 percent. If you were out of the market on the forty best days, which represent only 2 percent of the trading days, the return would drop to under 4 percent. The moral is that the penalty for being out of the market on the wrong days is severe—and human nature being what it is, those are exactly the days that most people are likely to be out of the market.

**What are the traits of the people who are successful in this business?**

They're open-minded and flexible. They're also risk takers, because they believe in what they're doing.

**I understand that you have several people at your firm trading their own small funds. Did you train these people?**

Yes, none of them had any previous experience in the business before starting with us. There are three people involved, and they're all doing very well.

**I guess that means that you believe successful trading can be taught?**

It can be taught as long as the person has an open mind. I like to say that the mind is like a parachute—it's only good when it's open. Of course, each person must still develop an individual philosophy and tailor basic trading concepts to his or her own personality.

**How did you fare during the October 1987 crash?**

We had a very tough month. The Small Cap Fund was down 34 percent. Fortunately, the fund was up 46 percent coming into October. We finished the year down 3 percent. About one week before the crash, I sensed something significantly negative was going to happen in the market.

**How did you realize that?**

Buying had dried up, there was a sense of fear in the market, and I was also worried about the burgeoning use of portfolio insurance. Because of my concern about the increased risk exposure in the market, I had a substantial portion of my portfolio up for sale on the Thursday and Friday before the crash. Unfortunately, I wasn't able to liquidate as much stock as I wanted to.

**You were unable to liquidate your position because the tone of the market was so bad?**

The atmosphere was horrible.

**When we were talking about entering orders on extreme price moves, you mentioned the necessity of using market orders instead of limit orders, which are unlikely to get filled in such situations. If you felt that strongly, why did you use limit orders instead of market orders in this case?**

We *were* trying to sell the stocks at the market. However, many of the issues we hold are very thin and the size we wanted to sell was just too large relative to what the market could handle. For example, one stock we held was nominally trading at $36 bid/$38 offered, and while we were willing to sell our entire thirty-thousand-share position at $34, there were no bids of any size even well below the market.

**Did you come in on Monday, October 19, knowing that it was going to be a very bad day?**

Yes, but I had no idea how extreme it would be.

**Were you still trying to sell stock that day?**

We managed to sell some.

**Did you stop trying to sell as the day wore on?**

After a while the break was so severe that it didn't seem to make any sense to try to sell unless the financial world was coming to an end.

**Could you describe your emotions on that day?**

I was actually very calm. I felt detached—as if I had transcended the situation. I almost had a sense of observing myself and everything that was going on.

**After the smoke cleared on October 19, you must have realized that you had just lost one-third of your wealth in one day's time. [Driehaus keeps almost all his money in his own funds.] Is there a feeling that goes with that?**

Yes, get it back! [He laughs loudly.] Actually, I had lost much more than that in 1973–74.

**Did that help?**

Yes, it did help. It showed me that you could survive that type of break. I had the confidence that I could make it back and the commitment to do it. As Nietzsche said, "What does not destroy me, makes me stronger."

**I get the impression that you really don't suffer any major market-related stress, even in extreme situations such as the October 1987 crash. Is that because you believe that things will work out in the end?**

I believe that's exactly right.

**When did you get that degree of confidence?**

I believed in my investment philosophy from the very beginning, but I acquired the true confidence when I applied this philosophy to the fund I managed at A. G. Becker and found that I had placed in the top 1 percent of all funds surveyed. I couldn't believe how well the approach worked. My confidence in this trading philosophy has never wavered.

**You've been a portfolio manager for nearly twenty years, during which time you outperformed the industry averages by a wide margin with enviable consistency. What do you consider the key to your sustained success over such a long period?**

The essential element is having a core philosophy. Without a core philosophy you're not going to be able to hold on to your positions or stick with your trading plan during really difficult times. You must fully understand, strongly believe in, and be totally committed to your trading philosophy. In order to achieve that mental state, you have to do a great deal of independent research. A trading philosophy is something that cannot just be transferred from one person to another; it's something that you have to acquire yourself through time and effort.

**Any final advice?**

If you reach high, you just might amaze yourself.

---

Driehaus's basic philosophy is that price follows growth and that the key to superb performance in the stock market is picking the companies with the best potential earnings growth. Everything else is secondary. Interestingly, the high growth stocks that meet Driehaus's criteria often sell at extremely high P/E ratios. Driehaus contends that the so-called prudent approach of buying only stocks with average to below-average P/Es will automatically eliminate many of the best performers. The stocks that Driehaus tends to buy are also often companies that are not followed by, or only lightly followed by, industry analysts, a characteristic that Driehaus believes leads to greater inefficiencies and hence greater profit opportunities.

Driehaus's stock selection ideas are fundamentally based. However, to confirm his selection and to aid in the timing of purchases, Driehaus is a great believer in technical analysis. With rare exception, before he buys a stock, Driehaus wants to see its price rising and high relative strength (i.e., a stock that is performing significantly stronger than the broad market). These technical characteristics mean that when Driehaus buys a stock, it is frequently near its recent high. He believes that fortunes are made by jumping on board the strongest fundamental and technical performers, not by picking bargains.

Most investors would find the typical stock in Driehaus's portfolio hard to buy. Think of a broker espousing the same strategy in a telephone solicitation. "Hello, Mr. Smith. I have a real interesting stock for you to consider." (*Pause*) "What is the P/E ratio? Well, it's 60 to 1." (*Pause*) "How far is it from its low? Well, it's making new highs. Mr. Smith? Hello? Mr. Smith?"

Driehaus's method provides yet another example of the principle that successful strategies often require doing what most people find instinctively uncomfortable. Quite simply, the natural inclination of most people toward comfortable approaches (e.g., buying stocks that are near their lows, buying stocks with low P/Es) is one of the reasons the vast majority of investors experience such poor results.

Another example in which Driehaus's ability to do what is uncomfortable enhances his profitability is his willingness to buy a stock on extreme strength following a significant bullish news item. In such situations, most investors will wait for a reaction that never comes, or at the very least will place a price limit on their buy order. Driehaus realizes that if the news is sufficiently significant, the only way to buy the stock is to buy the stock. Any more cautious approach is likely to result in missing the move. In similar fashion, Driehaus is also willing to immediately liquidate a holding, even on a sharp one-day decline, if he feels a negative news item has changed the outlook for the stock. The rule is: Do what is right, not what is comfortable.

Another important point to emphasize is that a small percentage of huge winners account for the bulk of Driehaus's superior performance. You don't have to be right the majority of the time, but you do have to take advantage of the situations when you are right. Achieving this dictate requires two essential elements: taking larger positions when one has a high degree of confidence (e.g., Home Shopping Network was

Driehaus's largest position ever) and holding such positions long enough to realize most of the potential. The latter condition means avoiding the temptation to take profits after a stock has doubled or even tripled, if the fundamental and technical conditions still point to continued higher prices. The steely patience necessary to hold such positions to fruition is one of the attributes that distinguishes the Market Wizards from less skilled traders. Even though Driehaus and Druckenmiller employ dramatically different approaches, "home run" trades are an essential ingredient to the success of each.

Perhaps Driehaus's most fundamental piece of advice is that in order to succeed in the market (any market), you must develop your own philosophy. Carefully researching and rigorously verifying a trading philosophy is essential to developing the confidence necessary to stay the course during the difficult times—and there will always be such times, even for the most successful approaches.

# *Gil Blake*

## THE MASTER OF CONSISTENCY

Gil Blake calls his management company Twenty Plus. This name ties into the logo on his business card and stationery, which shows a probability curve with a +20 percent return falling two standard deviations to the left of the mean. For those not statistically inclined, the implication is that he has a 95 percent probability of realizing an annual return of at least 20 percent. The sketch of the probability curve does not extend to a 0 percent return, let alone into negative returns—which says a great deal about Blake's confidence.

Blake's confidence is obviously not misplaced. In the twelve years since he began trading, he has averaged a 45 percent annual return. Although this is an impressive figure, the most striking element of Blake's performance is his consistency. True to his logo, he has never had a year with a return below 20 percent. In fact, his worst performance was a 24 percent gain in 1984. But even in that subpar year, Blake had a consolation—he made money in all twelve months! To really appreciate Blake's consistency, you have to look at his monthly returns. An amazing 134 months (ninety-six percent) in his 139-month track record were either breakeven or profitable. He even had one streak of 65 months without a loss—a feat that would qualify him as the Joe DiMaggio of trading (Joe's streak ended at 56).

Blake's confidence in his approach also permeates his unique fee arrangement. He charges his clients 25 percent of total annual profits, but—and here's the unusual part—he also agrees to pay 25 percent of any losses and 100 percent of losses incurred in a new account during the first twelve months. Obviously, he has not had to pay out on these guarantees yet.

By now you probably want to know where to send your check. Save your stamp. Blake stopped accepting client funds five years ago. He has made only two exceptions since then; both times for close friends.

Blake is a mutual fund timer. Generally speaking, mutual fund timers attempt to enhance the yield return on a stock or bond fund by switching into a money market fund whenever conditions are deemed unfavorable. In Blake's case, he doesn't merely switch back and forth between a single mutual fund and a money market fund but also makes the additional decision of which sector in a group of sector funds provides the best opportunity on a given day. Blake uses purely technical models to generate signals for the optimum daily investment strategy. His holding period tends to be very short, typically ranging between one and four days. By using this methodology, Blake has been able to show consistent monthly profits even in those months when the funds in which he invested registered significant declines.

Blake prides himself on being a Wall Street outsider. After graduating from Cornell, he served three years as a naval officer on a nuclear submarine. He subsequently attended the Wharton Business School, graduating with highest honors. Following business school, Blake spent three years as an accountant with Price Waterhouse and nine years as chief financial officer for Fairfield Optical. During this entire time, he had no serious thoughts about trading. Indeed, he still generally believed in the truth of the random walk theory, which he had been dutifully taught in school. (This theory basically implies that trying to beat the markets is a futile endeavor.)

Blake's life changed when he strolled into his friend's office one day and was presented with some evidence of nonrandom market behavior that he assumed must have been a fluke. In doing the research to prove this point, he instead convinced himself that there were indeed substantial pockets of nonrandom behavior in the markets that provided unbelievable profit opportunities. Thus, fifteen years after graduating from college, Gil Blake became a trader.

Are great traders born or made? In Blake's case, the following note from his nursery school teacher, which his mother proudly saved, provides some insights:

> His claywork, painting, and carpentry all show an amazing meticulous precision. He enjoys working with small things, and is a perfectionist about it. Everything he does is made up of many small parts instead of one, big splashy form that is more usual for a child of his age. He has an extraordinary interest and grasp of numbers, and shows a real talent toward things mathematical.

I interviewed Blake at his suburban Massachusetts home on a Saturday afternoon during the peak of the fall season. I arrived there shortly after lunchtime. Thoughtfully, assuming that I would not have eaten, he had picked up sandwiches. I found Blake to be very low-key and unassuming. He seemed genuinely flattered that I considered him worthy enough to be included in a book of top traders. In terms of return relative to risk, Blake has few, if any, peers, but you would never guess that from his demeanor.

---

**You became a mutual fund timer long before it became popular. What was your original inspiration?**

Well, I really owe it to a friend. I remember the day as if it were yesterday. I wandered into a colleague's office, and he said, "Hey, Gil, take a look at these numbers." He had invested in a municipal bond fund to take advantage of the prevailing high interest rates, which at the time were about 10 to 11 percent tax free. Although he was getting a high interest rate, he discovered that his total return was actually declining rapidly because of the steady attrition in the net asset value [NAV].

He handed me a sheet with about a month's worth of numbers, and I noticed that the trend was very persistent: the NAV had declined for approximately twenty-two consecutive days. He said, "Fidelity allows you to switch into a cash fund at any time at no charge. Why couldn't I just switch out of the fund into cash when it started to go down and then switch back into the fund when it started to go back up?"

My reaction was, "Nick, I don't think the markets work that way.

Have you ever read *A Random Walk Down Wall Street?*" I pooh-poohed his idea. I said, "The problem is that you don't have enough data. Get some more data, and I bet that you'll find this is not something you could make any money on over the long run."

He did get more data, and, amazingly, the persistency of trends seemed to hold up. I quickly became convinced that there was definitely something nonrandom about the behavior of municipal bond funds.

**How did you perceive that nonrandomness?**

In fact, it was the simplest approach that proved the best. We called it the "one penny" rule. In the two years' worth of data we had obtained, we found that there was approximately an 83 percent probability that any uptick or downtick day would be followed by a day with a price move in the same direction. In the spring of 1980, I began to trade Fidelity's municipal bond fund in my own account based on this observation.

**And that worked?**

Yes, it worked exceedingly well.

**That's almost hard to believe. I know that in the bond market, switching a position each time there's a daily price change in the opposite direction is a disastrous strategy.**

That may well be true. However, you have to keep in mind two things. First, there were no transaction costs involved in switching in and out of the fund. Second, there seemed to be some sort of smoothing process operating in the NAV numbers of the municipal bond fund. For example, there was one three-month period around early 1981 when there were virtually no upticks in the NAV of the fund—the days were all either down or flat—while at the same time, the bonds were certainly having some uptick days. In fact, this price behavior was exhibited by virtually all municipal bond funds.

**How can you explain that?**

I don't know the answer. Maybe someone can explain it to me some day.

**Of course, you couldn't directly profit during the declining periods, since you obviously can't go short a fund.**

That's right, during those periods we were in cash.

**Given that you could be only long or flat and the bond market was collapsing, were you still able to come out ahead?**

When I started in March 1980, the NAV of the fund was approximately $10.50. By the end of 1981, the NAV had steadily eroded to about $5.65—a drop of nearly 50 percent. Nevertheless, using the above method, I was able to achieve gains in excess of 20 percent per year, not counting interest income, which added another 10 percent. The odds appeared to be so favorable that I started to seriously think about how I could get more funds to trade. I ended up taking out four successive second mortgages over a three-year period, which I was able to do because housing prices in the Northeast were rising at a fast clip.

**Weren't you at all reticent about doing that?**

No, because the odds were so favorable. Of course, I had to overcome the conventional wisdom. If you tell someone that you're taking out a second mortgage to trade, the response is hardly supportive. After a while, I just stopped mentioning this detail to others.

**If it took only a one-day change in the direction of the NAV value in order for you to get a signal, it sounds like you would be switching an incredible number of times during the year.**

Actually, it only worked out to about twenty or thirty times per year, because the trends were so persistent.

**Wasn't there any limit to the amount of times that you could switch? Even twenty to thirty times per year sounds like a high number.**

Fidelity's guideline was four switches per year, but they didn't enforce that rule. In fact, I even discussed the excess switching with them, and they said, "Just don't abuse it too much."

I asked, "What if I make twenty or thirty trades per year?" The reaction was, "Well, don't tell too many people about it." My impression was that the rule was there as a fallback provision but that they didn't worry too much about it—at least they didn't in the beginning.

As the years went by, I got an occasional letter from Fidelity stating: "It has come to our attention that you are switching more than four times a year, and we would appreciate your cooperating with the guideline."

**Did you just ignore these letters?**

No. I would use the municipal bond fund for four trades, then the high-yield municipal bond fund for four trades, and then the limited-term municipal bond fund for four trades, and so on.

**So, technically, you did adhere to the four-trades-per-year-rule; you merely switched to different funds.**

That's right.

**I assume that, nowadays, the NAV must change direction much more frequently.**

That's right. The next step in my evolution as a trader began when that pattern started to go away—as most of these things eventually do.

**The probabilities of a price change in the same direction as the previous day started dropping?**

To some extent, but, more importantly, the high volatility started to disappear. During 1979 to early 1984, the volatility in these funds averaged approximately one-quarter to one-half of a percent per day. The daily volatility eventually dropped to only about one-tenth to two-tenths of a percent. Also, the reliability or persistency of the prices dropped from 80 percent to below 70 percent.

**What happened when the reliability of the trend persistence and the volatility in the bond funds both started to decline precipitously? Was the method still profitable?**

Yes, but the potential annual return in municipal bond funds began to look like about 20 percent.

**And that was not good enough?**

I really wanted to look for something better. I thought that if I were able to find profitable inefficiencies in municipal bond funds, then it was possible that similar opportunities could be found in equity funds. From the fall of 1984 through the spring of 1985, I practically lived at the local library, extracting years of data on perhaps a hundred mutual funds off the microfilm machine. I was looking for another needle in a haystack.

I found that there were tradable patterns in equity funds but that the prospective returns were only around 20 to 25 percent per year. Even with higher volatility, the daily price persistency of about 60 percent was just not high enough. Through most of this research, I had ignored the Fidelity sector funds, because they charged a $50 fee per switch. I couldn't see paying this charge when there were so many funds that had no switch fee at all.

Two insights really contributed to a breakthrough. First, I had found early on that commodity-related funds (such as the gold and oil sectors) seemed to work better than more broadly based funds. Second, I discovered separately that the technology, oil, and utility indexes were each significantly less random than a broad market index. I went back to examine the sector funds and was just amazed by what I found. I couldn't believe that I had ignored sectors during my earlier research. I had almost missed it.

**What did you find?**

Generally speaking, I found that a price change that was larger than the average daily price change in a given sector had anywhere between a 70 to 82 percent chance of being followed by a move in the same direction on the following day. This finding was tremendously exciting because of the volatility in the sectors. For example, the biotech group moved an average of 0.8 percent a day and the gold sector an average of 1.2 percent a day, compared with the volatility of the municipal bond funds, which had shrunk to a mere 0.1 to 0.2 percent by that time. Therefore, I was applying the same batting average to markets that offered more than five times the profit potential.

The icing on the cake was that the sector funds allowed unlimited switching per year, instead of the four-switch limit applicable to most of the other funds. You could switch a hundred times a year if you were willing to pay the $50 fee per transaction.

**Why do you believe the sectors proved so tradable?**

That's my favorite question. Not just because I think I may have an answer, but also because I have not encountered the mathematical explanation elsewhere.

In researching the price behavior of individual stocks, I have found that significant daily price changes (with relative strength) have about a 55 percent chance of being followed by a similar directional move on the following day. After allowing for commissions and bid/ask spreads, that is not a sufficient probability edge to be tradable.

Now, as an analogy, assume you have a stack of coins, and each has a 55 percent chance of landing on heads. If you toss a single coin, the odds of getting heads are 55 percent. If you toss nine coins, the odds of getting more heads than tails go up to 62 percent. And if you toss ninety-nine coins, the odds of getting more heads than tails go up to about 75 percent. It's a function of the binomial probability distribution.

Similarly, assume you have ninety-nine chemical stocks, which on average are up 1 or 2 percent today, while the broad market is flat. In the very short run, this homogeneous group of stocks tends to behave like a school of fish. While the odds of a single chemical stock being up tomorrow may be 55 percent, the odds for the entire chemical group are much closer to 75 percent.

**I assume that this pattern does not extend to the broader stock market. That is, once you extend beyond a given sector, including more stocks may actually reduce the probability of an index persisting in its trend on the following day.**

The key ingredient is that the stocks making up the index or sector are homogeneous. For example, Fidelity's leisure fund, which was the least homogeneous sector at the time, including such diverse stocks as Budweiser, Pan Am, and Holiday Inn, was also the least persistent of all the sectors. Conversely, funds like savings and loans and biotech, which were more homogeneous, also tended to be the most persistent.

**How did you anticipate the direction of the daily price changes in the sector funds in time to enter a switch order, or did you just enter the order with a one-day lag?**

I found that I could sample ten or twenty stocks in each sector and get a very good idea where that sector was going to close that day. This observation allowed me to anticipate the signal by one day, which proved to be critically important, as my research demonstrated that the average holding period for a trade was only about two to three days, with approximately 50 percent of the profit occurring on the first day.

**How did you pick the stock sample groups?**

Initially, I used the Fidelity holdings for that sector as indicated in their quarterly reports.

**I assume that the holdings turned over infrequently enough so that this proved to be an adequate estimate.**

Actually, I subsequently discovered that this procedure was a lot less important than I thought. I found that I could take a sample consisting of fifteen stocks that Fidelity held in a given sector, and it would give me a very good estimate of that sector. On the other hand, I could also use a sample of fifteen stocks in that sector, none of which Fidelity held, and it would still give me a very good indication. As long as the number of stocks in my sample was large enough relative to the stocks in that sector, it didn't make much of a difference.

**What percentage of your account were you betting each day?**

One hundred percent.

**How many different sectors might you invest in on a given day?**

I traded one sector at a time.

**Did you consider diversifying your money by trading different sectors at the same time?**

I'm not a big fan of diversification. My answer to that question is that you can diversify very well by just making enough trades per year. If the odds are 70 percent in your favor and you make fifty trades, it's very difficult to have a down year.

**How did you select which sector to invest in on any given day?**

Imagine a board containing flashing lights, one for each sector, with red lights indicating liquidate or avoid and green lights indicating buy or hold. I would rank each sector based on a combination of volatility and historical reliability, which I call persistency. Essentially, I would take the brightest green light, and when that green light eventually turned red, I would take the new brightest green light. Very often, however, when one light turned red, they would all turn red.

**And if they all turned red, you would then go into cash.**

Correct, but I needed only one green light to take a position on any day.

**When did you get involved in taking on clients?**

Most of my clients today actually started with me when I was still trading municipal bond funds. I took on my first client in 1982. It made no sense to be borrowing at 15 percent from Phil Rizzuto at The Money Store when I could manage $100,000 of client money, share 25 percent of the gains and losses, and effectively be borrowing $25,000 for nothing. That was the point at which I decided to start the business. I still kept the second mortgage, though, because I wanted to trade that money as well. It didn't make sense to me to pay off a mortgage at 15 percent when I was making 35 to 40 percent on the money.

**How did you go about soliciting accounts?**

All my accounts were either friends or neighbors. For example, I would invite a neighbor over for a beer in the evening and say, "I've been doing this for a couple of years now, and I'd like you to take a look at it." Some people had no interest at all and others did.

It's interesting how different people are when it comes to money. Some people don't do any homework at all and give you their money immediately. Others wouldn't dream of giving you $10, no matter what you showed them. Finally, there are those that do a lot of homework and ask the right questions before they invest. Everyone falls into one of these three categories.

**Which of those categories do your clients generally fall into? Obviously, one category is automatically eliminated.**

Most of my clients did the type of homework that I like. They asked the right questions. They told me about their tolerance for risk.

**How large were these accounts?**

They ranged from $10,000 to $100,000.

**What kind of fee structure did you use?**

I took 25 percent of the capital gains. However, I guaranteed to take 25 percent of any losses as well. I also assured each of my investors that I would cover 100 percent of losses if the account were down after twelve months.

**Heads you win one; tails you lose four. You must have been awfully confident to offer that type of guarantee.**

What I was confident in was the probability of winning after fifty trades per year.

**For how long did you maintain the 100 percent guarantee against first-year losses?**

I still maintain that offer, but I've accepted only two new clients during the past five years.

**Given your performance, I assume that implies that you're no longer accepting any new accounts.**

I stopped accepting new accounts five years ago. I made an exception in these two cases because they were very close friends.

**Why did you stop accepting new accounts? Did you feel there was a limit to the amount of money you could handle without it negatively impacting your performance?**

It's not a limit to how much money I can handle but rather a limit to how much money may be welcome in the funds I'm trading. I'm very sensitive to any potential impact I might have on the fund manager or on the other shareholders who don't move as actively as I do. I prefer to restrict the amount of money I move to only a couple of million dollars in a fund of several hundred million dollars, so that the impact will be minimal. Also, I have found that when I enter orders, I often get a comment like, "You're getting out? Most of the calls we're getting today are getting in."

**What does that tell you?**

It tells me that I'm running counter to a lot of money that's being switched in and out; hence, the impact of my activities is not great. I've also been told by fund employees that most of the people who do a lot of switching in their own accounts end up doing worse than if they had done no switching at all.

**Did you decide to limit your size to a certain dollar amount in order to not rock the boat?**

The most important factor here is my risk. Sharing 25 percent of both profits and losses is the exact equivalent of leverage. What I did not fully appreciate at first was the psychological importance of finding and maintaining a stable proportion of client money to my own capital. Actually, I prefer this proportion (or leverage) to decline over time.

**Did you ever find yourself managing funds beyond your comfort level?**

In 1986 I took on new money too rapidly. I found myself rationalizing taking 50 percent positions. For example, a green light would come on, and I would trade only $200,000 of a $400,000 account. I would think, "Yes, I'll feel much more comfortable tomorrow having only $200,000 in." I soon realized that as a result of my caution, I was reducing my clients' return by one-half. I decided that a better approach was to have fewer clients, if necessary, and to trade all of them fully.

When I first cut back on the percentage of an account that I was trading, I wasn't aware of the motivations for my actions. In hindsight, I came to understand that I was really uncomfortable with the size of the risk. It wasn't just a matter of whether I won or lost the next day but also how I would feel until the verdict came in. I have a routine of internalizing how I would feel given what might happen on the next day.

**That routine being what?**

My approach is to confront losses even before they materialize. I rehearse the process of losing. Whenever I take a position, I like to imagine what it would be like under the worst-case scenario. In doing so, I minimize the confusion if that situation actually develops. In my view, losses are a very important part of trading. When a loss happens, I believe in embracing it.

**Why is that?**

By embracing a loss, really feeling it, I tend to have less fear about a potential loss the next time around. If I can't get over the emotions of taking a loss in twenty-four hours, then I'm trading too large or doing something else wrong. Also, the process of rehearsing potential losses and confronting actual losses helps me adapt to increasing levels of risk over time. The amount of money I'm managing is growing by 15 to 20 percent a year, which means that the dollar risk I'm taking is increasing at the same rate. The best way I can deal with that reality is by being willing to feel the risk at each level.

**How is it that the amount you're managing is growing by only 15 to 20 percent per year when your rates of return are more than double that amount?**

Until two or three years ago, growth probably averaged 50 percent, but recently I've tried to limit this. It helps that more money is now withdrawn by clients each year for paying my fees, income taxes, and other bills. Also, I've encouraged reductions in accounts, and I've asked a few clients with multiple accounts to close one.

**Are there any clients that you've dropped completely?**

One of my clients was someone I didn't know personally. He opened an account with me in response to another client's recommendation. The money he invested represented an inheritance his wife had received, and he was very nervous about the account. I couldn't have started in a worse situation. It was the fall of 1985, and I had two disastrous trades in healthcare. I entered the first trade on the day the industrialized nations announced a plan to weaken the dollar. The dollar cracked and drug stocks took off. The next day, everyone was saying the plan wouldn't work; the dollar rebounded, drug stocks got clobbered, and I was out with a big loss. Only about a week later, I went back into healthcare. The following day, Hospital Corporation of America reported surprisingly bad earnings, and the sector got hit extremely hard again.

**How big a hit were these trades?**

About 2 or 3 percent each. Anyway, this particular client was extremely nervous about his investment. The account had gone from $70,000 down to about $67,000. I told him, "Don't worry, I'll cover 100 percent of your losses." I went down to the bank and sent him a cashier's check for $3,000. I told him, "If in two weeks we're down $3,000, then I'll send you another check. Just hold onto the check; it's as good as cash."

**Normally, you wouldn't make up the difference until the end of the year—is that right?**

That's right, but this guy was so nervous that I always wanted him to have the $70,000. About a month later, the account was back over $70,000. I have to admit that I did inquire whether he cashed the check, and it turned out that he had. A year or two later, when I was reducing my clients, he was the first to go, because his actions were indicative of a lack of trust.

**Why do you believe Fidelity went from a policy of virtually encouraging switching in its sector funds to imposing onerous restrictions that made active switching all but impossible?**

I suppose they thought that the profits being made by some market timers were coming out of shareholders' pockets. I would submit, however, that the profits were coming mostly from unsuccessful market timers.

An example of Fidelity's attitude toward market timing was their response to a *Wall Street Journal* article in early 1989 that mentioned my track record and that I traded the Fidelity sector funds. Two days after the article appeared, I called to place an order and was told, "I'm sorry, Mr. Blake, but the hourly investment limit in energy service has been lowered to $100,000." (The previous limit had been 1 percent of the fund's assets, or about $500,000.) I suspect they checked and found that energy service was a sector that I traded exclusively for a half-dozen clients and that I had been doing very well.

**Why had you used this fund more actively?**

Because energy service contained the most reliable pattern that I had ever found. A year or so after Fidelity introduced hourly pricing of sector funds in 1986, I discovered that energy service had an extraordinarily strong tendency to trade near its daily low at the beginning of the day. When I first analyzed the hourly data, I found there was a 90 to 95 percent probability of realizing a gain by simply buying this fund at ten, eleven, and twelve o'clock, for different clients and then selling at the close. Remarkably, this extremely high probability continued to hold up in the year or two that I traded this fund.

**It's amazing that such a simple pattern could exist with such consistency. Does this pattern still exist today?**

It might, but it's of little value. In November 1989, Fidelity began charging a fee of 0.75 percent on trades held less than thirty days.

**I assume that the management of your funds takes only a small part of your day.**

A tiny part. I spend most of my day researching new methods.

**Do you find new strategies that are better than the ones you're using and shift your approach accordingly?**

All the time.

**Presumably, since you can't use everything at the same time, you must have a lot of viable methods on the shelf that you're not even using.**

I do.

**Do you follow your trading signals absolutely? Or do you ever stray from a straight mechanical approach?**

For me, it's important to be loyal to my system. When I'm not, which happens occasionally, then, win or lose, I've made a mistake. I usually remember these for years.

It's not disloyal, however, to question a trade. Sometimes, based on prior experience, a trade just doesn't look right. If I can complete the necessary research before the close and the results so dictate, then I make a permanent amendment to the rules.

**How important is the performance of the funds you're using to your overall performance?**

It's not nearly as important as you would think. The difference between trading a fund that rises 20 percent in a year versus a fund that loses 20 percent in a year is surprisingly small. For example, if a fund has an average daily volatility of 1 percent, an annual return of 20 percent would imply that approximately 54 percent of the days were up and 46 percent were down, and vice versa for a fund that loses 20 percent. [Assuming 250 trading days per year and an average 1 percent price change per day, a net 20 percent return would imply 135 up days and 115 down days, and 135 is 54 percent of 250.] For my strategies, the difference between trading a fund that's up 54 percent of the time and one that's up 46 percent of the time is not that significant.

**Any trades that are particularly memorable?**

When I was just starting out, there was one day when I didn't get the closing price over the phone. I knew it had been a pretty good day, but I didn't know to what extent. I woke up in the middle of the night and remembered that I hadn't checked the closing price. I called and found that it had been a huge up day—twice what I had expected. I think I made a few thousand dollars. You have to remember this was back when I had just started. I was so excited that I couldn't sleep. I was like a kid at Christmas. I'll always remember that feeling.

**Are there any other trades that stand out for one reason or another?**

On July 7, 1986, the stock market fell 62 points (a record then, I think). I knew that morning that I would be out of my positions at the close. However, since this was before hourly switching was available, there was nothing I could do in the interim. That afternoon I had a windsurfing lesson. I thought that I would be able to get back well before four o'clock to place a call to liquidate my positions. Unfortunately, I hadn't mastered the sport well enough and got blown to the other side of the lake. I knew time was running out, and I paddled back as hard as I could to try to beat the close. I didn't make it, and it cost me.

**Any other trades come to mind?**

In August 1987 I took a position in the gold sector fund. The day after I entered the trade, the fund dropped, giving me a red light, but I stayed in.

**Why did you stay in?**

I honestly don't remember. Anyway, the next day, the gold stocks were down big, while a bright green light in technology was staring me in the face. I remember that I found it extremely difficult to exit all my clients from the gold sector at a big loss—a loss that I knew I shouldn't have taken in the first place—and immediately place them at risk again in the technology fund, which was already up sharply. I think the thing that made it so difficult was that I had violated my rule. As it turned out, the subsequent gain in technology more than made up for the loss in gold.

**So in the end you did follow your system.**

Yes, but I almost didn't. The lesson for me was that if you break a discipline once, the next transgression becomes much easier. Breaking a diet provides an appropriate analogy—once you do it, it becomes much easier to make further exceptions.

**Have the markets changed in the past decade?**

In a micro sense—yes; in a macro sense—no. Opportunities change, strategies change, but people and psychology do not change. If trend-following systems don't work as well, something else will. There's always money being lost, so someone out there has to win.

**What do you believe are the major myths about markets?**

A prevailing myth on Wall Street is that no one can consistently beat the market year in, year out, with steady returns of 20 or 30 percent a year. On the other hand, the sales side would have you believe that it can be done by anyone. Neither is really the truth.

**Why do traders lose?**

First of all, most traders don't have a winning strategy. Second, even among those traders who do, many don't follow their strategy. Trading puts pressure on weaker human traits and seems to seek out each individual's Achilles' heel.

**What makes a good trader?**

A critical ingredient is a maverick mind. It's also important to have a blend between an artistic side and a scientific side. You need the artistic side to imagine, discover, and create trading strategies. You need the scientific side to translate those ideas into firm trading rules and to execute those rules.

**Can people be successful using a purchased system?**

I believe that systems tend to be more useful or successful for the originator than for someone else. It's important that an approach be personalized; otherwise, you won't have the confidence to follow it. It's unlikely that someone else's approach will be consistent with your own personality. It's also possible that individuals who become successful traders are not the type to use someone else's approach and that successful traders don't sell their systems.

**How would you respond to Burton Malkiel [the author of *A Random Walk Down Wall Street*]?**

Well, I'm more in agreement than in disagreement with him. The markets *are* mostly random, and most people *can't* beat or "time" the market. One hundred money managers each believe that they can consistently outperform the market. My feeling is that the number is a lot closer to zero than one hundred. Trading is probably more of an art than most people want to believe. I guess I'd also be tempted to show him my numbers.

**What advice would you give to a novice trader?**

There are five basic steps to becoming a successful trader. First, focus on trading vehicles, strategies, and time horizons that suit your personality. Second, identify nonrandom price behavior, while recognizing that markets are random most of the time. Third, absolutely convince yourself that what you have found is statistically valid. Fourth, set up trading rules. Fifth, follow the rules. In a nutshell, it all comes down to: Do your own thing (independence); and do the right thing (discipline).

At the core, the quality of open-mindedness is responsible for Blake's success and, for that matter, his entire career. For many years, Blake sincerely believed that the markets were random. When confronted with contradictory evidence, he didn't dig in his heels and argue his position—the reflexive response most people would have in such a situation. Instead, he researched the question, and when the evidence suggested that his prior views had been wrong, he changed his mind. The ability to change one's mind is probably a key characteristic of the successful trader. Dogmatic and rigid personalities rarely, if ever, succeed in the markets.

Another attribute that has allowed Blake to excel is his adaptability. The markets are a dynamic process, and sustained trading success requires the ability to modify and even change strategies as markets evolve. Blake began by trading municipal bond funds. However, when the reliability and profitability of his approach in that sector started to diminish, he didn't just blindly keep repeating the same strategy that had worked for him in the past. Instead, he used the changing market conditions as a spur to start an intensive research project, which eventually yielded an entirely new and even more effective approach. When hourly switching became available in the Fidelity sector funds, he altered his methods accordingly. Then, when Fidelity made it virtually impossible to use its funds for switching strategies (by imposing prohibitively high fees), Blake switched to different fund families and different strategies. Blake's ability to adapt has allowed him to maintain a remarkable consistency of performance, despite profound changes in his trading environment.

Perhaps Blake's most important message lies in his amazingly consistent track record, which provides compelling empirical evidence that the markets are indeed nonrandom. Of course, this nonrandomness is hardly blatant. If it were, we would all be millionaires. However, Blake's ability to win in an astounding twenty-five months for every month he loses, allows us to say "Yes, Virginia, the markets can be beat."

How can the markets be beat? Certainly not by buying the answer. Even if the answer were for sale, the odds are that it wouldn't fit your personality and that you wouldn't have the confidence to follow it.

Essentially, there are no shortcuts. Each trader must find his or her own solution to the market puzzle. Of course, most such research efforts will end in failure. If, however, you are able to uncover nonrandom market patterns and can convincingly demonstrate their validity, only two steps remain to achieve trading success: Devise your trading rules and then *follow* your trading rules.

# *Victor Sperandeo*

## MARKETS GROW OLD TOO

Victor Sperandeo started his career on Wall Street straight out of high school. It was certainly an unglamorous beginning, working first as a minimum-wage quote boy and then switching to a slightly higher paying job as a statistical clerk for Standard & Poor's. Sperandeo found this work, which basically involved copying and transferring columns of numbers, "stupifyingly boring." He had a difficult time keeping his mind on his work. To his relief, he was eventually fired for making too many errors.

After a stint at another nontrading job in a Wall Street accounting department, Sperandeo talked his way into an option trading position. Over the next two years, he was a dealer in the over-the-counter (OTC) options market, matching up buyers and sellers and "making the middle."

In the midst of the 1969 bear market, Sperandeo switched firms in a search for greater autonomy in his trading decisions. At this new firm, he was offered a percentage of the spread he earned on each option transaction, as opposed to the flat fee compensation structure at his former company. The new firm, however, would not commit to a salary because of a cautious posture fostered by the ongoing bear market. Sperandeo gladly accepted the offer, confident that he could substantially increase his income by sharing in a percentage of his transaction earnings.

After six months on the job, Sperandeo had earned $50,000 in commissions. His boss, who earned an annual salary of $50,000, called him in for a talk. "Victor," he said, "you're doing such a good job, we decided to put you on a salary." Somehow, the offer of a $20,000 salary and an ambiguous commitment to some sort of bonus in lieu of his existing compensation arrangement just didn't sound like good news. Three weeks later Sperandeo switched jobs. Unfortunately, he found that his new firm played the same song only in a different key—when he received his monthly profit/loss statements, he discovered that his profits were being eaten away by enormous expense allocations.

After about six months, Sperandeo finally decided that if he were going to get a fair deal, he would have to make it himself. After finding a partner to finance the operation, Sperandeo launched his own firm, Ragnar Options, in 1971. Sperandeo claims that Ragnar was the first option dealer to offer guaranteed quotes on options without charging exceptionally high premiums. If they couldn't find an existing option contract in the market to meet a buyer's request (which they could purchase and resell at a premium), they wrote the option themselves. (At the time, options were tailor-made to the customer's specifications, as opposed to being traded as uniform instruments on an exchange.) As a result of this policy of offering reasonable firm quotes, according to Sperandeo, within six months Ragnar was the largest OTC option dealer in the world.

Ragnar was eventually merged with another Wall Street firm. Sperandeo stayed on for a while but then joined Interstate Securities in 1978. At Interstate, Sperandeo was given a company account and a few private accounts to manage at a 50/50 split (expenses as well as profits). Sperandeo had finally landed the perfect job: complete independence to trade any markets in any way he desired, capital backing, and a meaningful split of profits (and losses). This ideal arrangement finally came to an end in 1986 when Interstate went public and decided to dissolve its trading group. Sperandeo traded his personal account for a little over a year before deciding to start his own money management firm—Rand Management Corporation.

Throughout his entire career, Sperandeo has placed a greater emphasis on loss avoidance than on scoring large gains. He was largely successful at this objective, stringing together eighteen consecutive winning years before registering his first loss in 1990. Over this period, his average annual gain was 72 percent, with results ranging from a single loss of 35 percent in 1990 to five years of triple-digit gains.

Although Sperandeo never bothered to finish the credits for his nighttime college degree, over the years he has done an enormous amount of reading. In addition to books about the market, Sperandeo has read widely in the somewhat related fields of economics, psychology, and philosophy. Overall, he estimates that he has read approximately twenty-five hundred books on these subjects.

The interview was conducted at Sperandeo's "office," which is located in the basement of his house, the main section of which he has converted to a lounge, complete with a fifteen-foot bar, seating for seventy-five, and an elaborate sound system. You almost expect Bill Murray to pop up and do his "Saturday Night Live" lounge singer act. I couldn't help but smile at the image of a starchy pension fund trustee doing an on-site inspection of Sperandeo's operations in considering him as a prospective manager for its funds. I found Sperandeo very relaxed and friendly—the type of person who is instantaneously likable.

**After nearly two decades as an independent or quasi-independent trader, why did you finally decide to start a money management firm?**

In 1987 I did enormously well catching the huge break in the stock market. My success in this market led to unsolicited offers to manage some large sums of money. I realized that if I had been managing money, as opposed to simply trading my own account, my profit potential would have been enormously greater.

**How have you done in your trading since you started your own management company?**

I did well in 1989, which was the first year of the firm's existence, but I lost money in 1990. Actually, I found it somewhat ironic that my first losing year in the markets occurred after having gained more knowledge than ever.

**How do you explain that?**

That's what you call being a human being. [He laughs loudly and long.]

**How did you become a trader?**

I think my first related interest was an enthusiasm for poker. As a teenager, I literally earned a living by playing poker. When I first started playing, I read every book I could find on the game and quickly learned that winning was a matter of managing the odds. In other words, if you played only the hands in which the odds were in your favor and folded when they were not, you would end up winning more times than you lost. I memorized the odds of every important card combination, and I was very successful at the game.

Although I did quite well, I realized that being a professional card player was not what I wanted to do with my life. When I was twenty years old, I made a complete survey of the *New York Times* employment section and discovered that three professions offered more than $25,000 per year as a starting salary: physicist, biologist, and OTC trader. Now, I didn't even know exactly what an OTC trader did, but, since I obviously didn't have the educational background for being a physicist or biologist and OTC trading sounded a little bit like playing cards—they both involved odds—I decided to try for a career on Wall Street. I landed a job as a quote boy for Pershing & Company.

**How did you learn about trading and markets? Did you have a mentor?**

No. At the time, Milton Leeds, who was a legendary tape reader and trader of his day, worked at Pershing. I found observing him inspirational, but I didn't work directly for him. Basically, I learned about the markets by reading everything on the subject that I could get my hands on.

**When did you actually first become a trader?**

After working on Wall Street for almost three years, first at Pershing and then some other short-lived jobs, I decided that I wanted to try trading. I considered the different areas of trading that I could go into.

There was stocks—kind of boring. There was bonds—really boring. Then there was options—very sophisticated. In the late 1960s, probably only about 1 percent of all stockbrokers even understood options. I thought that if I undertook the most esoteric form of trading and mastered it, then I would have to make a lot of money. So I applied for a job as an options trader.

**What did you know about options trading at the time?**

Nothing, but I knew that was what I wanted to do. I tried to make an impression on the senior partner who interviewed me by telling him that I was a genius.

He said, "What do you mean?"

I told him that I had a photographic memory—which, incidentally, I don't.

He said, "Prove it."

I told him that I had memorized all the stock symbols—which I had. I had taken a memory course years before. This fellow had been on Wall Street for thirty-five years and didn't know all the symbols. He tested me, and I knew them all. He offered me the job.

**You said earlier that you were drawn to a trading career because of the analogy to playing cards. Do you then see trading as a form of gambling?**

I'd say that *gambling* is the wrong term. Gambling involves taking a risk when the odds are against you. For example, betting on a lottery or playing a slot machine are forms of gambling. I think successful trading, or poker playing for that matter, involves speculating rather than gambling. Successful speculation implies taking risks when the odds are in your favor. Just like in poker, where you have to know which hands to bet on, in trading you have to know when the odds are in your favor.

**How do you define "the odds" in trading?**

In 1974 I missed the huge October–November rally in the stock market. That error served as a catalyst for an intensive two-year study. I wanted

256 / FUND MANAGERS AND TIMERS

to know the answer to questions like: How long do bull and bear markets last? What are the normal percentage price moves a market makes before it forms a top or a bottom?

As a result of that research project, I found that market price movements are like people—they have statistically significant life-expectancy profiles that can be used to measure risk exposure. For example, the median extent for an intermediate swing in the Dow during a bull market is 20 percent. This doesn't mean that when the market is up 20 percent, it's going to top; sometimes it will top earlier, sometimes later. However, what it does mean is that when the market is up more than 20 percent, the odds for further appreciation begin to decline significantly. Thus, if the market has been up more than 20 percent and you begin to see other evidence of a possible top, it's important to pay close attention to that information.

As an analogy, consider life insurance, which deals with the life expectancy of people instead of price moves. If you're writing life insurance policies, it's going to make a great deal of difference whether the applicant is twenty years old or eighty years old. If you're approached by an out-of-condition twenty-year-old, you might judge that the odds of his survival are pretty good. However, you'd be a lot less anxious to write a policy on an eighty-year-old. If the eighty-year-old is the Jack LaLanne of eighty-year-olds—he can do two hundred push-ups; he can swim the English Channel—then fine, you can write him a policy. But let's say the same eighty-year-old smokes three packs of Camels a day, drinks a quart of scotch a day, and has pneumonia—then you probably wouldn't want to write him a policy. The older the individual, the more significant the symptoms become.

Similarly, in a market that is in a stage of old age, it is particularly important to be attuned to symptoms of a potential end to the current trend. To use the life insurance analogy, most people who become involved in the stock market don't know the difference between a twenty-year-old and an eighty-year-old.

In my opinion, one reason why many types of technical analysis don't work too well is because such methods are often applied indiscriminately. For example, if you see a head-and-shoulders pattern form in what is the market equivalent of a twenty-year-old, the odds are that the market is not likely to die so quickly. However, if you see the same chart formation in the market equivalent of an eighty-year-old, there's a much better chance of that pattern being an accurate indicator of a price top. Trading the market without knowing what stage it is in is like selling life insurance to twenty-year-olds and eighty-year-olds at the same premium.

**When you say that the historical median length of a bull move has been 20 percent, how are you defining a bull move?**

I'm talking about intermediate upmoves in a long-term bull market. With very rare exceptions, I define "intermediate" as a price move lasting a minimum of three weeks to a maximum of six months. Of course, there are analogous figures for all other types of market movements categorized by type of market (bull or bear), length of move (short term, intermediate term, or long term), and location within market cycle (first swing, second swing, and so on).

Incidentally, there's remarkable consistency in the 20 percent median upmove figure, which I based on a study of all years since 1896. When I looked only at markets up through 1945, I found that the corresponding figure was virtually identical at 19 percent. I think there are two reasons that help explain the stability of this approximate 20 percent figure. The first factor is related to value. Roger Ibbotson did a study spanning sixty years of data in which he compared the returns of different forms of investment. He found that, over the survey period, the stock market returned an average of 9.2 percent annually, including dividends. Therefore, if the market rises 20 percent in, say, 107 days—which happens to be the median time duration of an intermediate upmove—then you've squeezed out a lot of value in a very short amount of time. The market as a whole has become much less of a value.

The second factor is psychological. Let's say you go to the supermarket to buy ingredients for a salad. A head of lettuce is selling for $1.00, and a pound of tomatoes is selling for $1.00. You go back two weeks later and lettuce is still selling for $1.00, but tomatoes are now $1.50. In that situation, a lot of people will look for a substitute for tomatoes. They're going to say, "I'm just not paying that much for tomatoes." Does the fifty cents really matter? I've done the same thing when my income was in the seven figures. It really doesn't matter, but you don't want to pay up beyond a certain number.

**And you're saying that 20 percent is that type of number?**

That's my hypothesis. Obviously, I can't really prove it.

**Do you use your statistical studies of the normal duration and magnitude of price moves to set targets either in terms of price or time?**

Absolutely not. To use extent and duration profiles to predict exact market turning points would be like an insurance company telling you when and how you will die on the day you buy your policy. They don't have to do that to make a profit. All they need to do to make a profit is to know what the odds are.

**How then do you analyze a situation in which a market has reached the median age of historical upmoves?**

Once a price move exceeds its median historical age, any method you use to analyze the market, whether it be fundamental or technical, is likely to be far more accurate. For example, if a chartist interprets a particular pattern as a top formation, but the market is only up 10 percent from the last relative low, the odds are high that the projection will be incorrect. However, if the market is up 25 to 30 percent, then the same type of formation should be given a great deal more weight.

**When you miss a major turning point, such as the October 1974 low you mentioned before (which was the low point of the market since that time), how do you eventually get back into the market?**

Markets go up in stepwise fashion. I wait until a situation arises that looks like there's another major relative low. In the case of 1974, I went long the world on December 6. That day proved to be the exact bottom of the market. Ironically, I actually ended up losing money on the trade.

**Before I ask you to explain that apparent paradox, first tell me what made you so sure that it was the bottom of the market?**

To begin, there was a Dow Theory buy signal—the Dow Jones Industrial index had made a new low, but the Transportation index and the S&P 500 had not. In addition, the volume on the break to new lows was relatively light. Also, we had been in a bear market for a long time, and bearish sentiment was pervasive. Finally, bad news was starting to lose its impact on the market—bearish news stories would come out, and stocks would essentially lie flat.

**Now tell me how you managed to lose money buying the December 1974 low.**

I had an incredibly profitable year up to that point. I took one-third of my profits for the year and bought out-of-the-money calls expiring in January. As one example, at the time, Kodak was trading at 64, and I bought the January 70 calls, which were trading near 1. On January 27, which was the expiration day of the January option series, Kodak had rebounded to 69. The calls obviously went out worthless. One week later, Kodak was trading at 80. The same type of experience was repeated in a dozen other positions.

**So your mistake was buying options that were too far out of the money and too short in duration?**

They weren't too far out of the money. My mistake was that I didn't allow enough time until expiration. This episode preceded my study on the duration and magnitude of historical price moves, which we discussed earlier. After I completed my study in 1976, I realized that the second legs of bull markets tend to be relatively extended. I'm certain that if I encountered a similar situation after 1976, I would have bought the April options instead of the January options. But at the time, I simply didn't have enough knowledge about the probabilities of various market moves.

**How did you eventually get back into the market?**

I got long in February 1975 and did very well. By the way, that was very hard to do because I was getting back into the market at a point at which stock prices were trading much higher than when my options expired worthless in January.

**I don't completely understand your statistical study of the longevity of price moves. It appears that we've been in an extended**

bull market since 1982, which at the time of this interview [April 1991] would make the current bull market nine years old. Doesn't that place the age of this bull market off the charts in terms of your historical studies? Wouldn't you have been inclined to look for a major top far too prematurely?

I look at it from a completely different perspective. By my definitions, the bull market that began in 1982 ended in November 1983.

**How do you objectively make those kinds of classifications?**

What defines an uptrend? One essential criterion is that you do not take out a prior major relative low. The bear phase that lasted from June 1983 to July 1984 consisted of two major downswings—that is, you took out a prior major relative low. Also, by my definitions, to qualify as a bear market, the price move must last a minimum of six months and be equal to at least 15 percent. Both of these conditions were met by the price decline from the June 1983 high to the July 1984 low. Thus, in terms of all my criteria, the price upmove that began in July 1984 marked the beginning of a new bull market.

**By your classification, when did the bull market that began in July 1984 end?**

In my view, that bull market ended in October 1989, making it the second longest bull market since 1896 (the start of my statistical survey). The bull market didn't end in August 1987 because the subsequent price break lasted only three months. Therefore, although that price decline was extraordinarily sharp, it did not meet the minimum time duration definition for a bear market, namely, six months from top to bottom.

**Is there anything you consider unique about your money management approach?**

Yes, I analyze risk by measuring the extent and duration of price swings. For example, if the market has risen 20 percent in roughly 107 days, even if I'm still extremely bullish I'll have a maximum position size of 50 percent, because statistically we've reached the median historical magnitude and duration of an upmove.

**In other words, you vary the size of the bet relative to your perception of the market risk. Do you do anything differently in terms of cutting loses?**

Losses are always predetermined so that I can measure my risk.

**By "predetermined" you mean that you decide where you're getting out before you get in?**

Exactly. Let me give you an example to illustrate why this principle is so important. Take the typical trader who gets a call from his broker. "Listen," his broker says, "I have some information from a reliable source that stock XYZ is going to be a takeover play. It's only trading at $20; it could go up to $60!" The trader buys the stock, and two weeks later it's trading at $18. The action just doesn't seem right, so he promises himself to get out when he's even. The next week the stock is down to $17. Now he's beginning to feel a little bit concerned. "I'll get out on the first rally," he vows to himself. One week later the stock is down to $15, and the trader, who has bought the stock on margin, suddenly realizes he's lost half his money. Two days later the stock is at $14, and he calls up his broker in a state of desperation and exclaims, "Get me out!" He gets filled at $13, and that's the bottom of the market. Sound familiar?

Think about the psychological process involved. At the beginning, the trader fell for the lure of making easy money. When the stock declined to $18, he felt a little anxious. When it fell to $17, he felt the onset of panic. When the stock slid to $15, it was pure panic. When he finally got out, he felt a sense of relief—which is somewhat ironic since he had just lost 70 percent of his money. There's nothing logical about this process. It's all an emotional pitfall. Planning where to get out before putting on the trade is a means of enforcing emotional discipline.

**Is predetermining an exit point something that you've done for the last few years?**

No, that's something that I've done since my first day in the business. I've always had a point where I knew that I was getting out.

**Does taking a loss have an emotional impact on you?**

None. Taking a loss never affects me, but I don't take big losses.

**Never? Wasn't there ever any instance in which you deviated from your risk control guidelines?**

Well, actually, there was one instance in November 1984. That situation was dramatic because it ended up costing me over $1 million. At the time, the Fed was easing, and I was convinced that we were in a bull market. The market had started to sell off because Congress was considering a change in the tax code. However, when the newspapers reported that the proposed change in the tax code would be "revenue neutral," I decided to go long. I put on a huge position because I trade at my biggest when I'm making money, and I had experienced a great year up to that point. I was long the world—two legal-size pages of positions. My smallest position was one hundred options and my biggest position—I'm not exaggerating—was two thousand options.

What I failed to realize was that, even though the proposed change in the tax code was revenue neutral, the plan called for taking money from corporations and giving it to individuals. When you're long stocks, you don't want any plan that takes money away from corporations [*he laughs*].

When the market went down four days in a row, I knew I was wrong. I wanted to be out. The market just kept on falling. On the sixth straight down day, I got out. If I had sold after the fourth down day, my loss would have been only half as large.

**I thought you had a rule about getting out?**

I did. My rule would have had me out on the fourth day.

**So you violated your rule?**

Yes, but it wasn't a matter of my hoping that the market would go up. The reason that I didn't get out was that the decline seemed extremely overdone. My plan was still to liquidate, but to wait for the first day the market rallied.

**Did you end up getting out at the bottom?**

No, the market actually declined for nine consecutive days.

**What lesson did you learn from that experience?**

Whenever there's a tax proposal, or some other major legislative uncertainty, I now get flat immediately. The market will always run to the sidelines until it knows what will happen.

**Is there any more general lesson that would apply?**

Yes, when you're trading at your biggest, you should be making money instantaneously.

**In other words, when you have a large position, you should cut your bet size quickly unless that position starts making money right at the start?**

Exactly. When you're trading large, you need to have an especially short fuse in regard to cutting losses. My goal on Wall Street was never to get rich but to stay in business. There's a big difference. If you're out of the business, you can never get rich. That's why you have to be especially cautious when you're trading a larger position size.

**Any other trades that stand out as being particularly dramatic?**

On one of the expiration days in the S&P in 1985 or 1986—I forget the exact date—the spread action between the S&P and OEX convinced me that a major buy program was going to hit the market. The Major Market Index [MMI] was trading at about 349. I bought four thousand of the 355 options at 1/8 and five hundred of the 350s at 1 3/4.

The market moved higher, and at 3:30—one half-hour before the close—the 355s were trading at 2 and the 350s were trading at 5 1/2. I sold the five hundred 350 options, giving me a free ride on the rest of the position. At that point, one of the major Wall Street firms hit the market with an extremely large sell program, and prices collapsed. With less than a half-hour remaining until expiration and the options out of the money, there was no way to get out of anything. The market finished down sharply for the day.

After the close, I remember going to Michael's One and telling the bartender, "I need a drink. I just made $100,000 today—the only problem is that an hour ago I was ahead $800,000."

**Your track record shows that you made substantial withdrawals from your account during the 1980s. You don't seem to be the type of person who's an extravagant spender. Therefore, I assume that this money was reinvested in some form. What alternative investments did you choose? Why didn't you simply let the money compound in your account, since you were doing so well?**

One of my major investments was starting a trading company. I hired other traders, taught them what I did, and gave them my capital to trade.

**Why did you do that?**

Because I wanted to be the McDonald's of trading rather than an egotistical, solitary trader. This venture, of course, didn't work out as well as McDonald's [he laughs loudly].

**What was the outcome?**

Over a five-year period, I trained thirty-eight people. Each of these people spent several months by my side while I taught them virtually everything I knew about the market. Out of these thirty-eight people, five made money.

**How did you choose the people you selected for training?**

I wasn't very scientific about it. Basically, I went with my instincts and whims about who might be a good trader. The people I selected were a very diverse group.

**Was there any correlation between intelligence and success at trading?**

Absolutely, but not in the way you think. For example, one of the people I picked was a high school dropout, who I'm sure didn't even know the alphabet. He was one of the five who made me a great deal of money.

**Why did you pick him?**

He was my phone clerk on the American Stock Exchange, and he was very aggressive and alert. Also, he had been in Vietnam and had a hand grenade explode near him, leaving shrapnel in his pancreas. As a result of this experience, he was always afraid of everything. When it came to trading, he was more worried about losing than winning. He took losses very quickly.

On the other extreme of the intelligence spectrum, one of the people I trained was a genius. He had a 188 IQ, and he was on "Jeopardy" once and answered every question correctly. That same person never made a dime in trading during five years.

I discovered that you can't train people how to trade by just imparting knowledge. The key to trading success is emotional discipline. Making money has nothing to do with intelligence. Think of all the bright people that choose careers on Wall Street. If intelligence were the key, there would be a lot more people making money trading.

**You almost seem to be implying that intelligence is an impediment to successful trading. How would you explain that?**

Assume that you're a brilliant student who graduates Harvard summa cum laude. You get a job with a top investment house, and within one year, they hand you a $5 million portfolio to manage. What would you believe about yourself? Most likely, you would assume that you're very bright and do everything right. Now, assume you find yourself in a situation where the market is going against your position. What is your reaction likely to be? "I'm right." Why? Because everything you've done in life is right. You'll tend to place your IQ above the market action.

To be a successful trader, you have to be able to admit mistakes. People who are very bright don't make very many mistakes. In a sense, they generally *are* correct. In trading, however, the person who can easily admit to being wrong is the one who walks away a winner.

Besides trading, there is probably no other profession where you have to admit when you're wrong. Think about it. For example, consider a lawyer who, right before a big case, goes out with his girlfriend and stays up half the night. The next day, he's drowsy and inadequately prepared. He ends up losing the case. Do you think he's going to tell the client, "I'm sorry, I went out last night and stayed up too long. If I were sharper, I would have won the case. Here's your money back." It will never happen. He can always find some excuse. He would probably say something like, "I did the best I could, but the jury was biased." He will never have to admit he was wrong. No one will ever know the truth except him. In fact, he'll probably push the truth so far into his subconscious that he'll never admit to himself that his own actions caused the loss of the case.

In trading, you can't hide your failures. Your equity provides a daily reflection of your performance. The trader who tries to blame his losses on external events will never learn from his mistakes. For a trader, rationalization is a guaranteed road to ultimate failure

**Typically, how much money did you give these trainees to trade, and what was their cutout point?**

In most cases, I started people out with $25,000 to $50,000. In a few cases, I started trainees out with accounts as large as $250,000. Their cutout point was when they lost it all [*he laughs*]. I never had to fire anyone, they just self-destructed.

**On balance, did you lose money on this trainee trading program?**

No, because the five of the thirty-eight trainees who were successful made mcre money than all the others combined lost. The only unfortunate thing was that these five people made so much money that they quit. That was one outcome I didn't consider at the onset.

**In the end, though, you still ended up with net profits on the deal.**

Yes, but not very much considering the effort that went into this venture. I certainly wouldn't do it again.

**Why do you think the majority of people you trained lost money?**

They lacked what I call emotional discipline—the ability to keep their emotions removed from trading decisions. Dieting provides an apt analogy for trading. Most people have the necessary knowledge to lose weight—that is, they know that in order to lose weight you have to exercise and cut your intake of fats. However, despite this widespread knowledge, the vast majority of people who attempt to lose weight are unsuccessful. Why? Because they lack the emotional discipline.

**If you were going to repeat this experiment again—which obviously you are not—do you think that you'd be able to pick a higher percentage of winning traders?**

Yes, because this time around I would pick people on the basis of psychological traits.

**Specifically, what traits would you look for?**

Essentially, I would look for people with the ability to admit mistakes and take losses quickly. Most people view losing as a hit against their self-esteem. As a result, they postpone losing. They think of all sorts of reasons for not taking losses. They select a mental stop point and then fail to execute it. They abandon their game plan.

**What do you think are the greatest misconceptions people have about the market?**

In my opinion, the greatest misconception is the idea that if you buy and hold stocks for long periods of time, you'll always make money.

Let me give you some specific examples. Anyone who bought the stock market at any time between the 1896 low and the 1932 low would have lost money. In other words, there's a thirty-six-year period in which a buy-and-hold strategy would have lost money—and that doesn't even include the opportunity loss on the funds. As a more modern example, anyone who bought the market at any time between the 1962 low and the 1974 low would have lost money.

If something happens once, I think logic tells you that it can happen again. Actually, I believe that anything can happen, but certainly if it has happened before, it can happen again. From 1929 to 1932, the market dropped an average of 94 percent. In fact, it has even happened in more modern times—during 1973–74, the "nifty fifty" stocks lost over 75 percent of their value.

**Is your point that we could get a bear market that would be far worse than most people could imagine?**

Exactly, and people who have the notion that buying and holding for the long term is the way to go can easily go bankrupt.

**Wouldn't your own duration and magnitude rules lead you astray if we get a market that goes down 80 or 90 percent?**

Not at all. Remember that I use these statistical studies as only one among many tools.

**How do you handle losing streaks?**

We all go through periods when we're out of sync with the market. When I'm doing things correctly, I tend to expand my rate of involvement in the market. Conversely, when I start losing, I cut back my position size. The idea is to lose as little as possible while you're in a losing streak. Once you take a big hit, you're always on the defensive. In all the months I lost money, I always ended up trading small—sometimes trading as little as 1 percent of the account.

When I get into a losing streak, I like to read a nonfiction book to learn something new. That action accomplishes two things. First, it takes my mind off of trading; second, by enhancing my knowledge, I help improve my self-esteem. The key is to do something positive.

**Do you sometimes pull yourself away from the markets totally?**

Yes.

**For how long?**

Sometimes for as long as a month or two.

**Do you think that taking such extended withdrawals from the market is a good practice?**

Without a doubt. You don't want to keep losing if you're in a rut, because that will only destroy your self-confidence even more.

**How do you get back into trading?**

Ty Cobb once was asked why he never had slumps. He said that whenever he felt himself getting into a slump, he wouldn't try to get a hit, but he would simply try to make contact with the ball. To relate that concept to trading, when you're in a slump, try to be patient and wait for a trade that you feel very confident about and keep the bet size small. Your goal should not be to make lots of money but rather to get your confidence back by making correct decisions.

**Why do most people lose money in the market?**

I know this will sound like a cliché, but the single most important reason that people lose money in the financial markets is that they don't cut their losses short. It is a curiosity of human nature that no matter how many books talk about this rule, and no matter how many experts offer this advice, people still keep making the same mistake.

**What other mistakes do people make?**

They don't approach trading as a business. I've always viewed trading as a business.

**Can you elaborate on your business plan for trading?**

I view the objectives in trading as a three-tiered hierarchy. First and foremost is the preservation of capital. When I first look at a trade, I don't ask, "What is the potential profit I can realize?" but rather, "What is the potential loss I could suffer?" Second, I strive for consistent profitability by balancing my risk relative to the accumulated profits or losses. Consistency is far more important than making lots of money. Third, insofar as I'm successful in the first two goals, I attempt to achieve superior returns. I do this by increasing my bet size after, and only after, periods of high profitability. In other words, if I have had a particularly profitable recent period, I may try to pyramid my gains by placing a larger bet size assuming, of course, the right situation presents itself. The key to building wealth is to preserve capital and wait patiently for the right opportunity to make the extraordinary gains.

**What is your opinion about chart analysis?**

I've made too much money trading on technical observations to dismiss technical analysis as many pure fundamentalists do. However, I do believe that technical analysis is insufficient as a sole method of analyzing and trading the market.

Back in 1974, I was approached by a technical analyst who talked a convincing game about how he could help improve my trading. I hired him as an advisor on a trial basis for $125 a week. I also offered to pay him a percentage of the profits on his recommendations. Well, this fellow was very industrious. He worked sixteen-hour days and analyzed his charts in ways that I still don't understand. However, whenever I asked him for a specific recommendation, he would show me the chart and say things like, "This stock might be forming a top." He could never give me a straight answer when I asked him if I should buy or sell. My most distinct memory about him is that his shirtsleeves were frayed and he ate homemade tuna fish sandwiches for lunch.

**Do you use chart analysis?**

Yes, but I like to keep it simple. My primary methodology is a three-step process to define important trend changes. Let me take the example of trying to identify a top in a rising market. The first step is waiting for the uptrend line to be broken.

**In my experience, I have not found trend lines to be particularly reliable.**

It is essential that you draw the trend line correctly. Most people draw trend lines incorrectly.

**What is the correct way of drawing a trend line?**

In the case of an uptrend line, you draw the line from the lowest low to the highest low immediately preceding the highest high, making sure that the connecting point you select does not result in the trend line passing through any prices between the two points.

**I interrupted you. You said you used a three-step process of chart analysis. What are the remaining two steps?**

Once the trend line is broken, I then look for an unsuccessful test of the recent high. This failure may take the form of prices reversing below the previous high or, in some instances, prices might actually penetrate the previous high by a modest amount and then break. In the case where prices penetrate the previous high, a pullback below that high would serve as confirmation of a failed test of the high. The third and final confirmation of a trend change would be the downside penetration of the most recent relative low.

**In the second criterion you mentioned—the failed test of the previous high—you indicated that sometimes the rebound will fall short of the high and sometimes it will penetrate the high before prices break. Is the pattern more reliable if the previous high is penetrated before prices pull back?**

As a matter of fact, yes. In fact, this one pattern alone can sometimes catch the virtual exact high or low. In my view, these types of price failures are probably the most reliable and important chart patterns. The reason these types of failures often mark major turning points is related to the mechanics of the trading floor. Many traders tend to set their stops at or near the previous high or low. This behavioral pattern holds true for both major and minor price moves. When there is a heavy concentration of such stops, you can be reasonably sure that the locals on the floor are aware of this information. There will be a tendency for the locals to buy as prices approach a concentration of buy stops above the market (or to sell if the market approaches heavy sell stops below the market). The locals try to profit by anticipating that the activation of a large pocket of stops will cause a minor extension of the price move. They will then use such a price extension as an opportunity to liquidate their positions for a quick profit. Thus, it's in the interest of the locals to try to trigger heavy concentrations of stop orders.

In cases where there are valid fundamental reasons for the continuation of a price move beyond the previous high (or low), the move will tend to extend. However, if the move to a new high (or low) was largely caused by local trading activity, once the stop orders are filled, prices will tend to reverse, falling back below the prior high (or rebounding above the prior low). In effect, the triggering of the stops represents the market's last gasp.

The process I have just described applies to an open outcry type of market, such as futures. However, a similar process also operates in specialist-type markets, such as the stock exchange. The specialist trades one stock or several stocks. It's the specialist's job to make a market in these stocks. For providing this service, the specialist is paid a flat fee per hundred shares traded. Obviously, it's in his interest to have prices move to the levels that will result in the execution of the largest amount of orders. These points will normally be prices just above the prior high or just below the prior low. Also, keep in mind that the specialist has the advantage of knowing ahead of time the location of all the orders for his stock. In addition, the locals on the stock exchange floor will have a similar type of interest in triggering stops as do the locals on, say, the futures market exchanges.

The primary point I'm trying to make is that key chart patterns are often based on the activity of the professionals on the floors.

**Do you use any technical indicators?**

I use them as a secondary type of input. In the stock market, the one indicator I give the greatest weight is the two-hundred-day moving average. I wouldn't recommend this indicator as a sole input for making trading decisions, but it does add a bit of useful information to supplement other methods and forms of analysis. In fact, one study I saw demonstrated that by simply using the two-hundred-day moving average on the Dow Jones stocks, an investor could have earned an average annual return of 18 percent over the fifty-year survey period—approximately double the return that would have been realized by a straight buy-and-hold method.

**I know that you're a self-taught student in economics, having read scores or possibly even hundreds of books on the subject. Has this study been a purely intellectual endeavor, or does it yield some practical benefits in terms of trading?**

There have been a number of incidents in which I believe my knowledge of economics and economic history helped me profit from the markets. A classic example occurred when François Mitterrand, a self-proclaimed socialist, won a surprise victory in the 1981 French presidential election. In his campaign, Mitterrand had promised to nationalize segments of industry and to introduce massive social welfare programs. I understood that the economic implications of Mitterrand's programs would spell disaster for the French franc. I immediately sold the franc, which was then trading at approximately a four-to-one exchange rate to the dollar. I covered that position a mere three weeks later when the franc was trading at six to one to the dollar. In my view, that trade was about as close as you can get to a sure thing. Incidentally, the franc eventually sank to a ten-to-one rate against the dollar.

**Probably your best-publicized market call was a prediction for a major top in the stock market, which you made in *Barron's* in September 1987—one month before the crash. What made you so confident about an impending collapse in stock prices?**

At the August 1987 high, the stock market had gained nearly 23 percent in ninety-six days. These figures were almost exactly in line with the historical medians for the magnitude and duration of intermediate bull market moves. This consideration was only a cautionary note. If all the other factors were positive, then fine. However, to recall an analogy I used earlier, this market was no Jack LaLanne. In August, the Dow Jones Industrial index made a new high, but the advance/decline ratio did not—a bearish divergence. The price/earnings ratio at the time was at its highest level in twenty-five years. Government, corporate, and consumer debt were at record levels. Virtually any indicator you looked at was screaming caution against the possibility of an impending collapse.

**Were you short going into the October 19 crash? If so, what considerations did you use to actually time your entry into the market?**

The first major timing signal came on October 5, when I read Fed Chairman Greenspan's comment in the *Wall Street Journal,* in which he was quoted as saying that interest rates could become "dangerously high" if inflation fears were to "mushroom" in the financial markets. Although Greenspan indicated that he felt such concerns were unwarranted, he also hinted that the discount rate might have to be raised to alleviate such worries. On October 15, Dow Theory gave a sell signal, and I initiated my short position.

The straw that broke the camel's back was Secretary of State James Baker's dispute with Germany, in which he urged Germany to stimulate its economy. When Germany refused to cooperate, Baker made a weekend announcement that the United States was prepared to "let the dollar slide." In my opinion, there's no doubt that this statement was the trigger for the October 19 stock market collapse. An unknown devaluation of a currency is not something that any foreign investor wants to live with. What does "slide" mean? Five percent? Ten percent? Twenty percent? How much are you going to let it slide? Investors who hold dollar-denominated securities are going to sell until they know what "slide" means.

At that point, I was absolutely convinced that the stock market was going to collapse because of this unknown dollar devaluation. On Monday morning, I immediately added to my short position, even though the Dow Jones index opened over 200 points lower.

**I know that you also caught the October 1989 minicrash. Was the analysis process similar to that in October 1987?**

Very much so. In October 1989, the market had been up for 200 days without an intermediate downtrend [by Sperandeo's definition, a decline of fifteen days or longer], versus a historical median of 107 days. Moreover, the market was up over 24 percent, and my historical studies had shown that seven out of eight times when the market was up by that amount, a correction eventually occurred that carried prices back below that point. In other words, the odds for the market continuing to move higher were very low. Consequently, I was out of longs and very attuned to signs that the market was ready to die. Statistically, this market was like an eighty-seven-year-old.

**Any final words?**

Being involved in this business requires tremendous dedication and desire. However, you shouldn't make trading your whole life. You have to take time off. You need to spend time with loved ones. You need to balance your life.

When I did my exhaustive study on historical stock trends, my daughter, Jennifer, was in her preschool years. That's a critical age for the child in terms of development and a wonderful age for parents to enjoy their children. Unfortunately, I was so involved with my project that when I came home from work, I would eat and immediately head for my study. When my daughter wandered into my office, I had no time to share with her. It was a mistake that I regret to this day.

Some traders make this business their entire life and, as a result, they may make more money, but at the expense of living a more rounded, balanced, and satisfying life.

---

One way or another, it all comes down to odds. Unless you can find some way to get the odds in your favor, trading, like any other 50/50 game with a cost to play (commissions and execution slippage in this case), will eventually be a losing proposition. Sperandeo has taken the definition of odds to an actuarial-like extreme. Just as insurance companies guarantee that the odds are in their favor by classifying policyholders according to risk, Sperandeo categorizes the stock market by risk. When it comes to the stock market, he can tell the difference between a twenty-year-old and an eighty-year-old.

Another somewhat related element behind Sperandeo's success is that he varies his bet size considerably. When he implements a position in a market that he perceives to be in the beginning stages of a new trend and various indicators confirm the trade, he will tend to trade much larger than in situations where these conditions are lacking. In this way, Sperandeo places his largest bet when he estimates that the odds are most favorable. (Incidentally, this strategy is essentially the key to success in games such as blackjack; see the Hull interview.) Sperandeo emphasizes, however, that when trading large, it is essential that the market go immediately in your favor; otherwise, the position should be pared down quickly. This measure is essential to ensure financial survival when you are wrong in a situation that you thought was highly favorable.

While his view is hardly universal, Sperandeo downplays the significance of intelligence to trading success. Based on his experience in training thirty-eight traders, Sperandeo concluded that intelligence was virtually irrelevant in predicting success. A far more important trait to winning as a trader, he says, is the ability to admit mistakes. He points out that people who tie their self-esteem to being right in the markets will find it very difficult to take losses when the market action indicates that they are wrong.

One sacred cow that Sperandeo believes is really a bum steer is the standard advice to use a buy-and-hold strategy in the stock market. Sperandeo provides some examples of very extended periods in which such a strategy would have been disastrous.

# PART V

# *Multiple-Market Players*

# Tom Basso

## MR. SERENITY

To be frank, Tom Basso was not on my list of interview subjects for this book. Although his track record is solid, it is by no means striking. As a stock account manager, he has averaged 16 percent annually since 1980, approximately 5 percent above the S&P 500 return. Quite respectable, considering that the majority of managers underperform the index, but still not the stuff of legends. As a futures fund manager, Basso has averaged 20 percent annually since 1987 with only moderate volatility. Here, too, the results are significantly better than the industry average, but hardly extraordinary. And yet, in an important sense, Basso is perhaps the most successful trader I have interviewed. To paraphrase a recent commercial, how do you spell success? If your answer is M-O-S-T B-U-C-K-S, then Basso doesn't make the grade. If, however, your answer is G-O-O-D B-U-C-K-S, G-R-E-A-T L-I-F-E, then Basso has few peers.

When I first met Basso, I was immediately struck by his incredible ease about trading. He has learned to accept losses in trading not only in an intellectual sense but on an emotional level as well. Moreover, his feelings of exuberance about trading (or, for that matter, about life) bubble right out of him. Basso has managed to be a profitable trader while apparently maintaining complete peace of mind and experiencing great joy. In this sense, I can't think of a more worthy role model for a trader. I knew within minutes of meeting Basso that he was someone I wanted to include in this book. I also realized that my method of selecting interview subjects strictly on the basis of numbers was a somewhat myopic approach.

Basso started out as an engineer for Monsanto Company. He found that this job didn't fully absorb his energies, and he began dabbling in the investment field. His first foray into the financial markets was a commodity (futures) account, which proved to be an immediate disaster. Although it took many years before Basso was able to trade futures profitably, he persisted until he finally succeeded.

In 1980, he began managing equity accounts as an outgrowth of an involvement in an investment club. In 1984 he expanded his management scope to include futures accounts as well. The small size of most of these futures accounts (many as small as $25,000) resulted in excessive volatility. Basso realized that in order to reduce volatility to a reasonable level while still maintaining adequate diversification, he would have to drastically raise his minimum account size. In 1987, he raised his minimum to $1 million and returned the funds of all clients with smaller accounts. Today, he continues to manage both stock and futures accounts.

Basso and I met at a psychology investment seminar run by Dr. Van Tharp and Adrienne Toghraie. The seminar was held in the somewhat unlikely locale of Newark, New Jersey. The interview was conducted over lunch at a local diner.

---

**One of the things that immediately struck me about you is that you have this aura of incredible relaxation—almost bliss—about your trading. It's the antithesis of the mental state people typically associate with traders. Have you always had this attitude about trading?**

Not at all. I still remember my first trade. In 1975, I opened a commodity account for $2,000. I bought two corn contracts and immediately lost $600. My stomach was turning. I couldn't concentrate on my work. (I was an engineer in those days.) I called my broker every hour.

**Do you remember your motivation for that trade?**

I put on the trade because of a rather naive study I did in which I found that a certain very infrequent chart pattern had been followed by a price advance 100 percent of the time. Several years ago I heard you give a speech in which you talked about "the well-chosen example." I laughed to myself when I heard you use that phrase because it reminded me of my first trade, which was the epitome of the well-chosen example.

[The well-chosen example Basso is referring to represents one of my pet peeves. The basic contention is that virtually any system ever invented can be made to look great if one simply illustrates the approach by selecting the historical market that proved most favorable for the particular method. I first became aware of this concept in the mid-1980s, when I read an article on a simple, fully disclosed trading system. At that time I was working on a rather complex system of my own. To my shock and dismay, this very simple system seemed to have outperformed the far more complicated system I had spent so much time developing—at least for the one illustration provided.

I reread the article with greater scrutiny. The proposed system consisted of only two conditions. I and Norman Strahm, my partner in system development at the time who did all our programming, had tested one of the conditions before. We knew it to be a net winning, albeit only moderately performing, trading rule. The other condition was a rule that we considered to have such a poor prospect of success that we never even bothered testing it. However, if the system described in the article were really that good, its superiority had to come from including this second condition—a trading rule we had dismissed out of hand.

Naturally, we tested this second condition. Its performance for the market illustrated in the article was exactly as indicated. However, the time period selected for the example just happened to be the single best year in a ten-year test period for that market. In fact, it was the single best year for any of the twenty-five markets we tested for that ten-year period. No wonder the system had appeared to be that good—we were looking at the single best case out of the 250 possible market and year combinations we tested. What a coincidence! I'm sure hindsight had nothing to do with it.

But that's not the end of the story. The system did dismally in the remainder of the test sample. In fact, for the ten-year period tested, seventeen out of twenty-five markets actually lost money once transaction costs were taken into account. Ever since that time, I have had an ingrained sense of skepticism regarding the illustrations used in trading system articles and advertisements.]

**Do you believe that most of the people who sell trading systems using these well-chosen examples know better? Or are they really fooling themselves—as you admittedly did in your first trade?**

I think it's probably a bit of both. Some people are just selling garbage and they know it, while others are kidding themselves—they believe they have something that's worthwhile, but they really don't. This type of self-delusion occurs frequently, because it's psychologically comforting to construct a system that looks very good in its past performance. In their desire to achieve superior past performance, system developers often define system conditions that are unrealistically restrictive. The problem is that the future never looks exactly like the past. As a result, these well-chosen models fall apart when they're traded in the future.

After my years of experience in the markets, I now try to keep my models as flexible as I possibly can. I try to imagine scenarios that would almost make good movie plots. As an example, the U.S. government falls, causing the Treasury to default on its T-bill obligations and the U.S. dollar to drop by 50 percent overnight.

**How can you possibly design systems that can cope with those types of extreme situations?**

I don't necessarily design systems that will cope with those situations, but I mentally live through what will happen to my positions, given one of these scenarios.

**How does that help?**

It helps prepare me for all the different market conditions that can arise. Therefore, I know what I'll do in any given situation.

**In your description of your first trade, you come across as being filled with tension and anxiety. How did you go from that mind-set to your current extraordinarily relaxed attitude?**

I realized that every time I had a loss, I needed to learn something from the experience and view the loss as tuition at the College of Trading. As long as you learn something from a loss, it's not really a loss.

**When did you adopt that mental attitude?**

Very early; probably right after the corn trade.

**Did it help?**

Definitely. By adopting that perspective, I stopped looking at the losses as problems and started viewing them as opportunities to elevate myself to the next plateau. Over the next five years, I gradually improved and lost less each year.

**After losing money for five consecutive years from your start in trading, didn't you ever think that you might not be cut out for this endeavor?**

No, never.

**What gave you the confidence? You obviously weren't getting any reinforcement from the market.**

My reinforcement came when my losses gradually became smaller and smaller. I was getting very close to the breakeven point. I also kept my losses at a manageable level. I always traded a very small account—an amount that I could afford to lose without affecting my life-style.

**Did you stop trading when you lost whatever amount of money you had set aside to risk in a given year?**

That never happened. I had developed the concept of never taking a trade that would jeopardize my ability to continue trading. I always limited the risk on any trade to a level that I knew would permit me to come in and play the game again if I were wrong.

**What lessons stand out most vividly from the period during which you attended your so-called College of Trading?**

An absolutely pivotal experience occurred in 1979, about four years after I had started trading. My parents, who lived in Syracuse, New York, came in for a week-long visit. I was busy playing tour guide and fell behind in my work. Unbeknownst to me, that same week, silver broke out violently on the upside. The next week, I updated my work and discovered I had missed a buy signal in silver.

**Were you trading a system at the time?**

Yes. I was following a specific system and had taken every trade for nine months straight. In other words, there's no question that I would have taken the trade had I updated my work. Over the next few months, silver skyrocketed. The end of the story is that missing that single trade meant an opportunity loss of $30,000 profit per contract.

**What was your trading account size at the time?**

It was very small—about $5,000. So that trade would have meant an approximate sixfold increase in the account size. From that point on, no matter what system I was using, I always made certain that I would take all the trading signals.

**Were any other trades pivotal in shaping your overall trading approach?**

In 1987 my wife and I had an account that, at the time, had an equity level of about $130,000. We were long several contracts of silver when the market exploded. We watched the account go up by about $500,000 in one month and then surrender 80 percent of that profit in only a week.

That trade taught me a lot about my own stomach lining. When your account has these massive swings up and down, there's a tendency to feel a rush when the market is going your way and devastation when it's going against you. These emotions do absolutely nothing to make you a good trader. It's far better to keep the equity swings manageable and strive for a sense of balance each day, no matter what happens. That trade was the catalyst for my adopting a formula that limited both my profits and drawdowns by notching back the number of contracts traded in each market to a tolerable level. The key is that the number of contracts traded fluctuates in accordance with each market's volatility.

**Getting back to my first question, can you explain how you manage such a composed attitude in trading the markets?**

When I come to work each day, I know that the risk and volatility in my portfolio is exactly the same as it was yesterday, last week, and last month. So why should I let my emotions go up and down if I'm in exactly the same exposure all the time?

**I assume that being able to have that attitude requires great confidence in your system.**

It's a matter of both having confidence and being comfortable in the approach you're using. For example, if I gave you my exact system, I'm sure that within a month you would be making changes to fit your own ideas. For one reason or another, you probably wouldn't be comfortable with what I gave you. It would be even worse if I gave you the system as a black box [a computer program that generates buy and sell signals based on undisclosed rules]. That would drive you crazy. Since you wouldn't have any idea what went into the program, the first time the system had a losing streak, you would probably abandon it altogether. You would say, "Tom may be a nice guy, but how do I know he just didn't develop this system off of some well-chosen examples?"

**That is precisely the reason why I believe people almost invariably fail to make money on trading systems they buy. Even if they are lucky enough to purchase a system that works, they almost never have the confidence to stay with the system when it hits its first major drawdown period—and every system in the world will have a drawdown.**

I couldn't agree more.

**What would you say to the trader who says, "I'm making money overall, and I'm using stops to limit my losses, but I still have a lot of anxiety about trading. I still can't stand to lose."?**

I would tell that trader to think of each trade as one of the next one thousand trades he's going to make. If you start thinking in terms of the next one thousand trades, all of a sudden you've made any single trade seem very inconsequential. Who cares if a particular trade is a winner or a loser? It's just another trade.

**Do you do any mental exercises to relax, or is that not necessary now that you're fully computerized?**

I probably do more mental exercises now than I ever did. Each morning while I'm driving to work, I make a conscious effort to relax. I mentally rehearse any conflict that might happen that day. The process of mentally organizing and relaxing before I get to work helps me start my day in a very positive frame of mind.

**In effect, are you visualizing all possible crises or tensions that might occur and how you would respond to them, so that if they do arise, they're not stressful?**

Exactly.

**Can you give me an example in which that mental attitude was put to the test of fire?**

A good example is the recent Gulf War. On the evening of January 16, 1991 [the night the United States launched the air war against Iraq], I had come into the office to do some computer work. While I was there, the news of the war broke, and crude oil prices shot up to $40. I happened to have a substantial long position at the time. My first thought was ...

**"We're going to have a great day tomorrow."**

Actually, I think my most immediate thought was, "We're going to have a lot of volatility and risk control alarms going off tomorrow, and we better be prepared." I called our managing director, George, at home to make sure he was aware of the situation.

He said, "I know, it's on all three networks. I'll be in early."

The next morning, I was drying my hair after coming out of the shower, while my wife was watching the news in the next room. I thought I heard the newscaster say that crude oil prices were at $22. Of course, I couldn't believe the number. I thought to myself, "Was that $42? Or maybe $32?" I walked into the bedroom and asked my wife, "Did he say $22?"

"I'm sorry," she said, "I didn't hear it."

I waited for the story to come back on and found that the price was indeed $22. I called up George and asked him, "Did you see the news? We're really going to have our work cut out for us this morning."

We both got in early, ran all the programs, worked out all our risk alarms, and called in all the orders before the openings. We did everything we had planned to do. By 9:30, everything was done—all our orders had been placed, we had received our execution prices, and we had our new position balances figured out. I sat back, let out a sigh of relief, and asked George, "What do you think we lost on this today?"

"I would guess about 15 percent," he answered.

"Yeah, I would guess about the same amount," I said.

I sat there for a moment and thought about all the events and actions of the previous evening and that morning. I realized that there was not a single thing I would have done differently. Despite having just lost 15 percent in our portfolios overnight, I felt phenomonally good at that point.

**Because you had done everything that you were supposed to do?**

Exactly.

**When you went to sleep the night before, was the market still trading above $40?**

Yes.

**Did you assume it was still going to be up the next morning?**

Sure.

**It must have been a great shock then to discover that crude oil prices had gone from being up $8 the night before to being down $10 the next morning. What were your gut emotions when you real-**

ized that your profits of the previous evening had suddenly been transformed into a gargantuan one-day loss?

I wondered how my programs were going to deal with the volatility in crude oil going from $1,000 per day [per contract] to $18,000 per day. I was both excited and horrified at the thought of how my programs would handle the situation. I hoped that I had done a good job in preparing for a catastrophic event.

**But on the inside, didn't you have any hurt or depressed feelings?**

No, I was more curious.

**That is exactly the attitude I find so fascinating. Your portfolios went from being up sharply the night before to a 15 percent loss the next morning. Most people would have some very negative emotions in that type of situation. How were you able to respond with such emotional aloofness?**

You have to put it into perspective. I'm fond of thinking of trading in terms of scores of years. If I live long enough, I'll trade for fifty or sixty years. I figure that, over that time span, I'll see devastating declines, spectacular advances that I virtually can't believe, and everything in between. If you have done mental rehearsals to see how you would react in different catastrophic situations, then when such an event occurs, you become curious.

**Curious to see if you're going to follow your mental rehearsal?**

Exactly. You feel like you've already seen this movie once before, and you wonder whether it's going to come out the same way.

**How do you handle such situations in your mental rehearsal?**

My mental rehearsal for a catastrophic event is to picture a doctor in a triage situation. He's in a battlefield emergency operating room. In come fifty bodies. Some are going to live; some are going to die. The doctor has been trained to handle the situation. He's going to make all the necessary decisions. "This patient goes to operating room number one." "This patient gets pushed aside." He's calm and collected, not nervous. He knows that he has the best chance of saving the maximum number of lives. He knows that he can't save them all, but he's going to do the best he can with what he has.

**You just stay focused on what you have to do.**

Exactly.

**Does that focus actually shut out any negative emotions that might arise?**

Who knows? You don't really think about it at that point. You don't get thrilled at the gains either.

**Actually, being thrilled about the gains isn't so desirable. One trader described the emotional flux to me as follows: "When I'm losing money, I'm upset because I'm losing. When I'm making money, I'm anxious because I worry that I won't be able to keep it up."**

I liken emotions in trading to a spring, with emotions being stretched up and down, up and down. While it's going up and down, it's kind of thrilling, but eventually the spring wears out. Burnout sets in, and you realize that maybe it isn't so much fun to be on this emotional roller coaster. You find that if you can just keep your emotions in balance in the middle, it's actually a whole lot more fun.

**How do you achieve that balance?**

I focus my total attention on trading well, and let the results take care of themselves.

**It sounds almost as if you're viewing yourself from the outside, completely detached.**

When I was in high school I had an extreme fear of getting up in front of the class and talking. My knees would literally tremble. I eventually learned to deal with the situation by disassociating and observing myself. I was able to have this observer show up in times of stress. When I found myself shaking, my observer would say, "Why are you shaking, Tom? Just relax. You're talking too fast. Slow down a little bit."

Eventually, I found that the observer was there all the time. If you're watching yourself doing everything, you get pretty close to watching a movie. The observer is watching you play a role in this movie called *Life*.

**Is this advice that you give to people in general—try to be an observer of yourself?**

Absolutely. I couldn't recommend it more. If instead of saying, "I'm going to do this trade," you say, "I'm going to watch myself do this trade," all of a sudden you find that the process is a lot easier.

**How does having this observer help your trading?**

The observer is able to say, "You're getting greedy on this trade, watch out." You might be straining and struggling because some of your indicators are bullish and some are bearish, and you don't know what to do. The observer might say, "How about doing nothing? You don't have to trade."

This concept is something I would recommend not only for trading but for life in general. There's no reason why you have to struggle and strain and claw your way through life.

**But if you're observing your life, you're not living it. It sounds so detached.**

That's what a lot of people think, but it's not like that at all. Think of life as a movie in which you'll see what you're seeing right now only one time. You'll never see it exactly the same way again. Absorb it; be aware of it; enjoy it.

**What advice would you have for people who feel stressed out?**

First, keep things in perspective. The universe is overwhelming. It was here before you were born, and it will be here after you die. In the general scheme of things, your problems are not that important. Also, it helps if you view your life as a movie. If you go to a video store and rent a horror movie, you're voluntarily letting yourself be horrified, and it's not stressful because deep down you know it's just a movie. What if you had the same attitude about life?

**Earlier you mentioned that you envisioned yourself trading for about fifty or sixty years. Do you really expect to continue trading all the way through old age? Have you ever considered an earlier retirement once you reach some specified monetary goal?**

Actually, I briefly toyed with the idea of retirement several years ago. My wife asked, "What would you do if you retired?"

"Well, I would set up my computers and quote screen at the house," I answered. "I would do some trading and spend most of the time on research developing new systems. I would take some time each morning to read the *Wall Street Journal* and other financial periodicals."

My wife listened patiently and said, "That sounds exactly like what you're doing right now. The only difference is that now you have a staff to back you up when you want to go on vacation."

Of course, she was right. I realized that I was really doing what I loved to do and would be doing it anyway if I were retired.

**Your trading approach is obviously heavily computerized. Is it entirely mechanical or do you still make some discretionary decisions when entering trades?**

My intuitive feelings about the markets are probably right more often than they are wrong. However, having observed myself as I do, I notice that sometimes the trading signals that I'm intuitively most nervous about turn out to be the best trades. Therefore, over the long run, I think my performance is best served by following my systems unquestioningly.

There's another aspect to why I prefer a purely systematized approach. I find that using systems gets the monkey off your back. If you lose money today, it's not your fault; it's the system that had the problem. There is an element of disassociation involved. Even though you designed the system, you start taking losses less personally. At least that's what happened to me. Once I was fully computerized, I found that I was less and less emotionally involved in each trade.

I now have much more time available to pursue a variety of work projects and personal interests because I'm not tied to a quote machine watching every tick go up and down. In the process, life has become much more fun.

**If you were starting out as a trader today, knowing what you know now, what would you do differently than the first time around?**

I started out by worrying about the system I was going to use to trade. The second factor I worked on was risk management and volatility control. The third area I focused on was the psychology of trading. If I had it to do over again, I would reverse the process completely. I think investment psychology is by far the most important element, followed by risk control, with the least important consideration being the question of where you buy and sell.

---

If there is a single theme that keeps recurring in this volume, as it did in *Market Wizards,* it is that psychology is critical to success at trading. Certainly this idea is repeated strongly in the Basso interview. However, there is a more important lesson here: In order to achieve success in life, you must have the right mental attitude, without which success in trading is a Pyrrhic victory.

If trading (or any other job or endeavor) is a source of anxiety, fear, frustration, depression, or anger, something is wrong—even if you are successful in a conventional sense, and especially if you are not. You have to enjoy trading, because if trading is a source of negative emotions, you have probably already lost the game, even if you make money.

Basso is far from being the most successful trader I have interviewed in terms of performance statistics, but he is probably one of the first I would choose as a role model. Essentially, adopting such a model implies the following prescription: Combine your enthusiasm, energy, focus, devotion, and discipline to becoming the best trader you can be, but once you have done that, there is no point in agonizing over the details. Maintain the perspective of viewing unfolding market events as you would view a movie. Don't worry about the adverse market moves if you've got it right in a long-term sense. And if you haven't yet developed a fully sound approach, then learn from your losses and view them as tuition for trading lessons (always making sure you never risk more than you can afford to lose).

Basso's advice to view your life as a movie may sound passive on the printed page, but that is not the feeling that comes across on a personal level. Basso is suggesting that you enjoy and experience your life with the same involvement and intensity you would an engrossing movie, but at the same time, maintain the sense of perspective you would have if you were watching a movie. Don't take your problems too personally. The universe will still be there tomorrow.

# *Linda Bradford Raschke*

## READING THE MUSIC OF THE MARKETS

L inda Bradford Raschke is so serious about trading that she traded right through the last day of her pregnancy. "You didn't trade while you were in labor?" I asked her half-jokingly. "Well, no," she said, "but then again, it was four A.M. and the markets weren't open. I did, however, put on a trade about three hours after I gave birth to my daughter. I was short some currency contracts that were expiring that day. It seemed like such a good trade that I couldn't bring myself to give up the opportunity of rolling the position over into the next contract month." As I said, Linda Raschke is very serious about her trading.

Raschke knew that she wanted to be involved in the markets from an early age. When she was unable to land a job as a stockbroker after graduating from college, she got into the routine of hanging out on the floor of the Pacific Coast Stock Exchange every morning before work. Although the driving motivation for her daily visits to the exchange floor was her fascination with the markets, this routine eventually led to an opportunity to become a trader. One of the exchange locals befriended Raschke and taught her the basics of options. Impressed by Raschke's enthusiasm and quick ability to grasp market concepts, he provided her with a trading stake.

Raschke spent six years as a floor trader, initially at the Pacific Coast Stock Exchange and then at the Philadelphia Stock Exchange.

With the exception of one catastrophic event early in her trading career, Raschke made money steadily as a floor trader.

In late 1986, when injuries suffered in an accident forced Raschke to trade from an office, she discovered that she much preferred off-the-floor trading. Thereafter, she set up her trading office at home. Although many floor traders who try to make the transition to office trading encounter major difficulties in the first year of the changeover, Raschke's first year off the floor was actually her best ever. She continued to be a consistently profitable trader in subsequent years.

When I first met Linda Raschke, I was impressed by her ebullient demeanor. I was shocked when she told me that she was suffering from Epstein-Barr Syndrome—a malady whose hallmark symptom is chronic loss of energy. "What you don't know," she said, "is that I have spent the better part of the past four days resting to build up enough energy to make this trip." (Although I had offered to travel to her home to do the interview, Raschke wanted an excuse to make a day trip to New York.) Even so, I could hardly imagine what she must be like when she is fully healthy.

Raschke believes that she contracted her ailment because she had just pushed herself too far—simultaneously trading full-time, taking care of an infant, dealing with hordes of workers as her home was being remodeled, and actively pursuing her hobby of training and riding horses. Raschke even manages to be upbeat about her illness. "I feel a tremendous amount of good has come out of this," she explains. "Instead of trying to cram in everything before I turn thirty-five, I now realize that at thirty-three I'm still really young and that I have many years of great opportunities ahead of me."

The first few hours of the interview were conducted at my office. We then continued our conversation at a local Wall Street area restaurant. I kept eyeing my watch and hastening our conversation along throughout dinner, because I was aware that missing her next scheduled bus home would mean a four-hour wait. Although Raschke seemed relaxed and unconcerned, I didn't want to be responsible for her being stranded at Port Authority Bus Terminal for that length of time. There are far better places to spend four hours (a Turkish prison, to name only one).

**When did you first get involved with the markets?**

My father loved to trade the markets, although he never made any money at it. Being the oldest of four children, I was enlisted to help him leaf through hundreds of stock charts, looking for some specific types of patterns. My first real involvement in the markets came when I attended Occidental College. The school had a program wherein ten students were selected each year to manage a trust set up by an anonymous donor.

**What did you know about the markets at that time?**

Not much. We made decisions based almost strictly on fundamentals. Anyone in the group could come up with an idea, and it would be implemented if approved by the majority.

**What did you learn from that experience?**

I just learned that it was an awful lot of fun.

**Did you get a market-related job after finishing college?**

After graduating college, I went up to San Francisco to try to find a job as a stockbroker. I must have applied to every brokerage firm in the city, and I was turned down by all of them. They didn't take me seriously. To them, I was just a young kid who had graduated college. I was repeatedly told to come back in four or five years. I finally ended up taking a job as a financial analyst with Crown Zellerbach, a paper company.

As fate would have it, my office was only two blocks away from the Pacific Coast Stock Exchange. Since I didn't have to be at work until 8:30 and the exchange opened at 7:30, I started spending the first hour of my day at the exchange.

**What did you do there?**

I just watched what was going on. After a while, people noticed I was there, and some of them went out of their way to explain things. One trader explained the pricing of options to me, and I thought, "Gee, I can do that." It didn't sound like such a big deal. The truth is that once you get down on the trading floor, you find that the traders come from all walks of life. You don't have to be a rocket scientist to be a trader. In fact, some of the best traders whom I knew down on the floor were surf bums. Formal education didn't really seem to have much to do with a person's skill as a trader.

**How did your transition from observer to participant come about?**

The person who had explained the basics of the options market to me thought that I would make a good trader and offered to back me. At the time, I was applying to graduate schools to get an M.B.A. I thought to myself, "I can either go to business school to get my M.B.A., or I can trade on the floor of the stock exchange—hmm, which do I want to do?" It wasn't a hard decision.

**On what basis was he willing to back you as a trader?**

What has impressed me about other people whom I have ended up training or backing is their level of interest. If someone has a strong enough interest or desire, it usually overcomes other obstacles. I think he was impressed with my interest in the markets.

**How big a stake did he give you?**

As was standard procedure for traders backing other traders, we set up a partnership, in which I was the general partner and he was the limited partner. He put up $25,000, with the agreement calling for a 50/50 split of the profits.

**How were you making your trading decisions?**

I would just buy options that were underpriced or sell options that were overpriced and hedge the positions with other options or stock.

**Wasn't it difficult for you as a novice to be competing with more experienced brokers trying to do the same types of trades?**

No, the options market was just incredibly inefficient in the early 1980s. You didn't really need an IQ over 100 to make money. After my first three months, I had made about $25,000.

Around that time, I got involved in selling calls on Cities Service, because the options were overpriced. And why were they overpriced? Because the stock was a takeover candidate.

**Did you know that at the time?**

Oh sure.

**But did you know how to factor that situation into the price?**

I thought that I did. At the time, the stock was trading at $32. At the prices at which I was able to sell the options, I knew I would be okay as long as the stock price didn't go above $55. Unfortunately, the takeover was announced the afternoon before the options expired, and the stock jumped from about $34 to $65. Suddenly, I discovered that you could lose $80,000 overnight.

**So overnight you lost all your profits and your initial stake, and you were still in the hole for $30,000. Who was responsible to make up that deficit?**

I was, since I was the general partner.

**Do you remember your emotional response at the time?**

It wasn't so bad emotionally, because I had seen other traders around me lose much greater amounts in sudden takeover situations. They were able to survive after taking hits of several million dollars. In comparison, my situation didn't seem that extreme. Also, I felt that in any business where you could lose money that quickly, you had to be able to make it back.

**It almost sounds as if you were able to shrug it off.**

I don't want to make light of this experience, because it was intimidating being faced with a mountain of debt at the age of twenty-two. In fact, I still had $10,000 in debt left over from college student loans. Fortunately, I was able to find another backer, and everything worked out. Overcoming that experience gave me the confidence that I could overcome anything that might happen in the future.

**How did you do after that point?**

I made money steadily.

**What made you decide to abandon floor trading for trading from an office?**

In late 1986, I had a bad horse riding accident. I fractured my ribs, punctured my lung, and dislocated my shoulder. I found it physically very uncomfortable to stand on the floor. That was the first time I started sitting upstairs and trading off a quote machine. I thought it was great! There were all these indicators and different markets I could watch at the same time. Over time, I evolved my own trading style in the S&P futures.

**What is your trading style?**

My niche is short-term trading, which is how I make my bread and butter. The occasional long-term trades are frosting on the cake. I believe that only short-term price swings can be predicted with any precision. The accuracy of a prediction drops off dramatically, the more distant the forecast time. I'm a strong believer in chaos theory.

[A basic concept of chaos theory is that for aperiodic systems—i.e., systems that never exactly repeat themselves and hence never find a steady state, such as weather or the markets—slight differences in variable values or measurements can be magnified to have huge effects over increasing periods of time. The technical name for this phenomenon—sensitive dependence on initial conditions—has become better known as the Butterfly Effect. As James Gleick described it in his excellent book, *Chaos: Making a New Science,* "In weather, for example, this translates into what is only half-jokingly known as the Butterfly Effect—the notion that a butterfly stirring the air today in Peking can transform storm systems next month in New York."]

There are too many unpredictable things that can happen within two months. To me, the ideal trade lasts ten days, but I approach every trade as if I'm only going to hold it two or three days.

I'm also a firm believer in predicting price direction, but not magnitude. I don't set price targets. I get out when the market action tells me it's time to get out, rather than based on any consideration of how far the price has gone. You have to be willing to take what the market gives you. If it doesn't give you very much, you can't hesitate to get out with a small profit.

I put a great deal of effort into getting the best entry price possible. I feel this is probably one of my strongest skills. In day trading, a good entry price is critical because it buys you time to see how the market will react. If you buy because you think the market should bounce, but it only goes sideways, you'd better get out. Part of the trading process is a matter of testing the water. If your entry timing is good enough, you won't lose much even when you're wrong.

Some of the best trades come when everyone gets very panicky. The crowd can often act very stupidly in the markets. You can picture price fluctuations around an equilibrium level as a rubber band being stretched—if it gets pulled too far, eventually it will snap back. As a short-term trader, I try to wait until the rubber band is stretched to its extreme point.

**How do you determine when the market is near such an extreme?**

One of my favorite patterns is the tendency for the markets to move from relative lows to relative highs and vice versa every two to four days. This pattern is a function of human behavior. It takes several days of a market rallying before it looks really good. That's when everyone wants to buy it, and that's the time when the professionals, like myself, are selling. Conversely, when the market has been down for a few days, and everyone is bearish, that's the time I like to be buying.

I also track different indicators. I don't think the specific choice of indicators is that critical, as long as you have a good feel for interpreting the indicators that you use. Personally, I pay close attention to the tick [the difference between the number of issues whose most recent tick was up and those whose most recent tick was down], TRIN [a measure that relates the price and volume of advancing issues to the corresponding figures for declining issues], and premium [the premium, or discount, of stock index futures to the theoretically equivalent cash index price]. For example, if the tick is at an extreme level and falling— –480, –485, –490, –495—and then just pauses—–495, –495, –495— and the other indicators I watch are also oversold, I'll often go in and buy at the market. Sometimes, I've actually bought the low tick of the day using this method.

I really have no fear of buying into breaks or selling into rallies. Sure, once in a while the market will keep on going, and I'll immediately be down a full point or more on the S&P. However, by waiting for a sufficient extreme, even in such situations, the market will often snap back enough to let me out near even. Perhaps my number one rule is: Don't try to make a profit on a bad trade, just try to find the best place to get out.

**So when you have a bad trade, you don't dump it immediately.**

That's right. I find that I can usually get out at a better price if I have a little patience, since the reason I got into the trade in the first place was because the market was so overdone that a reaction seemed overdue. Once I'm out, it's easy for me to get back in. If I buy back at a higher price, I just look at it as a fresh trade.

**When did you set up your home trading office?**

About three months after leaving the floor.

**After spending years surrounded by people on the floor, did you find it difficult to adjust to the isolation of trading from home?**

For the first four years, being off the floor was great—no distractions, no outside opinions. Last year, however, the isolation started to really bother me. I got lonely. I tried talking to other traders on the phone during the day, but I found that it was distracting and lowered my productivity. I also tried establishing a trading office with another trader, which worked great for a while until he left to establish a trading operation in New York. And I tried hiring an assistant, but it didn't add to my bottom line.

Now I try to deal with the isolation by scheduling projects outside of the trading day in order to keep me involved with the outside world. I'm a member of the Market Technicians Association and I try to attend every meeting. I have also worked with a programmer to develop neural network trading indicators, which I'm now using as a market tool. [A key characteristic of neural network programs is that they are not static; rather, they evolve as they "learn" from the data.] This project has also led to lots of calls to other people across the country who are working on applying neural networks to trading.

I recognize that isolation has become a problem, and I keep on trying to find different solutions. I think that eventually I might like to have one or two traders sharing my office again.

**Since you're primarily a trader of stock index futures, I'm curious about what your experiences were during the incredible crash of October 1987.**

Ironically, I stopped trading about a month before the crash. I had a phenomenal year up to that point, making more than half a million dollars, which was nearly twice as much as I had made the year before. I couldn't believe how well I was doing. I had caught all the major market swings. I had a feeling that I had just been too hot and shouldn't press my luck anymore. At the same time, I had the opportunity to apprentice with a horse trainer whom I had been working with. I decided that it would be a good time to take a trading hiatus.

**So you weren't involved in the market at the time of the October 1987 crash?**

Not exactly. I had no positions at the start of that week. However, during the period in which I had stopped trading, I called my husband (he's a market maker on the Philadelphia Stock Exchange) each morning to find out what was happening in the markets. When I called him from the stables that morning, he said, "You'd better get home and watch this day! All the world markets have crashed, and it looks like the Dow Jones is going to open 200 points lower!" When I heard that, I thought to myself, "Boy, this is great. This is the buying opportunity I've been waiting for."

I rushed home and turned on the news. Everyone was talking panic,

panic, panic. Silly old contrarian me is thinking, "This is terrific. Let's see how low we can open the market." As you recall, the market kept plummeting all through the day. I had to force myself to hold back from buying. Finally, in the early afternoon, I couldn't wait any longer. I bought one S&P futures contract. In the final hour of trading, I kept on buying, as the market moved lower. By the end of the day, I was long ten contracts.

**When the market closed, were you down for the day?**

Oh sure. The market closed near its lows. I was down about a $100,000.

**Did that bother you?**

No, not really. Of course, I was a little annoyed with myself for not being more patient, because I could have gotten a better average price if I had waited. However, I really wasn't concerned about the initial loss on the position. The futures market was at such a large discount relative to the cash stock index that I was sure it would open higher the next day, which it did.

**Did you get out on the higher opening?**

I took profits on only part of the position. My plan was to stay long. I thought that we had seen such a level of stupidity in the market, with people virtually throwing away stocks that had value, that I felt it just had to be a selling exhaustion point. As one example, I remember when I first went down to the floor of the Philadelphia Stock Exchange, Salomon Brothers stock was trading at $32. It eventually ran up to over $60. Here it was on the day of the crash down to $22. To me, it seemed ridiculous that people were pricing stocks that way.

**You make it sound like you completely shrugged off the panic that engulfed the markets that week.**

I don't think I underestimated the risk of the trade when I bought ten S&P futures on the day of the crash. However, in retrospect, I certainly was naive in having faith that the markets, clearing firms, and banks would continue to function. The subsequent realization that if the Fed had been less aggressive, my clearing firm, along with many others, could have gone bankrupt, obliterating my account equity in the process, really shook me up.

**Does it ever bother you when you lose?**

Not at all. It never bothered me to lose, because I always knew that I would make it right back. I always knew that no matter what happened, I could go into any marketplace, with any amount of money, and make a living.

**Could you describe the mistakes you've made in your trading career that served as learning experiences?**

My own particular weakness has always been being a bit premature on entering positions. As the saying goes, "The pioneers are the ones with the arrows in their backs." I've learned to think to myself, "Patience, patience, patience." I try to wait until things set up just right before I take a trade. Then, when I'm ready to take the trade, I slowly count to ten before I pick up the phone. It's better to have the wrong idea and good timing than the right idea and bad timing.

Another mistake I've frequently made is participating in too many markets at one time, which leads to sloppy trading. I've also found that it's my smallest positions that cause my biggest losses, because they tend to be neglected. It's natural to be cautious and attentive to big positions. With the small positions, it's easy to fall into the trap of being complacent. My awareness of this pitfall has made me more careful with such positions.

I realize that I'm only human, and that I'll always make mistakes. I just try to make them less frequently, recognize them faster, and correct them immediately!

**What percentage of your trades are profitable?**

About 70 percent.

**Is your average winner also larger than your average loser?**

On my short-term trades, on a per contract basis, my average win is about $450 (the figure would be higher if I included longer-term trades), and my average loss is just over $200.

**With both the percentage and average magnitude of your winning trades outdistancing the losers by a better than two-to-one ratio, it sounds like you would be profitable in every month.**

Every month! My philosophy is to try to be profitable every day! Of course, I don't quite achieve that consistency, but that's my goal. I'm probably profitable nearly every week. Remember, I do this for a living, and I use my own money. I really value the fact that I've learned to trade as a craft. Like any craft, such as piano playing, perfection may be elusive—I'll never play a piece perfectly, and I'll never buy the low and sell the high—but consistency is achievable if you practice day in and day out.

**I assume that, in part, your consistency can be attributed to the intensity with which you follow the markets. When you described your trading earlier, it sounded like you virtually followed a market tick by tick. I assume this type of approach must limit the number of markets you can trade. How many markets do you follow at one time?**

It varies. I analyze twenty markets. But at any given time, I trade no more than about six markets. Ideally, I would like to trade every market, every day, but I know that's physically impossible.

**Couldn't you train assistants to apply your methodologies to the markets you can't watch?**

I've tried that. I hired and trained someone for a year. He was the nicest person you could hope to meet. Any organization would have been proud to have him as an employee. He was extremely hardworking and loyal. He was in perfect physical shape—he ate well and practiced karate every day. Emotionally, he was on such an even keel that I never once saw him get angry at anyone.

I put a lot of time and effort into training him. I even gave him his own account, because I thought that the only way he could learn to trade was by doing it. Unfortunately, it didn't work out.

**What went wrong?**

He didn't seem to have any passion for trading. He couldn't pull the trigger. I think he didn't like the idea of taking risks. [Linda describes a typical conversation with her assistant:]

"OK, Steve, what's your game plan for today?"

"I think I'm going to buy wheat today," he says, explaining his reasons for the trade.

"That's great!" I say, trying to encourage him.

At the end of the day, I ask him, "Did you buy the wheat?"

"No," he answers.

"Well, what did you do?"

"I watched it go up."

[She laughs wholeheartedly at the recollection.]

**Why do you believe you have excelled as a trader?**

I believe my most important skill is an ability to perceive patterns in the market. I think this aptitude for pattern recognition is probably related to my heavy involvement with music. Between the ages of five and twenty-one, I practiced piano for several hours every single day. In college, I had a dual major of economics and musical composition. Musical scores are just symbols and patterns. Sitting there for hours every day, analyzing scores, probably helped that part of my brain related to pattern recognition. Also, practicing an instrument for several hours every day helps develop discipline and concentration—two skills that are very useful as a trader.

**Could you elaborate some more on the parallels between music and the markets?**

A musical piece has a definite structure: there are repeating patterns with variations. Analogously, the markets have patterns, which repeat with variations. Musical pieces have quiet interludes, theme development, and a gradual crescendo to a climax. The market counterparts are price consolidations, major trends, and runaway price moves to major tops or bottoms. You must have patience as a musical piece unfolds and patience until a trade sets up. You can practice, practice, practice, but you're never going to play a musical piece perfectly, just as you're never going to buy the low and sell the high on a trade. All you can hope to do is to play a piece (or trade) better than before. In both music and trading, you do best when you're relaxed, and in both you have to go with the flow.

A final analogy may explain the type of trading I've gravitated toward. You must be able to read individual notes and learn a piece of music measure by measure before you can play the whole piece through. Perhaps that's why I spend most of my energy on short-term trades rather than analyzing the long-term picture.

**There are so few full-time women traders. Do you believe there are any obstacles to women trying to get into the field?**

I have sometimes felt that I had to work twice as hard to gain respect or to be taken seriously. But, quite honestly, that perception was probably based on my own beliefs rather than grounded in reality. In retrospect, I don't think that being a woman has ever really hindered me. In fact, if anything, it sometimes seemed that people made an extra effort to be helpful to me, perhaps because there are so few women traders.

Of course, there may be pockets in the industry in which women do encounter barriers—for example, the large New York institutional firms and banks. I have known women who felt that sexism interfered with their ability to land a job on a trading desk. But, again, I have never personally encountered such difficulties.

I would strongly encourage women who have the confidence to become traders to make the effort. There is no reason for women to feel any fears of intimidation. Trading, more than any other field, is a bottom-line business. People look at your performance numbers. They don't care if you're a man or a woman. If you perform well, you'll get financial backing. Conversely, if you're incompetent as a trader, just being a man is certainly not going to help.

Women may also have intrinsic advantages over men as traders. For example, women are less likely to use trading as an ego trip. They aren't prone to making the macho-type trades [putting on a large position with the intent of feeling a sense of power in moving the market], which I have seen lead to the financial ruin of a number of male traders. Even the largest women traders I know tend to be very low-key, almost reserved, as traders.

**Are there any other differences between women and men as traders?**

Women may be more intuitive. I certainly feel that I can see patterns that other people can't, but I don't know if that's because I'm a female. I think it's often more acceptable for a woman to rely on intuition than it is for a man to do so, and intuition certainly comes into play in trading. For example, when I'm watching the price quotes, I never say something like, "Oh, the market is down exactly 62 percent, I have to buy right here." Rather, I might think, "Gee, it looks like we've corrected enough and the price has stopped going down, so I'd better buy."

**In our initial phone conversation, you mentioned that you've shared your trading methods with other traders. Aren't you concerned that revealing your approach could destroy its effectiveness as other people start to use it?**

I truly feel that I could give away all my secrets and it wouldn't make any difference. Most people can't control their emotions or follow a system. Also, most traders wouldn't follow my system, even if I gave them step-by-step instructions, because my approach wouldn't feel right to them. They wouldn't have the same confidence or comfort in the trading method as I do. But for argument's sake, let's say that showing my methods to other traders did eventually cause some of the patterns that I follow to change. If these patterns changed, new ones would be created, and I'm confident that I would find them.

**What advice would you give novice traders?**

Understand that learning the markets can take years. Immerse yourself in the world of trading and give up everything else. Get as close to other successful traders as you can. Consider working for one for free.

Start by finding a niche and specializing. Pick one market or pattern and learn it inside out before expanding your focus. My favorite exercise for novice traders is pick one market only. Without looking at an intraday chart, jot down the price every five minutes from the opening to the close. Do this for an entire week. Be in tune to the patterns. Where are the support and resistance levels? How does price act when it hits these levels? What happens during the last half-hour? How long does each intraday price move last? You won't believe how much you can learn from this exercise.

Never fear the markets. Never fear making a mistake. If you do make a mistake, don't complicate the position by trying to hedge it—just get out.

Stay actively involved with the market. Don't just sit passively in front of a monitor, or simply stare at charts. Notice how many old-timers who have been successful for years still construct their own point-and-figure charts by hand intraday. They keep the same routine day after day. Develop your own routine for taking periodic market readings.

Never be greedy. It's OK to leave money on the table. If you can't get in at a favorable price, let the trade go and start looking for the next trade.

Finally, remember that a trader is someone who does his own work, has his own game plan, and makes his own decisions. Only by acting and thinking independently can a trader hope to know when a trade isn't working out. If you ever find yourself tempted to seek out someone else's opinion on a trade, that's usually a sure sign that you should get out of your position.

### What are your goals?

There's no better satisfaction than playing a piece well, whether the instrument is a piano or the markets. I measure my progress not in dollars but in my skill in predicting market patterns—that is, in how close I can come to pinpointing my entries and exits to the market turns. I believe that I can go into any market with just a quote machine and out-trade 98 percent of the other traders. Over the next ten years, I would like to significantly step up my trading size. I really believe that I can become one of the best traders around.

Certainly one of the primary common characteristics I have found among the great traders is an almost compelling sense of confidence in their ability to succeed. Linda Raschke personifies this type of confidence as well as any trader I have interviewed. There is not the slightest doubt in my mind that she could start over in any market with minimal funds and excel. She truly believes that she will become one of the best traders ever, and I for one certainly wouldn't take the other side of that bet.

Are traders like Raschke confident because they succeed, or do they succeed because they are confident? Probably a little bit of both. However, the key point is that exuberant confidence appears to be one of the essential elements in exceptional achievement as a trader, and I assume in many other endeavors as well.

Occasionally, an interview provokes me to reassess my view of reality. I have long assumed that markets might be predictable over the long term but that short-term price movements are largely random. Raschke holds exactly the opposite point of view. She believes that in the markets, much as in weather forecasting, short-term predictions can be quite accurate but long-term forecasting is a virtual impossibility. With her ability to see patterns that others don't, she has been able to trade short-term price swings with a consistency that would defy the laws of probability, if indeed there were no patterns in these movements. Raschke has made me a believer. Clearly, there are predictable movements in price even over periods as short as a few days or a single day.

Raschke reminds us that traders are people who do their own work, make their own decisions. One particularly insightful observation made by Raschke is that the temptation to seek out other peoples' opinions on a trade is a sure sign that the trade should be liquidated.

Among the characteristics that Linda Bradford Raschke cites as essential to being a good trader are a passion for trading, self-reliance in developing trading ideas and making trading decisions, the willingness to take risk, the ability to correct mistakes immediately (because they are inevitable), and patience, patience, patience.

# PART VI

# *The Money Machines*

# CRT

## THE TRADING MACHINE

Y ou guys make money every day," said the floor broker to Mark
Ritchie in a reference to CRT (Chicago Research and Trading).
His voice was a mixture of envy, disgust, and admiration. He was holding a long position, and the market had moved locked limit-down
against him, in one of the periodic painful setbacks that are a bane to
even successful traders. The amazing thing is that the exasperated broker was exaggerating only slightly. CRT may not make money every
day, but it is profitable virtually every month, if not every week. Think
about that!

The story of CRT is one of the most incredible in the investment
world. A mere fifteen years ago, Joe Ritchie (Mark's brother), the
firm's founder and leading force, was so broke that he had to borrow
his brother's wholesale suit to visit the Chicago Board of Trade. Today,
Joe is the helmsman of a trading company of eight hundred employees,
including a primary dealer of government securities, that has been estimated to have garnered close to $1 billion in trading profits. To gener-
ate that profit, Joe Ritchie estimates that the firm has done over $10 tril-
lion in transactions. (That's trillion like the figures used to describe the
total U.S. debt—we're talking big numbers here.)

CRT doesn't go for home runs. It is in the business of extracting the
many modest profit opportunities that are continually created by the

313

small inefficiencies in the marketplace. Are options on one exchange slightly higher priced than equivalent options on another exchange? If so, CRT uses its state-of-the-art information and execution capabilities to buy the option that is low and sell the one that is dear. Do options in a given market provide a better risk/reward profile than the underlying market? Or vice versa? If such a discrepancy exists, CRT trades one position against the other. There are literally hundreds, if not thousands, of variations on this theme.

CRT is constantly tracking approximately seventy-five different markets, traded on nineteen worldwide exchanges, with sophisticated trading models instantaneously signaling which financial instruments are relatively underpriced and which are overpriced. Other models continuously evaluate the net risk of all the firm's positions, with the goal being to reduce net exposure as close to zero as possible. In taking advantage of these small profit opportunities and keeping net risk to a minimum, CRT has come as close as any firm to creating a successful trading machine.

How does CRT operate? Floor brokers have sheets generated by the firm's proprietary computer models, telling them what price they can bid or offer for each option at any given market price level. The calculated figures take into account not only the matter of determining the option's value but also how that option interrelates with the firm's overall position. For example, if a given option position helps bring the firm's net risk exposure closer to zero, the indicated bid price for that option might be skewed upward.

The floor traders are supported by teams of upstairs traders, who use the firm's computer models to monitor the impact of fluctuating prices and the firm's constantly changing portfolio on option values. The upstairs traders feed the floor traders a constant stream of updated information. On very volatile trading sessions, runners may bring the floor traders revised computer valuation sheets as often as twenty times in one day.

When the floor trader implements an option trade, he or she immediately offsets the positions with an equivalent opposite trade in the outright market. For example, if a trader sells T-bond 98 calls, he will buy the equivalent amount of T-bond futures to counterbalance the position. This hedge is implemented instantaneously. As soon as the floor trader posts the option trade, he hand signals an arbitrage clerk standing on the top step of the bond futures pit fifty feet away. Within a second or two, a futures trader has placed the offsetting order, and the transaction is complete.

The initial hedge placed in the outright market virtually eliminates any significant near-term risk on the position. However, as the market moves, the position will become unbalanced. Once the initial trade and offsetting hedge are booked, the responsibility for managing the position is transferred to an upstairs position manager. The job of this manager is to keep the risk exposure of the firm's constantly changing portfolio as close to zero as possible. CRT is so rigid about risk control that it even has a backup risk control group. The backup group assures that the firm is always ready to handle even the most extraordinary trading events (e.g., the October 1987 stock market crash and huge price moves triggered by the outbreak of the Persian Gulf War).

The complexity of monitoring the positions placed by hundreds of traders, reevaluating thousands of interrelationships between different market instruments traded worldwide, and tracking the firm's portfolio risk balance continuously, all while prices and positions are changing every second, requires enormous computer support. CRT has nearly an entire floor in its office building devoted to computers. There are departments for developing new proprietary software, and the firm even has its own on-site hardware repair unit.

CRT's computer software programs are highly sophisticated. Every effort has been made to translate data into graphic displays, reflecting the belief that the human mind can draw information much more readily if it is in visual form. A new generation of CRT software, which was in an advanced stage of development when I visited the company, provides three-dimensional displays. These computer images will allow the traders to view the firm's real-time position for an option market across both a range of strike prices and a range of expiration dates in one picture, with different colors used to represent different concentrations of positions.

All the high tech aside, ask anyone at CRT about the firm's success, and they will tell you that teamwork is the key. It may sound corny, but it is obviously an absolutely essential element of CRT's philosophy. You either buy into that philosophy or you are in the wrong place. Self-centered maverick traders, no matter how talented, need not apply.

Here is how one former CRT floor trader (who now handles a variety of other roles) describes the advantages of CRT's teamwork approach versus the situation at most other firms:

> If you have the confidence that the person upstairs is not going to blame you, it makes life so much easier. When I worked on the floor, I often saw screaming matches between people trying to make sure the blame didn't get laid on them. The broker would blame the clerk; the clerk would blame the person on the other side of the phone; and the person on the phone would blame the customer. That never happened to me. When a five-hundred-lot order came into the pit, I knew I could use discretion to act on it right away, whereas many of the other traders at competing firms would have to first call upstairs to get permission to do anything more than a fifty-lot.

Another CRT trader echoed a similar theme:

> Our competition has traders in the pit who on expiration day will hand the clerk a $100 bill to give them special attention. I don't have to hand my clerk a $100 bill. I let him know that I believe in him and the company values him. I get better service from my clerk by making him feel that way than that other broker does by handing his clerk a $100 bill.

The teamwork philosophy also extends to compensation. As one employee describes it: "Joe is absolutely committed to sharing the wealth. Instead of thinking about how little he can pay people and get away with it, he seems to be more concerned about how he can split up the profits fairly."

Mark Ritchie gave me my first perfunctory tour of CRT, walking me through the main trading floor. The workspaces appeared very attractive and comfortable. However, something seemed out of place. I thought of those childhood puzzles with the caption "What's wrong with this picture?" When we walked past the receptionist area, Mark was told that he had a phone call holding. While he was on the phone, the nature of the oddity finally struck me. The trading floor was quiet! I mean, you might have thought we had toured the offices of a university or law firm. The shouting, turmoil, activity, anxiety, stress, cheering, swearing, and other assorted noises and emotions that normally permeate a trading floor were all missing.

CRT is a laid-back firm in many ways that go beyond the extraordinary calm in which trades are planned, monitored, and executed. No suits and ties here, unless of course that's your preference. Jeans and sport shirts are the common attire. There is a cafeteria in the center of the trading floor, which is available to all employees—and the food is home-cooked, not the typical cafeteria variety. There is even a lounge area on the floor. Again, not your typical trading operation.

One development that has raised a few eyebrows is CRT's growing relationship with the Mitsubishi Trust and Banking Corporation. On the surface, the informal, entrepreneurial CRT doesn't seem to mesh with the organizational structure of one of the world's major financial institutions and the largest trust bank in Japan. CRT, however, sees this partnership as complementary, blending different product, geographic, and personal strengths.

The following two chapters contain interviews with two of CRT's initial four founding members: Mark Ritchie and Joe Ritchie. Mark actually drifted away from CRT years ago, preferring to trade on his own, unencumbered by additional managerial obligations. Joe's involvement with CRT, however, remains strong. He is still the firm's primary visionary and guiding force, albeit the responsibilities for the day-to-day operation of the firm have been transferred to a senior management team. Although Mark is no longer actively involved with CRT, his interview is placed first, maintaining the order in which the conversations actually transpired.

# *Mark Ritchie*

## GOD IN THE PITS

The subtitle of this chapter is taken from Mark Ritchie's autobiographical book—a highly unusual blend of spiritual revelations, exotic experiences, and trading stories. It certainly does not mean to imply, however, that Ritchie believes he has deity-like trading prowess. On the contrary, the title refers to Ritchie's convictions about the presence of God that he perceives in his life.

It is hard to imagine an educational background further removed from trading—Mark Ritchie attended divinity school. (No, it doesn't help in praying for positions.) While attending school, he barely scraped by, working a variety of part-time jobs such as correctional officer (night-time shift) and truck driver. In those days, he was so poor that when he drove a truck, he sometimes could not even afford to fill the tank. Mark initially got hooked on trading when he accompanied his bother, Joe, on a visit to the Chicago Board of Trade.

Mark spent most of his trading career on the floor of the Chicago Board of Trade, specializing in trading the soybean crush (explained in the interview). Although he was consistently successful as a floor trader, about five years ago he decided to try trading from an office.

Realizing that this type of trading was completely different from the trading he had been accustomed to, Mark Ritchie devoted himself to researching various possible trading approaches. The first year was fairly tough because his inexperience led him down many blind alleys. Despite these early difficulties, his off-the-floor trading proved remarkably successful. His trading account, which started with $1 million in 1987, registered an average annual return of 50 percent over the next four years.

Ritchie's interests have ranged far beyond the world of trading. In recent years, he has become intensely involved in philanthrophic efforts aimed at helping a primitive Amazonian tribe. His involvement has not been confined to monetary contributions, but has included numerous extended stays living among the tribespeople. Ritchie has compiled a series of narratives told from the perspectives of the Indians into a recently completed manuscript, *Victim of Delusion.*

My first contact with Mark Ritchie occurred when he sent me his book, *God in the Pits* [MacMillan, 1989], inscribed with a beautiful compliment of my own first book. I responded with a letter, and further correspondence ensued. This book of interviews, however, provided the catalyst for our first meeting. I found Mark Ritchie to be very personable, low-key, and sincere. The interviews were conducted over several sessions in CRT's offices.

---

**I think you're an ideal person to whom to address this question, since you've made a life of blending the trading business (much of it on the floor) with an obvious deep sense of ethics. There has been a lot of publicity about the ethics of floor brokers, as particularly highlighted in the relatively recent FBI sting operation on the Chicago futures exchange floors. Are we talking about a small fringe element, like in any other industry, or does the temptation of large dollar amounts actually lead to a more serious problem of dishonesty? Without mentioning any names, of course.**

If I mentioned any names, I know you wouldn't print them. How could you [*he laughs*]? You're starting off with the heavy stuff here.

It varies drastically from pit to pit. Each pit is almost a culture in itself. A pit has its own personality. I used to spend 90 percent of my time in the soybean meal pit, and the traders there are some of the nicest and most honest people I've known in my life. In one sense, you have to be awfully honest to be in this business, where huge transactions take place with a nod of the head. Having said that, though, there's tremendous opportunity to cheat. However, I don't believe there are any more cheats in this business than, say, among plumbers or lawyers.

**Now *there* is a raving endorsement. It reminds me of a sign I saw for sale in a country store saying simply, "Honest Lawyer."**

[*Laughing*] That's probably the only one they made, and they're still waiting to sell it! There's no industry that has a corner on crooks. Think of the jokes we can make about dishonest politicians. Essentially, I think there's probably the same percentage of dishonest people in our business as in any other. The difference is in the payoff for a dishonest act. There are people on the exchanges who would fill orders for nothing, simply for the opportunity to bucket trades. In fact, I have been told there are brokers who would even pay to fill orders—if they could do it with a straight face. The broker who told me this said that the conflict of interest between trading his own account and filling customer orders was so great that the only way he could sleep at night was to refuse to ever do any customer orders.

**What is your own opinion of the FBI's sting operation? Do you think it uncovered a real problem, or was it overblown?**

I think that all the honest people in this business were thankful that something was finally done. For years, I've been saying that if we didn't clean up our own business, someone else would do it for us, and we wouldn't like the result. Instead of a scalpel, they'd likely use a dull chainsaw.

**Let's switch the subject. In your estimate, what percentage of the people who come to the trading floor to make their fortune actually succeed?**

Well, I really don't know, but I'll give you my best guess. I'd say roughly 10 percent do well, and maybe 1 percent do extremely well. But that's only a wild guess. I'd be willing to accept anybody else's percentages.

**That's a relatively low success rate. What would you say is the primary reason so many apparently fail?**

Lots of people in this business who pass themselves off as successes are really failures. I know one person in particular who to this day writes articles in industry publications and is often quoted by the press, yet he hardly knows the first thing about successful trading. One time, I was holding a position in a volatile interest rate spread. The trade was going against me, and I was nervous about the position. This particular trader was holding the same position and seemed quite worried.

"Do you think I'm overtrading?" he asked me.

I questioned him about his account size and the number of contracts he held. "I have $25,000 in the account," he said, "but I can't afford to lose it, and I have a fifty-contract position."

My mouth fell open. I had about $1,000,000 in my account for a position that was only twice as large, and I was even worried about that. "Overtrading, wouldn't even begin to communicate it," I said.

So he takes off half the position and says, "I'm OK now, right?"

"You're not OK," I said. "You haven't even begun."

There's no way you can communicate with a person like that. I remember saying to the people who were clearing his orders that he was a walking time bomb.

**Did he eventually self-destruct?**

Absolutely, and he left the clearing firm with a huge debit, which he had to work off.

**How do you decide when a position is too large?**

I have a rule that whenever I'm still thinking about my position when I lay my head on my pillow at night, I begin liquidation the next morning. I'm hesitant to say this because it could be misconstrued. You know that I'm a praying person. If I find myself praying about a position at any time, I liquidate it immediately. That's a sure sign of disaster. God is not a market manipulator. I knew a trader once who thought he was. He went broke—the trader, I mean.

**I assume this sensitivity to trading too large or letting losses get out of line is one of the ingredients that has made you successful.**

Absolutely. Magnitude of losses and profits is purely a matter of position size. Controlling position size is indispensable to success. Of all the traits necessary to trade successfully, this factor is the most undervalued.

As soon as you mention position size, you also bring up the topic of greed. Why did the trader I just mentioned hold a huge position backed up by only $25,000 he couldn't afford to lose? I will not presume to be judgmental. A person must look inside for these answers. But it would be foolish to overlook the human vice of greed. The successful trader must be able to recognize and control his greed. If you get a buzz from profits and depressed by losses, you belong in Las Vegas, not the markets.

**What other traits do you think are important to be successful as a trader?**

You have to be able to think clearly and act decisively in a panic market. The markets that go wild are the ones with the best opportunity. Traditionally, what happens in a market that goes berserk is that even veteran traders will tend to stand aside. That's your opportunity to make the money. As the saying goes, "If you can keep your head about you while others are losing theirs, you can make a fortune."

**Actually, I thought that line ended with, ". . . then you haven't heard the news."**

[Laughing] That's right. That's the risk. Maybe you haven't heard the news. But, on the other hand, it's also often an opportunity. If it looks too good to be true, the rest of the market may know something that you don't. But usually the way we miss opportunities in this business is by saying, "It looks too good to be true," and then not doing anything. Too often we think that everybody else must know something that we don't, and I think that's a critical mistake.

How many times have you heard someone put down an idea you're excited about by saying, "If it's such a good idea, why isn't everyone doing it?" This is the battle cry of mediocrity. Think about it for a minute. Any investment opportunity that everyone else is doing is by definition a bad idea. I would always recommend doing the opposite. The reason markets get out of line is because everyone is doing the wrong thing. The good trader always sticks with his own ideas and closes his ears to the why-isn't-everyone-doing-it cry of the crowd. He'll make a trade against the crowd at a conservative level that he can afford, and then get out if he's wrong. That's what a stop is for.

You need to have the courage to stand up against the crowd, decide your position, and execute it. One experience that really brought this home to me was when I was taking flying lessons. I had the theory down, but not very much experience. I was coming in for what was my second or third landing. When I was only about twenty or thirty feet above the runway, several gusts of wind blew the plane all over the place. I fought the plane down for what was probably the worst landing ever in history. When I finally brought the plane to a stop, I was actually chuckling at how terrible a landing it was, wondering what the instructor would say.

"Well, that was really impressive," he said.

I laughed a little more and asked, "What was impressive about that? I thought it was terrible."

He replied, "I have never seen any other beginner do that. Any other beginner would have taken his hand off the stick, given up, and expected me to land the thing. You hung in there and implemented the program all the way until the landing was complete." He paused for a moment and added, "You're right, though, it was terrible. Just terrible."

I thought about that later and realized that that is the trait you have to have to trade.

**That trait being what?**

The ability to implement your ideas despite adverse conditions. There is no opportunity in the market that is not an adverse condition situation.

**So the ability to think clearly and have courage when others are in a panic is an element of a successful trader?**

Indispensable.

**Is that an innate ability? I assume you either have it or you don't. You can't quite train yourself to act that way, can you?**

I'm not sure, but I don't think it's innate. You can prepare for it by having a game plan. Once I had a coach who when I stepped up to the plate would yell, "Have an idea?! What are you going to do?" Investing is the same. You have to know what you're going to do when the market gets out of line. Generally speaking, it's human nature to hesitate.

**What do you do to prepare?**

I go through a mental process. I decide what I'm going to do when X, Y, or Z happens. If X, Y, or Z is a surprise, then you're part of the crowd.

**Your book *God in the Pits* was extraordinarily personal. Didn't you have any reticence about being so open in print?**

I remember one reviewer called the book "embarrassingly personal." Sure there was some reluctance to be that vulnerable. In the first few months after the book was released, I could hardly look anybody in the eye who said they had read it, because I felt they knew more about me than was necessary.

**Does that imply that you had second thoughts? Would you do the same thing all over again?**

Yes, I would. My hope was that the book would make people take a long, honest look at themselves—at their relationship to others and their relationship to God. How could I expect people to honestly confront these questions unless I was willing to do the same. I'm sure that after having read the book, most people are probably disappointed when they meet me, because I can't be as honest in person as I tried to be in print.

**How did you first get involved in this business?**

In the early 1970s, my brother, Joe, was working for a silver coin dealer in Los Angeles. He had come to Chicago to explore the possibility of setting up a silver arbitrage operation between the Chicago and New York markets. [Silver is traded in both New York and Chicago. Theoretically, the price should be the same in both locations. However, occasionally, large influxes of either buy or sell orders in one market or the other may result in a temporary price disparity. Arbitrageurs tend to profit from this aberration by buying silver in the lower-priced market and simultaneously selling an equivalent amount in the higher-priced market. Since many arbitrageurs are competing to profit from these transitory distortions, the price in the two markets will never get too far out of line. In essence, arbitrageurs try to lock in small, virtually risk-free profits by acting very quickly to exploit inefficiencies in the marketplace.]

Joe asked me to join him in visiting the Chicago Board of Trade. He also needed to borrow a suit. At the time, I had only two suits to my name. One was ragged and the other I had picked up wholesale for $60. Since Joe would do the talking, I gave him my good suit.

When we arrived at the exchange, we inquired at the president's office about memberships and trading privileges. Upon seeing us, one of the exchange officials slowly eyed us from head to toe and back again and said, "You boys have got to be in the wrong place!"

**Was that the end of the conversation?**

No, but the whole conversation was about as strained as you might expect after an opening comment like that. Joe asked him about the possibility of getting a membership, but the exchange official just couldn't get the smirk off his face. "Do you know the financial requirements to become a clearing member?" he asked disdainfully.

**Did you?**

No, of course not [*laughing*]. We had no idea! We couldn't have guessed within two decimal places. The whole conversation was almost a joke. I was glad I wasn't the one doing the talking.

After that inauspicious start, we made our way to the visitors' gallery. I had heard rumors about the floor of the exchange being a wild place. We stood there watching for a bit. Although everyone was running around and there was a lot of noise, it didn't seem as wild or exciting as we had expected. Suddenly, we heard this ear-shattering dong and the floor erupted into sheer pandemonium. Obviously, we had been watching the market before the opening. And this was a particularly hectic trading session. The crowd in the pits flowed from the bottom up and back again in waves. Our mouths dropped open in astonishment. At that moment, both Joe and I decided that this was the place for us. It just looked like a barrel of fun.

**Did you have another job at this time?**

Actually, I was going to seminary school, majoring in philosophy of religion. I had a job as a correctional officer working the midnight-to-eight shift. It almost covered the rent and tuition.

**Did you ever finish divinity school?**

Yes, after I got into the business. It took me seven years to complete the degree.

**Were you planning to use your religious training?**

I wasn't headed to be a member of the cloth, although that was an option. I was mainly in seminary to answer some personal spiritual questions that were nagging me. I had no specific plans.

**You had no real plans about how you were going to earn a living?**

No, I was too idealistic for that. This was the late 1960s and early 1970s. We had the feeling that if you just did right, everything else would take care of itself. You remember, this was the attitude that society thought was so naive.

**How did you first get on the exchange floor?**

About six months after our visit to the exchange, Joe's company sponsored him to start a silver arbitrage floor operation. Several months later, I got a job with the company as a phone clerk on the floor. That job lasted for over a year. Then the volatility in the silver market declined sharply from the hectic levels of the 1973–74 period, and the arbitrage opportunities dried up. Or, perhaps more accurately, the opportunities were still there, but too small to justify an operation that was paying nonmember clearing rates. In any case, the company let me go.

**Did you try to stay in the business?**

I found a job for a company that was marketing commodity options to the public.

**Now correct me if I'm wrong, but as I remember it, this was well before exchange-traded options, and the companies that were selling options at the time were charging the public exorbitant premiums. [The "premium" is the price of an option.]**

Unconscionable prices. Rip-off levels. Their markup was approximately 100 percent. They would buy an option for $2,000 and sell it for $4,000.

**When you went to the interview, did you turn down the job because you were aware of what was involved?**

I had no idea what was going on.

**Were you offered the job?**

Yes.

**Then what happened?**

I worked there for about a day and realized that the entire operation was basically involved in cold calling. They had lists of possible investors and they called these people to convince them to buy options.

**In other words, you found yourself in a boiler room operation?**

Exactly [laughing]. I was introduced to what the other side of the business was all about.

After I was hired, I went to their training program, which was aimed at teaching us how to sell options. Since, at the time, U.S.-traded options did not yet exist, they were buying the options in London and selling them to the public at a high markup. They had written scripts on how to sell. You'd call up somebody and say, "Hello Mr. so-and-so. We understand that you are a wealthy investor, and that is how we got your name. You are obviously the type of intelligent person who can appreciate this kind of opportunity." You'd butter him up.

I'm sitting there with a trader's mentality, and I'm thinking to myself that if I'm going to sell something to somebody, I want to know the track record.

**Did you ask the instructor?**

Certainly. He answered, "We make money for our clients."

So I asked him, "How much? Exactly what am I going to tell the people whom I'm calling? What kind of percentage return can they expect?"

He stared at me as if I were asking frivolous questions, and with a suspicious look said, "Why would you want to know about all that stuff?"

**In other words, was his attitude: What difference does it make?**

Of course, that was exactly his attitude. "The point is to sign the guy up," he said.

**Well, what were you supposed to tell people when they asked you how much they could make on the investment?**

Oooooh, "You're going to make big bucks! Sugar is going to double!" Or you might hype a special sale. Sometimes they would come up with these specials where a $4,000 option was being sold for $3,000. My guess is that it was probably an option they had bought at $2,000, which was running out of time and about to expire worthless, and they just wanted to dump it. So they would call up all their people and tell them they had a special on this option.

**How were you supposed to handle the question from the potential** *investor*—**and I use the term loosely—who asked to see a track record?**

I asked a question exactly like that. The instructor said, "Our records show that 62 percent of our clients make money."

**Was he lying outright?**

Well, I think he had some figures, but it was difficult to say what they meant. Maybe 62 percent of the clients had made a profit on a trade at one time or another. However, for all I know, most of them were wiped out. So I kept pressing the question.

**Was his attitude: Stop bothering me kid?**

Was it ever! Anyway, I kept on pressing the issue. I asked him, "Look, I'm selling an option for $4,000. At what price can the buyer sell it back?" You can always tell very quickly whether a market is legitimate by simply asking for a quote on the other side.

He gave me this funny look and asked, "Why would he want to sell it? He's buying it from you. He's going to hold it until he makes a lot of money."

So I said, "Hypothetically, if he wanted to sell it the next day, what price could he sell it at? I'm used to a market. A market means that there are buyers and sellers." He kept on evading the issue, and this went back and forth for a while. Finally I said, "Just tell me what you paid for the $4,000 option."

He gave a deep sigh, leaned on his desk and said, "Now look. If you go into a furniture store and refuse to buy the furniture until the salesman tells you what he paid for it, he's not going to tell you. You can ask that question all day, but eventually he's going to tell you to fuck off. And that's exactly what I'm telling you." There was a long silence in the classroom.

**How was the rest of the class reacting to this whole interchange?**

They were beginners to the business and didn't have a clue to what was going on. One of the trainees had seen a company salesman drive up in a Corvette, and that was all he needed; he was signed up right then and there.

**Were you asked to leave?**

No. But I was kind of embarrassed by the whole situation. I eventually mumbled something along the line that if most people were making money then it was probably all right.

**But you didn't really believe that, did you?**

No, of course not. In fact, at one point, the phone rang and the instructor answered saying, "He's on the trading floor, let me get him." I thought to myself, "I didn't know there was a trading floor in this building." He opens the door to this big room, packed with people at desks—the so-called trading floor, which you have aptly described as a boiler room—and yells at the top of his voice: "Hey Bob, pick up the phone!" They loved that trading-floor-pandemonium ambience. I said to myself, "Trading floor? This thing is nothing but a con operation. These people are conning themselves." In fact, a lot of dishonesty in this business begins when people are dishonest with themselves.

**Do you really believe that they had glossed over the facts so much in their own minds that they didn't realize they were completely ripping off the public?**

I think so. I believe the majority of crooks have told themselves enough lies that they begin to believe them. For example, the floor brokers who were indicted in the FBI sting operation that we talked about earlier generally said, "Hey, I wasn't doing anything anybody else wasn't doing." It's not true, but I think they believe it.

**Did you quit at that point?**

I made a few half-hearted calls on the first day following the training session, but it had a feel of scam written all over it. I left after that and never came back.

**Are there any trades that you would consider particularly memorable?**

One that comes to mind occurred on the day the Falklands war broke out. People off the floor have the idea that the traders on the floor are the first to know what's going on. Nothing could be further from the truth. The market erupts long before we ever get the news. We're the last to hear what's driving the market. On that day, I had taken a large position in soybean meal at what looked like a great price. By the time I got out of the position, in what was probably only one minute, I had lost $100,000.

**Any other memorable trades?**

I've always lost money faster than I've made it. One particularly striking instance concerned the roaring gold market during the period from 1979 to early 1980. Gold was sitting at around $400 when Iran took the hostages. I thought that the heightened tensions aroused by this situation would push gold prices much higher. But the market responded sluggishly, so I hesitated. The market eventually did go higher; it went to almost $500 over the next month. This was a classic example of not doing what you know should be done.

**In other words, you failed to act decisively, a trait you cited earlier as one of the key ingredients to being a successful trader.**

Exactly. I eventually ended up buying gold at just under $500 an ounce. And as you might guess, it went down the limit the day I bought it. Locked limit-down, in fact.

**Did you think of getting out?**

No. The hostage situation was still completely unresolved. Also, around the same time, the Soviet Union had invaded Afghanistan. I still felt the market would eventually continue to go higher. So I stuck with it. Of course, as you know, the market did go sharply higher.

**Did you have a plan for getting out?**

Yes, my plan was to get out whenever the market dropped 10 percent from its high.

**Basically, your plan was to let the market run until there was some sign of meaningful weakness.**

Right. Unfortunately, when the market dropped, it lost 25 percent of its value in one day. Needless to say, that was a particularly painful loss. But the point is that I still ended up with a large profit on the trade.

In fact, this trade raises the whole question of how you view drawdowns. Most people don't distinguish between drawdowns in open equity and drawdowns in closed equity. [The distinction is that *open equity* refers to unrealized profits on an existing position. In effect, what Ritchie is implying is that he views a given loss differently if it is a partial surrender of profits on a winning trade as opposed to if it is a drawdown in a losing trade.] If I protected open equity [i.e., open profits] with the same care I protected closed equity, I would never be able to participate in a long-term move. Any sensible overall risk control measure could not withstand the normal volatility in such a move.

**In other words, in order to score the really large gains, you have to be willing to see those gains erode significantly before getting out of the market.**

I can't see any other way. If you get too careful about not risking your gains, you're not going to be able to extract a large profit.

**How much do you risk on any single trade or idea (measured from trade initiation, not peak equity)?**

About one-half of 1 percent. I think it's generally a good idea that when you put a trade, it should be so small that it seems almost a waste of your time. Always trade at a level that seems too small.

**You spent approximately the first ten years of your trading career on the floor and then made a transition to trading from an office. Since you were very successful as a floor trader, I'd like to under-**

**stand your motivation for making the switch. First, tell me, would I be safe in assuming that while you were a floor trader, virtually every month was profitable?**

Yes.

**Let's take it one step further. What percentage of your weeks would you estimate were profitable during that period?**

Ninety percent.

**Most people would say, "My God, 90 percent of the weeks this guy makes a profit!" Why would you ever leave that type of an edge?**

First I'll give you my short answer: old age. Also, the soybean market had lost much of its volatility, which reduced trading opportunities. It seemed like the right time to try trading off the floor.

**Did you have a plan on how you would approach trading from upstairs?**

I had no idea. I checked out lots of things. I tried a number of advisory services but found that they were often not worth the time it took to listen to the phone tape. I eventually gravitated toward trying to develop my own systems. One of the things that amazed me was the unreliability of information by the so-called pros of the industry. For example, when I started working on testing and developing systems, I purchased price data from a company that marketed what they called a "perpetual" contract. [The perpetual price is derived by interpolating between the nearest two actual futures contracts to obtain a hypothetical price series that is always a constant amount of time forward from the current date (e.g., ninety days). The resulting price is a theoretical concept that will be a hybrid of two different contracts and cannot be replicated by any real-world trading instrument(s).]

I used this data for over six months before I realized that it was not a reflection of the real market. For example, the perpetual series could show a large price move that implied a profit that you could not have realized in the real market. When I discovered this, I almost fell off my chair. I couldn't understand how anyone who had ever traded anything could have constructed this type of series.

I asked myself, "How can all these professionals who obviously know what they're doing be following data that's fundamentally foolish?" The question was easy enough to answer. After all, I had used it myself for six months. I had to go back to square one and start over. I never again trusted anyone else's work.

**Did you buy any commercial trading systems at the time?**

Yes, I did buy a couple. One of them—I don't want to mention the name—was essentially a simulation package. I had assumed that if I could get a tool that would allow me to develop optimized trading systems, it would be a thousand times more effective than trying to approach the market by using charts. [Optimization refers to the process of testing a particular system, using many different values for the key inputs, and then choosing the single combination of values that worked best for past history. Although this procedure can yield wonderful performance for the past, it usually wildly overinflates the implied performance for the future.] Instead, I found the software was worthless. There again, I was amazed at the magnitude of ignorance of the people who had developed this system.

**In what way was it worthless?**

The software was a system that allowed you to optimize the market to death. In fact, this organization even recommended reoptimizing the system every week. In other words, curve-fit the program to last week so the trades this week will match what should have been done the previous week. I just got the overwhelming impression that whoever had developed the ideas for this system had never traded himself.

**Did you ever find out if that was true?**

[A long sigh] I asked that question, but they just dodged it. In fact, I remember the company salesman showing me how to enter the data manually. Personally, I prefer to get the data by computer, because manual entry just seems like too much work. Anyway, this fellow, who was himself a trader, said, "I don't even pay for the price of the *Wall Street Journal*. I have a friend photocopy the price page for me." I thought to myself, "Here's a guy who's marketing a program that's being represented as the premiere trading system software on the market, and he doesn't even have enough money to buy the *Wall Street Journal*."

**Did you actually try trading the system?**

Yes, but the results were just spasmodic. Moreover, I was extremely uncomfortable with the idea of trading a black box [trading system computer software that generates buy and sell signals without revealing the rules of how the signals are generated]. I swore to myself that I would never purchase a black box system again.

**Is your advice to people then: Forget what's out there and do your own work?**

My advice to people has always been: Stay out of the business; stay completely away from the market. For novices to come in and try to generate profit in this incredibly complex industry is like me trying to do brain surgery on the weekends to pick up a little extra cash.

I have a friend who knows three doctors who got together to invest in a stud race horse. When they took delivery of the horse, they found that it was a gelding. My friend was teasing them about this and asked if they had ever thought of inspecting the horse. You won't believe this, but it turns out that they had thought of it, but they didn't go any further. So he said, "Well, you guys are all doctors; did you ever bend over and take a look under there to make sure he had the necessary tools?"

If you asked those three doctors today what their mistake was, I'm sure they would tell you that they should have inspected the horse's valuables. They still wouldn't have learned the lesson: DON'T INVEST WHERE YOU DON'T KNOW WHAT YOU'RE DOING. If they invest in another horse, they won't get a gelding, but they'll make some other mistake just as laughable.

**Do you mean to imply that people should just put their money in T-bills?**

I think they can go with some of the managed funds or trading advisors that have proven track records. But I would take very seriously the standard disclaimer that says, "Past performance is no guarantee of future results." Also, I don't think you can make money unless you're willing to lose it. Unless you have money that you can afford to lose and still sleep at night, you don't belong in the market. My willingness to lose is fundamental to my ability to make money in the markets.

**And that's not true of most people?**

That's right. Most people come into this business without a willingness to lose money. They also enter the market with unrealistic expectations. Even if they're lucky enough to pick a successful trading advisor, they're likely to pull their money out the first quarter he has a drawdown. So they end up losing even though they may have been in a winning situation.

**Actually, my empirical research has demonstrated the exact same conclusion. Several years ago, part of my job was evaluating outside trading advisors. In the process, I found out something particularly interesting. There was a handful of advisors who had made money every year. Yet even for this select group, less than 50 percent of their closed client accounts showed a net profit. That really brought home to me how poor most people are in deciding when to enter and exit investments. I think the natural tendency is to invest money with a manager after he has had a hot streak and to withdraw it after a losing streak.**
    **Although you discourage people from getting into this business, let's say that somebody comes to you with a serious interest in becoming a trader. What do you tell them?**

I know this is going to sound patronizing, but honestly, I tell them to read your first book [*The Complete Guide to the Futures Markets*]. I slow them down by telling them to come back to me after they have digested half of that book, knowing full well that most of them will never do that.

**So that's the way you turn people away from the business. Now *there's* a ringing compliment on my work if I ever heard one.**

Actually, just picking the book up is a threatening experience. Seriously, I think your book gives people a good idea of the amount of work it takes to become competent in this business.

**Is one of your motivations for trading having the ability to give a portion of your profits to charity?**

Precisely, although I hate to put it that simply. In my youth, I was so idealistic that I thought the dollar was that unholy Mammon that one must resist in order to do humanity some higher good. I eventually learned that wealth has a great deal of inherent value. When you see somebody starving, what he needs is money.

**I assume that you probably long ago passed the point where your trading profits took care of any personal needs or financial security you might envision. In your own case, if the charity aspect were not there, do you think you would still be trading?**

I'm not sure that I would be. I just don't know. Incidentally, let me correct your use of the term *charity*. I don't think in terms of charity. I think in terms of investing in the poor. If someone is starving and you hand him a buck, you've taught him that what he needs is for someone to give him a handout. I prefer to *invest* in the poor—to provide capital so they can enhance their own productivity. What the poor need are cottage industries that allow them to become self-sufficient. That's the type of funding I believe in, and it may not fit the conventional view of charity.

I know what I'm going to say can be easily misconstrued, but if I could set up a system where I could make money off the poor, then I would have achieved my goal. I know that sounds crass. Of course, my objective is not to make money off the poor, but the point is that charity tends to spawn dependency. That's why the Great Society war on poverty was such a failure. In contrast, if I can establish someone in a business where he can return my money, then I know his situation is stable.

**Would you mind saying roughly what percentage of your income you funnel into these efforts to help the poor?**

As a sweeping generalization, roughly one-third goes to Uncle Sam, one-third I put back into my account to increase my trading size, and one-third I dispense to these various projects.

**I know that you've become involved with Indians in the Amazon jungle whose tribal customs include killing members of neighboring tribes. Wasn't there an element of fear in visiting this area?**

No. They kill only each other; they don't bother outsiders. One of their beliefs is that whenever someone dies, his death must be avenged by killing someone from another village. When that person is killed, his village will then seek revenge in turn, and so on.

**You mean every time someone dies, they blame the death on a member of another village? It sounds like there wouldn't be anybody left before too long.**

They don't blame the deaths of older people or young children on the evil spirits of another village member, but otherwise the answer to your questions is yes. Fortunately, their killing practices are not too efficient. However, their numbers have diminished drastically over the years, partially because of disease and malnutrition, but also because of this particular custom. I should add that the village I visited has been converted to Christianity and has given up this practice.

**What has been your own involvement with this village?**

I've gone down there for extended visits about four or five times since 1982. My efforts are directed to helping them progress. For example, I helped make all the arrangements for setting up a sawmill operation. The last time I visited the village, they were building gorgeous houses. If you had seen the squalor they once lived in—children playing with cockroaches on dirt floors, rubbing filth all over their little faces—then you could understand the euphoria I felt when I saw their new homes.

**Aren't you concerned that by helping Westernize these villages, their way of life will be destroyed to their ultimate detriment?**

It's a commonly held belief here in the civilized West that the cultures and life-styles of isolated peoples are to be valued and preserved. And I find that view romantically attractive. I would be inclined to agree with this premise if only I could find someone in one of these cultures who would stop laughing at it.

An Indian I know named Bee was once read a newspaper article about his beautiful culture. Bee responded by asking, "Where does this man live that he could be so foolish?" He was told that the man lived and worked in Caracas. "Why does he sit up there in his comfortable office and write this nonsense about us?" Bee asked. "Why doesn't he come down here with his family and join us? Then we can all enjoy this beautiful place together." They're mystified by our lack of compassion. Academics make compelling arguments extolling the beauty and virtues of Indian culture, but I agree with the Indians.

**So the Indians generally accept the intrusion of civilization?**

Yes. I have never met an Indian who didn't want progress. Sure, some of them want to maintain their beliefs and customs, but they all want the benefits of civilization. [Author's comment: Although I question the generalization that civilization is beneficial to tribal societies, having read Ritchie's *Victim of Delusion,* which describes the unimaginable brutality of life and death in this society (told from the perspective of the Indians), it is hard to rue the loss of their way of life.]

**Let me make a rather abrupt transition from the Amazon to the world of trading. I know that you're considering shifting from being a private trader to managing public funds. Since you have already been quite successful trading your own funds and have a sizable personal account, wouldn't it just be easier to continue to do the same thing? Why undertake all the headaches that come with money management?**

If dramatically increasing the amount of money traded is going to substantially reduce your profit per trade, then your implication is right: the profit incentive fees may not provide sufficient compensation for the degradation in trading profits.

**But in your own case, you obviously feel that your approach is not volume sensitive.**

That's right, because it's so long term.

**Let's talk about specifics. On average, how many times a year will your approach signal a shift from long to short or vice versa in a given market?**

Generally speaking, between one and five times per year in each market.

**That's probably far fewer than most people would think.**

Right. Of course, I would prefer only one trade per year. In fact, perhaps my best trade ever was one that I held for over four years.

**What trade was that?**

I was long soybean meal and short soybean oil and just kept rolling the position over.

**What kept you in that trade for so long?**

Monthly profits.

---

[At this point, Joe Ritchie enters the room. He is carrying a tray of coffee and dessert. The interview with Joe continues in the next chapter.]

---

Five basic trading principles appear to be elemental to Mark Ritchie's trading success. These can be summarized as follows:

1. Do your own research.

2. Keep each position size so small that it almost seems to be a waste of your time.

3. Have the patience to stay with a winning position as long as that position is working, even if it means keeping a single position for years.

4. View risk of open profits differently from the risk as measured from starting equity in a trade. The point is that in order to ride winning positions to their maximum potential, it is necessary to endure periodic losses in open profits greater than the risk level that would be advisable when a position is first implemented.

5. Recognize and control your greed.

# Joe Ritchie

## THE INTUITIVE THEORETICIAN

Joe Ritchie is the founder and driving force behind CRT. It is his ideas, concepts, and theories that serve as the blueprint for the complex strategies that guide the firm. Although he has never taken an advanced math course, Joe Ritchie is considered by many to be a math genius—a natural. He would have to be, given the intricate mathematical nature of the trading models employed by CRT. Joe describes math as something he almost feels or intuitively understands.

Ritchie would be the first to emphasize that the success of CRT is hardly a solo act. There are many individuals that are integral to the company's achievements. In our interviews, Joe insisted that I also talk to some other CRT personnel. Here is how one key employee described Ritchie's philosophy: "Joe believes in empowering people. He trusts people. I sincerely believe that one of the reasons we can make so much money is that Joe makes us feel absolutely comfortable to risk his money."

Ritchie makes a lot of business decisions based on his gut feeling about the people involved. If he feels any discomfort with the people, he has no reservation about walking away from even the most lucrative

Note: Readers unfamiliar with options may wish to read the Appendix in order to understand the trading-related references in this chapter.

venture. On the other hand, he has been known to initiate major operations on not much more than a handshake.

A recent case in point is his venture in launching a computer company in the former Soviet Union. The company is involved in every phase of the production and marketing chain, including developing software, importing hardware, establishing service and trading centers, and implementing a distribution system. This whole elaborate operation sprang to life because Ritchie was impressed by an entrepreneurially inclined Russian whom he met. His trust and confidence in this man was all it took to convince Ritchie to make the investment commitment. As one CRT employee explained, "While every other U.S. company involved in a joint venture in this region is trying to write three-hundred-page legal documents to protect themselves, which don't hold water there anyway, Joe asked the Russian to write a contract that he thought was fair, and Joe signed it on his next trip to Moscow."

As might be expected of a man who has built one of the world's most successful trading operations, Joe Ritchie is dynamic, energetic, and brilliant. Work is truly fun for him because it is an endless challenge and an ever-changing puzzle. But there is another key aspect that delights Joe Ritchie about his work: the people. "I love to come to work," he booms. And he means it. It's not just that he loves what he does, but he considers CRT an extended family. He appears to exude a genuine affection for his employees.

---

**When you first started doing silver arbitrage, you had hardly invented the wheel. Other people were already doing the same thing. Did you do anything differently in order to succeed?**

We tried to do a better job of understanding the interrelationships between markets and assessing the probabilities involved. We also traded more aggressively and for a narrower margin than the other brokers. We did the same thing years later in options, when by using more accurate pricing models we were able to quote such narrow bid/asked spreads that our main competitors assumed we were making markets that were too tight to be profitable. If you really have the mechanics or theoretical value nailed, you can do a lot more volume at a smaller margin.

**How did the other floor brokers respond to your competing for the same type of business?**

They resented us because we were so aggressive and were eating into their volume.

**But I imagine that back then you had very low capitalization. How could you have been much of a threat to their business?**

That's true. We probably had one of the smallest capitalizations on the floor. Some of the other key players might do a five-hundred-lot arbitrage order, whereas if we did fifty, we would be up to our limit. However, we traded it back and forth much more aggressively, so we ended up with a much larger proportion of the volume than might be expected relative to our typical order size.

**Was that a matter of your willingness to take a smaller edge than the other brokers?**

That was certainly part of it. But there were a hundred other small things. For example, getting better phone clerks, or coming up with faster ways to communicate between the Chicago and New York silver floors.

**I don't understand. Doesn't everyone use the telephone? How much faster can you get?**

You're going to find this hard to believe. When I first came to Chicago, we found that a lot of the people who were doing silver arbitrage didn't even have a phone clerk because they didn't want to pay for one. Instead, they had a telephone with a little light above it, and when the market changed in New York, the New York floor clerk would pick up his phone, which would cause the phone light to flash in Chicago. When the Chicago broker saw the light, he would run over to the phone, get the quote, hang up the phone, and run back to the pit to do the trade. The transmission time that was involved was so slow that we thought we could easily beat it by getting good phone clerks.

**Were most people doing it that way?**

About half of them were. But even the ones who were using phone clerks still had a transmission time of about three to ten seconds. We found that if we got the best phone clerks, motivated them, and did everything else right, we could cut that time down to about two seconds.

**Essentially, you were doing the trades faster and taking the trades before the spreads widened to the point where other brokers would do them. I assume that approach didn't make you very popular.**

It made us very unpopular. In fact, they tried to throw us off the floor.

**On what grounds?**

For rule violations, such as the phone clerk verbally calling orders into the pit. Technically, the orders are supposed to be written down and carried to the pit by a runner. However, it was standard operating procedure for orders to be called into the pit. The exchange realized that they needed the arbitrage activity to provide liquidity, so the rule was not enforced. However, that didn't stop them from pulling us in front of the committee for violating this rule. In the end, they had to drop the issue when they realized that trying to enforce the rule against one party and letting everyone else violate it was not going to work.

**You make it sound like a real insider's club.**

It was.

**Is that true of most exchanges?**

[Long sigh] It varies a great deal from exchange to exchange, but it's a lot less prevalent than it used to be. The competition has just forced changes.

**The silver arbitrage operation eventually came to an end. What happened?**

The silver arbitrage was very profitable during 1973–74 because the market was so volatile. However, when the volatility died down in 1975, the silver arbitrage became a very slow business. I tried to convince the fellow who owned the company I worked for to try something else. I thought that the soybean crush was the business of choice at the time.

[Soybeans are crushed into two constituent products: meal and oil. If soybean prices are low relative to the product prices, then crushing plants can lock in very attractive profits by buying soybeans and selling an equivalent amount of products. This activity will cause soybean prices to gain relative to product prices. Conversely, if soybeans are highly priced relative to products, causing the profit margins to be low or negative, crushing activity will be reduced. In effect, this development will reduce soybean demand, which will decrease soybean prices and reduce product supply, which will increase product prices. Essentially, these economic forces will cause soybean and soybean product (meal and oil) prices to maintain a broadly defined relationship. The soybean crush trader tries to buy soybeans and sell products when soybeans are priced relatively low versus products and do the reverse trade when soybeans are priced relatively high.]

**What did you do differently to give you an advantage over other brokers who were doing the crush?**

Very simple things. Many of the same things we did in silver. We would keep the best clerks by paying a good wage and providing them with the opportunity for growth. We also constructed our own crude slide rules that would show the implied price for soybeans given different price combinations for soybean oil and soybean meal. This tool allowed us to instantaneously calculate the value of the market, which helped us take advantage of the order flow more quickly. I can't tell you why the other brokers weren't doing the same thing, but they weren't.

**Were you still associated with your original company at the time?**

Yes. I reached an agreement to switch from silver arbitrage to doing the soybean crush, wherein I would be responsible for all losses but would split any profits with the company 50/50.

**It sounds like heads you win fifty, tails you lose one hundred—not a very good deal. Why did you stay with the company under that arrangement? Did you need the use of their seat?**

No. It was probably a combination of inertia and loyalty to the company for having given me my start in the business. But eventually I went off on my own.

**Was that the start of CRT?**

Yes, although the name and the partnership arrangement came later. The move into the soybean complex was also characteristic of what was to become one of our principles all along—namely, not being tied to any one business but rather moving to the markets where something interesting was going on. When we first formed a partnership, the company name was Chicago Board Crushers. Then some time later we changed the name to Chicago Research and Trading.

[Mark Ritchie, who has been sitting in for the interview, interjects.] One of the reasons we changed the name from Chicago Board Crushers was that our secretary got tired of explaining to people who called in why we couldn't crush their boards.

**You're joking.**

No, seriously.

**You just mentioned the idea of being flexible enough to switch to the markets that had the best trading opportunities. As I recall, you became involved with silver again during the wild 1979–80 market. Were you just trading the arbitrage, or did you do some directional trades?**

Almost exclusively arbitrage. When the volatility expands dramatically, the opportunities for profit in arbitrage are greatly enhanced.

There was one trade, however, that you could term directional. This is one of those stories that proves that it's better to be dumb and make a profit than be smart and take a loss. In early 1979, some mystery buyer came in and bought twenty thousand contracts of silver. Nobody knew who it was. I did some digging around and found that the person who was managing this trade was a Pakistani. I happened to know a Pakistani who was from the upper crust, and the upper crust of that country is relatively small. So I asked her if there were any Pakistanis who could have that kind of money. She said, "No, but there are two Pakistanis that manage money for the Saudis." She gave me the two names. Sure enough, with a little secret investigating, we found that one of these guys was connected to the buying. We thought we had a nice bit of information.

At the time, silver options were traded only in London. The out-of-the-money silver calls were trading at very low prices. Even though the market was not that liquid, I bought a huge amount of calls. I took a ridiculously large position relative to our equity base, knowing that our downside was limited. [Essentially, an out-of-the-money call gives a buyer the right to buy a contract (silver in this instance) at a specified price above the current price. If the market fails to rise to that price, the option will expire worthless, and the entire premium paid for the option will be lost. On the other hand, if prices exceed the specified price (called the strike price), then the right to buy offered by the call position can result in profits. If the strike price is significantly exceeded, the profit potential can be huge.]

We had lots of theories about who might be buying all this silver. But there was one theory that we had never considered. It turns out that some guy had passed off a $20 million bum check to a brokerage office in Dallas.

**What did that have to do with the Saudis?**

Absolutely nothing. Apparently, he wasn't related to the Saudis. He was just someone who passed a bad check. So while we thought we were being very clever, all our analysis actually proved to be inaccurate. The brokerage company finally caught this guy, sold out his position, and silver prices slid down to under $6. I couldn't even get out of my position because the market was so illiquid and I held so many options that I would have gotten virtually nothing for the contracts if I had tried to sell. Essentially, I ended up being married to the position.

At that time, I went away for a vacation, which was fortunate, because the Hunt buying started to push silver prices sharply higher.

I'm sure that if I were around, I would have gotten out at the first opportunity of breaking even. By the time I came back, the silver calls were in the money [i.e., the market price had risen above the strike price].

Although I thought the market was going to continue to go up, I couldn't stand the volatility. One day, I decided to go into the silver pit just to get a feel for what was going on. I promised myself that I would keep my hands in my pocket. At the time, silver was trading at $7.25. I decided to sell twenty-five contracts against my calls just to lock in some profits. Before I knew it, I had liquidated my entire position. By the time the calls expired, silver prices had gone up to about $8.50.

**The 1979–80 silver market was one of the great bull markets of all time. [Silver soared from $5 per ounce to $50 per ounce in a little over a year.] Did you have any inkling of how high prices might go?**

None whatsoever. In fact, even $10 per ounce seemed extremely far-fetched. I don't know anybody who bought silver at relatively low prices and got out at over $20. The traders who bought silver at $3, $4, $5, and $6 did one of two things. Either, by the time silver got up to $7, $8, or $9 they got out, or they rode the position all the way up and all the way down. I'm sure there are exceptions, but I've never met one. I did, however, know traders that went short silver at $9 and $10 because the price seemed so ridiculously high and ended up riding the position until they had lost their entire net worth. That happened to some of the best professionals I knew in the silver market.

**Would Hunt have succeeded if the exchange didn't step in and change the rules by allowing trading for liquidation only, thereby averting a delivery squeeze?**

The exchanges didn't have to change the rules to prevent Hunt from taking delivery. According to the rules, the exchange has the power to step in and say, "Ok, you want silver, you can have your silver, but you're going to have to spread out the delivery periods." Or they can allow trading for liquidation only. If the exchanges had just stood aside and allowed a noneconomically driven demand for delivery, they would have been abrogating their responsibilities.

At the time that the Hunts were standing for delivery of April silver, the forward contracts were trading at huge discounts. The Hunts had no immediate economic need for delivery. If all they really wanted was ownership of the silver, they could have switched their April contracts into the discounted forward months, locking in a huge net saving and also freeing up their capital for use in the interim. Or they could have purchased silver coins in the free market at $35 per ounce when the April contract was at $50. When instead of these economically sensible alternatives they insist, "No, no, no, we want to take delivery of the silver in April," it indicates that they're playing a game. That's not what these markets are here for. So I feel that the Hunts got exactly what they had coming to them.

A lot of innocent parties were hurt by the Hunt activity. For example, take a mine down in Peru whose cost of production is under $5 per ounce. When the price gets up to $15, the mine decides to lock in a huge profit by hedging their next two years' worth of production in the silver futures market. This makes all the economic sense in the world. However, when the price keeps on going up to $20, $25, $30, $35, they have to keep putting up more and more variation margin on their short futures position. Eventually, they run out of money and are forced to liquidate their position, going broke in the process.

**I know that CRT's basic emphasis is option arbitrage, but I'm curious, do you do any directional trading?**

Yes, for my own account. I've always believed that technical trading would work. From time to time I dabbled in it, and in each case it worked very well. However, I didn't like the way directional trading distracted me all the time. I turned my ideas over to CRT staff members who had both an interest in technical trading and the appropriate skills. They followed up by developing technical trading systems based on these concepts and assuming the responsibility for the daily trade executions. I rarely look at the system anymore, except for an occasional glance at the account statements.

**How long has the system been operational?**

Five years.

**How has it done?**

The system has been profitable in four of the five years it has traded, with an average annual gain of 40 percent for the period as a whole.

**Did you do anything different in the losing year?**

Ironically, it started out as a fantastic year. About halfway through the year, the system was really smoking, so we started increasing the position size very quickly. At one point, we must have nearly tripled it. That was the only time we increased trading size rapidly. As it turned out, if we had held the trading size constant, the system would have had a winning year.

**Is there any human judgment involved in this system, or is it totally mechanical?**

Early on, there was about a six-month period when human judgment was employed.

**And it was usually detrimental?**

Unbelievably detrimental.

**It's amazing how often that's true.**

Everyone says that.

**What is your view of fundamental analysis versus technical analysis?**

Back in the late 1970s, I once gave a talk on technical analysis at a seminar. At lunch I ended up sitting at the same table as Richard Dennis. I asked him what percentage of his trading was technical and what percentage was fundamental. He answered with scorn in his voice, "I use zero percent fundamental information." The way he answered, I was sorry I had asked the question. He continued, "I don't know how you escape the argument that all fundamental information is already in the market."

I asked, "How do you escape the argument that all the technical information is already in the market?"

He said, "I never thought of that." I admired him for that. He had a humility about him that I think explains a lot of his success.

My basic argument was that there are a number of technicians trading with the same information and the distribution of success is a matter of who uses that information better. Why shouldn't it be the same with fundamentals? Just because all the information is in the market doesn't mean that one trader can't use it better than the next guy.

**To a major extent, CRT's prominence is due to options. I assume that CRT is, in fact, the world's largest trader of options. How did someone without any mathematical training—you were a philosophy major, as I recall—get involved in the highly quantitative world of options?**

I have never had a course in math beyond high school algebra. In that sense, I am not a quant. However, I feel math in an intuitive way that many quants don't seem to. When I think about pricing an option, I may not know calculus, but in my mind I can draw a picture of how you would price an option that looks exactly like the theoretical pricing models in the textbooks.

**When did you first get involved in trading options?**

I did a little dabbling with stock options back in 1975–76 on the Chicago Board of Options Exchange, but I didn't stay with it. I first got involved with options in a serious way with the initiation of trading in futures options. By the way, in 1975 I crammed the Black-Scholes formula into a TI-52 hand-held calculator, which was capable of giving me one option price in about thirteen seconds, after I hand-inserted all the other variables. It was pretty crude, but in the land of the blind, I was the guy with one eye.

**When the market was in its embryonic stage, were the options seriously mispriced, and was your basic strategy aimed at taking advantage of these mispricings?**

Absolutely. I remember my first day in the T-bond futures options pit, when the market had been trading for only several months. Someone asked me to make a market in a back month. [The back months have considerably less liquidity than nearby months.] Since it was my first day, I felt really out of step. I was too embarrassed not to make a market. So I gave him a fifty-point bid/ask spread on a hundred-lot order. I said, "Look, this is my first day, and I don't really trade the back months. I'm sorry, but this is the best I can do."

His jaw dropped and he said, "You're making a fifty-tick market on a hundred-lot!" He couldn't believe anybody was making that tight of a market.

**The bid/ask spreads were that wide back then?**

Yes, there was far less volume than now. A fifty- or hundred-lot was considered a really large order.

**Once you put on a position because the market provided you with a large edge for taking the other side, I assume that you tried to hedge the position to eliminate the risk. However, when you went to implement an offsetting position, didn't you face the same problem of wide bid/ask spreads?**

The first thing you would normally do is hedge the option position by taking an opposite position in the outright market, which had much broader volume. Then the job becomes one of whittling down positions that can bite you, and there are so many ways to do it. For example, if on the original trade I sold a call, I would now be looking to buy other calls and could afford to become the best bidder in the pit.

**Obviously, in those early years, the option market was highly inefficient. It's pretty easy to see how, in that type of situation, you could put on positions that were well out of line, hedge the risk, and make lots of money. However, I'm sure that with the dramatic growth in volume over the years, the market has become much more efficient, and those types of trades no longer exist. What kind of concepts can be used in today's market to make money?**

Yes, the market has become much more competitive, but so have we. As long as we stay a notch better than our competition, there will still be good profit opportunities.

**So there are still mispricings in the market?**

Absolutely. There will always be mispricings in the market. The notion that the market will trade at its precise theoretical fair value implies that someone will hold it there without getting paid. Why should anyone do that? The service of making a market, like any other labor, is one that people are not going to want to do for free, anymore than they would want to wait on tables for free. There's work involved. There's risk involved. The market has to pay someone to do it. It's only a question of how much.

**Is that payment a bid/ask spread?**

Yes. If that edge did not exist, when someone walked in with a large buy or sell order, who would be there to take the other side?

---

The following section deals with theoretical questions related to options. Explanations for the layperson are provided within the bracketed portions of text.

---

**What do you think are some of the conceptual flaws in standard option pricing models?**

I don't know how I can answer that question without disclosing information we don't want to talk about.

**Well, let me take the initiative. For example, is one of the flaws in the standard models that they don't give enough probability weight to extreme price moves? In other words, actual price distributions have fatter tails than are implied by normal probability curves. Therefore, people using the standard models might then be inclined**

**to sell out-of-the-money options at lower prices than would be warranted by the way markets really work.**

Yes, that's a flaw in the standard Black-Scholes model. When we first started, even our biggest competitors didn't seem to have that figured out, and a lot of our profits came through that crack. By now, however, all the serious players have figured it out, and I assume that many commercially available models allow for it.

I would add, however, that it's one thing to recognize that the tails are fatter than normal, and it's another to know where to go from there. For example, do you simply fit your distribution to your empirical observations, and price options accordingly? That path has some serious problems. Do you take into account your hedging strategy? Are there other variables that none of the available models allow for? And, if there are, would their inclusion introduce so much complexity into the model as to make its application unweildly?

In other words, knowing that the distribution isn't log-normal only opens a can of worms. Frankly, though, I still can't understand why back then the competition hadn't at least gotten the lid off the can.

**Well, I think I can answer that for you. The standard mathematical curves that allow for specific probability statements just don't look that way [i.e., don't have fatter price tails].**

I think that probably explains a lot of it, but it presupposes that reality matches the curve in a mathematician's head. Believing that can get expensive.

**Let me try another one. Standard option pricing models are price neutral—that is, they assume the most likely point is an unchanged price. Do your option pricing models differ by incorporating a trend bias?**

They don't, but I think some people believe that they do. There used to be a rumor that CRT gave this line about being price neutral and hedged but that we really made our money on direction. We didn't try to dissuade people from believing that, because it made people more willing

to trade with us. But now, since the cat is probably out of the bag anyway, I'll confirm it. Our price models are neutral.

**Hypothetically, let's say that you developed a model that had a 60
percent probability of being right on the direction of the market. If
you incorporated that trend projection, then your option pricing
model would be skewed, and theoretically you could do better.**

The obvious rejoinder to that question is that if you think there is a
directional bias, set up a separate account to trade that idea, but in your
option account, trade flat. You'll get the same benefit, and if nothing
else you'll segregate the results due to each approach.

**Do you believe that over the long run there's an edge to being a
seller of premium?**

Not that I'm aware of.

**Which do you consider a better predictor of future actual volatility:
historical volatility or implied volatility? [Theoretical models
employed to estimate an option's value use a number of known
inputs (e.g., current price of the underlying market, number of
days until the option expiration) and one key unknown factor: the
volatility of the market until expiration. Since this factor is
unknown, all the standard option pricing models assume that the
future volatility will be equal to the recent volatility. The option
price indicated by this assumption is called the fair value. Some
people assume that if the market price for the option is higher than
the fair value, the option is overpriced, and if it is lower than the
fair value, it is underpriced.**

    **An alternative interpretation is that the market is simply
assuming that volatility in the period remaining until the option's
expiration will be different from the recent past volatility, called the
*historical volatility*. The volatility assumption embedded in the market price is called the *implied volatility*. If option prices are a better
predictor of future volatility than is the recent past volatility, then
the question of whether an option is overpriced or underpriced is
not only irrelevant but actually misleading. In essence, the question**

posed above is equivalent to asking whether there is any reason to assume that the strategy of buying options priced below their fair value and selling those that are above their fair value has any merit.]

Implied volatility seems better to me.

**Conceptually or empirically?**

To me it seems pretty obvious conceptually. The implied volatility is a statement of what all the players in the market, having cast their votes, believe is a fair price for future volatility. Historical volatility is nothing more than a number representing past volatility.

**In the early days of option trading, however, when the markets were highly inefficient, did you use a strategy of buying options that were well below their historical volatility-based fair value and selling those that were well above their fair value?**

No, we didn't even do it back then. We never assumed that the historical volatility was a reliable guide to an option's true value.

**How, then, did you determine when an option was out of line?**

By making a bid/ask spread where you believed you could find some other trade to lay off the volatility risk and still leave a profit margin. We were making judgments only about whether an option was overpriced or underpriced relative to other options, not about whether it was mispriced relative to the underlying market.

**There's been a lot of time and energy expended in developing improved option pricing models. If the model-derived price is not as good an indicator of an option's true value as the current market price, does it really make all that much difference which theoretical model is used to derive option values?**

I think it does. You still need the model to determine relative values. In other words, you're trying to determine whether a given option is overpriced or underpriced relative to other options, not necessarily whether it's underpriced or overpriced in any absolute sense. If two models have different opinions about the relative values of two options, then the people using those two models are going to trade with each other, and they can't both be right. Yet neither trader may have an opinion about whether a given option is overpriced or underpriced, simply about whether it is overpriced or underpriced relative to other options.

**Do you believe then that your ability to develop option pricing models that provide more accurate measurements of relative option values than do the standard option pricing models is part of the explanation behind CRT's success?**

The models are important, but the critical element is the people. To make a company this size work like a clock takes extremely unusual people.

---

During the interview, three other CRT employees—Gene Frost, Gus Pellizzi, and Niel Nielson—had entered the room and now begin to partake in the conversation.

---

**How does CRT differ in this respect from other trading companies?**

GUS: People who have interviewed here have told me that what separates us from other companies is that the other firms appear to be solely interested in their technical competence—their education and experience. CRT, on the other hand, also tends to place a large emphasis on the person and how well that person will interrelate with the other people in the work group.

**What kind of people does CRT look for?**

GENE: In the earlier years, we placed some emphasis on hiring the brightest people. One person we hired was a world champion go player. He had a great mind. It was like putting a human computer in the pit. One day he made a bad trade, panicked, and couldn't bring himself to cover the position and admit he had made a mistake. He waited until the end of the day and still didn't get out. Luckily, Joe caught the error at night, but it still ended up costing us $100,000. Even though this fellow was brilliant, he had a character flaw that allowed the error to get out of hand. Whether this guy cracked because of some insecurity in not wanting to look bad, or because of some other reason, in the end it comes down to a character flaw. Joe has made the comment that he would rather have a good trader he could trust than a brilliant trader he couldn't. When we hire people, we look for three things: character, character, and character.

GUS: I think we try to hire people who are less self-centered and more team players than is typical for this industry. A lot of other firms may also use these words, but I don't think they are as integral a part of the company as they are at CRT. It doesn't mean that we always get it right, but just trying seems to have put us ahead.

JOE: I would describe our people as those who take as much pleasure in the success of their group as they do in their individual success. We're not looking for people who sacrifice their good for the good of someone else, but rather people who can take pleasure in the success of the group. People with this attitude enhance the value of everyone around them. When you put together people who are not worried about whether they, individually, are getting enough credit, you have a tremendous advantage over the competition.

**How do you identify whether someone is doing a good job if many people are inputting into the final result?**

JOE: You can tell. The people who work with the person know, and you can ask him and he'll tell you. I recently spent some time reviewing an employee at CRT. He had written out pages of information showing what he was doing and an outline of his priorities. After about an hour of this, I finally said, "Look, how do you think you have been doing? How would you rate yourself? Not how busy have you been. Not how hard have you worked. But how have you really been doing?"

He thought for a minute and said, "Well, I think I should have been fired." He proceeded to give me an honest evaluation, including his shortcomings. He knows how he's doing, better than if I were looking over his shoulder, and he really wants to do the right thing. In general, if I trust someone to evaluate himself, he'll do so and tend to be his own toughest critic.

**Look, not everyone may have the right talents to do the job properly. Someone can come in here and sincerely say, "I love the idea of CRT and I want to be a team player," but still lack the innate talent to do the job. Or a person might think he can do the job and find out later that he can't. Maybe he's not quick enough, or maybe he's too emotional. That has to happen. How do you deal with that type of situation in an organization like this?**

JOE: Just like you do anyplace else. But the difference is that if the person is not self-centered, it's so much easier to find out that he's not right for the job. He'll admit it so much more quickly. When you get the right type of person, and he finds out that he can't do the job, he'll come to you.

**Do the other people on the team sometimes come and say, "This person is just not working out"?**

NIEL: Sure, that happens. But when it does, there's a very strong effort to find a place somewhere else at CRT for that person. That has happened over and over again.

**And does that work?**

NIEL: When we have a person whom we believe has the right type of attitude, it succeeds far more often than it doesn't.

**What distinguishes traders who succeed from those who fail?**

JOE: Successful traders tend to be instinctive rather than overly analytical.

**Why is being analytical detrimental to being a good trader?**

JOE: Because it seems to mask intuitive traits and abilities. In fact, the most analytical people tend to be the worst traders.

**What other traits distinguish the good traders?**

JOE: Humility—the ability to admit when they're wrong.

**Doesn't the fact that there's more competition from other sophisticated firms doing the same type of trading strategies cut into your profit margins?**

GUS: It has. The margins are a lot thinner than they used to be.

**How do you handle that?**

JOE: The margins go down, but the volume goes up. Also, in any business, the profit margin shrinks only up to a certain point. The margin can't shrink so much that an efficient person in that business can't put bread on the table. Therefore, if you can be the most efficient, there should always be a profit margin—maybe not all the time but certainly over the long run. I believe that's true of virtually any business.

**CRT is the preeminent firm of its type. What makes the company different?**

JOE: At CRT we believe in the philosophy that people work best when they work for each other. People think that CRT's success is due to some secret computer model. However, I believe that CRT has succeeded because we build teams. We try to give people a lot of authority and pay them what they're worth. I'm often asked what is the reason for CRT's success, and I'm willing to tell people because (A) they won't believe me and (B) even if they did believe me, they couldn't train themselves to do the same thing—to trust people and to give up absolute control.

Other people who do this type of trading often approach it too mechanically. People who are mathematically oriented believe that if you can just get the formula right, it solves the whole problem. It doesn't. Most businesses tend to think that you work with one brain and a whole bunch of mechanical executioners. To build a machine that uses many different brains that are qualitatively contributing different things is an art. Most people don't want to do it that way. Usually someone wants to believe that it's his thinking that is making things run, and there doesn't tend to be sufficient credit or responsibility given to other people. That's not the way things work here.

For me, there's a kind of magic around here, and I don't know if that's something you can pick up on or not. Without that, CRT would have been a much smaller trading company. We could have stayed in business and made a profit, but nothing compared to where we are now.

**When you say "without that," are you referring to the interrelationship among the people?**

JOE: Yes, that's the stuff that makes it a blast to come to work. I consider myself to be unbelievably lucky to be able to come to work in this kind of environment, with these people.

---

Joe Ritchie provides living proof that creative thinking can be more powerful than complex analysis. Although he has no formal mathematical training, by just thinking about how options should work Ritchie was able to develop an option pricing model that, judging by CRT's performance, must be better than all the academically derived models commonly in use.

The type of trading done by CRT has little direct relevance to individual traders. The primary lessons to be drawn from this interview, I believe, are not related to trading, but rather management. The enormous financial success and widespread employee loyalty enjoyed by CRT is no doubt a consequence of Joe Ritchie's managerial philosophy: Share the responsibility and share the profits. This policy makes so much common sense that you wonder why more companies don't use it. Corporate America, are you listening?

# Blair Hull

## GETTING THE EDGE

B lair Hull came to trading by way of the blackjack tables. This is not as strange as it may sound, since there are actually very strong parallels between the two activities. The point is not that success in trading is akin to luck in gambling, but rather that consistent winning in both is a matter of strategy and discipline, not luck. Luck plays a role only over the short term, where its potential adverse impact must be neutralized by money management controls.

After the casinos caught on to Hull's blackjack team, he sought another avenue for applying probability theory to making money. He found the same general principles could be employed to profit from the mispricings that occurred in the option markets. Hull started with $25,000 in late 1976 and by the start of 1979 had multiplied his stake twentyfold. He continued to score consistent profits in the subsequent years, averaging roughly 100 percent per year (excluding those years in which he took sabbaticals).

In 1985, he launched Hull Trading Company to allow for a more widespread application of his trading strategies. The company, which began with a skeleton staff of five, expanded rapidly, reaching nearly one hundred employees by mid-1991. If the growth in personnel can be

Note: Readers unfamiliar with options may wish to read the Appendix in order to understand the trading-related references in this chapter.

described as arithmetic, the expansion of computers was geometric. HTC has an entire floor in its office building devoted to its computer equipment. Another option trader with the Chicago Board Options Exchange (CBOE) who maintains an office in the same building quipped, "The building had to put in another bank of air conditioners on the roof because Hull's computers were sucking up all the cool air."

Hull's company employs complex strategies, trading a broad range of interrelated option markets against each other in order to profit from temporary mispricings, while simultaneously keeping the firm's net risk exposure to minimal levels. HTC is a market maker on a wide variety of exchanges, including the CBOE, the Chicago Mercantile Exchange, the American Stock Exchange, the New York Stock Exchange, and various foreign exchanges. They account for over 10 percent of the total trading volume in a number of options in which they make markets.

All the positions taken by the company's traders, who now number twenty-five, are constantly monitored in real time. Strategies are continuously revised to take into account changes in both market prices and positions held by the firm, with a real-time lag of only two seconds. Now you get the idea why Hull needs all those computers.

A graph of HTC's trading profits looks like a simulation in one of those trading system ads, except in this case the results are real. A starting stake of $1 million in 1985 grew to $90 million by mid-1991, after expenses. (The gross trading profits during this period were substantially greater, approximating $137 million.) The really remarkable achievement is the firm's apparent modest risk level despite these very substantial gains. Since its inception, HTC has been profitable in fifty-eight of six-nine months (after expenses), with only five of these months registering a net trading loss (before expense allocations).

This interview was conducted in a conference room at HTC. I found Hull relatively relaxed and open in discussing his career. I particularly liked his candidness in talking about his blackjack-playing experiences.

---

**How did you first get involved in the markets?**

My interest probably dates back to when my grandfather charted stocks. I didn't really understand what he was doing, but the idea of having capital working for you was appealing. The desire to learn about the financial markets led me to business school at Santa Clara University. After graduating, I got a job as a security analyst at Blair and Company. Exactly three months after I started, the West Coast research department was eliminated during the bear market of 1969.

**Did you learn anything about the markets during your brief stint there?**

I learned what financial analysts do. I learned about Graham and Dodd and fundamental analysis.* I thought that approach was too subjective; it couldn't be quantified or systematized. So I didn't want to have anything to do with it.

**After your job was eliminated, did you get another position as an analyst?**

No, I got a job selling time on large computers. However, that position was essentially a marketing slot, and I was interested in doing analytical work. After about a year, I left to take a job in operations research for Kaiser Cement. At that time, I got interested in playing blackjack by reading a book called *Beat the Dealer* by Ed Thorp. From 1971 to 1975, I went to the Nevada casinos regularly.

**Did you live in Nevada at the time?**

No, I lived in California. But I would take a blackjack trip every chance I got. I probably spent about five days a month in Nevada during that time. In a sense, I owe everything that I have to the state of Nevada. It not only provided me with my original trading stake, but the betting experience taught me a lot of things that allowed me to become a successful trader.

**Would it be fair to say that Thorp's book was in some way responsible for your success as a trader?**

---

*Hull is referring to the book *Security Analysis* by Graham and Dodd, which is considered by many to be the bible of fundamental analysis in the stock market.

The book certainly taught me about the methodology of blackjack. Without this knowledge, I don't think I would be in the trading business today.

**What was the basic strategy espoused by the book?**

In the basic rules of blackjack, the house has a small edge. However, if a lot of small cards have been dealt—that is, the deck is rich in tens and aces—then the odds can shift in favor of the bettor by, say, 1 to 2 percent. [Tens refer to the point value of the cards and include all picture cards as well as tens.]*

**Would it be a matter of keeping track of the cards and placing very small bets, or not betting at all, whenever there were a relatively large amount of aces and tens out?**

Right. That's essentially what I did. I would place maybe five bets an hour using that method.

**My image of a blackjack table is where you sit down and are continually dealt hands. From a practical standpoint, how do you bet so selectively without it appearing awkward?**

My strategy was to play only the hands that had an advantage. I stood back and did what was called back-counting. You can get away with that if you're betting small amounts of money.

**Were you immediately successful using this technique?**

Actually, in my first attempt, I made only about fifty bets and ended up with a net loss. At that point, I got a little more involved in calculating

---

*The object of blackjack is to get a total card count greater than the dealer, but not higher than twenty-one. Each card has a point value equal to its face, except for picture cards, which each have a value of ten, and aces, which can be counted as either one or eleven at the option of the player. A blackjack is a two-card hand consisting of an ace and a ten-card. If a player is dealt a blackjack, he wins one and one-half times his bet, unless the dealer draws the same hand, in which case the result is a tie. If the dealer alone draws a blackjack, all players lose automatically. A player may draw as many cards as he wants as long as his total remains under twenty-one. If his total exceeds twenty-one, he loses automatically. The more concentrated tens and aces are in the deck, the better the odds for the player.

how many bets it would take to make sure that I would be a winner over the long run.

**In other words, the reason fifty bets didn't work was that fifty was too small a number and still left the odds of winning too close to even.**

Right. I knew that if I kept on playing with the edge in my favor, eventually I would come out ahead. Following Thorp's advice, I started with a base of $120 and placed bets between $1 and $4. After two years, I was ahead about $10,000.

Around this time, I became friends with another blackjack player who told me about a team of players that were doing quite well. He said, "This is a very secretive team, so I can't give you the leader's name. But I will give him your name, and maybe he'll contact you." A couple of months later, my friend was killed in an automobile accident, and I assumed that put an end to any chances of contacting the team. About a year later, the organizer of the team called me.

Actually, during the interim, I had tried to put together my own team. However, I wasn't too successful in recruiting qualified members. For example, one time we were supposed to meet at the Sahara in Las Vegas, which is the city we always played in. One of the players, however, knew only of a Sahara in Lake Tahoe. So that's where he went. All weekend long, we couldn't figure out where he was.

**Why were you interested in a team approach instead of continuing to play solo?**

Whether you're playing blackjack or trading, your profitability depends on your edge and how many times you get to apply that edge. The team approach provides two advantages. First, assume that over a weekend of playing, the odds of my coming out ahead are two out of three. By combining banks with another person, the total number of trading days would be doubled and, as a result, the probability of winning would rise to three out of four. The more players you combine, the better your chances of a successful outcome.

**In other words, if you have the edge, by greatly increasing the number of bets, the probability of success approaches certainty. It**

**sounds as if you had created a minicasino within a casino, with the casino taking the sucker bets. What is the other advantage you referred to?**

The team approach allows you to increase the maximum bet size. Theoretically, the largest bet you can make should be one-fiftieth of your capital. If you have $1,000, that means your biggest bet should be $20. If five players with $1,000 apiece combine, however, the maximum bet size increases to $100.

**Are you saying that each person could determine his maximum bet size based on the combined capital base of all the players without any increase in his individual risk?**

That's correct.

**Did the team accept you as a member?**

The team had a series of tests that one had to take in order to become a member. I thought I was a very skillful player, but I actually failed the test. I had to increase my skills in order to become a member of the team.

**What were your shortcomings?**

They were in all areas. I had some flaws in basic strategy. I didn't count the cards fast enough. I didn't estimate decks accurately.

**How do you estimate the size of the deck?**

The casinos typically used four-deck shoes. The team used eight different deck sizes in one-half deck increments. You would practice identifying these different stacks, until you could tell them apart from across the room.

**What method did the team use to count cards?**

They used a method called the Revere Advance Point Count: twos, threes, and sixes were assigned a value of two, fours a value of three, fives a value of four, sevens a value of one, eights a value of zero, nines a value of minus two, and tens a value of minus three; aces were kept as a separate count. The higher the count—that is, the more high cards remaining undealt—the more favorable the odds for the players.

**Did the count have to be standardized by the number of cards remaining?**

Yes. The true count is the raw count divided by the number of decks remaining. So if the raw count is ten and there are two decks remaining, the true count is plus five. If there is only one-half deck remaining, the true count is plus twenty. What you're really concerned about is the density of high cards in the undealt deck.

**Did Thorp use a similar approach in his book?**

Thorp started out with a ten and non-ten count. In his second book, he revised that so twos through sixes had a value of plus one, sevens, eights, and nines were neutral, and tens and aces had a value of minus one.

**So, in essence, the Revere Advance Point Count was a more sophisticated version of the Thorp approach.**

Right. There's a basic trade-off between accuracy and difficulty in keeping the count. Even the Revere approach doesn't represent the optimal solution based on probability theory. But if you use a more complicated (and presumably more accurate) counting method, you would be prone to making more errors.

**Was it hard to keep track of the true count?**

It takes a lot of practice, and you need to have discipline. Also, you develop mental shortcuts. For example, if you see a five and a ten together, you automatically associate the combination as plus because the five has a value of plus four and the ten a value of minus three.

**How much time did you actually spend in honing these skills?**

Initially, it takes a lot of time. After a while, it's a matter of practicing a couple of hours before each trip.

**Were you shocked when you flunked the team's test? What happened afterwards?**

There was a battery of ten different tests. I was informed as to the lack of my knowledge. I practiced for about a month and retook the test successfully.

**How many people were part of the team at the time?**

When I joined, there were eight members, but it eventually grew to about twenty.

**Does this type of operation depend on a great deal of trust and honesty? If you combined banks and played independently, how did players know how the other members were really doing?**

In the later stages, we actually started using polygraphs. I have both taken and administered them. In the early days, there weren't any polygraphs; people just trusted each other.

**At what point did people start becoming suspicious of other members of the team?**

[*He laughs.*] It became obvious that one of the players was skimming off the top.

**Because there's a lot of controversy about polygraphs, I'm curious about whether you believe that the tests actually work.**

Generally speaking, I believe they're about 85 percent accurate. I've taken four and administered about six. There's no question that the process of getting ready for the polygraph and administering the test can get information from people. In one case, I literally saw the blood drain from a person's face when I asked a question. I've had admissions before, during, and after polygraphs. Sometimes the information you turn up is minor—for example, a person not accounting for expenses accurately. Sometimes there are bigger issues involved. For example, one fellow was playing for another team at the same time he was playing for us, which involved passing on proprietary information to a competitor.

**Did the team operate as a team or just simply separate individuals using a common bank?**

There were several versions of teams. This particular large team used a method in which there was a Big Player and several card counters. The card counters were spread out over several tables and would bet relatively small. They would then signal the Big Player when the count was very favorable.

**Was this done to be less obvious?**

Right. If this guy isn't looking at the cards, how could he be counting them?

**How long did it take for the casinos to learn of the team's existence?**

A little over six months. We started playing very big. We just kept building and building, and pretty soon we were playing limit, and they knew who we were.

**Did they know you were all part of the same team, or did they just know you individually?**

They knew each of us, but then they slowly started to pick up the associations. There was a detective agency the casinos employed that specialized in finding card counters. The agency classified card counters in the same category as dice cheats or slot machine drillers. Essentially, the casinos don't want to have skillful players. And I understand that. I wouldn't either if I owned a casino.

**Is it easy to spot a card counter because he's not playing every hand?**

It's easy to spot him even if he *is* playing every hand.

**Because of the variation of bet size—betting low on low-probability hands?**

Yes. If I stood behind someone playing with a large amount of money, I could tell very quickly at what level of advantage or disadvantage he was playing.

**Did you originally think the team would last longer before the casinos caught on?**

I think if we had been a little more discreet, the team could have lasted longer. One of the problems was that one of the members of the team was more interested in writing a book than in the continued success of the team. [The book Hull is referring to is *The Big Player,* by Ken Uston; Holt, Rinehart and Winston, 1977.] Ironically, I was the one who talked the other partners into allowing him to be a Big Player. It proved to be the start of the team's downfall. People have a basic need to be recognized. He had a need to be recognized—even by the casinos. Until you get barred, the casinos haven't recognized that you're a good player. There are direct parallels to trading in the markets.

**Let's talk about that connection.**

It's the same thing. The people who want to be recognized as the greatest traders are probably not the greatest traders. Egos get in the way of the process. In my opinion, you never want to be the largest player in the pit.

**Before I get to the connection between blackjack and trading, I'm just curious: Is it still possible to beat the casinos using the card counting method today?**

Absolutely. If I didn't have any money, there's no doubt in my mind about where I would go.

**Then why don't the casinos use larger decks or reshuffle more frequently so as to make card counting unfeasible?**

First of all, the prevalence of blackjack strategy books actually helps the casinos by giving people the hope of winning. Also, it's not the mathematical skill that's critical to winning, it's the discipline of being able to stick to the system. There are very few people who can develop the skills to get the edge, and far fewer still who can withstand the losses emotionally and still stick with the system. Probably only one in five hundred people has the necessary discipline to be successful.

**Did the teams on which you played help enforce the necessary discipline?**

To some extent, the team helps you to develop discipline. It's almost like the army—you have to do things under certain conditions and you have to have a certain skill level. The discipline is imposed by the team as a self-regulatory process. It's very difficult for an individual to have the same level of discipline.

**So the casinos leave it feasible to win in blackjack by card counting because there are more people who misapply the strategies for winning.**

Absolutely.

**What element of the blackjack playing experience do you believe contributed to your success as a trader?**

The experience of going through extensive losing periods and having the faith to stick with the system because I knew that I had the edge was something that helped me a great deal when I went into the pit. Also, the risk control experience was very beneficial. In blackjack, even if you have the edge, there are going to be periods of significant losses. When that happens, you have to cut back your bet size in order to avoid the possibility of ruin. If you lose half your stake, you have to cut your bet size in half. That's a difficult thing to do when you're down significantly, but it's essential to surviving.

**The way you express it, blackjack and trading are very similar.**

That's right. All you need is a mathematical advantage and the money management controls to assure that you stay in the game. Everything else takes care of itself.

**What happened after the team was uncovered?**

For a while, I used the same principles to organize smaller teams. I kept a low profile by being a counter instead of the Big Player and playing in other locations, like Atlantic City. When I got tired of traveling so much, I tried to find other ways of applying probability theory. For a while, I tried poker, but I found that, although I had all the mathematics down pat, I didn't have the appropriate skills. Every time I had the hand and bet large, everybody folded, and every time I bluffed, everybody stayed in.

**Now correct me if I'm wrong. In blackjack, the rules are absolutely dictated. The dealer has to draw another card or he has to stick, depending on his card count, whereas in poker, people have more choice, and reading your opponent becomes a factor. Therefore, even if you have the edge mathematically, if people can read your emotions correctly or you can't read theirs, you lose the edge.**

Right, you lose the edge in a major way. Bluffing is an essential element of the game. There's a mathematician who has written some very good books on poker strategy, but he's never been able to make any money playing poker.

**Do you believe that some of the successful floor traders are successful because they're good at reading people?**

Absolutely. To some extent, you can sense when another market participant is in trouble. In other words, he's offering at a quarter and you can just read that he needs to get out. So even if you want to buy at a quarter, you'll wait, because you know he's eventually going to reduce his offer to an eighth. This approach was never an important element in my own trading, however. Most of the money I've made has been the result of being on the right side of the theoretical value.

**When did you actually get involved in trading?**

During the period when I was winding down my involvement in blackjack, I started to work on some option valuation models.

**Was your model similar to the standard models, such as Black-Scholes?**

Actually, the paper on this model was published in 1973. I was unfamiliar with the literature, so in 1975 I was busy constructing this model, which in fact had already been developed. In late 1976, I applied to be a market maker on the Pacific Stock Exchange.

**What was your trading method?**

Each day, I ran a computer program that generated theoretical value sheets, which told me what each option was worth at a certain stock price. Essentially, I walked around the pits with these sheets, and any time an option was out of line with my theoretical model, I bought or sold it.

**So when you first started in option trading, you were looking for options that were out of line with their theoretical value.**

That's right.

**That raises an interesting question. Since theoretical values are based on historical volatility, doesn't that approach imply that historical volatility is a better predictor of future volatility than implied volatility? [For a detailed discussion of the concepts underlying this question, see the Joe Ritchie interview, pages 356–57.]**

No. Actually, empirical studies have shown that implied volatility is better than historical volatility in predicting the actual future volatility.

**Then how could you make money by trading based on mispricings relative to your model?**

The real key is relative value. It doesn't matter what model you use, as long as you apply it consistently across all option prices. What I was really concerned about was the price of options relative to each other. I would adjust the model-implied prices so that the at-the-money implied price was in line with the market price. For example, if the model said the at-the-money option was worth 3 but the option was actually trading at 3 1/2, then I would raise the volatility assumption in the model so the at-the-money option would also be priced at 3 1/2. Once you make that adjustment, all the other option values should be in line with the market. Then I would merely buy those options that were trading cheaper and sell those that were more expensive.

**In other words, we're not talking about looking at whether the market is out of line with the model, but rather whether the individual options in a specific market are out of line relative to each other.**

Yes. I would say that in the early periods, most of my money was made in those types of trades.

**Besides the fact that the mathematical models are forced to estimate the unknown future volatility by using past volatility, are there any other potential pitfalls in using these models?**

Most of the models assume that stock options follow a log-normal distribution. In fact, I found out that the actual price distributions of virtually all financial markets tend to have fatter tails than suggested by the log-normal distribution.

**To put that in lay terms, you're saying that the standard mathematical models do not provide an accurate reflection of how options should be priced in the real world because of the tendency of extreme price moves to occur far more frequently than implied by the standard assumptions in these models.**

Correct.

**This would imply that it makes more sense to be a buyer of deep out-of-the-money options than might be assumed based on a model.**

That's true—especially in potential takeover situations.

**Given this bias, might you not be misled to be willing to sell a deep out-of-the-money option versus another option more readily than you should?**

Yes, absolutely. In all classes of options, if you believed the model, you would sell more of these options.

**Were you losing money doing that?**

No. I was consistently making money, but that kind of strategy—selling deep out-of-the-money options—only leads to consistent profits until a catastrophe arises. Then you lose it all, plus some.

**Were you lucky not to hit a catastrophe using that approach?**

I was lucky in hitting catastrophes that did not take me out of the game, even though that could have happened.

**Can you give me a specific example?**

In 1981, I had financed a trader on the American Stock Exchange who sold out-of-the-money options in a takeover situation. I lost about one-third of my capital in that one trade. Emotionally I handled it very well. Unfortunately, about a week later, I had another large loss in a short out-of-the-money call position in Kennecott. Ironically, even though my position was relatively small, the overnight move was so enormous that the loss was substantial. After these two takeovers, I had lost about half my money.

**How long had you been trading at that time?**

About four and a half years.

**Am I understanding you correctly? These two trades alone wiped out approximately half of the cumulative profits you had made on the presumably thousands of trades up to that point?**

Right.

**How had you done over the four years up to this point in time?**

In my first two years in the business, I had back-to-back 400 percent returns. Thereafter, I averaged roughly 100 percent per year.

**What about 1981, the year in which you had these two big hits?**

I still ended the year with a net profit.

**Were your trading profits made strictly by taking advantage of mispricings?**

Right. The speculators are usually on one side of the market. For example, they may be buying out-of-the-money calls. At the same time, institutional investors might be doing buy writes, which would be selling long-term calls. To some extent, a smart market maker is a risk transfer agent. He would buy the calls from the institutions and sell the other calls to the speculators, trying to balance the overall position so that there is as little net risk as possible.

**Were you always totally hedged?**

I always tried to be relatively hedged. In a takeover situation, however, you might think that you are hedged, but the price move occurs so quickly that you really aren't.

**You mentioned that speculators are usually on the buy side of options. In general, do you believe there is a mispricing that occurs because people like to buy options?**

If you compare historical graphs of implied volatility versus historical volatility across a spectrum of markets, you will see a distinct tendency for implied volatility being higher—a pattern that suggests that such a bias exists.

**Does that imply that being a consistent seller of options is a viable strategy?**

I believe there's an edge to always being a seller, but I wouldn't trade that way because the implied risk in that approach is too great. But to answer your question, generally speaking, I believe the buyer of options has the disadvantage.

**In takeover situations, are there sometimes clues that something is going to happen—for example, an option suddenly starting to trade significantly beyond where it should be trading?**

Of course. In fact, in recent years, some of the regulatory people have started to look at these things. There are also some traders who use indicators called wolf detectors. These traders monitor the markets for unusual price moves in the underlying stock, or sudden increases in volume, or a jump in implied volatility for the out-of-the-money options. These types of indications are used as a warning that there may be a wolf out there, so to speak. But that's not my approach.

**How do you protect yourself against the possibility that there may be a surprise takeover in a stock in which you hold a significant short out-of-the-money call position?**

In individual stocks, you play the high capitalization issues, which tend to have information that is already in the marketplace. You tend to get far fewer sudden moves when trading the high capitalization stocks.

**Do you ever do any directional trades?**

Maybe a couple of times a year, I might get a strong idea for a directional trade. Although these types of trading ideas are infrequent, they're usually right.

**Can you give me an example?**

When I was trading on the Pacific Stock Exchange, I bought thousands of calls in McDonnell Douglas. At the time, there had been a number of DC-10 crashes, and there was some speculation that they would never fly again. I went home and told my wife about the large position I had in these calls. She was absolutely horrified. She said, "Those planes [DC-10s] are never going to fly again. We're going to be broke."

**Was this opinion based on the news coverage prevalent at the time?**

Yes. It was the climax of fear in the public. You could say my wife taught me to be a contrarian. That trade taught me a lot about the marketplace. When nobody wants to touch the market, that's the time you have to step up.

**Do you remember any other directional trades?**

On the day following the 508-point crash in the Dow Jones index [October 19, 1987], due to a combination of pervasive fear in the market and the increased capital requirements by the clearing firm, we couldn't find anybody to execute our orders in the Major Market Index [MMI] traded on the Chicago Board of Trade. As a result, I was forced to go over there and trade in the pit myself.

I heard rumors that the Chicago Mercantile Exchange was considering calling a trading halt. [The CME trades the S&P 500 index futures contract.] If true, this would have represented a drastic action. I immediately ran to call up my desk to try to research what had happened after past trading halts. However, after about thirty minutes, they couldn't find out anything. I sensed that the CME was about to halt trading. I called back the desk and said, "Make sure that we're long on any trading halt."

**Why did you want to be long?**

Because the fear was all out of proportion to reality. I had to be a buyer. We have a philosophy that involves always trying to provide liquidity to the market. The Merc eventually halted trading and about three minutes later a commission house broker was trying to get a bid on a one-hundred-lot sell order. The market was trading at 290 and nobody was bidding any size. I bid 285 and he sold me a hundred. A few minutes later, he sold me another fifty at the same price. Those were the only trades transacted at 285. The market closed at 400 that day.

**Of course, in hindsight, that was a great trade—you ended up buying the low. But couldn't the rationale of buying because fear was out of proportion to reality also have been used as a reason to go long the previous day when the Dow Jones collapsed by over 500 points?**

There was a specific event tied to the timing of that trade: the CME was going to halt trading.

**Any other directional trades that come to mind?**

I went long the stock market on the morning of January 15, 1991, the day of Bush's original midnight ultimatum deadline to Hussein. Everybody thought the market would go down 150 points if the war started. I thought, "How bad can this war be?"

**Your assumption was that Bush would move as soon as he could?**

My assumption was that the uncertainty had to diminish, and therefore I had to be long the market. My strategy was to put on half the position that morning just before the deadline expiration and the other half after the war had started.

**Putting on the first half before the start of the war certainly proved to be the right move. But do you remember why you didn't wait to put on the entire position until after the war had actually started?**

It was just a matter of the fear and uncertainty in the market. My head trader put that trade in the LTG account. A few years earlier, I had criticized one of my arbitrage traders for wanting to take a net long position by saying, "What do you think, you have a line to God?" So putting the trade in the LTG account was his way of making fun of me.

**Did you end up buying the other half of the position after the war had started?**

No. I would have put it on if the market had opened down, but instead the market opened up sharply higher.

**Your main profitability, however, doesn't come from directional trades?**

That S&P 500 trade amounted to close to $4 million in about thirty minutes, which certainly helped our P and L for that day. But overall, I would say that those types of trades account for only about 5 percent of the firm's total trading profits. Our basic methodology is still buying undervalued securities and selling overvalued securities. It all goes back to the blackjack philosophy that, if you have the edge, in the long run, you'll make more money by doing a lot of transactions.

**Have your strategies changed from the basic concept of buying the cheap options and selling the more expensive ones?**

Speed has become much more important and strategies have become much more complex.

**Is that because the easier plays are gone?**

This is always a horse race, and unless you're running very fast, they're going to catch you.

**Do you now have to focus on intermarket trades instead of intra-market trades? Has the single market mispricing disappeared?**

Absolutely. Your return on capital would be very small if you weren't trading across markets.

**There are many other major firms, such as CRT, utilizing similar trading strategies. Don't you find yourself competing with these other firms for the same trades? How do you avoid getting in each other's way?**

You have to realize who is driving the market. None of us would be here if it weren't for the institutions who want to do the trades. They have a need to alter their risk profile, and we take the other side. Also, we do differ from some of these other firms you mentioned in that we look for the less obvious offsets.

**What does that mean?**

It's an outgrowth of my days as a floor trader. I was one of the slowest floor traders ever. Because someone else would always get to the primary market first, I had to look someplace else. I would end up offsetting a trade in a market that was not as highly correlated. For example, if the OEX options were priced high and the arbitrage traders were sellers, they would offset these positions in the S&P 500. Instead, I would end up hedging the position in the NYFE [New York Futures Exchange] and MMI, because the other OEX traders would already have hit the S&P 500. [The OEX contract is based on the S&P 100, which is extremely highly correlated with the S&P 500 but less correlated with the other stock indexes, such as the NYFE and MMI.]

**Having toured your operation, I find it difficult to believe that you're still one of the slowest traders.**

Well, probably not anymore. We're highly automated now. But my on-the-floor experience has made us much more inclined to look for less obvious markets in which to offset trades. We look for trading opportunities between less correlated markets.

**Do you try to keep the firm's total position basically hedged all the time?**

I try to have a zero delta portfolio [a portfolio that is neutralized relative to directional moves in the market]. The net delta of the firm's portfolio [i.e., the contract equivalent net long or short position] is reevaluated within two seconds each time any of the traders makes a new trade. There is a feedback process so that each trader knows this information instantaneously and therefore knows in which direction to lean.

**In other words, if the firm's net position is long, the traders lean to finding mispricings that require implementing a position with a bearish bias.**

Exactly. In essence, each trader is really trading a firm strategy.

**Is each trader responsible for hedging his own trades?**

No. We have twenty-five traders, one of whom is responsible for doing the hedging [i.e., assuring that the firm's net exposure to price changes is as close to zero as possible]. You might say he's the air traffic controller.

**So the individual traders can buy whatever they think is cheap and sell whatever they think is high, even if it's a one-sided trade, because they know that the air traffic controller will make sure that the firm's net position stays close to neutral.**

Exactly. When there's an edge on a trade, part of the cost of taking that trade is that you have to give up some of that edge to somebody else in order to hedge it. The beauty of this system is that the cost of hedging is very small.

**Covered calls [buying a stock and selling a call against it] are frequently promoted as trading strategies. As we both know, doing a covered call is identical to selling a put. Is there ever any strategic rationale for implementing a covered call instead of a short put, or is the former promoted because it involves a double commission, or perhaps for semantic reasons— that is, even though the two trades are identical, the covered call *sounds* like a less risky proposition than a short put position?**

I don't know how to articulate the fraud that is sometimes perpetrated on the public. A lot of strategies promoted by brokers do not serve the interest of their clients at all. I almost feel guilty when taking the other side of a covered call position, because it's obvious that the customer is operating under a misconception.

**Then you agree that anyone who wants to do a covered call would be better off simply selling a put, assuming that he plans to initiate and liquidate the stock and call positions simultaneously?**

Right. If you want to guarantee an inferior strategy, do covered calls.

**I could never understand the logic....**

You've got the game.

**On expiration, small moves in the underlying stock can make a big difference in whether an option expires profitably or unprofitably. It seems like there must be a tremendous temptation for people with a large option position to try to influence the price of the stock at expiration. Does that happen?**

When I was a trader on the Pacific Stock Exchange, two smaller market makers wanted to pin the price of a particular stock to the strike. They wanted to sell the stock on the expiration date and make sure all the calls and puts went out worthless. They enlisted the aid of a large market maker in this scheme. The large market maker agreed to join their group and pin the stock at the strike. Instead, he took the opposite position and took them both out of the game. [He laughs at the recollection.]

Actually, there is a natural tendency for stocks to finish at or near the strike. A few years ago I did some statistical work that was quoted in the *Wall Street Journal.* Speculators tend to be long the slightly in-the-money calls and they usually sell their option positions prior to expiration because they don't want to exercise them. For example, let's say a stock is trading at 60 1/2. Most of the open interest will be in the 60 calls. The public, which is long the 60 calls, will tend to sell this position as expiration approaches. The market maker will be on the other side of this trade, and in order to hedge himself he has to sell the stock. This chain of events tends to push the price of the stock toward the nearest strike price at expiration. I found that, statistically, a stock is about twice as likely to finish within one-quarter of a point of the strike price at an option expiration than might be expected if there were no correlation involved.

**Do you use this finding in any way?**

Yes, we play this strategy because it provides an edge.

**Any advice for the nonprofessional who trades options?**

The OEX RAES (Remote Automatic Execution System) is the public's edge. The system provides an automatic execution within ten seconds or so.

**Why do you say it's the public's edge?**

Because market makers have agreed to be on the other side. When markets turn extremely volatile, the market makers cannot update these quotes fast enough. Therefore, the public customer has a tremendous edge in those types of markets.

**Why should a customer ever go to an open outcry execution if he can use this automatic system?**

The RAES only accepts orders of ten contracts or less. If the order size does not exceed this limit, the customer would generally be better off using this execution system.

**What do you think are some of the key characteristics or traits of a successful options trader?**

You can't listen to the news. You have to go with the facts. You need to use a logical approach and have the discipline to apply it. You must be able to control your emotions.

**Anything else?**

Consistency. You need to go for the small theoretical edges instead of home runs.

**Is there a certain personality type that is best suited to being a successful trader?**

Based on my experience with the traders I've hired, I would say that successful blackjack, chess, and bridge players are more likely to fit the profile of a good options trader.

**What are some of the misconceptions you have found people have about the market?**

They tend to listen to rumors. They're too interested in who's buying or selling. They think that type of information is important; yet it rarely means anything.

**Do you feel that your past experience on blackjack teams influenced you in moving toward a team trading approach?**

The experience was helpful in being able to successfully build a trading team.

**Did you enter this business thinking you were going to be a team trading leader as opposed to an individual trader?**

I actually went into the business thinking I could automate everything and that a machine would do it all.

**When did you realize that wasn't going to happen?**

I haven't realized that yet. I'm still working on it [he laughs]. We reward people who automate. We want people to work toward that goal.

---

Some people are fond of saying, "Even a poor system could make money with good money management." This contention is complete nonsense. All that good money management will do for a poor strategy is to assure that you will lose money more slowly. For example, no money management system can ever be designed to make money playing roulette, because the edge is against you. (The odds would be exactly even, but the zero and double zero give the house a decisive advantage.) In fact, if you are playing a poor strategy (one where the edge is against you), your best chance for coming out ahead is to apply the extreme of bad money management—risk everything on one trade. Why? Because the longer you play with a negative edge, the greater the probability of eventual financial ruin.

Probably the most basic requirement for successful trading is that you must have some well-defined method, or, in other words, a specific approach that gives you an edge. That approach could be buying under-valued securities and selling overvalued securities, as it is for Hull, or it could be some better-than-breakeven way of selecting price directional trades. Without such a method, or edge, you will eventually lose, because the odds are 50/50 before transaction costs. If you don't know what your method is, you don't have one. (By the way, buying a stock because your brother-in-law gives you a tip is not a method.)

The Hull interview also helps underscore the distinction between gambling and betting or trading with an edge. Participants in the market may well be gambling. If you don't have a method (i.e., an edge), then trading is every bit as much a gamble as betting in the casinos. But with a method, trading—or for that matter, even blackjack—becomes a business rather than gambling. Fortunately for traders, whereas the casinos can bar players because they become too proficient, the market has no way of eliminating the skillful traders (other than behaving in a manner that seems to confound the greatest number of people the greatest amount of time). Therefore, if you can devise a method to beat the market, no exchange can come to you and say, "We've noticed that you're making too much money. You can't trade here any more."

Once you have a method, you still need money management to prevent an adverse streak from taking you out of the game. It is critical to keep in mind that even if you have the edge, you can still lose all your money. Therefore, the bet or trade size must be small enough to keep the probability of such an event very low. So the appropriate quote is, "Even a good system can lose money with poor money management," rather than the fallacious contortion of this theme quoted at the start of this section.

This same theme is colorfully described in Ken Uston's *The Big Player*, the book written about the blackjack team that Hull described in the interview:

> Listening to Barry narrate his horror story, Ken thought back to a day several weeks earlier when a broker friend who counted cards had come over to his apartment to discuss his favorite subject—losing. Ever since extreme negative swings had led to his personal Las Vegas wipeout several years ago, the man approached the blackjack pit conservatively. He warned Ken about the dangers of the team's escalating betting level. "Those swings are wild, Kenny. I'm telling you, they

can really hurt you. Watch out. So far you guys have been lucky, but those swings are there."

Another pertinent lesson that Hull applied to blackjack, as well as trading, is that if you have a winning method, you must have the faith to keep applying it even during losing periods. The trick, however, is to reduce the risk by reducing your bet or trade size so that the ratio between risk and equity stays relatively constant.

Although Hull is predominantly an arbitrage trader, he occasionally takes directional trades, which have tended to be quite successful. Hull's rules for directional trading, although not explicitly stated, can be inferred from the interview:

1.  Trade infrequently and only when you have a strong idea.
2.  Trade the opposite side of the predominant news stories.
3.  Time your trade to coincide with an event that has the potential to lead to a panic climax.

# Jeff Yass

## THE MATHEMATICS OF STRATEGY

Jeff Yass started as an option trader on the floor of the Philadelphia Stock Exchange in 1981. He was so enthralled by the opportunities in option trading that he enticed a number of his college friends to try trading careers. During the early 1980s, he trained six of these friends as traders. In 1987, Yass and his friends joined to form Susquehanna Investment Group. The firm has grown rapidly and now employs 175 people, including 90 traders. Today, Susquehanna is one of the largest option trading firms in the world and one of the largest entities in program trading.

Yass seeks out nuances of market inefficiencies through complex refinements of standard option pricing models. However, the essence of Yass's approach is not necessarily having a better model but rather placing greater emphasis on applying mathematical game theory principals to maximize winnings. To Yass, the market is like a giant poker game, and you have to pay very close attention to the skill level of your opponents. As Yass explains it in one of his poker analogies, "If you're the sixth best poker player in the world and you play with the five best players, you're going to lose. On the other hand, if your skills are only

Note: Readers unfamiliar with options may wish to read the Appendix in order to understand the trading-related references in this chapter.

**390**

average, but you play against weak opponents, you're going to win." Yass will factor in his perception of the skill and knowledge of the person on the other side of a trade and adjust his strategy accordingly. He is willing to subjugate or revise his own market views based on the actions of those he considers better-informed traders.

Yass has a quick mind and talks a mile a minute. We started the interview in his Philadelphia office after market hours and finished at a local restaurant. Although I had my doubts about Yass's restaurant selection abilities (for reasons that will quickly become evident), the food was superb. Unfortunately, the food quality was matched by the restaurant's popularity, and hence noise level, leaving me with cassette recordings worthy of the deciphering capabilities of the CIA. We obviously appeared to be a bit strange to a group of nearby diners who upon leaving couldn't resist inquiring why we were recording our dinner conversation.

---

**When did you first get interested in markets?**

When I was a kid. I loved the stock market. I used to tear the paper out of my father's hands to check the stock quotes.

**Did you trade any stocks as a kid?**

I loved TV dinners. The first time I tried a Swanson's TV dinner, I thought it was so delicious and such a great idea that I wanted to buy the stock. I found out that Swanson's was owned by Campbell, and I got my father to buy ten shares of the stock for me.

**Do you still love TV dinners?**

Yes, and I also love all airplane food. I agree with Joan Rivers, who says she's suspicious of anyone who claims they don't like airplane food.

**I'm not sure I still want to go to dinner with you later. So what happened to Campbell after you bought it?**

The stock never went anywhere.

**I'm not surprised.**

It went up *eventually*. I would have done OK if I had held on to it for the next thirty years.

**Was that your first stock market transaction?**

Yes.

**How old were you then?**

Eleven.

**Did you buy any other stocks as a kid?**

When I was about thirteen, I bought Eastern Airlines. I flew to Florida at the time, and I thought it was a good airline. I also bought a realty company that eventually went bankrupt. I always lost. I remember my father saying to me, "The stock was around a long time before you bought it. Just because you bought it now doesn't mean that it suddenly has to go up."

In high school, I discovered options. I would check the option closing prices and find what I thought were huge mispricings. For example, one time Alcoa closed at $49 and the 50 call was trading only $2 1/2 above the 45 call. By buying the 50 call and selling the 45 call, I would lose $2 1/2 if the stock went down $4 or more, but I would win $2 1/2 if the stock went up $1 or more. It seemed like a great bet. I convinced my father to do the trade for me. The stock went up, and the trade worked out.

**Did you do any other option trades in high school after that?**

No, I discovered that the closing option price printed in the newspaper was really just the last sale, which could be very stale. For example, an option might have finished the day 11 bid/12 offered, but if the last sale was at 13, that's the price that would be printed in the paper. Once I discovered that these quotes were not real, I realized that most of the trading opportunities that I found were really nonexistent.

**How did you even know about options in high school?**

The company my father worked for issued warrants when they went public. I asked my father to explain warrants to me. Since a warrant is nothing more than a long-term option, I understood the basic concept.

**After you graduated from college, did you go on to graduate school? Or did you go directly to work?**

My plan was to take a year off and travel across the country. I did, however, end up going on one interview with an investment house, which I won't name. I was interviewed by the head of the options department. I think I might have insulted him, and I didn't get the job.

**Since you're not naming the firm, why don't you be more specific.**

Well, our conversation went something along the following lines: He said, "So, you think you can make money trading options." I then told him about what I thought was important in making money in the options market. He asked me, "Do you know this year's high and low for IBM?"

I answered, "I think the low was 260 and the high was 320, but it's absolutely irrelevant. If you're wasting your time thinking about that, you're on the wrong track completely."

He said, "Well, *I know* what it is; I think it is very important."

I replied, "Great! Just hire me and I'll show you why it's immaterial."

In our subsequent conversation he indicated that he didn't know the definition of *beta* [a technical term used to describe a stock's volatility relative to the overall market]. He said, "I don't bother myself with that kind of stuff."

I said, "Terrific! Just hire me, and I'll explain it to you and show you how to use it." Amazingly, I didn't get the job. [*He laughs heartily at the recollection.*]

**I know that you're a serious poker buff and apply many of the strategies of the game to options. When did you first develop an interest in poker?**

I started playing poker during college. My friends and I took poker very seriously. We knew that over the long run it wasn't a game of luck but rather a game of enormous skill and complexity. We took a mathematical approach to the game.

**I assume that you've played at casino poker games. I'm curious, how does the typical Las Vegas game break down in terms of the skill level of the players?**

In a typical game with eight players, on average, three are pro, three are semipro, and two are tourists.

**That sure doesn't sound like very good odds for the tourists!**

You have to be a very good player to come out ahead over the long run.

**Given that high skill level, what percentage of the time do you actually walk away a winner?**

On average, I guess that I win about 55 percent of the time.

**Does it bother you when you lose?**

It doesn't bother me at all. I know that I'm playing correctly, and I understand that there is nothing that you can do to smooth out the volatility. I rarely second-guess myself when I lose, since I know that in the short run most of the fluctuations are due to luck, not skill.

**Is the strategy in poker primarily a matter of memorizing the odds for various hand combinations?**

No, memorization plays a very small role. Understanding the probabilities sufficiently well to know which hands to play and which hands not to play is important, but that's just basic knowledge. The really great poker players have an understanding of proper betting strategy. What information do you get when your opponent bets? What information do you give up when you bet? What information do you give up when you don't bet? We actually use poker strategy in training our option traders, because we feel the parallels are very strong. I believe that if I can teach our trainees the correct way to think about poker, I can teach them the right way to trade options.

**Can you give me a specific example?**

Assume that you're certain that you have the best hand, and the last card has just been dealt. What do you do? A novice trader would say, "I would bet the limit." However, that is often not the right move—even if you're sure that your opponent will call. Why? Because sometimes when you pass, he'll bet, giving you the opportunity to raise, in which case you'll win double the bet size. If you think that the probability is better than 50 percent that he'll bet, you're better off checking. By using that strategy, sometimes you'll win nothing extra when you had a sure chance to win a single bet size, but more often, you'll win double the bet size. In the long run, you'll be better off. So, whereas betting when you have the best hand may seem like the right thing to do, there's often a better play.

**What is the analogy to option trading?**

The basic concept that applies to both poker and option trading is that the primary object is not winning the most hands, but rather maximizing your gains. For example, let's say you have the opportunity to buy one hunded calls of an option you believe is worth 3 1/4 at 3, giving you an expected $2,500 profit. Most market makers would say that you just buy the option at 3 and try to lock in the profit. However, in reality, the decision is not that simple. For example, if you estimate that there is a 60 percent probability of being able to buy the same option at 2 3/4, your best strategy would be to try to buy at 2 3/4, even though doing so means that 40 percent of the time you're going to miss the trade entirely. Why? Because 60 percent of the time you're going to win $5,000. Therefore, over the long run, you'll average a $3,000 gain [60 percent of $5,000] in that type of situation, which is better than a sure $2,500 gain.

**Were you aware of that analogy when you first started trading options?**

Yes, the poker world is so competitive that if you don't fully capitalize on every advantage, you're not going to survive. I absolutely understood that concept by the time I got down to the options floor. I learned more about option trading strategy by playing poker than I did in all my college economics courses combined.

**Are there any other examples you can give that provide an analogy between poker strategy and option trading?**

A classic example we give all our trainees is the following: Assume you're playing seven card stud, and it's the last round of betting. You have three cards in the hole and four aces showing; your opponent has the two of clubs, three of clubs, nine of diamonds, and queen of spades showing. You're high with four aces. The question we ask is: "What bet do you make?" The typical response is, "I would bet as much as I can, because I have four aces and the odds of my winning are huge." The correct answer is ...

**You pass, because if he can't beat you, he's going to fold, and if he can beat you, he'll raise and you'll lose more.**

That's right. He might have the four, five, and six of clubs in the hole. You can't win anything by betting; you can only lose. He knows what you have, but you don't know what he has.

**So what is the analogy to option trading?**

Let's say that I believe an option is worth $3. Normally, I would be willing to make a market at 2 7/8 / 3 1/8 [i.e., be a buyer at 2 7/8 and a seller at 3 1/8]. However, let's say a broker whom I suspect has superior information asks me for a quote in that option. I have nothing to gain by making a tight market because if I price the option right, he'll pass—that is, he won't do anything—and if I price it wrong, he'll trade, and I'll lose.

Along the same line, if a broker with superior information is bidding significantly more for an option than I think it's worth, there's a very good chance that he's bidding higher because he knows something I don't. Therefore, I may not want to take the other side of that trade, even though it looks like an attractive sale.

The point is that option trading decisions should be based on conditional probability. I may have thought that an option was worth X, but now that someone else wants to bid X + Y, I may have to revise my estimate of the option's value. The lesson we try to teach our traders is that anything that seems very obvious should be double-checked.

A great example to illustrate this concept is a puzzle posed years ago by Fisher Black of the Black-Scholes option pricing model fame. Imagine that you're on "Let's Make a Deal," and you have to pick one of the three doors. You pick door No. 1. Monty Hall says, "OK, Carol, open door No. 2." The big prize is not behind door No. 2. Monty Hall, of course, knows which door the prize is behind. The way he played the game, he would never open the door with the real prize. Now he turns to you and asks, "Do you want to switch to door No. 3?" Do you stay with door No. 1 or switch? [Reader: You might wish to think of your own answer before reading on.]

**The obvious answer seems to be that it doesn't make a difference, but obviously that must be the wrong answer.**

The correct answer is that you should always switch to door No. 3. The probability that the prize is behind one of the two doors you did *not* pick was originally two-thirds. The fact that Monty opens one of those two doors and there is nothing behind it doesn't change this original probability, because he will always open the wrong door. Therefore, if the probability of the prize being behind one of those two doors was two-thirds originally, the probability of it being behind the unopened of those two doors must still be two-thirds.

**I don't understand. This show was watched by millions of people for years, and yet no one realized that the odds were so heavily skewed in favor of switching!**

You have to remember that you're talking about a show where people had to wear funny rabbit ears to get picked.

The thing that confuses people is that the process is not random. If Monty randomly chose one of the two doors, and the prize was not behind the selected door, then the probabilities between the two remaining doors would indeed be 50/50. Of course, if he randomly selected one of the two doors, then sometimes the prize would be behind the opened door, which never happened. The key is that he didn't randomly select one of the doors; he always picked the wrong door, and that changes the probabilities. It's a classic example of conditional probability. If the probability of the prize being behind door No. 2 or door No. 3 is two-thirds, given that it's not door No. 2, what is the probability that it's door No. 3? The answer, of course, is two-thirds.

---

Ironically, four weeks after my interview with Jeff Yass, the *New York Times* ran an article on the exact same puzzle. The *Times* article reported that when Marilyn Vos Savant answered this puzzle correctly in her *Parade* column in response to a reader's inquiry, she received nearly a thousand critical (and misguided) letters from Ph.D.s, mostly mathematicians and scientists. The *Times* article engendered its own slew of letters to the editor. Some of these provided particularly lucid and convincing explanations of the correct answer and are reprinted below:

To the Editor:
 Re "Behind Monty Hall's Doors: Puzzle Debate and Answer?" (front page, July 21): One reason people have trouble understanding the correct solution to the puzzle involving three doors, two with goats behind them and one with a car, is that the problem uses only three doors. This makes the assumed, but incorrect, probability of picking the car (1 in 2) appear too close to the actual probability (1 in 3) and the solution difficult to arrive at intuitively.
 To illustrate better the right answer—that a player should switch the door picked first after one of the other two has been opened by Monty Hall, the game-show host—suppose the game were played with 100 doors, goats behind 99 and a car behind 1.
 When first offered a door, a player would realize that the chances of picking the car are low (1 in 100). If Monty Hall then opened 98 doors with goats behind them, it would be clear that the chance the car is behind the remaining unselected door is high (99 in 100). Although only two doors would be left (the one the player picked and the unopened door), it would no longer appear that the car is equally likely to be behind either. To change the pick would be intuitive to most people.
 Cory Franklin
 Chicago, July 23, 1991

To the Editor:

As I recall from my school days, when you are dealing with tricky, confusing probabilities, it is useful to consider the chances of losing, rather than the chances of winning, thus:

Behind two of the three doors there is a goat. Therefore, in the long run, twice in three tries you will choose the goat. One goat-bearing door is eliminated. Now two times out of three when you have a goat, the other door has a car. That's why it pays to switch.

Karl V. Amatneek
San Diego, July 22, 1991

And finally there was this item:

To the Editor:

Your front-page article July 21 on the Monty Hall puzzle controversy neglects to mention one of the behind-the-door options: to prefer the goat to the auto. The goat is a delightful animal, although parking might be a problem.

Lore Segal
New York, July 22, 1991

---

The point is that your senses deceive you. Your simplistic impulse is to say that the probabilities are 50/50 for both door No. 1 and door No. 3. On careful analysis, however, you realize that there is a huge advantage to switching, even though it was not at all obvious at first. The moral is that in trading it's important to examine the situation from as many angles as possible, because your initial impulses are probably going to be wrong. There is never any money to be made in the obvious conclusions.

**Can you give me a trading example of a situation where the obvious decision is wrong?**

Let's say a stock is trading for $50 and an institution comes in with an offer to sell five hundred of the 45 calls at $4 1/2. The instinctive response in that type of situation is: "Great! I'll buy the calls at $4 1/2, sell the stock at $50, and lock in $1/2 profit." In reality, however, nine times out of ten, the reason the institution is offering the call at $4 1/2 is because it's fairly certain that the stock is going lower.

**Does this type of situation ever happen—that is, an institution offering to sell options at a price below intrinsic value [the minimum theoretical value, which is equal to the difference between the stock price and strike price—$5 in Yass's example]?**

It happens all the time.

**I don't understand. What would be the motive to sell the option below its intrinsic value?**

In the example I gave you, the institution may be very certain that the stock is going to trade below $49 1/2, and therefore a price of $4 1/2 for the 45 call is not unreasonable.

**Even if they have good reason to believe that the stock will trade lower, how can they be *that* sure of the timing?**

The straightforward answer is that they know they have a million shares to sell, and that they may have to be willing to offer the stock at $49 to move that type of quantity. It all comes down to conditional probabilities. Given that this institution is offering the option at below its intrinsic value, which is more likely—they're so naive that they're virtually writing you a risk-free check for $25,000, or they know something that you don't? My answer is, given that they want to do this trade, the odds are you're going to lose.

When I first started out, I would always be a buyer of options that were offered at prices below intrinsic value, thinking that I had a locked-in profit. I couldn't understand why the other smart traders on the floor weren't rushing in to do the same trades. I eventually realized that the reason the smart traders weren't buying these calls was that, on average, they were a losing proposition.

**If it's not illegal, why wouldn't the institutions regularly sell calls prior to liquidating their positions? It seems that it would be an easy way to cushion the slippage on exiting large positions.**

In fact, that is a common strategy, but the market makers have wised up.

**How has the option market changed in the ten years that you have been in the business?**

When I first started trading options in 1981 all you needed to make money was the standard Black-Scholes model and common sense. In the early 1980s, the basic strategy was to try to buy an option trading at a relatively low implied volatility and sell a related option at a higher volatility. For example, if a large buy order for a particular strike call pushed its implied volatility to 28 percent, while another call in the same stock was trading at 25 percent, you would sell the higher-volatility call and offset the position by buying the lower-volatility call.

**I assume these types of discrepancies existed because the market was fairly inefficient at the time.**

That's correct. At that time, a lot of option traders still didn't adequately understand volatility and basic option theory. For example, if a call was trading at a 25 percent volatility, which was relatively low for the options in that stock, many traders didn't understand that you didn't have to be bullish on the stock to buy the call. If you were bearish on the stock, you could still buy the underpriced call by simultaneously selling the stock, yielding a combined position equivalent to a long put. The more mathematical market makers understood these types of relationships and were able to exploit pricing aberrations. Now everybody understands these relationships, and you no longer see situations in which different options in a same stock are trading at significantly different volatilities—unless there's a good fundamental reason for that difference in pricing. Now that everybody understands volatility, the major battle is in the skewness in option pricing.

**Can you explain what you mean by "skewness"?**

To explain it by example, the OEX today was at 355. If you check the option quotes, you will see that the market is pricing the 345 puts much higher than the 365 calls. [The standard option pricing models would actually price the 365 calls slightly higher than the 345 puts.]

**Are options prices always skewed in the same direction? In other**

**words , are out-of-the-money puts always priced higher than equiv-
alently out-of-the-money calls?**

Most of the time, puts will be high and calls will be low.

**Is there a logical reason for that directional bias?**

There are actually two logical reasons. One I can tell you; the other I
can't. One basic factor is that there is a much greater probability of
financial panic on the downside than on the upside. For example, once
in a great while, you may get a day with the Dow down 500 points, but
it's far less likely that the Dow will go up 500 points. Given the nature
of markets, the chance of a crash is always greater than the chance of an
overnight runaway euphoria.

**Did the markets always price puts significantly higher than calls
for that reason?**

No. The market didn't price options that way until after the October
1987 crash. However, I had always felt that the chance of a huge down-
move was much greater than the chance of an upmove of equivalent
size.

**Did you reach the conclusion about the bias in favor of larger
downmoves based on a study of historical markets?**

No, nothing that elaborate. Just by watching markets, I noticed that
prices tend to come down much harder and faster than they go up.

**Does this directional bias apply only to stock index options? Or
does it also apply to individual stock options?**

The options on most major stocks are priced that way [i.e., puts are
more expensive than calls], because downside surprises tend to be
much greater than the upside surprises. However, if a stock is the subject of a takeover rumor, the out-of-the-money calls will be priced
higher than the out-of-the-money puts.

**Do your traders use your option pricing models to make basic trading decisions?**

Anyone's option pricing model, including my own, would be too simplistic to adequately describe the real world. There's no way you can construct a model that can come close to being as informed as the market. We train our market makers to understand the basic assumptions underlying our model and why those assumptions are too simplistic. We then teach them more sophisticated assumptions and their price implications. It's always going to be a judgment call as to what the appropriate assumptions should be. We believe we can train any intelligent, quick-thinking person to be a trader. We feel traders are made, not born.

**Essentially then, you start off with the model projections and then do a seat-of-the-pants adjustment based on how you believe the various model assumptions are at variance with current realities.**

Exactly.

**Can you give an example of how this adjustment process works?**

A current example is NCR, which is a takeover target of AT&T. AT&T's bid is $110, and the stock is currently trading at approximately $106. If the takeover goes through, the buyer of the stock stands to make about $2. (About half of the difference between the current price and the takeover bid represents interest rate costs on carrying the stock.) If, on the other hand, the takeover falls through, then the stock can drop sharply—to about $75 based on current market estimates. In this particular case, the relatively close calls are essentially worthless, because the stock is unlikely to go above $110. On the other hand, the much further out-of-the-money 90 puts have some chance of gaining significant value in the event the takeover fails. Thus, in this type of situation, the out-of-the-money puts will be priced much higher than the equivalent out-of-the-money calls.

**In other words, this is an example of how an option pricing model could yield very misleading projections in a real-world situation.**

Right, because the standard model assumes that the probability of any individual tick being up or down is 50/50. That, however, is not the case here because there's a much greater probability for a large price decline than a large price rise.

At one time, the mathematical types traded straight off their models, and in a situation like the one I have just described, they would sell the out-of-the-money puts because they appeared to be priced too high. However, the seat-of-the-pants types would look at the situation and realize that there was a real possibility of the stock witnessing a large decline [i.e., a breakdown in the case of a takeover]. The traders using a commonsense approach would end up buying the out-of-the-money puts from the mathematical types and taking them to the cleaners in the process. Eventually, the mathematical types caught on.

**In your day-to-day operations, do you basically start off by looking at the model and then making certain mental adjustments?**

Exactly. Our basic philosophy is that we have tremendous respect for market opinion. For example, if we believe an option is worth $2 and a knowledgeable market maker is bidding $2 1/2, we assume that nine times out of ten he's going to be right, because he's trading one stock and we're trading five hundred. We will then try to figure out why he's bidding $2 1/2. If we can identify the reason and we disagree with it, then we may sell the option because it's overpriced. But most of the time, we'll decide that his knowledge is better than ours, and we'll end up adjusting our valuation on the other options in that stock and then buying these other options or the stock itself.

**When you adjust your option valuations because someone else is bidding at a price that appears to be removed from the theoretical value, are you simply assuming that they know more about the given company?**

Yes, information doesn't exactly flow perfectly, like they teach you in Finance 101. Frequently, the information will show up first in the option market. A lot of these insider trading cases involve options, and we're the people who lose the money.

For example, just today they caught an employee of Marion Labs who obviously had inside information that Dow was going to offer a takeover bid for the company. This person had bought five hundred of the July 25 calls at $1 [total cost: $50,000], and the next day the options were worth $10 [total position value: $500,000]. In the old days—before options—someone with this type of information might buy the stock, and even assuming 50 percent margin, the profit percentage wouldn't be that large. However, now, by buying options, traders with inside information can increase their profit leverage tremendously. Sometimes I feel sorry for some of these people because, until the recent barrage of publicity regarding insider trading, I'm not sure that many of them even realized they were breaking the law. However, since they come to the options market first, we're the ones on the other side of the trade getting picked off.

**I don't understand. Doesn't the SEC scrutinize the order flow when there's an announced takeover to make sure there are no suspicious orders?**

Yes, they do, and they're getting particularly effective in catching people trading on insider information. They have also become much more efficient in returning money to those on the other side of these trades. However, in earlier years, the process took much longer.

One famous example involved Santa Fe, an oil company that was a takeover target by the Kuwaitis in 1981. At the time, the stock was at $25 and the option traders on the floor filled an order for one thousand 35 calls at $1/16. Shortly afterwards, the stock jumped from $25 to $45 and the options went from $1/16 to $10. The floor traders had a virtual overnight loss of about $1 million. Although they eventually got their money back, it took years. If you're a market maker and you're broke, waiting to get your capital back is not pleasant. You live in fear that you're going to be the one selling the option to an informed source.

Eventually, everyone gets picked off, because if you try to avoid it completely, you're going to pass up a lot of good trading opportunities. In a nutshell, if you're too conservative, you won't do any trades, and if you're too aggressive, you're going to get picked off a lot. The trick is to try to strike a balance between the two.

**Can you think of a recent example in which you were picked off?**

The options for Combustion Engineering are traded on the Pacific Coast Exchange. The options rarely trade. One morning, we received a call from the board broker (the exchange employee responsible for managing order imbalances). He said there was an order to buy several hundred options and inquired whether we wanted to take the other side. The stock was trading at around $25, and we agreed to sell three hundred of the 25 calls at approximately $2 1/2. Ten minutes later, trading in the stock was halted, and there was an announcement that the company was being taken over by a European corporation. When trading resumed several minutes later, the stock reopened at $39, and we were out over $350,000 in a matter of minutes. It turned out that the buyer was on the board of directors of the acquiring company.

**What ultimately happened?**

In this particular case, we've already gotten our money back. The SEC identified the buyer quickly, and because the individual was a high-level foreign executive who didn't even realize he was doing anything illegal, he returned the money without any complications.

**Given that consideration, aren't you always reticent to fill a large option order in a market that normally doesn't trade very often?**

There's always that type of reticence, but if you want to be in the business, it's your job to fill those types of orders. Besides, in the majority of cases, the orders are legitimate and nothing happens. Also, under normal circumstances, we hedge the position after we fill the option order. In the case of Combustion Engineering, the stock stopped trading before we had a chance to buy it as a hedge against our position. We still would have lost money, but not as much as we did being completely unhedged.

The more successful the SEC is in catching people trading on inside information—and lately they seem to be catching everyone—the tighter the bid/ask spreads will be. Every trade we do involves some risk premium for the possibility that the other side of the trade represents informed activity. Therefore, if everyone believes that the SEC is going to catch all inside traders, then the market will price away that extra risk premium. In essence, it's really the average investor who ends up paying for insider trading through the wider bid/ask spreads.

**When stocks have large overnight moves, is that type of price action normally preceded by a pick up in the option volume?**

Almost always. If you go over the volume data for stocks that were taken over, you'll find that there was almost always a flurry of option trading before the event.

**Do you do any directional trading?**

None. It's my firm belief that the market's wisdom is far greater than mine. In my opinion, the market's pricing of an item is the best measure of its value. The odd thing about believing in efficient markets is that you have to surrender your beliefs and ego to the markets.

Several years ago, a director of the Office of Management and Budget made a statement that budget projections should be based on the assumption that long-term interest rates would eventually decline to 5 to 6 percent, at a time when rates were over 8 percent. The market-implied interest rate level reflects the net intelligence of thousands of traders battling it out daily in the bond market. In comparison, the OMB director's personal opinion doesn't mean anything. If he's basing government policy on the assumption that long-term interest rates will be 5 to 6 percent, when the market's best guess is 8 percent, he's doing grave harm to society. Presumably, if he were smart enough to predict interest rates better than the market, he could make a fortune trading the bond market, which he obviously can't do.

My guess about where interest rates will be in the next twenty years is better than that of almost any economist, because all I have to do is look at where the bond market is trading. If it's trading at 8 percent, that's my projection. Someone can spend millions of dollars developing an elaborate interest rate forecasting model, and I'll bet you that over the long run the bond market's forecast will be better. The general principle is that if you can give up your ego and listen to what the markets are telling you, you can have a huge source of information.

**I know that your bottom-line advice to people regarding trading is: Don't think that you can beat the market. However, is there any advice you can offer for those who do participate in the markets?**

If you invest and don't diversify, you're literally throwing out money. People don't realize that diversification is beneficial even if it reduces your return. Why? Because it reduces your risk even more. Therefore, if you diversify and then use margin to increase your leverage to a risk level equivalent to that of a nondiversified position, your return will probably be greater.

**I tend to agree. I like to say that diversification is the only free lunch on Wall Street.**

The way I would put it is that not diversifying is like throwing your lunch out the window. If you have a portfolio and are not diversifying, you're incinerating money every year.

---

The type of professional option arbitrage trading in which Yass engages obviously has little direct relevance to most ordinary traders. However, there are still some significant messages here that have broader application. Perhaps Yass's most important point is that it is critical to focus on maximizing gains rather than the number of wins. One obvious application of this concept is that regardless of your trading style, a betting (i.e., trading) strategy that increases the stakes on trades deemed to have a higher probability of success could significantly enhance the final results. Another point emphasized by Yass is that our initial impressions are often wrong. In other words, beware of acting on the obvious.

# PART VII

# *The Psychology of Trading*

*"We has met the enemy, and it is us."*

*The famous quote from Walt Kelly's cartoon strip, "Pogo," would provide as fitting a one-line summation of the art of trading as any. Time and time again, those whom I interviewed for this book and its predecessor stressed the absolutely critical role of psychological elements in trading success. When asked to explain what was important to success, the Market Wizards never talked about indicators or techniques, but rather about such things as discipline, emotional control, patience, and mental attitude toward losing. The message is clear: The key to winning in the markets is internal, not external.*

# Zen and the Art of Trading

One of the hazards of doing a book of this sort is that you can go through the arduous process of transforming a rambling 250-page raw transcript into a readable 25-page chapter only to have the interview subject withhold permission to use the material. (In order to provide an atmosphere conducive to openness on the part of those I interviewed, I felt it necessary to offer them the right of final refusal.) One of the traders I interviewed, an individual who had made several hundred million dollars in trading profits for his firm, felt that the resulting chapter, which contained a lot of copy related to intuition, dreams, Eastern philosophy, and trading anecdotes, presented an image of him that would be viewed askance by his corporate clients. I prevailed upon him, however, to allow me to use the following excerpt anonymously, as I felt it offered an unusual and insightful perspective on trading.

---

**I still don't understand your trading method. How could you make these huge sums of money by just watching the screen?**

There was no system to it. It was nothing more than, "I think the market is going up, so I'm going to buy." "It's gone up enough, so I'm going to sell." It was completely impulsive. I didn't sit down and formulate any trading plan. I don't know where the intuition comes from, and there are times when it goes away.

**How do you recognize when it goes away?**

When I'm wrong three times in a row, I call time out. Then I paper trade for a while.

**For how long do you paper trade?**

Until I think I'm in sync with the market again. Every market has a rhythm, and our job as traders is to get in sync with that rhythm. I'm not really trading when I'm doing those trades. There's trading being done, but I'm not doing it.

**What do you mean you're not doing it?**

There's buying and selling going on, but it's just going *through* me. It's like my personality and ego are not there. I don't even get a sense of satisfaction on these trades. It's absolutely that objective. Did you ever read *Zen and the Art of Archery?*

**No, I have to admit, I missed that one.**

The essence of the idea is that you have to learn to let the arrow shoot itself. There's no ego involved. It's not, "I'm shooting the arrow, and I'm releasing it." Rather, the arrow is shot, and it's always right.

The same concept applies to trading. There's no sense of self at all. There's just an awareness of what will happen. The trick is to differentiate between what you *want* to happen and what you *know* will happen. The intuition knows what will happen.

In trading, just as in archery, whenever there is effort, force, straining, struggling, or trying, it's wrong. You're out of sync; you're out of harmony with the market. The perfect trade is one that requires no effort.

**You talk about knowing what will happen. Can you give me an example?**

The current decline in the mark versus the yen is something that I just knew would happen.

**Before the mark went down versus the yen, it had trended in the other direction for quite some time. How did you know when the timing was right for the trade?**

The trigger was actually a Freudian slip. I was talking about the yen/mark rate with another trader when it was trading at 87.80. I kept on referring to the price as 77.80. The other trader finally said, "What are you talking about?" I realized that I was off by ten big figures in my price references. Obviously, there was some part of me that was looking for the rate to go down to that level. It was literally bubbling out of me.

# Charles Faulkner

## THE MIND OF AN ACHIEVER

Charles Faulkner abandoned graduate school (he was studying psycholinguistics at Northwestern University) after becoming enamored with two early books written by Richard Bandler and John Grinder, the cofounders of Neuro-Linguistic Programming (more on NLP in the interview). Starting in 1981, Faulkner studied extensively with Grinder and then with Bandler and other key NLP codevelopers, becoming a certified NLP trainer in 1987. Faulkner's focus has been on modeling human excellence, with projects that have included accelerated learning, physician decision making, and futures trading. Faulkner is also a consultant, NLP seminar leader, and program designer and author of several audio tape programs applying the techniques of NLP.

I met Charles Faulkner when he approached me after a talk I had given at a futures industry symposium. During my speech, I had made several references to this volume, which at the time was about half-completed. Faulkner explained that he had been doing research and consulting directed at helping traders overcome mental impediments to success. I told him that I was quite interested in his work because it

Note: In several instances in this interview, where I thought it would help clarify or expand the information, I supplemented Faulkner's responses with adapted excerpts from the Nightingale-Conant tape series *NLP: The New Technology of Achievement NLP*, for which Faulkner was the program designer and principal coauthor.

might fit as a feature in the new book but that my scheduling on that trip did not leave enough time for an interview. He gave me a boxed tape set, asking me to see what I thought about it.

The tape series dealt with applying NLP to various aspects of achievement. Although there are a number of NLP elements that I have trouble relating to, certain segments of the series made great sense to me and seemed helpful in increasing motivation and focusing goals. Overall, I was sufficiently impressed with Faulkner's tape series to schedule another trip to Chicago to interview him.

A portion of NLP is concerned with studying the cues people provide through their gestures, eye movements, language, and voice intonations. Faulkner has obviously had a great deal of experience honing these interpretative skills, and he struck me as being extremely perceptive. He had thoughtfully arranged for the use of a private conference room in a hotel near the airport in order to maximize our time together.

---

**You're a Neuro-Linguistic Programming trainer. That's not going to mean very much to most readers of this book. Let's start with a layperson's definition of NLP.**

Actually, Natural Learning Processes might have been a better name. NLP's principal cofounders, Richard Bandler, an information scientist, and John Grinder, a professor of linguistics, define NLP as the study of human excellence. NLP studies great achievers to pinpoint their mental programs—that is, to learn how great achievers use their brains to produce results. They began their study with extraordinarily talented therapists—individuals who consistently produced positive changes in the lives of others. Succeeding there, they went on to study talented people in other fields—managers, negotiators, athletes, and artists—to find what those individuals did to get their outstanding results. The models of the natural learning processes these people used to become extraordinary in their fields can be used by anyone wishing to excel.

To understand how NLP works, let me make an analogy to the beginning of modern skiing. Until the 1950s, most people thought skiing was a matter of natural talent. You either had the talent to do it, or you didn't. Then something happened that changed the sport forever. Films were made of some of Europe's great skiers to identify all the movements that characterized them. It was found that they all had certain techniques in common. Beyond that, it was discovered that the techniques of these exceptional skiers could be taught to anyone. All kinds of people could learn to be very good skiers. The key was to identify the movements that made a great skier—the essence of their skills—so it could be taught to others. In NLP we call that essence a model. The same basic principles can be applied to any other endeavor or to various aspects of human interrelationships. I like to describe NLP as software for the brain. It provides mental programs that allow you to develop new abilities and have more of the kinds of experiences you want.

**As evident by NLP's middle name, linguistics plays a pivotal role. I'm not at all clear how linguistics can dramatically affect behavior. Can you give me an example?**

How do our brains process language? The answer is very, very literally. People often say things like, "Don't worry" or "Don't think about it." What happens if I tell you not to think about a problem? Well, despite what I said, you'll think about that problem. That's because our brains cannot understand putting something in negative language. In order to know what not to think about, our brains have to first think of it.

Consider the example of experienced traders telling new traders, "Don't think about the money. Remember, don't think about the money." Although that may sound like good advice, what's going to happen? The new traders will repeat that phrase to themselves until they are literally obsessing about the money.

Because of the way our brains process language, which is literally, NLP recommends taking negative thoughts and stating them in positive terms. Instead of saying what you don't want, state what you do want. Instead of advising a trader, "Don't think about the money," it would be far more effective to say, "Focus your attention on following your method."

**What are the basic principles of NLP?**

NLP is based on principles different from those in psychology. Five essential principles or presuppositions guide NLP. The first is: The map is not the territory. The map is our thoughts and feelings; the territory is reality. We respond to our thoughts and feelings about reality; we don't respond to reality. This is good news because it means that it is possible to get a better map—a better way to think and feel.

The second fundamental principle of NLP is: Experience has a structure. In other words, the way in which memories are arranged in our minds determines what they will mean and how they will affect us. If we can change the structure of our memories, we will experience those events in our lives differently. Change the structure of our thoughts and our experiences will change automatically.

The third major principle of NLP is: If one person can do it, anyone else can learn to do it. This is the great promise of NLP. Excellence and achievement have a structure that can be copied. By modeling successful people, we can learn from the experience of those who have already succeeded. If we can learn to use our brains in the same way as the exceptionally talented person, we can possess the essence of that talent.

The fourth basic principle is: The mind and body are part of the same system. If you change your mind about something, your abilities will change. If you change your posture, breathing, or other parts of your physiology, your thoughts will change. The great psychiatrist R. D. Laing used to say, "Change your mind, change your body. Change your body, change your mind."

The fifth principle is: People have all the resources they need. In NLP, an image, a sound, or a feeling is a resource. Our brain has the ability to see inner pictures. Whether these pictures begin as fuzzy or clear, they can be built up into great motivating visions. Inner voices can criticize us or they can encourage and guide us. Any feeling we've had in our lives—confidence, challenge, indomitable will, whatever it is—even if we've only had it once, can be transferred to any situation in our lives where we want or need it.

**When you say, "The map is not the territory," do you mean that people have distorted views of reality that lead them astray?**

NLP believes that all maps (mental and physical) are a distorted, or selected, view of reality. A topographical map, a street map, and a weather map all provide different views of the same territory and all are true representations. Usefulness, rather than truthfulness, will guide you to want a different map at different times. The different forms of market analysis can be seen as different maps of the same territory. Outstanding traders seek to have maps that most closely match the market territory in a way that is useful for them.

Of course, not all maps are true or useful. Let me offer one example that is particularly significant for traders. It relates to the statistical concept of regression to the mean. This mathematical phenomenon implies that if you do extremely well, you're likely to do more poorly the next time, while if you do very poorly, you're likely to do better the next time. This pattern is an inevitable consequence of the law of averages and tends to skew traders' perceptions and evaluations of their own performance.

For example, if a trader does very well in one period and only average in the next, he might feel like he failed. On the other hand, if the trader does very poorly in one period, but average in the next, he'll probably feel like he's doing dramatically better. In either case, the trader is very likely to attribute the change of results to his system or his feelings rather than to a natural statistical tendency. The failure to appreciate this concept will lead the trader to create an inaccurate mental map of his trading ability. For example, if the trader switches from one system to another when he's doing particularly poorly, the odds are that he'll do better at that point in time even if the new system is only of equal merit, or possibly even if it is inferior. Yet the trader will attribute his improvement to his new system. In contrast, supertraders understand the concept of regression to the mean and use it to their advantage instead of being misled by it.

Incidentally, the same phenomenon also explains why so many people say they do better after they have gone to a motivational seminar. When are they going to go to a motivational seminar? When they're feeling particularly low and inactive. In a sense, it doesn't matter what the presenter does, because statistically, on average, these people will do better in the period afterwards anyway—whether or not they attended the seminar. But since they did, they'll attribute the change to the seminar.

**In the seminar example you just cited, isn't it also possible that people will feel and perform better because of the placebo effect? For that matter, isn't it possible that the results attributed to NLP may also be a placebo effect?**

In part, this contention may be valid, and it fascinates me that this is supposed to be a criticism. Medical science researchers take the view that the placebo effect is something bad. You can hear it in their language: "We have to rule out the placebo effect." However, Bandler and Grinder looked at it differently. They saw the placebo effect as a natural human ability—the ability of the brain to heal the rest of the body. This actually presents exciting possibilities. What if this ability can be called forth when we want it or need it? What if our brains can literally make us feel better? NLP is concerned with results. If the favorable results are partially due to the placebo effect—that is, the natural ability of the brain to affect how we feel, heal, and function, mentally and physically—let's use it deliberately.

**NLP makes claims of being able to change behaviors and feelings very quickly through simple mental exercises. Can you give me an example of such an exercise in order to give readers who are completely unfamiliar with NLP some flavor of the approach?**

Let me offer an example that will probably be of use to most of your readers. We've all been in trading situations where the market moved dramatically against our position. The question is: How unsettling or disconcerting was it? What happens when you're in a similar situation a couple of weeks or even a couple of months later? If you begin to experience some of the same unsettling feelings just thinking about it, you've conditioned yourself just like Pavlov's dogs. This is what NLP calls "anchoring." If these feelings are disturbing your trading decision concentration, use the following NLP technique to neutralize them.

Quickly go through your movie of that disturbing situation and pick out one frame, like a still photograph, that symbolizes for you the whole disappointment. When you've found it, notice whether you see yourself in that still snapshot of that time. That is, do you see that earlier you, dressed as you were back then, in that photo? You probably won't, and this is usually the case. So in your mind's eye, begin to pull back so that more and more of the scene becomes visible, until you can see your earlier self in the scene.

Imagine that scene rendered in the style of a famous painter, as if it were a Renoir, a van Gogh, or even a Lichtenstein. Now consider what kind of frame might be most appropriate around this picture. Perhaps a big old-fashioned gold frame might seem right, or maybe you'll choose a modern steel frame. You might even want to add a museum light. Take a moment to appreciate this picture as one of the framed memories in your mind. Now notice your feelings about that time. Most people will find that their disturbed or anxious feelings have been greatly reduced, or even completely eliminated. This NLP process detaches our emotions from the memory. It's like an emotional reset button and provides a real-world example of the NLP principle: Experience has a structure. By changing the structure, we change the experience. Taking just the few minutes to do this exercise will allow a trader to regain his emotional objectivity.

Another way to change disturbing memories is to do the following: Think of that incident of disappointment and run it back to the beginning, like it's a movie. Now put on circus music, or the *William Tell* Overture, better known as the theme to the "Lone Ranger" TV series. Any rich, compelling music will do, especially if it mismatches the emotions of your memory. Pick a tune, and start it playing nice and loud as you rewatch that incident in a new way. Once the memory has played through to its end with the music, then rewind it to the beginning. Now play that scene again without the music. Notice your response to it this time. For some people, the incident has become humorous, even ludicrous. For many, the previous feelings of disappointment have been neutralized, or at least greatly mitigated.

Obviously, one approach is more visual and the other more auditory. Depending on whether a person has a stronger visual or auditory sense, one of these two approaches will work better than the other.

**Good, that helps clarify the type of process involved. Give me another example.**

The following is an example of how to transfer feelings of confidence (or for that matter any emotional state) from one time of your life to another. As with many NLP techniques, the following will work more deeply and completely when done in a relaxed, interruption-free environment.

There are many times in your life when you've felt confident. Go back in your memories to a particular time when you felt abundantly confident. Relive the moment, seeing what you saw and hearing what you heard. As you begin to reexperience that confidence and feel it building, imagine a colored circle on the floor around you. As the feeling gets strong, exhale as you step out of the circle, leaving those confident feelings inside the circle. (I am fully aware that these sound like strange instructions.)

Now think of a specific time in the future when you want to have that same confidence. As you begin to think about that specific future time and place, step back into the circle and spontaneously feel those confident feelings again. You have just anchored together that future time and your feelings of confidence from your past. To test whether this has worked, think of that specific future time. You'll feel some of that confidence as you do. This feeling is now automatic and will be there without your thinking about it when that future situation arrives. This exercise can be repeated for as many different future occasions and as many different feelings as you would like.

**Why doesn't success bring happiness? What does?**

I think it's because people base their ideas of success on outdated models or patterns of what it means to be successful. For example, someone might have the idea that in order to be successful he or she must have a certain kind of house, a certain kind of car, and a certain kind of spouse. They're using those things as evidence for whether they are a success, but they're leaving themselves out of the picture. They don't ever actually step into that picture and ask, "Do I really want to live this type of life?" So I recommend that people not merely visualize what it would be like to actually live the type of life they are trying so hard to achieve, but to step into that life and mentally experience several weeks or months. When people do this exercise, they may find there are things they want to change, and I recommend they make those changes. After all, since they're working so hard for this future, it ought to be one they'll enjoy when it arrives.

**Are you saying that the reason people don't find happiness after achieving their goals is because they have the wrong goals?**

It's because they aren't going for goals that will fulfill *them*. They're striving for goals that society, or their family, or the media told them to have. We are inundated with all these images of how we'll know whether we are successful. For example, what is valuable in this culture in a spouse? We know the answer from all the advertisements we see—someone who is young and attractive. But what else is important? I think people sometimes get lost; they don't explore what success means for them.

**How can people identify what goals would make them happy?**

One NLP exercise that deals with this question is having people imagine themselves at the end of their lives. Some people are reluctant to do this exercise, but when I tell them to go ahead and imagine that it's been a very long, healthy, and active life, they're more willing to try it. Then I ask them to look back on what they have accomplished, and see whether they wish they had done something else or something more. Although it's a mind trick, by adopting this end-of-life perspective, unconscious expectations are revealed, and people find it easier to make an assessment about what they really want to fill their lives. I ask my clients, "What is really worth the time of your life?"

The idea for this exercise came out of an experience I had when I was in college. I worked as an orderly in a hospital ward that typically had lots of elderly patients. Over the course of three years, I spoke to hundreds of people who were near the end of their lives. I asked these people how their lives had been, what they liked about their lives and what they regretted, if anything.

**What did you find out?**

I found out that falling in love at nineteen was important. I found out that the willingness to take risks into the unknown, like leaving one's small hometown, was important. On the other hand, just simply retiring because of age was something many of them felt was the biggest mistake of their lives.

One thing that really struck me was that not one of these people said they truly regretted anything they had actually done—what they regretted was what they hadn't done. They regretted that they had wasted their lives on petty pursuits. They hadn't identified their important values and then done everything they could to fulfill them. The lesson I learned from this experience was the same one emphasized years later in NLP: If we don't live true to our values and fulfill them, we experience disappointment and emptiness.

**How do you know whether the goals you're pursuing are the ones that will fulfill your values?**

It's useful to think in terms of a mission. A mission isn't something you force on yourself or construct out of your current concerns; rather, it's something that you discover within. As John Grinder once asked, "What do you love so much that you would pay to do it?" If you don't have strongly held values, it will be hard to clearly define a mission, and you will have little motivation to achieve your goals. However, if your goals support your values and you have a clear sense of mission, then your motivation will be equally strong.

**Is strong motivation a common characteristic of traders who excel?**

Strong motivation is a common characteristic among those who excel in any field. There are two different types of motivation, or what NLP calls two directions of motivation: either toward what we want or away from what we don't want.

For example, consider how people respond to waking up in the morning. When the alarm goes off, one person might mumble to himself, "Oh no, let me sleep just a little longer," and hit the snooze button. Then when the alarm goes off again, and he sees pictures of himself rushing to get ready for work, he thinks, "No big deal, I'll wear the same clothes as yesterday and skip breakfast," as he hits the snooze button another time. When the alarm goes off a few minutes later, his brain begins showing him pictures of getting to work late and having to explain it to his boss. He decides he'll drive to work faster and goes back to sleep again. But when the alarm goes off the next time, his inner voice says, "*You must get up!*" He sees pictures of his clients waiting impatiently and his boss yelling and screaming, threatening to fire him. When these pictures in his mind's eye become big enough, bright enough, close enough, and loud enough, then he says, "OK, I'll get up." He's finally motivated.

Another person, when he hears the alarm go off in the morning, thinks about all the great things he's going to do that day. He sees himself accomplishing new goals and wakes up raring to go. This person is also motivated. In fact, he probably wakes up before the alarm.

The person who wouldn't get up until he saw images like his boss yelling at him has an "Away From" motivational direction. His motivation is to get away from pain, discomfort, and negative consequences. He probably picks friends who won't bother him. He's not likely to make a career move until he can't stand his job anymore. He moves away from what he doesn't want. The person who can't wait to get out of bed has a "Toward" motivational direction. He moves toward pleasure, rewards, and goals. He probably picks friends who stimulate him. He makes career moves to reach bigger opportunities. He moves toward what he wants. People can have both types of motivation—Away From and Toward—but most people specialize in one or the other. They are very different ways of getting motivated, and both are useful in different situations.

**The benefits of Toward motivation seem pretty obvious, but how would an Away From motivation be beneficial?**

Your question reflects a common perception. The benefits of Toward motivation are more obvious. People who move toward goals are greatly valued in our society. You can see it in the language of the Help Wanted ads, which liberally use terms such as "self-motivated" and "go-getter." However, the Away From direction of motivation has gotten a bad rap. Another way of thinking about this motivation is that it is away from problems. Many people who use Away From motivation are problem solvers. You can hear it in their language. They'll say, "Excuse me, but we have a problem here." They see a problem and have to solve it. Sometimes they get so involved in the problem that they may forget where they are going, but they *will* solve the problem. The Toward motivated people are so motivated toward their goals that they might not even consider what problems they might run into or what difficulties to prepare for along the way. Therefore, both types of motivation are useful.

**Are you implying that people with Away From motivation are likely to be as successful as those with Toward motivation?**

That's right. The Toward motivation may be enshrined in success magazines, but the less appreciated Away From motivation individuals can also be very successful. A perfect example is Martin Zweig, the famous stock forecaster. He manages over a billion dollars in assets. His stock letter and books are among the most respected in the industry. When Zweig talks about strategy, he says, "DON'T fight interest rate trends. DON'T fight market momentum." He uses Away From motivation to minimize loss. Many outstanding traders reveal an Away From motivation when they talk about "protecting themselves" or "playing a great defense." They're only willing to take so much pain in the market before they get out. As Paul Tudor Jones said in your interview, "I have a short-term horizon for pain."

**Certainly there must be some disadvantages to having an Away From motivation.**

Sure. People who are motivated away from things often experience a lot of pain and worry before they are motivated. If they let the stressful anxiety level get too high, it will affect their health. Stress management classes are filled with these people. It would be more useful for them to learn to accept less pain before taking action than to learn to manage it better. Also, the further away they get from the problem, the less serious it appears, and hence they lose some of their motivation. As a result, Away From motivation tends to run hot and cold. Finally, people with Away From motivation won't necessarily know where they're going to end up because their attention is on what they don't want, not on what they do want.

**Do successful traders tend to have one type of motivation versus the other?**

Very often they come in with a developed Toward motivation—toward success, toward money—that's why they got into the markets in the first place. However, those that are primarily Toward motivated must spend the time and energy to develop the Away From motivation required for proper money management. In my studies of traders I've found that it's nearly impossible to be a really successful trader without the motivation to get away from excessive risk.

**Obviously, motivation is critical to achieving goals. Is that the only critical factor, or is there more to it?**

NLP research has shown that five conditions must be met in order for a goal to be achievable. First, the goal must be stated in positive terms. It's not getting rid of something—for example, "I don't want to lose money." Rather, it needs to be stated in positive terms—for example, "I want to protect my assets." The second condition is that the goal needs to be yours. "They want me to trade larger," is an example of a goal that does not meet this condition. Instead, if your goal is, "When market conditions warrant it, I'm going to double my trading size," you're much more likely to reach that goal. Third, the goal must be specific. Nothing ever happens in general. The more richly detailed the description of your goal—what you'll see, hear, and feel when you get it—the better. The fourth condition adds the when, where, and with whom. The fifth condition for achieving a goal is anticipating the effects of the goal. Is it worthwhile and desirable in itself and in its effects? This brings us full circle to having goals we really want and that will fulfill us.

**The very first condition you stated as critical in achieving your goal is that the goal be stated in positive terms. Wouldn't those with Away From motivation have difficulty in fulfilling this condition?**

The underlying motivation may be one of getting Away From something negative, but the goal can still be stated in positive terms. For example, someone's motivation for being a successful trader might be to get away from poverty. So the goal might be to set a personal record in profits for the coming year. An Away From motivation and a positive goal can work together to provide thorough motivation and outstanding results.

**How did you first get involved in working with traders?**

In 1987, I was approached by Steve Bianucci, a young Treasury bond floor trader who was working with Pete Steidlmayer's Market Logic School [Steidlmayer has since left the school] and looking to make the transition from the floor to position trading. He wanted to know if NLP could be used to build a working model of a great trader. I was intrigued by his question, and it served as the catalyst for a research process that is still ongoing.

**What kind of research?**

Observing great traders to construct a model of trading excellence.

**Wasn't it difficult to gain access to such traders? I have trouble imagining that many of them would willingly agree to be the subjects of extended observation and modeling.**

In the case of floor traders, such as Tom Baldwin [a phenomenally successful T-bond floor trader profiled in *Market Wizards*], direct observation was quite easy, requiring nothing more than access to the trading floor, which I got. In the case of Pete Steidlmayer [a highly successful futures trader and the inventor of Market Profile—an analytical methodology that relies heavily on the study of intraday volume], he offered classes and I was able to observe him directly. Finally, in the case of some supertraders, the observation was one step removed— watching video tapes of their trading and listening to their talks or interviews. Jimmy Rogers, Paul Tudor Jones, and Richard Dennis [three of the best traders of our generation, who were also profiled in *Market Wizards*] fall into this last category. I later saw Dennis on a futures industry panel that you moderated and determined my inferences about his trading strategies and emotional management style were accurate.

**Can you give me a typical example of a trader who came to you for help?**

I recently worked with a man who is a good trader. However, every time he gets ahead, he ends up giving back a good part of his profits. While I was working with him, it came out that he knew lots of traders who made money but who, in his words, were "not wonderful human beings." He wanted to be successful as a trader, but he was worried about becoming like them. His unconscious solution to the problem was to not become too successful.

His beliefs also had a very restricting effect on his personal life. He thought that he had to put trading first—that trading meant that he couldn't have a personal life or a family. Using NLP to change those beliefs helped evolve that part of himself that he had mistakenly thought was sabotaging his trading. This was a particularly gratifying experience for me, because I saw him reclaim a part of his life that he thought he couldn't have as a trader.

He recently called me to say he had tripled his position size to over a thousand contracts. By resolving his inner conflict, he freed up mental power to better watch for opportunities and improve his trading.

**What differentiates those who excel at trading from the vast majority of traders?**

One critical element is beliefs. In his book *Peak Performers,* Charles Garfield reported that the key element these individuals share is a total belief in the likelihood of their own success. Contrast this with Dr. Michael Lerner's research, published in his book *Surplus Powerlessness,* in which he found that most people feel that they have very little power over their lives. He based his conclusions on thousands of interviews conducted with people from a wide cross section of occupations. This general contrast between peak performers and the majority of the population serves equally well in explaining an essential difference between the outstanding traders and all other market participants. The supertraders have an absolute confidence in their ability to win—a confidence confirmed by competence in the markets. Contrast this with most traders who lack confidence in their system or approach and the typical tendency of many traders to blame others (their broker, floor traders, and so on) for their results.

**Beyond confidence in their own success, what are some of the other characteristics of successful traders?**

Another important element is that they have a perceptual filter that they know well and that they use. By perceptual filter I mean a methodology, an approach, or a system to understanding market behavior. For example, Elliott Wave analysis and classical chart analysis are types of perceptual filters. In our research, we found that the type of perceptual filter doesn't really make much of a difference. It could be classical chart analysis, Gann, Elliott Waves, or Market Profile—all these methods appear to work, provided the person knows the perceptual filter thoroughly and follows it.

**I have an explanation as to why that may be the case.**

I'd certainly be interested in hearing it.

**I believe a lot of the popular methodologies are really vacuous.**

[He laughs.] Aha! That's a pretty provocative statement. You've got my attention.

**All these technical methods are based on price. In effect, they're all different-colored glasses for looking at price. Proponents of RSI and Stochastics (two popular overbought/oversold indicators) would see price patterns filtered through these price-derived series. Gann analysis enthusiasts would see the price patterns through a Gann-based interpretation. In these cases and others, traders accumulate experience on price patterns—albeit from different perspectives. Some of the methodologies employed, however, are probably totally worthless. It's simply that instead of looking at prices through clear glass, traders who use these methods are looking at prices through different-colored tints. The method, or tint shade, is a matter of individual preference. To extend the analogy, I would compare these methods to nonprescription sunglasses: they change the view but don't necessarily improve the vision. The bottom line is that these methods seem to work only because the people who use them have developed some sort of intuitive experience about price.**

That actually fits pretty well with my own view. People need to have a perceptual filter that matches the way they think. The appropriate perceptual filter for a trader has more to do with how well it fits a trader's mental strategy, his mode of thinking and decision making, than how well it accounts for market activity. When a person gets to know any perceptual filter deeply, it helps develop his or her intuition. There's no substitute for experience.

**What other characteristics typify successful traders?**

Another important element among traders who excel is that they have an effective trading strategy. I'm using the word "strategy" in an NLP sense, meaning a series of internal representations, mental pictures, words, and feelings, leading to a desired outcome: winning trades. One trader can act decisively, while another may be paralyzed by indecision. The difference lies in their strategies.

**I'm afraid you've lost me. In your use of the word, what typifies the strategies of successful traders?**

An effective trading strategy will have the following characteristics. First, it will be automatic. Given a specific situation, the trader will know what to do without second-guessing himself. Second, a good strategy will be congruent—that is, it won't create any internal conflict. Third, the strategy will incorporate Away From motivation by including some specific risk control plans. Fourth, part of the strategy will involve imagining the trade from the perspective of already being in the position and considering what might be wrong with the trade *before* putting it on. Fifth, an effective trading strategy will provide specific evidence that will allow the trader to evaluate the merits of a trade.

**Are there any other characteristics common to successful traders?**

Management of one's emotional state is critical. The truly exceptional traders can stand up to anything. Instead of getting emotional when things don't go their way, they remain calm and act in accordance with their approach. This state of mind may come naturally. Or some people may have ways of controlling or dissipating their emotions. In either case, they know they want to be emotionally detached from feelings regarding their positions. When a position is going against him, Pete Steidlmayer's attitude appears to be: "Hmm, look at that." He observes his own positions with scientific detachment. By staying calm, outstanding traders get the necessary feedback to determine whether or not their approach needs to be revised.

**Is having the proper emotional state an intrinsic quality? Or can it be learned?**

Both. Some outstanding traders just appear to be that way—they have a natural scientific detachment—while others have learned to exercise a military-like control over their emotions. Either approach will work, but these traders are the exceptions. Trading actually tends to attract people who are ill suited to the task—those who are enamored with making lots of money; people who are willing to take high risks; individuals who seek excitement or who react to the world with emotional intensity.

**How do you teach these types of people to adopt the kind of mental state appropriate to successful trading?**

One thing I do is to have them actually get up, step back, and imagine seeing themselves sitting in their chairs. I get them to calmly watch as if they were observing someone else doing the trading. I also have them do other NLP exercises that are designed to achieve the same goal.

**And just doing this type of simple mental exercise is sufficient to create permanent behavioral changes? For example, are you implying that previously high-strung traders will automatically respond calmly in crisis situations, simply by virtue of having done such mental exercises?**

If someone is very high-strung, it means he's particularly emotional, and it may take more work to make sure the results stick, but overall, the answer is yes. I know that it sounds hard to believe, but our brains learn very quickly. If you change the way the brain perceives a situation, you will change the way it will respond to that situation forever.

Of course, sometimes there are other conflicting considerations. One of my earliest clients was a very emotional trader who had a successful system but couldn't follow it. I taught him some techniques for emotionally detaching from the market. I watched him applying these techniques one day, and it really worked. In just a few hours, he was up $7,000. But just as I was savoring a sense of self-satisfaction, he turned to me and in a monotone voice said, "This is boring." I thought to myself, Uh-oh. I would like to say that I helped him solve his problem and that he made millions of dollars and lived happily ever after. No, the guy blew out. He knew how to go into an emotionally detached state, but he didn't like to be there.

This experience taught me that some people are in the markets because they like the excitement. Since then, I've learned to help people who have that need for excitement to find it in other places in their lives and to schedule it, so their brain gets the idea that this process is not about denial but about appropriate times and means of expression.

**Anything to add regarding traits that differentiate winning from losing traders?**

A final critical characteristic distinguishing winning traders from losing traders relates to what I've termed "operating metaphors." An operating metaphor determines how we view the world, and it shapes our beliefs, actions, and life-styles. Some of the metaphors used by traders to describe the market are a woman, war, and a game, to name a few of the more common ones. As an example of the game or puzzle-solving metaphors, Richard Dennis says, "It's like playing a hundred chess games at once." Pete Steidlmayer says he's "solving the markets." Paul Tudor Jones sums it up with, "It's a game, and money is a way to keep score." Each operating metaphor will lead a trader's brain to a different set of beliefs and a different approach to the markets, with some being more effective than others.

Contrast the metaphors I just cited with some of the operating metaphors I've typically heard around the trading floor. "I got torn up today," makes the market into a beast of prey. "We took a hit" reflects thinking that the market is a war and the speaker a wounded participant. Which metaphor will result in your feeling more objective about the market—playing a game, even a high-stakes game, or defending yourself from an attacking wild animal? The answer is obvious. The difference is in what is suggested by the metaphor. In the game, there are winners and losers, but your survival isn't at stake, as it is with being attacked by a wild animal. You may respond brilliantly to save yourself from the beast, but that metaphor doesn't encourage you to learn and practice long-term strategies and tactics the way a game does. Having an operating metaphor appropriate to your trading style is fundamental to success.

**Can you tell who will be a successful trader and who will not?**

Yes, based on how well they match the profiles of successful traders in regards to the areas just discussed: beliefs, perceptual filter, strategy, emotional-state management, and operating metaphors. On a less technical level, I can say that after years of studying traders, the best predictor of success is simply whether the person is improving with time and experience. Many traders unconsciously acknowledge their lack of progress by continually jumping from one system or methodology to another, never gaining true proficiency in any. As a result, these people end up with one year of experience six times instead of six years of experience. In contrast, the superior traders gravitate to a single approach—the specific approach is actually not important—and become extremely adept at it.

**What is NLP's view of the relationship between the conscious and unconscious minds?**

The property of the conscious mind is to reflect on things. "Am I where I want to be?" "Is this a good trade?" In other words, it's concerned with evaluation. It's not the property of the conscious mind to change things. To offer you an analogy, when I lived in Colorado, I had a friend from the East visit me. One day, I suggested that we go horseback riding. We rented horses from a stable. I don't know if you've ever rented horses from a stable, but the horses know the paths, and they also assess the experience of the rider when he gets on. I had a little experience; my friend had none.

We got on our horses, and they began to trot. Off in the distance, there was a line of trees in front of us. The closer we got to the trees, the faster the horses began to run. I knew exactly what was going on. The horses were planning to knock us off by running through the trees and then go back to the stables and take the rest of the day off. I ducked down as my horse and I went through the trees. Meanwhile, I heard this "thump" behind me. I pulled my horse around, and there was my friend lying on the ground, half a dozen yards before the trees.

"Are you OK?" I asked.

He was kind of embarrassed and said, "Yeah, I'm alright."

"What happened?" I asked.

"The stupid horse was going to run into a tree, so I had to jump off," he replied.

Now here is someone who has obviously mistaken horses for cars. The conscious mind is like the rider. It evaluates the direction the horse is going. If the horse, or the unconscious, is not going where we want it to go, it doesn't mean that it's bad, or not following instructions, or about to run into a tree. It means that the unconscious has its own programs and is running them the best it can based on all its history and habits—just like that horse had the habit of knocking people off and going back to the stable.

With NLP, you can direct your conscious mind to notice when you're not where you want to be. What's more important, you can use NLP techniques to effectively introduce new patterns into your unconscious mind to bring about the changes you desire, instead of complaining or making up any one of a thousand reasons why you aren't where you want to be in your life.

**We talked earlier about taking the time to examine your goals—to make sure that they are indeed the goals you want and if they're not, changing the direction of your efforts accordingly. Assuming a person has done that, do you have any advice on how to best transform those goals into a reality?**

I can best answer that question by relating the experience of Gary Faris, an NLP trainer and colleague. Gary's study of this very question grew out of a compelling personal experience. Gary is an avid runner. Several years ago, while running down a farm road in California, he was hit by a pick-up truck. His injuries were so severe that the emergency room doctors weren't sure he would even live. When he survived after the first two of the six operations he would eventually undergo, the doctors said that the only reason he had made it was because he was in such good physical condition. They told him that he would never walk normally, and certainly never run again.

Over the next two years, Gary was in sports rehabilitation. He rebuilt his body, overcoming the pain. Today, he runs regularly and is the fittest trainer working for NLP Comprehensive [one of the first and foremost NLP training organizations]. Needless to say, the doctors were astounded. However, they were making their assessment based on the statistical evidence of similar cases. They didn't realize that Gary Faris had made himself into an exceptional patient.

Right after his accident, Gary began studying sports injury rehabilitation. He searched for the core characteristics of those athletes who had gone through successful rehabilitation. He examined their mental attitudes. He found that six basic mental patterns characterized all these people.

First, these athletes used both motivating directions. In other words, they were both moving toward and away from consequences. In this way, these athletes were utilizing their maximum motivation.

Second, these athletes were absolutely dedicated to regaining full strength and health. This standard became their guiding goal. Anything less was unacceptable. In fact, many of them not only wanted to regain full strength and health, but they strived to get in even better shape than they were before their injuries. They knew their capabilities and wouldn't accept anything less. These athletes knew they would succeed.

The third key element that these athletes had in common was that they approached their rehabilitation one step at a time. If you contemplate achieving a major project, such as overcoming a terrible injury, it's intimidating to think of the entire task all at once. However, if you can take it in chunks, or individual steps, you'll complete it. Each step becomes a new goal. For Gary, he had to survive before he could walk; he had to walk before he could run. Gary and the other athletes he studied derived great satisfaction from completing each step. Thus, they experienced succeeding at each of the milestones along the way to a major goal of full strength and health.

The fourth key element related to the way in which these recovering athletes perceived time. They were in the moment. In other words, they succeeded because they focused on the present. If, instead, they had focused too far into the future, it would have been easier to fall into a negative orientation by questioning whether they would achieve their ultimate objective.

The fifth element of their positive mental attitude was involvement. The more the athlete helped himself—even doing something as simple as placing ice on an inflamed area—the more complete and faster the recovery. When you participate, you feel you can influence what's going on, and that makes you more determined and aggressive.

The sixth and final key element was related to how the athletes judged their individual performance and progress. People have a natural tendency to compare themselves and their actions with others. This type of thinking begins at an early age and becomes more ingrained as we become adults. It is critical that recovering athletes not fall into this mental habit. Because of their injuries, they would compare poorly and would likely become discouraged. The successful athletes looked solely at their own progress. They made self-to-self comparisons. They asked themselves questions like, "How far have I progressed since last week, or last month?"

Incidentally, teaching kids to make self-to-self comparisons is one of the greatest gifts parents can give them. Let them know that in any endeavor they engage in, there will always be some people who are better and others who are worse. What is important is our own progress. By adopting this mental attitude, it's possible to look at other people's accomplishments as inspiration and models of excellence as opposed to targets of envy.

When these six elements are combined, they create a compulsion to succeed. In subsequent research, I found that these six core characteristics provided the basis of any positive mental attitude. Whether I looked at athletes, entrepreneurs, or executives, the more confident their mental attitude, the more they used these same six elements.

**You have become heavily involved in both NLP and trading. Do you see any similarities between these two endeavors?**

Trading and NLP are like mirrors of each other. Trading is concerned with market patterns, and NLP is concerned with the patterns of the mind. Both deal with tangible, not theoretical, results. Traders are judged by their results—the money in their trading accounts—not the beauty or intricacy of their market theories. NLP practitioners are judged by their results—clients quickly achieving the changes they are seeking in their lives—not the originality or insights of NLP theories about how the brain works. NLP seeks to model human excellence, and trading is an activity in which excellence is required for success, since only a small minority can win. I have been drawn to NLP and trading because I like the emphasis they both place on real-world results and excellence.

---

Does NLP work? My personal view on this question matters little because it would represent only a sample of one. There is certainly a tremendous amount of anecdotal evidence supporting the efficacy of NLP techniques. However, rigorous, double-blind scientific tests are in short supply. No doubt the paucity of hard scientific experimental evidence is due to the extreme difficulty of measuring the results of NLP, which deal largely with feelings and beliefs. However, one of the hallmarks of NLP is that it virtually guarantees quick results. Therefore, if you try NLP in one of its forms (books, tapes, seminars, or one-on-one sessions), you should be able to make a fairly quick determination of whether the approach has any validity for you.

The broader questions of NLP's merits aside, I did find certain aspects of Faulkner's message compelling. First, I found the concept of mission a highly useful mental construct for focusing goals and intensifying motivation. My listening to Faulkner's tapes coincided with a surge in my personal efforts to further a commodity trading advisory venture and significant progress in that regard. I also think there is a great deal of merit to Faulkner's list of the six key steps in achievement:

1. Use both Toward and Away From motivation.
2. Have a goal of full capability plus, with anything less being unacceptable.
3. Break down potentially overwhelming goals into chunks, with satisfaction garnered from the completion of each individual step.
4. Fully concentrate on the present moment of time—that is, the single task at hand rather than the long-term goal.
5. Personally involve yourself in achieving goals (as opposed to depending on others).
6. Make self-to-self comparisons to measure progress.

The above elements have important implications and applications to trading. As one example, the stress on self-involvement would imply that it is unlikely for people to succeed at trading by completely relying on someone else's system. As another, the focus on self-to-self comparisons implies that traders should judge their progress based on their own past performance, not the performance of other traders.

The image that Faulkner paints of a successful trader is in stark contrast to popular perceptions. Most people probably think of great traders as the Evil Knievels of the financial world—individuals willing to take great risks, drawn to their calling by the adrenalin-charged excitement. According to Faulkner, nothing could be further from the truth. Successful traders have learned to avoid risk, not seek it. Moreover, very few of them trade for excitement. On the contrary, based on Faulkner's observations, one of the hallmarks of successful traders is their ability to maintain a calm, detached emotional state while trading. They may get excitement in their lives, but it's not from trading.

Many of Faulkner's comments have relevance to more than just trading. Most people could probably benefit from the advice given by Faulkner and NLP to explore what success means for them. The one comment I found particularly striking concerned his conversations with hundreds of elderly patients: "Not one of these people said they truly regretted anything they had actually done. What they regretted was what they hadn't done."

# *Robert Krausz*

## THE ROLE OF THE SUBCONSCIOUS

I first learned of Robert Krausz through a letter in *Club 3000*—a publication that consists largely of letters written by subscribers who share an interest in trading. The trader who wrote the letter described how a set of subliminal tapes he had purchased from Robert Krausz, a member of the British Hypnotist Examiners Council, had improved his trading immensely. I was intrigued.

There is almost a Dickensian quality to Robert Krausz's life story. His early childhood years were spent in a ghetto in Hungary during World War II. At the age of eight, he and a friend escaped from a forced march to a death camp, bolting for the woods in opposite directions during a moment in which the guards were distracted. Having no place else to go, he made his way back to the ghetto, where he stayed until the end of the war. Krausz spent the years after the war in a succession of orphanages, finally ending up in an orphanage in South Africa. There he met a diamond magnate who took a liking to him. The wealthy industrialist began coming to the orphanage on Sundays to take Robert out on excursions—starting a relationship that ended in adoption. In this way, the orphan who had survived the horrors of war found a new life as a son of one of South Africa's wealthiest men.

Krausz's wartime experience made him an avid supporter of Israel.

As he grew older, he became more and more committed to Israel's survival. Troubled by the implied hypocrisy of convincing other young South African Jews to emigrate and join the Israeli armed forces while staying put himself, he eventually followed his own advice. Despite the protests of his father, whom he loved and respected, he joined the Israeli armed forces, serving as a paratrooper during the 1956 war with Egypt. The socialist undertone of the Israeli economy troubled Krausz, however, and he eventually emigrated to Great Britain.

In London, Krausz's artistic inclinations led to a career as a dress designer. He eventually developed his own line of clothes during the heyday of Carnaby Street and the Beatles era. Krausz's business subsequently expanded to include the design of fabric patterns and clothes for overseas manufacturers and the importation of the finished products back into the United Kingdom. In connection with this business, Krausz traveled very extensively throughout the Far East over a number of years. Although the business prospered, Krausz's increasing fascination with trading led to another major career change. In early 1988, he gave up his business and emigrated to the United States to begin a new endeavor as a full-time trader.

Krausz declined to comment on his specific results as a trader other than to say that he has done well enough to "earn a very comfortable living." When he discusses trading as a career, Krausz becomes animated. "This is the best business in the world!" he emphatically proclaims. "There is no other profession that is so black and white; you're either right or wrong." (As he says this, I am struck by what he is wearing—black slacks and a white shirt.) "Trading also appeals to me because you're totally dependent on your own talents and abilities."

I met Krausz at his Fort Lauderdale home. He is an openly friendly man. He insisted on personally picking me up at the airport and enthusiastically invited me to spend the night at the guest cottage adjoining his house.

My conversations with Krausz progressed through various stages throughout the day. Krausz speaks with a distinct South African accent (which, to the untrained American ear, would commonly be mistaken for a British accent), a factor that adds further color to his retelling of past experiences. We began our talks sitting on the patio, looking out onto the waterway and tropical forest preserve that borders the rear of his property—a most extraordinary backyard. The chill of a seasonally cool Florida winter day eventually drove us inside, and we continued the interview in Krausz's office. The office, which Krausz shares with his wife, a well-known financial astrologer, runs the width of the house, with the windows on one side facing the ocean and the windows on the other side overlooking the waterway and preserve; the Krauszes divide the office along the lines of their preferred views.

One can see that Krausz is a serious chartist, as a drafting table in his office is covered with three-by-two-foot charts that Krausz manually maintains. Unlike conventional charts, which use vertical bars to represent each day or time interval, Krausz's charts use price bars of varying widths as part of a methodology called Symmetrics, which is based on the assumed symmetry of price and time and was invented by Joe Rondinone, one of W. D. Gann's first students.

The interview was temporarily halted for a lengthy dinner break. If Krausz is as good a trader as he is a Hungarian cook, he will become a very wealthy man.

---

**You have mentioned that you consider being a trader an essential qualification as a hypnotherapist specializing in helping traders. Which came first, the trading or the training in hypnosis?**

The trading was the catalyst that led me to hypnosis. My first exposure to trading came during the record-setting 1979–80 bull market in gold. At the time, I thought that I was trading. Of course, it was not trading; it was just childish nonsense.

**How did you first get involved in trading?**

During that 1979 bull market, every two or three days the *Financial Times* carried another article bearing the banner "New Highs in Gold" or some other very similar headline. These repeated stories made an impression on me. I also had a friend who was involved in the gold market and making a great deal of money trading. We went out for dinner one evening, and he talked to me at length about the gold market. He considered himself a great expert. Of course, I later found out that he knew absolutely nothing about trading. He said to me, "Robert, you're a fool. You work from 7 A.M. to 7 P.M. every day, six days a week. I'm making more money working only a few hours a day. Who's better off?"

He gave me the name of his broker, and I opened up an account. Then the greatest tragedy happened: My first trade was an absolute winner. My second trade was also a winner. My third trade was breakeven. My fourth trade was another winner. On my fifth trade, I gave it all back. Then on my sixth trade, I lost more money than I had made in all my previous winning trades put together. The market had turned, and I lost a considerable amount of money—much more than the account-starting equity.

**In other words, you were meeting margin calls along the way.**

Exactly. I kept putting more and more money into the account. I kept on thinking, "The market is going to turn. The market is going to turn." Of course, it never turned.

**When did you finally give up the ship?**

I had a specific cutoff point. I was a 50 percent shareholder in a garment business, and I wanted to be absolutely certain that my losses would not endanger the business. When I reached my maximum loss point, I got out. The experience proved to be a substantial financial loss, but even more important, it was a tremendous infliction of pain to my ego. I was a reasonably successful businessman who up to that point had never failed in any venture. I couldn't believe how stupid I had been.

**While you were trading, were you making your own decisions, or was your broker giving you advice?**

Oh, my broker was very "helpful" in advising me on the trades. I later found out that he knew less than I did. But I've always taken responsibility for my actions, and this experience was no exception.

**What ultimately happened to your friend who enticed you to trade the gold market?**

He never gave up the belief. The man eventually went totally broke.

## Did you continue to agonize over your mistake after you were out of the market?

I found out a long time ago that one of the most damaging things a person can do is to harp on past mistakes. If you're constantly repeating to yourself, "I shouldn't have done that," it's like a cartwheel going over the same tracks. Eventually, the negative message gets so embedded in your psyche that it becomes very difficult to change your course of action.

At that point, I decided that either I was going to figure out what makes the market tick, or I was going to wipe my mouth, smile, walk away, and never trade another contract for as long as I lived. Since I'm not the type of person to walk away from a challenge, I chose the former course of action.

At the time, my business required me to travel extensively to remote regions in the Far East. Since there were few diversions in these areas, I had lots of free time. I used this time to do a great deal of reading on the markets. I also began to follow the gold market on a daily basis. I went so far as to have my partner telex me the daily open, high, low, and close in gold. My library grew and grew, as I was wolfing down every new book that came out on technical analysis. One of the books I read was alluringly titled *How To Make Money in the Commodity Markets—and Lots of It!* by Charles Drummond. I found that Drummond traveled down a different track from everyone else. The book espoused a unique methodology called point-and-line charting. It made sense to me, and I purchased Drummond's second book, which delved more deeply into the subject.

I then began trading again, using this point-and-line methodology. However, I found that I was hesitating in taking trades. The fear of loss had arrived. By this time, I had started communicating with Drummond, initially with questions regarding his techniques. He always graciously responded to my inquiries. In one of my telexes to Drummond, I mentioned my dilemma of being unable to make trades. Drummond telexed back, "You're experiencing what is known as the 'freeze,' which is purely a psychological problem."

Around this time, I had a chance meeting with an acquaintance who ran a large public company. He seemed to be very depressed, and I asked him what was wrong. He told me that he was getting a divorce and his business was doing very poorly. Three weeks later, I bumped into this same individual at a local restaurant. He was talking, laughing, and altogether quite jovial. I was quite curious about his sudden transformation. The next day over lunch, he told me how he had gone to a hypnotherapist and his life was now back on track. I got the number of this hypnotherapist and went to see him with the specific intent of seeking help with my trading problem.

For my first session, I brought along a copy of Drummond's book. He flipped through it and exclaimed, "My god, it's Japanese!" That was his idea of a joke. Of course, he had no concept of trading.

**Did his lack of familiarity with trading act as an impediment, or did the hypnosis help anyway?**

Yes, it helped. My trading quickly went to breakeven, which for me was quite an accomplishment. I was still experiencing some slight hesitation in taking trades, but the "freeze" was gone. I was so impressed by hypnotherapy that I sought out information on getting trained as a hypnotist myself. I found there was a group called the British Hypnotist Examiners Council [BHEC] that offered courses, which taught the techniques. I took the beginner's course.

**How long was this course?**

It was given over two weekends.

**And that's all it takes to become a qualified practitioner?**

No, of course not. The course teaches you only the basic techniques, which are actually quite simple. Over the next year, I spent about one day a week observing one of the instructors, John Cross, in his practice. After a while, John allowed me to work with some of his clients under his observation. I then took an advanced course, given by BHEC. At the end of all of this, I took the BHEC qualification exam.

**Tell me about your first client.**

He was a student who came to me for help in improving his grades. I was quite nervous, but, fortunately, he was an easily hypnotizable subject.

**What percentage of the population is hypnotizable?**

About 85 percent. Contrary to popular belief, intelligent and creative people are the most easy to hypnotize.

**Are you saying that as much as 85 percent of the population can be influenced under hypnosis to change their beliefs and behavior?**

Yes, providing you don't ask them to do anything that they wouldn't do in a normal waking state.

**How then do nightclub hypnotists get people to make fools of themselves on stage?**

The trick is that people who volunteer to go up on stage are the type of individuals who like to perform in public. Typically, they are people who want to show off—closet showbiz types who missed their calling. Hypnosis merely brings out these natural inclinations by bypassing the behavioral controls enforced by the conscious mind. It's virtually impossible to get a naturally shy person to do silly things on stage.

**How can you tell whether a person is really hypnotized or merely following instructions to please the hypnotist?**

There are a number of standard techniques. For example, one method involves telling the subject that his or her arm is a rigid piece of steel, and then instructing the person to extend the arm horizontally. If the person is really hypnotized, you won't be able to push the arm down, regardless of the force applied—even if the subject is a physically weak person.

**Was there anything memorable about your first trading client?**

I would like to say that the procedure was immensely successful, but the truth is that the person didn't experience any overnight transformation. It took many years before I realized why hypnosis was very effective with some traders but not others.

**What is the reason?**

Some traders have a valid methodology that they have adequately backtested and that their conscious mind is happy with. These are the traders who can usually be helped through hypnosis. The only thing hypnosis can do is to inform the subconscious mind that the person now has a valid methodology that the conscious mind has already accepted.

**But you must first be at that point.**

Absolutely. For a novice trader to try to become an expert trader through hypnosis is like a novice chess player seeking to become a master through hypnosis. The point is that a certain proficiency level is necessary before hypnosis can help.

**Besides aiding in your transformation from losing trader to winning trader, how else did the exposure to hypnosis affect you?**

It's no exaggeration to say that hypnosis changed my perception of reality.

**In what way?**

I discovered that there was another world that I was totally unaware of: the subconscious. I realized that the subconscious mind had the power to overcome the conscious mind. Today, of course, I no longer think in those terms. I now understand that the subconscious and conscious minds have to be in harmony. The more closely the conscious mind is aligned with the subconscious, the easier it is to generate winnings. To keep those winnings, however, your subconscious mind must believe only one thing: that you deserve your winnings.

**Is the absence of that belief the reason why people lose in the markets?**

YES! YES! YES!

**How can you be so certain?**

Because I've seen the process time and time and time again.

**Could you give me an anonymous case history?**

A few years ago, I worked with a man who had traded very successfully for over thirty years. All of a sudden, he started losing six-figure amounts monthly. He had been losing this amount for about five consecutive months when he came to me for help. It turned out that the onset of his losing streak coincided with his being left by his wife, who was a much younger woman. As soon as I helped him realize that the breakup of his marriage was not his own fault and that his wife's affections went only as deep as his pocketbook, his trading began to change dramatically. Within three days, he was breaking even, and within another three days, he was making money. Once he had begun winning again, I questioned him under hypnosis. "Have you changed your method?" I asked.

"No," he replied.
"Are you feeling more confident?" I asked.
"Yes," he answered.
"What has made the big difference?" I inquired.
He replied, "Robert, I feel I deserve my winnings again."

**Why did he feel he didn't deserve his winnings?**

That was exactly my next question. Apparently, he believed that the breakup of his marriage was due to his inability to perform sexually at the same level he had as a younger man. Because at the subconscious level he felt that he had failed his wife, he was punishing himself by losing in the markets. He felt he didn't deserve to win anymore because of his inadequacy.

**Is the implication that people always lose because they feel that they don't deserve to win?**

No. Some people lose because they feel they don't deserve to win, but more people lose because they never perform the basic tasks necessary to become a winning trader.

**What are those tasks?**

1. Develop a competent analytical methodology.
2. Extract a reasonable trading plan from this methodology.
3. Formulate rules for this plan that incorporate money management techniques.
4. Back-test the plan over a sufficiently long period.
5. Exercise self-management so that you adhere to the plan. The best plan in the world cannot work if you don't act on it.

**Typically, how do you work with someone who comes to you for help in improving his or her trading?**

The first thing I do is go though a series of about thirty questions that have only one purpose: finding out if the person has a methodology.

**What do you do if you determine that the person doesn't have an effective methodology?**

I tell them, "Go home; find yourself a methodology; and then see me if you still need to." Hypnosis is not a crutch. If you don't have a methodology and trading plan, all the hypnosis in the world won't help you.

**Does that happen frequently?**

It's not uncommon, but the typical person who seeks me out is serious about trading and already has a trading plan. The problem, however, is that in the past, this person may have suffered so many losses and so much pain using another methodology that the new trading plan is not permitted to seep through the subconscious mind as a new reality. In other words, the belief system has to be altered.

**Are you implying that the subconscious sabotages the trading?**

Exactly. Every time you have a losing trading plan, the memory is etched in your subconscious. The more losses, the deeper the impression and the deeper the pain. Let's say you start trading with Methodology A and take many losses. You then stop trading for one or two years. After much research and careful testing, you develop Methodology B, which your conscious mind is convinced is valid. However, the losses from your previous Methodology A are so ingrained in your subconscious that whenever you contemplate making a trade, the adrenaline starts to flow, and the fear of executing a trade arises. Some traders are literally immobilized by this fear at the moment when they need to act. This is the "freeze" that I encountered when I returned to trading years after my first painful experience.

If you have truly back-tested a methodology and are employing an effective trading plan, your conscious mind is already aware of its validity. It's your subconscious mind that prevents you from taking correct action in the market. The problem will persist until you convince the subconscious in a very direct manner that the new methodology is valid and that it has to forget about the old methodology.

**How is this transformation achieved?**

We must erase the previous pictures of impending financial disaster and paint new pictures in beautiful colors, showing a happy, confident, and successful trader. Through deep-relaxation techniques, achieved through hypnosis, we can bypass the critical faculty of the conscious mind and establish a direct connection to the subconscious mind. Deep relaxation or hypnosis is a state of mind, not a state of sleep. Because the subconscious mind is nonjudgmental, it will accept new input as facts. By informing the subconscious mind that the old fears are no longer valid and that the trader now has a well-tested and confident plan, the subconscious mind will begin to accept this new reality. One cannot truly be a winner until the subconscious mind is fully in tune with what the conscious mind has set out to achieve.

**Do you ever have people come to you saying that they want to be traders, but when you put them in a hypnotic state you find that they really don't want to be traders after all?**

Absolutely. This situation arises with alarming regularity. Some people try to punish themselves through the market. Of course, this all occurs on a subconscious level. There are people who feel they have to make retribution for some real or imagined wrong they have done to another person. For some people, the channel is suicide; for some people, it's doing their job poorly on purpose; and for some people, it's losing money in the markets—even though they may know better.

Quite simply, there are some people who just shouldn't be trading. By putting them under hypnosis you find that these people are not really comfortable trading; it's not their calling. When I find people who fall into this category, I bring them to and inform them as to what transpired during hypnosis. I tell them, "Here's your money; I can't help you. Do yourself and your family a great favor and forget trading."

**Is there a typical reaction when you present this type of person with the advice to give up trading?**

Total horror. I've even been threatened with physical violence. "I'll bash your f–ing head in!" one person shouted at me after I gave him this advice.

**Can you describe a specific situation in which you advised a client to give up trading?**

One person hated his wife but didn't have the courage to divorce her. Ironically, it was his wife who had sent him to me. He was a successful professional man who had been trading for two years and losing money steadily. Under hypnosis, it came out that the only way he saw out of his dilemma was to make himself church-mouse poor so that his wife would walk out on him. The strategy was to make his financial losses look legitimate. He couldn't make himself look bad through his own profession, because he was so good at it. So every month in which he made X thousand dollars in his profession, he would give back X thousand plus in the commodity markets.

**Did he admit all of this under hypnosis? Or was this your analytical interpretation?**

I asked him straight out under hypnosis, "Are you getting back at your wife? Do you feel that if you lose enough money in the markets, she'll walk out on you?"

He exclaimed, "That's the idea!"

**That was his subconscious talking?**

Absolutely. In his conscious mind this man would never admit to this motivation.

**Was this a person who believed he wanted to trade?**

Not only did he want to trade, he felt he had to trade. He emphatically told me, "I *love* to trade the markets. I prefer trading to my profession."

**Any other unusual case histories come to mind?**

There was one rather humorous situation that occurred while I was still in London. One day this man came to me and said, "Mr. Krausz, I've heard good things about you. I don't know whether you can help me, but do you ever work with traders' wives?"

"It would be a first," I admitted, "but I suppose it could be done. What seems to be the problem?" I asked.

He said, "Every day, my broker sends me my runs, but I never receive them. My wife pinches them."

"What do you mean she pinches them?" I asked.

"She hides them from me," he answered. "She meets the mailman and intercepts my statements before I ever get them. At first I didn't realize what was happening. I called up my broker and asked him why I wasn't getting my statements. However, he insisted that my daily runs were being sent out regularly. I am now convinced my wife is pinching them."

I said, "This is ridiculous. Can't you go out and meet the mailman first?"

"I can't go!" he exclaimed. "The mailman comes in the middle of the trading day; I'm busy watching the quote screen. We've got to find out why she's hiding my statements."

"Why don't you simply ask her?" I suggested.

"She denies it," he answered. "Go on and get her on the phone yourself. You'll see that she'll deny everything."

I called his wife and said, "I have your husband in my office. Exactly what is the problem with the missing statements?"

She replied, "Mr. Krausz, I promise you that I never touch his mail."

So I asked her, "What then do you think happens to his statements?"

"He hides them himself," she answered. "He never opens them."

I thought to myself, That's very interesting. I thanked her, hung up the phone, and said to her husband, "Why don't we just have a short hypnotherapy session right now; no charge. Maybe I can help you in figuring out how to handle your wife with this problem."

"Good idea," he enthusiastically replied.

There are various levels of hypnosis. After about half an hour, I had him at the level I wanted. I asked him, "What is happening to your brokerage statements?"

"Why, I hide them, of course," he answered.

"Do you open them?" I asked.

"Nooooooo," he said, slowly drawing out the word, "I don't want to see my mistakes."

"How then do you know when you're losing money?" I asked.

"My broker phones me and tells me that I have to put up another few thousand pounds on margin."

"And do you send the money in?" I queried.

"Oh yes," he replied. "I have to. Otherwise, I would have to stop trading—wouldn't I? My broker would just close the account."

I asked, "Would you like him to close the account?"

"Oh no, I love trading!" he trumpeted.

"Well, do you know that you're losing money?" I asked.

"Certainly, I'm not a fool," he said authoritatively.

"Where do you hide your statements?" I inquired.

"Oh, I can't tell you that," he whispered. "You'll just tell my wife."

"I promise that I won't tell her," I assured him. "But, tell me, what would happen if she found out?"

"She'd be very cross," he said. "She'd throw me out of the house."

"Why would she do that?" I asked.

"Because I'm losing money that I should be giving her to buy new dresses."

I thought to myself, The best favor I can do for this chap is to stop him from trading. I brought him out of hypnosis and made an appointment to see him again the following week. Before he left, he turned to me and asked, "Do you think you can get my wife to tell us where she's hiding the statements?"

I said, "We'll talk about that next time."

"Why don't I bring her along with me," he suggested.

"You know what," I said, "that's a good idea."

The following week they both showed up at the appointed time. I asked him, "Are we going to solve this problem?"

He answered, "Certainly we're going to solve this problem—as long as you can stop her from taking my mail."

I put him under hypnosis, and I told his wife exactly what had happened.

She nonchalantly replied, "Oh, I know he's hiding his statements. I even know where he's hiding them, but I dare not say anything, because it will destroy him."

She was obviously a very clever woman. Under hypnosis I told him, "Your wife has agreed to turn over to you *all* your back statements. Moreover, she has promised that she will never stop the mailman again, as long as you take responsibility for your own actions and stop playing the fool."

"Are you sure?" he asked.

"I'm sure," I replied. "In fact, I'm going to bring you out of hypnosis now, and your wife is going to put this agreement in writing."

He thanked me energetically, and I brought him out of hypnosis. Three days later, his wife called to tell me he had closed his account.

## What had been his motivation for trading?

Just thrills. He was leading a very boring life. He held a civil service position and this was just his way of seeking some excitement. [His job only required a minimal number of hours of attendance in a consulting capacity; hence he was able to trade during the day.]

## What motivated him to stop trading?

When he was confronted with the piece of paper stating that his wife would turn over all his past statements, he knew that she knew where he had been hiding them because that was the only way that she could give him the mail that she had supposedly intercepted. At this point, his conscious mind realized what had been happening.

His wife told me that, the next day, he pulled out the hidden statements, put them on the dining room table, and said, "Aha! I see that you have finally decided to give me all the mail."

She said, "Yes dear; here it is; take it."

The next day, he phoned his broker and closed the account.

**What is the most surprising thing you have discovered about human behavior or human nature since you started doing hypnosis?**

How ready we are to fool ourselves. I learned that people's perceptions of reality and true reality are not the same thing. It's a person's belief system, not reality, that really counts. The more I worked with hypnosis, the more I realized how often our lives are warped and misdirected by invalid beliefs that have their origins in childhood. These beliefs frequently cause people to live their lives with a distorted view of reality.

**Can you give me an example?**

A young boy of five watches his father fixing the family automobile in the garage. Wishing to help, he picks up one of his father's tools. The father, afraid that the boy will get hurt, shouts at him to put the tool down. This type of experience only has to happen a couple of times before the subconscious mind files it into permanent memory.

Fast forward the scene to when the boy is twelve. Now the father thinks his son is ready to learn how to use tools, and he asks his son to help him fix the car. Without knowing why, as soon as he picks up one of the tools, the boy feels uncomfortable. Whatever he tries, he does poorly. Eventually his father tells him not to bother, saying he's just clumsy with tools. That boy is now convinced for life that he's useless with tools.

What has happened in this example? The first experience at the age of five is filed away in the subconscious mind as, "If I touch these tools, my father will shout at me. Therefore it's bad." Then, when the boy is twelve and the father asks for help, the subconscious mind is reinforced at the conscious level by the belief that he's also clumsy. Unless a way is found to eradicate these false premises, they'll remain with the boy the rest of his life.

**Can you give me a trading analogy?**

We discussed one earlier. Based on past experiences, a person may believe he's a poor trader on a subconscious level, even after he has developed an effective trading methodology. The result may be fear based on beliefs that are no longer relevant.

**Why do most traders lose?**

Recently I conducted a two-day workshop with a group of thirty part-time traders. At one point, I presented them with a questionnaire. The key question asked the students to rank the following list in order of importance as to what they thought were their greatest weaknesses in the markets:

1. Execution (pulling the trigger)
2. Analysis
3. Lack of knowledge
4. Lack of confidence
5. No trading plan
6. Personal problems
7. Fear of loss
8. Not devoting enough time

[Note to reader: You may wish to answer this question yourself, before continuing on.]

Amazingly, 90 percent of this group picked the exact same four items for the top of their list, although the order varied:

1. Lack of confidence
2. No trading plan

3. Execution
4. Fear of loss

What single element is the root of the other three? What causes lack of confidence? What causes fear of loss? What causes poor execution? NO TRADING PLAN! This is the basic feature that separates losing traders from winning traders. Lack of confidence disappears in direct relation to the validity of a back-tested trading plan.

**What are the key characteristics of a winning trader?**

Persistence, patience, and a willingness to take risks.

**How has hypnosis changed your life?**

I learned through the use of creative visualization that I could set goals and achieve them—providing, of course, that the goals were realistic. Incidentally, traders who do not set goals or targets find it much more difficult to achieve high returns than traders who set such goals.

**What do you mean by "creative visualization"?**

Using trading as an example, in a deep-relaxation state you see yourself applying your methodology, and you then see this methodology succeeding. By mentally playing through these images, you can alter the negative beliefs in your subconscious and in the process enhance your chance of success. This is the same methodology employed by many top athletes.

**As a hypnotist, you've certainly been exposed to the gamut of human emotions. I assume that those people who want to succeed as traders want to do so because they believe it will make them happy. Let's deal with a more fundamental question: In your experience, what do you believe is the essential element in achieving happiness?**

I believe the single most important factor is having control of your own life. Everything else is secondary.

According to Krausz, the major factors traders cite as the reasons for why they lose—lack of confidence, fear of loss, and poor execution—are all a consequence of not having a trading plan. Clearly, based on this premise, the absolutely essential first step for a trader is to develop a trading plan. Once such a plan has been constructed, the trader must adequately back-test the method to gain the necessary confidence in the validity of the approach.

Thus far, the advice is sound but hardly unconventional. Krausz offers a more unique view in his discussion of the role of the subconscious as an impediment to trading success. Krausz explains that subconscious beliefs will dictate a person's actions. The point is that if the subconscious believes that a person is a losing trader based on prior experiences, it will continue to hold that view even after the trader has developed an effective methodology. These beliefs, predicated on past experiences, can cause a person to feel fears that may no longer be appropriate. These fears can lead to what Krausz's mentor, Charles Drummond, called the "freeze." Thus, Krausz believes that once an effective trading plan is developed, it is critical to convince the subconscious mind of the new reality. The greater the harmony between the conscious and subconscious minds, the better the chance for success. The techniques for achieving such harmony include hypnosis or deep relaxation and visualization.

Krausz's unstated motto might be: We become what we believe. If you accept this premise, then it becomes quite clear why psychology plays such an important role in trading success or failure.

# PART VIII

# *Closing Bell*

# Market Wiz(ar)dom

By now it should be clear that the methods employed by exceptional traders are extraordinarily diverse. Some are pure fundamentalists; others employ only technical analysis; and still others combine the two methodologies. Some traders consider two days to be long term, while others consider two months to be short term. Yet despite the wide gamut of styles, I have found that certain principles hold true for a broad spectrum of traders. After a score of years of analyzing and trading the markets and two books of interviews with great traders, I have come down to the following list of forty-two observations regarding success in trading:

## 1. FIRST THINGS FIRST

First, be sure that you really want to trade. As both Krausz and Faulkner confirmed, based on their experience in working with traders, it is common for people who think they want to trade to discover that they really don't.

## 2. EXAMINE YOUR MOTIVES

Think about why you really want to trade. If you want to trade for the excitement, you might be better off riding a roller coaster or taking up hang gliding. In my own case, I found that the underlying motive for trading was serenity or peace of mind—hardly the emotional state typical of trading. Another personal motive for trading was that I loved puzzle solving—and the markets provided the ultimate puzzle. However, while I enjoyed the cerebral aspects of market analysis, I didn't particularly like the visceral characteristics of trading itself. The contrast between my motives and the activity resulted in very obvious conflicts. You need to examine your own motives very carefully for any such conflicts. The market is a stern master. You need to do almost everything right to win. If parts of you are pulling in opposite directions, the game is lost before you start.

How did I resolve my own conflict? I decided to focus completely on mechanical trading approaches in order to eliminate the emotionality in trading. Equally important, focusing on the design of mechanical systems directed my energies to the part of trading I did enjoy—the puzzle-solving aspects. Although I had devoted some energy to mechanical systems for these reasons for a number of years, I eventually came to the realization that I wanted to move in this direction exclusively. (This is not intended as an advocacy for mechanical systems over human-decision-oriented approaches. I am only providing a personal example. The appropriate answer for another trader could well be very different.)

### 3. MATCH THE TRADING METHOD TO YOUR PERSONALITY

It is critical to choose a method that is consistent with your own personality and comfort level. If you can't stand to give back significant profits, then a long-term trend-following approach—even a very good one—will be a disaster, because you will never be able to follow it. If you don't want to watch the quote screen all day (or can't), don't try a day-trading method. If you can't stand the emotional strain of making trading decisions, then try to develop a mechanical system for trading the markets. The approach you use must be right for you; it must feel comfortable. The importance of this cannot be overemphasized. Remember Randy McKay's assertion: "Virtually every successful trader I know ultimately ended up with a trading style suited to his personality."

Incidentally, the mismatch of trading style and personality is one of the key reasons why purchased trading systems rarely make profits for those who buy them, even if the system is a good one. While the odds of getting a winning system are small—certainly less than 50/50—the odds of getting a system that fits your personality are smaller still. I'll leave it to your imagination to decide on the odds of buying a profitable/moderate risk system and using it effectively.

### 4. IT IS ABSOLUTELY NECESSARY TO HAVE AN EDGE

You can't win without an edge, even with the world's greatest discipline and money management skills. If you could, then it would be possible to win at roulette (over the long run) using perfect discipline and risk control. Of course, that is an impossible task because of the laws of probability. If you don't have an edge, all that money management and discipline will do for you is to guarantee that you will gradually bleed to death. Incidentally, if you don't know what your edge is, you don't have one.

### 5. DERIVE A METHOD

To have an edge, you must have a method. The type of method is irrelevant. Some of the supertraders are pure fundamentalists; some are pure technicians; and some are hybrids. Even within each group, there are tremendous variations. For example, within the group of technicians, there are tape readers (or their modern-day equivalent—screen watchers), chartists, mechanical system traders, Elliott Wave analysts, Gann analysts, and so on. The type of method is not important, but having one is critical—and, of course, the method must have an edge.

### 6. DEVELOPING A METHOD IS HARD WORK

Shortcuts rarely lead to trading success. Developing your own approach requires research, observation, and thought. Expect the process to take lots of time and hard work. Expect many dead ends and multiple failures before you find a successful trading approach that is right for you. Remember that you are playing against tens of thousands of professionals. Why should you be any better? If it were that easy, there would be a lot more millionaire traders.

### 7. SKILL VERSUS HARD WORK

Is trading success dependent on innate skills? Or is hard work sufficient? There is no question in my mind that many of the supertraders have a special talent for trading. Marathon running provides an appropriate analogy. Virtually anyone can run a marathon, given sufficient commitment and hard work. Yet, regardless of the effort and desire, only a small fraction of the population will ever be able to run a 2:12 marathon. Similarly, anyone can learn to play a musical instrument. But again, regardless of work and dedication, only a handful of individuals possess the natural talent to become concert soloists. The general rule is that exceptional performance requires both natural talent and hard work to realize its potential. If the innate skill is lacking, hard work may provide proficiency, but not excellence.

In my opinion, the same principles apply to trading. Virtually anyone can become a net profitable trader, but only a few have the inborn talent to become supertraders. For this reason, it may be possible to teach trading success, but only up to a point. Be realistic in your goals.

### 8. GOOD TRADING SHOULD BE EFFORTLESS

Wait a minute. Didn't I just list hard work as an ingredient to successful trading? How can good trading require hard work and yet be effortless?

There is no contradiction. Hard work refers to the preparatory process—the research and observation necessary to become a good trader—not to the trading itself. In this respect, hard work is associated with such qualities as vision, creativity, persistence, drive, desire, and commitment. Hard work certainly does not mean that the process of trading itself should be filled with exertion. It certainly does not imply struggling with or fighting against the markets. On the contrary, the more effortless and natural the trading process, the better the chances for success. As the anonymous trader in *Zen and the Art of Trading* put it, "In trading, just as in archery, whenever there is effort, force, straining, struggling, or trying, it's wrong. You're out of sync; you're out of harmony with the market. The perfect trade is one that requires no effort."

Visualize a world-class distance runner, clicking off mile after mile at a five-minute pace. Now picture an out-of-shape, 250-pound couch potato trying to run a mile at a ten-minute pace. The professional runner glides along gracefully—almost effortlessly—despite the long distance and fast pace. The out-of-shape runner, however, is likely to struggle, huffing and puffing like a Yugo going up a 1 percent grade. Who is putting in more work and effort? Who is more successful? Of course, the world-class runner puts in his hard work during training, and this prior effort and commitment are essential to his success.

## 9. MONEY MANAGEMENT AND RISK CONTROL

Almost every person I interviewed felt that money management was even more important than the trading method. Many potentially successful systems or trading approaches have led to disaster because the trader applying the strategy lacked a method of controlling risk. You don't have to be a mathematician or understand portfolio theory to manage risk. Risk control can be as easy as the following three-step approach:

1. Never risk more than 1 to 2 percent of your capital on any trade. (Depending on your approach, a modestly higher number might still be reasonable. However, I would strongly advise against anything over 5 percent.)

2. Predetermine your exit point *before* you get into a trade. Many of the traders I interviewed cited exactly this rule.

3. If you lose a certain predetermined amount of your starting capital (e.g., 10 percent to 20 percent), take a breather, analyze what went wrong, and wait until you feel confident and have a high-probability idea before you begin trading again. For traders with large accounts, trading very small is a reasonable alternative to a complete trading hiatus. The strategy of cutting trading size down sharply during losing streaks is one mentioned by many of the traders interviewed.

## 10. THE TRADING PLAN

Trying to win in the markets without a trading plan is like trying to build a house without blueprints—costly (and avoidable) mistakes are virtually inevitable. A trading plan simply requires combining a personal trading method with specific money management and trade entry rules. Krausz considers the absence of a trading plan the root of all the principal difficulties traders encounter in the markets. Driehaus stresses that a trading plan should reflect a personal core philosophy. He explains that without a core philosophy, you are not going to be able to hold on to your positions or stick with your trading plan during really difficult times.

## 11. DISCIPLINE

*Discipline* was probably the most frequent word used by the exceptional traders that I interviewed. Often, it was mentioned in an almost apologetic tone: "I know you've heard this a million times before, but believe me, it's really important."

There are two basic reasons why discipline is critical. First, it is a prerequisite for maintaining effective risk control. Second, you need discipline to apply your method without second-guessing and choosing which trades to take. I guarantee that you will almost always pick the wrong ones. Why? Because you will tend to pick the comfortable trades, and as Eckhardt explained, "What feels good is often the wrong thing to do."

As a final word on this subject, remember that you are never immune to bad trading habits—the best you can do is to keep them latent. As soon as you get lazy or sloppy, they will return.

## 12. UNDERSTAND THAT YOU ARE RESPONSIBLE

Whether you win or lose, you are responsible for your own results. Even if you lost on your broker's tip, an advisory service recommendation, or a bad signal from the system you bought, you are responsible because you made the decision to listen and act. I have never met a successful trader who blamed others for his losses.

## 13. THE NEED FOR INDEPENDENCE

You need to do your own thinking. Don't get caught up in mass hysteria. As Ed Seykota pointed out, by the time a story is making the cover of the national periodicals, the trend is probably near an end.

Independence also means making your own trading decisions. Never listen to other opinions. Even if it occasionally helps on a trade or two, listening to others invariably seems to end up costing you money—not to mention confusing your own market view. As Michael Marcus stated in *Market Wizards*, "You need to follow your own light. If you combine two traders, you will get the worst of each."

A related personal anecdote concerns another trader I interviewed in *Market Wizards*. Although he could trade better than I if he were blindfolded and placed in a trunk at the bottom of a pool, he still was interested in my view of the markets. One day he called and asked, "What do you think of the yen?"

The yen was one of the few markets about which I had a strong opinion at the time. It had formed a particular chart pattern that made me very bearish. "I think the yen is going straight down, and I'm short," I replied.

He preceded to give me fifty-one reasons why the yen was oversold and due for a rally. After he hung up, I thought: "I'm leaving on a business trip tomorrow. My trading has not been going very well during the last few weeks. The short yen trade is one of the only positions in my account. Do I really want to fade one of the world's best traders given these considerations?" I decided to close out the trade.

By the time I returned from my trip several days later, the yen had fallen 150 points. As luck would have it, that afternoon the same trader called. When the conversation rolled around to the yen, I couldn't resist asking, "By the way, are you still long the yen?"

"Oh no," he replied, "I'm short."

The point is not that this trader was trying to mislead me. On the contrary, he firmly believed each market opinion at the time he expressed it. However, his timing was good enough so that he probably made money on both sides of the trade. In contrast, I ended up with nothing, even though I had the original move pegged exactly right. The moral is that even advice from a much better trader can lead to detrimental results.

## 14. CONFIDENCE

An unwavering confidence in their ability to continue to win in the markets was a nearly universal characteristic among the traders I interviewed. Dr. Van Tharp, a psychologist who has done a great deal of research on traders and was interviewed in *Market Wizards*, claims that one of the basic traits of winning traders is that they believe "they've won the game before the start."

### 15. LOSING IS PART OF THE GAME

The great traders fully realize that losing is an intrinsic element in the game of trading. This attitude seems linked to confidence. Because exceptional traders are confident that they will win over the long run, individual losing trades no longer seem horrible; they simply appear inevitable—which is what they are. As Linda Raschke explained, "It never bothered me to lose, because I always knew that I would make it right back."

There is no more certain recipe for losing than having a fear of losing. If you can't stand taking losses, you will either end up taking large losses or missing great trading opportunities—either flaw is sufficient to sink any chance for success.

### 16. LACK OF CONFIDENCE AND TIME-OUTS

Trade only when you feel confident and optimistic. I have often heard traders say: "I just can't seem to do anything right." Or, "I bet I get stopped out right near the low again." If you find yourself thinking in such negative terms, it is a sure sign that it is time to take a break from trading. Get back into trading slowly. Think of trading as a cold ocean. Test the water before plunging in.

### 17. THE URGE TO SEEK ADVICE

The urge to seek advice betrays a lack of confidence. As Linda Raschke said, "If you ever find yourself tempted to seek out someone else's opinion on a trade, that's usually a sure sign that you should get out of your position."

### 18. THE VIRTUE OF PATIENCE

Waiting for the right opportunity increases the probability of success. You don't always have to be in the market. As Edwin Lefevre put it in his classic *Reminiscences of a Stock Operator,* "There is the plain fool who does the wrong thing at all times anywhere, but there is the Wall Street fool who thinks he must trade all the time."

One of the more colorful descriptions of patience in trading was offered by Jim Rogers in *Market Wizards:* "I just wait until there is money lying in the corner, and all I have to do is go over there and pick it up." In other words, until he is so sure of a trade that it seems as easy as picking money off the floor, he does nothing.

Mark Weinstein (also interviewed in *Market Wizards*) provided the following apt analogy: "Although the cheetah is the fastest animal in the world and can catch any animal on the plains, it will wait until it is absolutely sure it can catch its prey. It may hide in the bush for a week, waiting for just the right moment. It will wait for a baby antelope, and not just any baby antelope, but preferably one that is also sick or lame. Only then, when there is no chance it can lose its prey, does it attack. That, to me, is the epitome of professional trading."

As a final bit of advice on the subject of patience, guard particularly against being overeager to trade in order to win back prior losses. Vengeance trading is a sure recipe for failure.

### 19. THE IMPORTANCE OF SITTING

Patience is important not only in waiting for the right trades, but also in staying with trades that are working. The failure to adequately profit from correct trades is a key profit-limiting factor. Quoting again from Lefevre in *Reminiscences,* "It never was my thinking that made big money for me. It was always my sitting. Got that? My sitting tight!" Also, recall Eckhardt's comment on the subject: "One common adage ... that is completely wrongheaded is: You can't go broke taking profits. That's precisely how many traders *do* go broke. While amateurs go broke by taking large losses, professionals go broke by taking small profits."

### 20. DEVELOPING A LOW-RISK IDEA

One of the exercises Dr. Van Tharp uses in his seminars is having the participants take the time to write down their ideas on low-risk trades.

The merit of a low-risk idea is that it combines two essential elements: patience (because only a small portion of ideas will qualify) and risk control (inherent in the definition). Taking the time to think through low-risk strategies is a useful exercise for all traders. The specific ideas will vary greatly from trader to trader, depending on the markets traded and methodologies used. At the seminar I attended, the participants came up with a long list of descriptions of low-risk ideas. As one example: a trade in which the market movement required to provide convincing proof that you are wrong is small. Although it had nothing to do with trading, my personal favorite of the low-risk ideas mentioned was: "Open a doughnut shop next door to a police station."

### 21. THE IMPORTANCE OF VARYING BET SIZE

All traders who win consistently over the long run have an edge. However, that edge may vary significantly from trade to trade. It can be mathematically demonstrated that in any wager game with varying probabilities, winnings are maximized by adjusting the bet size in accordance with the perceived chance for a successful outcome. Optimal blackjack betting strategy provides a perfect illustration of this concept (see Hull chapter).

If the trader has some idea as to which trades have a greater edge—say, for example, based on a higher confidence level (assuming that is a reliable indicator)—then it makes sense to be more aggressive in these situations. As Druckenmiller expresses it, "The way to build [superior] long-term returns is through preservation of capital and home runs.... When you have tremendous conviction on a trade, you have to go for the jugular. It takes courage to be a pig." For a number of Market Wizards, keen judgment as to when to really step on the accelerator and the courage to do so have been instrumental to their achieving exceptional (as opposed to merely good) returns.

Some of the traders interviewed mentioned that they varied their trading size in accordance with how they were doing. For example, McKay indicated that it was not uncommon for him to vary his position size by as much as a factor of one hundred to one. He finds this approach helps him reduce risk during losing periods while enhancing profits during the winning periods.

## 22. SCALING IN AND OUT OF TRADES

You don't have to get in or out of a position all at once. Scaling in and out of positions provides the flexibility of fine-tuning trades and broadens the set of alternative choices. Most traders sacrifice this flexibility without a second thought because of the innate human desire to be completely right. (By definition, a scaling approach means that some portions of a trade will be entered or exited at worse prices than other portions.) As one example of the potential benefits of scaling, Lipschutz noted that it has enabled him to stay with long-term winners much longer than he has seen most traders stay with their positions.

## 23. BEING RIGHT IS MORE IMPORTANT THAN BEING A GENIUS

I think one reason why so many people try to pick tops and bottoms is that they want to prove to the world how smart they are. Think about winning rather than being a hero. Forget trying to judge trading success by how close you can come to picking major tops and bottoms, but rather by how well you can pick individual trades with merit based on favorable risk/return situations and a good percentage of winners. Go for consistency on a trade-to-trade basis, not perfect trades.

## 24. DON'T WORRY ABOUT LOOKING STUPID

Last week you told everyone at the office, "My analysis has just given me a great buy signal in the S&P. The market is going to a new high." Now as you examine the market action since then, something appears to be wrong. Instead of rallying, the market is breaking down. Your gut tells you that the market is vulnerable. Whether you realize it or not, your announced prognostications are going to color your objectivity. Why? Because you don't want to look stupid after telling the world that the market was going to a new high. Consequently, you are likely to view the market's action in the most favorable light possible. "The market isn't breaking down, it's just a pullback to knock out the weak longs." As a result of this type of rationalization, you end up holding a losing position far too long. There is an easy solution to this problem: Don't talk about your position.

What if your job requires talking about your market opinions (as mine does)? Here the rule is: Whenever you start worrying about contradicting your previous opinion, view that concern as reinforcement to reverse your market stance. As a personal example, in early 1991 I came to the conclusion that the dollar had formed a major bottom. I specifically remember one talk in which an audience member asked me about my outlook for currencies. I responded by boldly predicting that the dollar would head higher for years. Several months later, when the dollar surrendered the entire gain it had realized following the news of the August 1991 Soviet coup before the coup's failure was confirmed, I sensed that something was wrong. I recalled my many predictions over the preceding months in which I had stated that the dollar would go up for years. The discomfort and embarrassment I felt about these previous forecasts told me it was time to change my opinion.

In my earlier years in the business, I invariably tried to rationalize my original market opinion in such situations. I was burned enough times that I eventually learned a lesson. In the above example, the abandonment of my original projection was fortunate, because the dollar collapsed in the ensuing months.

## 25. SOMETIMES ACTION IS MORE IMPORTANT THAN PRUDENCE

Waiting for a price correction to enter the market may sound prudent, but it is often the wrong thing to do. When your analysis, methodology, or gut tells you to get into a trade at the market instead of waiting for a correction—do so. Caution against the influence of knowing that you could have gotten in at a better price in recent sessions, particularly in those situations when the market witnesses a sudden, large move (often due to an important surprise news item). If you don't feel the market is going to correct, that consideration is irrelevant. These types of trades often work because they are so hard to do. As a perfect example, recall the willingness of the trader in Lipschutz's group to aggressively sell the dollar into a collapsing market following the G-7 meeting. Another example of this principle is Driehaus's willingness to buy a stock heavily after it is already up very sharply on a bullish earnings report if he feels the new information implies the stock will go still higher.

## 26. CATCHING PART OF THE MOVE IS JUST FINE

Just because you missed the first major portion of a new trend, don't let that keep you from trading with that trend (as long as you can define a reasonable stop-loss point). Recall McKay's observation that the easiest part of a trend is the middle portion, which implies always missing part of the trend prior to entry.

## 27. MAXIMIZE GAINS, NOT THE NUMBER OF WINS

Eckhardt explains that human nature does not operate to maximize gain but rather the chance of a gain. The problem with this is that it implies a lack of focus on the magnitudes of gains (and losses)—a flaw that leads to nonoptimal performance results. Eckhardt bluntly concludes: "The success rate of trades is the least important performance statistic and may even be inversely related to performance." Yass echoes a similar theme: "The basic concept that applies to both poker and option trading is that the primary object is not winning the most hands, but rather maximizing your gains."

## 28. LEARN TO BE DISLOYAL

Loyalty may be a virtue in family, friends, and pets, but it is a fatal flaw for a trader. Never have loyalty to a position. The novice trader will have lots of loyalty to his original position. He will ignore signs that he is on the wrong side of the market, riding his trade into a large loss while hoping for the best. The more experienced trader, having learned the importance of money management, will exit quickly once it is apparent he has made a bad trade. However, the truly skilled trader will be able to do a 180-degree turn, *reversing* his position at a loss if market behavior points to such a course of action. Recall Druckenmiller's ill-timed reversal from short to long on the very day before the October 19, 1987 crash. His ability to quickly recognize his error and, more important, to unhesitatingly act on that realization by reversing back to short at a large loss helped transform a potentially disastrous month into a net profitable one.

### 29. PULL OUT PARTIAL PROFITS

Pull a portion of winnings out of the market to prevent trading discipline from deteriorating into complacency. It is far too easy to rationalize overtrading and procrastination in liquidating losing trades by saying, "It's only profits." Profits withdrawn from an account are much more likely to be viewed as real money.

### 30. HOPE IS A FOUR-LETTER WORD

Hope is a dirty word for a trader, not only in regards to procrastinating in a losing position, hoping the market will come back, but also in terms of hoping for a reaction that will allow for a better entry in a missed trade. If such trades are good, the hoped-for reaction will not materialize until it is too late. Often the only way to enter such trades is to do so as soon as a reasonable stop-loss point can be identified.

### 31. DON'T DO THE COMFORTABLE THING

Eckhardt offers the rather provocative proposition that the human tendency to select comfortable choices will lead most people to experience worse than random results. In effect, he is saying that natural human traits lead to such poor trading decisions that most people would be better off flipping coins or throwing darts. Some of the examples Eckhardt cites of the comfortable choices people tend to make that run counter to sound trading principles include: gambling with losses, locking in sure winners, selling on strength and buying on weakness, and designing (or buying) trading systems that have been overfitted to past price behavior. The implied message to the trader is: Do what is right, not what feels comfortable.

### 32. YOU CAN'T WIN IF YOU HAVE TO WIN

There is an old Wall Street adage: "Scared money never wins." The reason is quite simple: If you are risking money you can't afford to lose, all the emotional pitfalls of trading will be magnified. Druckenmiller's "betting the ranch" on one trade, in a last-ditch effort to save his firm, is a perfect example of the above aphorism. Even though he came within one week of picking the absolute bottom in the T-bill market, he still lost all his money. The need to win fosters trading errors (e.g., excessive leverage and a lack of planning in the example just cited). The market seldom tolerates the carelessness associated with trades born of desperation.

## 33. THINK TWICE WHEN THE MARKET LETS YOU OFF THE HOOK EASILY

Don't be too eager to get out of a position you have been worried about if the market allows you to exit at a much better price than anticipated. If you had been worried about an adverse overnight (or over-the-weekend) price move because of a news event or a technical price failure on the previous close, it is likely that many other traders shared this concern. The fact that the market does not follow through much on these fears strongly suggests that there must be some very powerful underlying forces in favor of the direction of the original position. This concept, which was first proposed by Marty Schwartz in *Market Wizards,* was illustrated in this volume by the manner in which Lipschutz exited the one trade he admitted had scared him. In that instance, he held an enormous short dollar position in the midst of a strongly rallying market and had to wait for the Tokyo opening to find sufficient liquidity to exit his position. When the dollar opened weaker than expected in Tokyo, he didn't just dump his position in relief; rather, his trader's instincts told him to delay liquidation—a decision that resulted in a far better exit price.

## 34. A MIND IS A TERRIBLE THING TO CLOSE

Open-mindedness seems to be a common trait among those who excel at trading. For example, Blake's entry into trading was actually an attempt to demonstrate to a friend that prices were random. When he realized he was wrong, he became a trader. Driehaus says that the mind is like a parachute; it's good only when it's open.

## 35. THE MARKETS ARE AN EXPENSIVE PLACE TO LOOK FOR EXCITEMENT

Excitement has a lot to do with the image of trading but nothing to do with success in trading (except in an inverse sense). In *Market Wizards,*

Larry Hite described his conversation with a friend who couldn't understand his absolute adherence to a computerized trading system. His
friend asked, "Larry, how can you trade the way you do. Isn't it boring?" Larry replied, "I don't trade for excitement; I trade to win." This
passage came to mind when Faulkner described the trader who blew
out because he found it too boring to be trading in the way that produced profits.

### 36. THE CALM STATE OF A TRADER

If there is an emotional state associated with successful trading, it is the
antithesis of excitement. Based on his observations, Faulkner stated that
exceptional traders are able to remain calm and detached regardless of
what the markets are doing. He describes Peter Steidlmayer's response
to a position that is going against him as being typified by the thought,
"Hmmm, look at that." Basso also talks directly about the benefits of a
detached perspective in trading: "If instead of saying, 'I'm going to do
this trade,' you say, 'I'm going to watch myself do this trade,' all of a
sudden you find that the process is a lot easier."

### 37. IDENTIFY AND ELIMINATE STRESS

Stress in trading is a sign that something is wrong. If you feel stress,
think about the cause, and then act to eliminate the problem. For example, let's say you determine that the greatest source of stress is indecision in getting out of a losing position. One way to solve this problem is
simply to enter a protective stop order every time you put on a position.

I will give you a personal example. One of the elements of my job
is providing trading recommendations to brokers in my company. This
task is very similar to trading, and, having done both, I believe it's actually more difficult than trading. At one point, after years of net profitable recommendations, I hit a bad streak. I just couldn't do anything
right. When I was right about the direction of the market, my buy recommendation was just a bit too low (or my sell price too high). When I
got in and the direction was right, I got stopped out—frequently within
a few ticks of the extreme of the reaction.

I responded by developing a range of computerized trading programs and technical indicators, thereby widely diversifying the trading

advice I provided to the firm. I still made my day-to-day subjective calls on the market, but everything was no longer riding on the accuracy of these recommendations. By widely diversifying the trading-related advice and information, and transferring much of this load to mechanical approaches, I was able to greatly diminish a source of personal stress—and improve the quality of the research product in the process.

## 38. PAY ATTENTION TO INTUITION

As I see it, intuition is simply experience that resides in the subconscious mind. The objectivity of the market analysis done by the conscious mind can be compromised by all sorts of extraneous considerations (e.g., one's current market position, a resistance to change a previous forecast). The subconscious, however, is not inhibited by such constraints. Unfortunately, we can't readily tap into our subconscious thoughts. However, when they come through as intuition, the trader needs to pay attention. As the anonymous trader in *Zen and the Art of Trading* expressed it, "The trick is to differentiate between what you *want* to happen and what you *know* will happen."

## 39. LIFE'S MISSION AND LOVE OF THE ENDEAVOR

In talking to the traders interviewed in this book, I had the definite sense that many of them felt that trading was what they were meant to do—in essence, their mission in life. Recall Charles Faulkner's quote of John Grinder's description of mission: "What do you love so much that you would pay to do it?" Throughout my interviews, I was struck by the exuberance and love the Market Wizards had for trading. Many used gamelike analogies to describe trading. This type of love for the endeavor may indeed be an essential element for success.

## 40. THE ELEMENTS OF ACHIEVEMENT

Faulkner's list of the six key steps to achievement based on Gary Faris's study of successfully rehabilitated athletes appears to apply equally well to the goal of achieving trading success. These strategies include the following:

1. using both "Toward" and "Away From" motivation;
2. having a goal of full capability plus, with anything less being unacceptable;
3. breaking down potentially overwhelming goals into chunks, with satisfaction garnered from the completion of each individual step;
4. keeping full concentration on the present moment—that is, the single task at hand rather than the long-term goal;
5. being personally involved in achieving goals (as opposed to depending on others); and
6. making self-to-self comparisons to measure progress.

### 41. PRICES ARE NONRANDOM = THE MARKETS CAN BE BEAT

In reference to academicians who believe market prices are random, Trout says, "That's probably why they're professors and why I'm making money doing what I'm doing." The debate over whether prices are random is not yet over. However, my experience with the interviews conducted for this book and its predecessor leaves me with little doubt that the random walk theory is wrong. It is not the magnitude of the winnings registered by the Market Wizards but the consistency of these winnings in some cases that underpin my belief. As a particularly compelling example, consider Blake's 25:1 ratio of winning to losing months and his average annual return of 45 percent compared with a worst drawdown of only 5 percent. It is hard to imagine that results this lopsided could occur purely by chance—perhaps in a universe filled with traders, but not in their more finite numbers. Certainly, winning at the markets is not easy—and, in fact, it is getting more difficult as professionals account for a constantly growing proportion of the activity—but it can be done!

### 42. KEEP TRADING IN PERSPECTIVE

There is more to life than trading.

# A Personal Reflection

I am frequently asked whether writing this volume and the first *Market Wizards* helped me become a better trader. The answer is yes, but not in the way people expect when they ask the question. No trader revealed to me any great market secrets or master plan unlocking the grand design of the markets. (If this is what you seek, don't despair, the answer is readily available—just check the ads in any financial periodical.) For me, the single most important lesson provided by the interviews is that it is absolutely necessary to adopt a trading approach precisely suited to one's own personality.

Over the years, I have come to clearly realize that what I really like about this business is trying to solve this master puzzle: How do you win in the markets? You have all these pieces, and you can put them together in a limitless number of ways, bounded only by your creativity. Moreover, to keep the game interesting, there are lots of pitfalls to lead you astray, and some of the rules keep changing in subtle ways. There is even a group of very intelligent people telling you that the game can't be won at all. The really fascinating thing is that, as complex as this puzzle is, there are a multitude of totally different solutions, and there are always better solutions. Trying to solve this wonderful puzzle is what I enjoy.

On the other hand, I have also come to realize that I do not like the trading aspect at all. I do not enjoy the emotionality of making intraday trading decisions. When I am losing, I am upset, and when I am on a hot streak, I am anxious because I know I can't keep it up. In short, it is not my style. In contrast, there are people who thrive on and excel at the actual trading. One person who in my mind epitomizes this type of approach is Paul Tudor Jones, whom I interviewed in *Market Wizards*. When you watch Paul trade, you can see he's really charged by the activity. He bubbles over with energy, taking in information from a hundred different directions and making instantaneous trading decisions. He seems to love it, as if it were some challenging sport. And loving it is probably why he is so good at it.

For many years, I participated in both descretionary trading and system trading. It is, perhaps, no coincidence that in the course of working on this book, I came to the conclusion that it was system trading that suited my personality. Once I increased my efforts and commitment to system trading, my progress accelerated and I felt that the approach fit like a glove.

It took me over a decade to figure out my natural direction. I'd suggest that you take the time to seriously ponder whether the path you are on is the one you want to be on. Perhaps your journey will then be shortened.

# *Appendix: Options—*
# *Understanding the Basics*

There are two basic types of options: calls and puts. The purchase of a *call option* provides the buyer with the right—but not the obligation—to purchase the underlying item at a specified price, called the *strike price* or *exercise price,* at any time up to and including the *expiration date.* A *put option* provides the buyer with the right—but not the obligation—to sell the underlying item at the strike price at any time prior to expiration. (Note, therefore, that buying a put is a *bearish* trade, whereas selling a put is a *bullish* trade.) The price of an option is called a *premium.* As an example of an option, an IBM April 130 call gives the purchaser the right to buy 100 shares of IBM at $130 per share at any time during the life of the option.

The buyer of a call seeks to profit from an anticipated price rise by locking in a specified purchase price. The call buyer's maximum possible loss will be equal to the dollar amount of the premium paid for the option. This maximum loss would occur on an option held until expiration if the strike price were above the prevailing market price. For example, if IBM were trading at $125 when the 130 option expired, the option would expire worthless. If at expiration the price of the underlying market was above the strike price, the option would have some

Note: This Appendix was adapted from Jack D. Schwager, *A Complete Guide to the Futures Market* (New York: John Wiley & Sons, 1984).

value and would hence be exercised. However, if the difference between the market price and the strike price were less than the premium paid for the option, the net result of the trade would still be a loss. In order for a call buyer to realize a net profit, the difference between the market price and the strike price would have to exceed the premium paid when the call was purchased (after adjusting for commission cost). The higher the market price, the greater the resulting profit.

The buyer of a put seeks to profit from an anticipated price decline by locking in a sales price. Like the call buyer, his maximum possible loss is limited to the dollar amount of the premium paid for the option. In the case of a put held until expiration, the trade would show a net profit if the strike price exceeded the market price by an amount greater than the premium of the put at purchase (after adjusting for commission cost).

Whereas the buyer of a call or put has limited risk and unlimited potential gain, the reverse is true for the seller. The option seller (often called the *writer*) receives the dollar value of the premium in return for undertaking the obligation to assume an opposite position *at the strike price* if an option is exercised. For example, if a call is exercised, the seller must assume a short position in the underlying market at the strike price (because, by exercising the call, the buyer assumes a long position at that price).

The seller of a call seeks to profit from an anticipated sideways to modestly declining market. In such a situation, the premium earned by selling a call provides the most attractive trading opportunity. However, if the trader expected a large price decline, he would usually be better off going short the underlying market or buying a put—trades with open-ended profit potential. In a similar fashion, the seller of a put seeks to profit from an anticipated sideways to modestly rising market.

Some novices have trouble understanding why a trader would not always prefer the buy side of the option (call or put, depending on market opinion), since such a trade has unlimited potential and limited risk. Such confusion reflects the failure to take probability into account. Although the option seller's theoretical risk is unlimited, the price levels that have the greatest probability of occurrence (i.e., prices in the vicinity of the market price when the option trade occurs) would result in a net gain to the option seller. Roughly speaking, the option buyer accepts a large probability of a small loss in return for a small probability of a large gain, whereas the option seller accepts a small probability of a large loss in exchange for a large probability of a small gain. In an efficient market, neither the consistent option buyer nor the consistent option seller should have any significant advantage over the long run.

The option premium consists of two components: intrinsic value plus time value. The *intrinsic value* of a call option is the amount by which the current market price is above the strike price. (The intrinsic value of a put option is the amount by which the current market price is below the strike price.) In effect, the intrinsic value is that part of the premium that could be realized if the option were exercised at the current market price. The intrinsic value serves as a floor price for an option. Why? Because if the premium were less than the intrinsic value, a trader could buy and exercise the option and immediately offset the resulting market position, thereby realizing a net gain (assuming that the trader covers at least transaction costs).

Options that have intrinsic value (i.e., calls with strike prices below the market price and puts with strike prices above the market price) are said to be *in the money*. Options that have no intrinsic value are called *out-of-the-money* options. Options with a strike price closest to the market price are called *at-the-money* options.

An out-of-the-money option, which by definition has an intrinsic value equal to zero, will still have some value because of the possibility that the market price will move beyond the strike price prior to the expiration date. An in-the-money option will have a value greater than the intrinsic value because a position in the option will be preferred to a position in the underlying market. Why? Because both the option and the market position will gain equally in the event of a favorable price movement, but the option's maximum loss is limited. The portion of the premium that exceeds the intrinsic value is called the *time value*.

The three most important factors that influence an option's time value are the following:

1. *Relationship between the strike price and market price*—Deeply out-of-the-money options will have little time value since it is unlikely that the market price will move to the strike price—or beyond—prior to expiration. Deeply in-the-money options have little time value because these options offer positions very similar to the underlying market—both will gain and lose equivalent amounts for all but an extremely adverse price move. In other words, for a deeply in-the-money option,

risk being limited is not worth very much because the strike price is so far from the prevailing market price.

2. *Time remaining until expiration*—The more time remaining until expiration, the greater the value of the option. This is true because a longer life span increases the probability of the intrinsic value increasing by any specified amount prior to expiration.

3. *Volatility*—Time value will vary directly with the estimated *volatility* (a measure of the degree of price variability) of the underlying market for the remaining life span of the option. This relationship results because greater volatility raises the probability of the intrinsic value increasing by any specified amount prior to expiration. In other words, the greater the volatility, the greater the probable price range of the market.

Although volatility is an extremely important factor in the determination of option premium values, it should be stressed that the future volatility of a market is never precisely known until after the fact. (In contrast, the time remaining until expiration and the relationship between the current market price and the strike price can be exactly specified at any juncture.) Thus, volatility must always be estimated on the basis of *historical volatility* data. The future volatility estimate implied by market prices (i.e., option premiums), which may be higher or lower than the historical volatility, is called the *implied volatility.*

# *Glossary*

**Advance/decline line.** The cumulative total of the daily difference between the number of New York Stock Exchange stocks advancing and the number declining. Divergences between the advance/decline line and the market averages, such as the Dow Jones Industrial Average (DJIA), can sometimes be viewed as a market signal. For example, if after a decline the DJIA rebounds to a new high but the advance/decline line fails to follow suit, such price action may be reflective of internal market weakness.

**Arbitrage.** The implementation of purchases in one market against equivalent sales in a closely related market based on the price relationship between the two being viewed as out of line.

**Arbitrageurs.** Traders who specialize in arbitrage. Arbitrageurs seek to make small profits from temporary distortions in the price relationships between related markets, as opposed to attempting to profit from correct projections of market direction.

**Averaging losers (averaging down).** Adding to a losing position after an adverse price move.

**Bear.** Someone who believes that prices will decline.

**Bear market.** A market characterized by declining prices.

**Boiler room operation.** An illegal or quasilegal phone sales operation in which high-pressure tactics are used to sell financial instruments or commodities at excessive prices or inflated commissions to unsophisticated investors. For example, contracts for precious metals (or options on precious metals) might be sold at prices far above levels prevailing at organized exchanges. In some cases, such operations are complete frauds, as the contracts sold are purely fictitious.

**Breakout.** A price movement beyond a previous high (or low) or outside the boundaries of a preceding price consolidation.

**Bull.** Someone who believes that prices will rise.

**Bull market.** A market characterized by rising prices.

**Call option.** A contract that gives the buyer the right—but not the obligation—to purchase the underlying financial instrument or commodity at a specified price for a given period of time.

**Chart.** A graph that depicts the price movement of a given market. The most common type of chart is the *daily bar chart,* which denotes each day's high, low, and close for a given market with a single bar.

**Chart analysis.** The study of price charts in an effort to find patterns that in the past preceded price advances or declines. The basic concept is that the development of similar patterns in a current market can signal a probable market move in the same direction. Practitioners of chart analysis are often referred to as *chartists* or *technicians.*

**Congestion.** See *Consolidation.*

**Consolidation.** A price pattern characterized by extended sideways movement. (Also known as *Congestion.*)

**Contract.** In futures markets, a standardized traded instrument that specifies the quantity and quality of a commodity (or financial asset) for delivery (or cash settlement) at a specified future date.

**Contrarian.** One who trades on contrary opinion (see next item).

**Contrary opinion.** The general theory that one can profit by doing the opposite of the majority of traders. The basic concept is that if a large majority of traders are bullish, it implies that most market participants who believe prices are going higher are already long, and hence the path of least resistance is down. An analogous line of reasoning would apply when most traders are bearish. Contrary opinion numbers are provided by various services that survey traders, market letters, or trading advisors.

**Cover.** To liquidate an existing position (i.e., sell if one is long; buy if one is short).

**Day trade.** A trade that is liquidated on the same day it is initiated.

**Discretionary trader.** In a general sense, a trader who has the power of attorney to execute trades for customer accounts without prior approval. However, the term is often used in a more specific sense to indicate a trader who makes decisions based on his own interpretation of the market, rather than in response to signals generated by a computerized system.

**Divergence.** The failure of a market or indicator to follow suit when a related market or indicator sets a new high or low. Some analysts look for divergences as signals of impending market tops and bottoms.

**Diversification.** Trading many different markets in an effort to reduce risk.

**Downtrend.** A general tendency for declining prices in a given market.

**Drawdown.** The equity reduction in an account. The *maximum drawdown* is the largest difference between a relative equity peak and any subsequent equity low. Low drawdowns are a desirable performance feature for a trader or a trading system.

**Earnings per share (EPS).** A company's total after-tax profits divided by the number of common shares outstanding.

**Elliott Wave analysis.** A method of market analysis based on the theories of Ralph Nelson Elliott. Although relatively complex, the basic theory is based on the concept that markets move in waves, forming a general pattern of five waves (or market legs) in the direction of the main trend, followed by three corrective waves in the opposite direction. One aspect of the theory is that each of these waves can be broken down into five or three smaller waves and is itself a segment of a still larger wave.

**Equity.** The total dollar value of an account.

**Fade.** To trade in the opposite direction of a market signal (or analyst). For example, a trader who goes short after prices penetrate the upside of a prior consolidation—a price development that most technically oriented traders would interpret as a signal to buy or stay long—can be said to be fading the price breakout.

**False breakout.** A short-lived price move that penetrates a prior high or low before succumbing to a pronounced price move in the opposite direction. For example, if the price of a stock that has traded between $18 and $20 for six months rises to $21 and then quickly falls below $18, the move to $21 can be termed a false breakout.

**Federal Reserve Board (Fed).** The governing arm of the Federal Reserve System, which seeks to regulate the economy through the implementation of monetary policy.

**Fibonacci retracements.** The concept that retracements of prior trends will often approximate 38.2 percent and 61.8 percent—numbers derived from the Fibonacci sequence (see next item).

**Fibonacci sequence.** A sequence of numbers that begins with 1,1 and progresses to infinity, with each number in the sequence equal to the sum of the preceding two numbers. Thus, the initial numbers in the sequence would be 1, 1, 2, 3, 5, 8, 13, 21, 34, 55, 89, etc. The ratio of consecutive numbers in the sequence converges to 0.618 as the numbers get larger. The ratio of alternate numbers in the sequence (for example, 21 and 55) converges to 0.382 as the numbers get larger. These two ratios—0.618 and 0.382—are commonly used to project retracements of prior price swings.

**Floor trader.** A member of the exchange who trades on the floor for personal profit.

**Frontrunning.** The unethical—and in some cases illegal—practice of a broker placing his own order in front of a customer order that he anticipates will move the market.

**Fundamental analysis.** The use of economic data to forecast prices. For example, fundamental analysis of a currency might focus on such items as relative inflation rates, relative interest rates, relative economic growth rates, and political factors.

**Futures.** See "Futures—Understanding the Basics."

**Gann analysis.** Market analysis based on a variety of technical concepts developed by William Gann, a famous stock and commodity trader during the first half of the twentieth century.

**Gap.** A price zone at which no trades occur. For example, if a market that has previously traded at a high of $20 opens at $22 on the following day and moves steadily higher, the price zone between $20 and $22 is referred to as a gap.

**Hedge.** A position (or the implementation of a position) used to offset inventory risk or risk related to an anticipated future purchase or sale. An example of a hedge trade is a corn farmer who, during the growing season, sells corn futures with a delivery date subsequent to his anticipated harvest. In this illustration, the sale of futures effectively locks in an approximate future sales price, thereby limiting risk exposure to subsequent price fluctuations.

**Hedger.** A market participant who implements a position to reduce price risk. The hedger's risk position is exactly opposite that of the speculator, who accepts risk in implementing positions to profit from anticipated price moves.

**Implied volatility.** The market's expectation of future price volatility as implied by prevailing option prices.

**Leverage.** The ability to control a dollar amount of a commodity or financial instrument greater than the amount of capital employed. The greater the leverage of the position, the greater the potential profit or loss.

**Limit position.** A maximum position size (i.e., number of contracts) that a speculator may hold. For many futures contracts, government regulations specify this limit.

**Limit price move.** For many futures contracts, the exchanges specify a maximum amount by which the price can change on a single day. A market that increases in price by this specified maximum is said to be *limit-up,* while a market that declines by the maximum is said to be *limit-down.* In cases in which free market forces would normally seek an equilibrium price outside the range of boundaries implied by the limit, the market will simply move to the limit and virtually cease to trade. For an advancing market, such a situation is referred to as *locked limit-up* or *limit-bid;* for a declining market, the analogous terms are *locked limit-down* or *limit-offered.*

**Liquidity.** The degree to which a given market is liquid.

**Liquid market.** A market in which there is a sufficiently large number of trades daily so that most reasonably sized buy and sell orders can be executed without significantly moving prices. In other words, a liquid market allows the trader relative ease of entry and exit.

**Local.** A synonym for *Floor trader,* typically used to connote an exchange member who trades for his or her own account.

**Long.** A position established with a buy order, which profits in a rising price market. The term is also used to refer to the person or entity holding such a position.

**Lot.** In futures markets, another name for contract.

**Mark to the market.** The valuation of open positions at prevailing settlement prices. In other words, if a position is marked to the market, there is no distinction between realized and unrealized losses (or gains).

**Mechanical system.** A trading system (usually computerized) that generates buy and sell signals. A mechanical system trader follows the signals of such a system without regard to personal market assessments.

**Money management.** The use of various methods of risk control in trading.

**Moving average.** A method of smoothing prices to more easily discern market trends. A *simple moving average* is the average price during the most recent fixed number of days. Crossovers (one series moving from below to above another, or vice versa) of price and a moving average—or of two different moving averages—are used as buy and sell signals in some simple trend-following systems.

**Naked option.** A short option position by a trader who does not own the underlying commodity or financial instrument.

**Open interest.** In futures markets, the total number of open long and short positions are always equal. This total (long or short) is called the open interest. By definition, when a contract month first begins trading, the open interest is zero. The open interest then builds to a peak and declines as positions are liquidated approaching its expiration date.

**Options.** See the Appendix.

**Outright position.** A net long or short position (as opposed to spreads and arbitrage trades, in which positions are counterbalanced by opposite positions in related instruments).

**Overbought/oversold indicator.** A technical indicator that attempts to define when prices have risen (declined) too far, too fast, and hence are vulnerable to a reaction in the opposite direction. The concept of overbought/oversold is also often used in association with contrary opinion to describe when a large majority of traders are bullish or bearish.

**P and L.** Shorthand for profit/loss.

**Pattern recognition.** A price-forecasting method that uses historical chart patterns to draw analogies to current situations.

**Pit.**   The area where a futures contract is traded on the exchange floor. Also sometimes called the *Ring.*

**Position limit.**   See *Limit position.*

**Price/earnings (P/E) ratio.**   The price of a stock divided by the company's annual earnings.

**Put/call ratio.**   The volume of put options divided by the volume of call options. A put/call ratio is one example of a contrary opinion or overbought/oversold measure. The basic premise is that a high ratio, which reflects more puts being purchased than calls, implies that too many traders are bearish and the ratio is hence considered bullish. Analogously, a low put/call ratio would be considered bearish.

**Put option.**   A contract that provides the buyer with the right—but not the obligation—to sell the underlying financial instrument or commodity at a specific price for a fixed period of time.

**Pyramiding.**   Using unrealized profits on an existing position as margin to increase the size of the position. By increasing the leverage in a trade, pyramiding increases the profit potential as well as the risk.

**Reaction.**   A price movement in the opposite direction of the predominant trend.

**Relative strength.**   In the stock market, a measure of a given stock's price strength relative to a broad index of stocks. The term can also be used in a more general sense to refer to an overbought/oversold type of indicator.

**Resistance.**   In technical analysis, a price area at which a rising market is expected to encounter increased selling pressure sufficient to stall or reverse the advance.

**Retracement.**   A price movement counter to a preceding trend. For example, in a rising market, a 60 percent retracement would indicate a price decline equal to 60 percent of the prior advance.

**Reversal day.**   A day on which the market reaches a new high (low) and then reverses direction, closing below (above) one or more immediately preceding daily closes. Reversal days are considered more significant ("key") if accompanied by high volume and a particularly wide price range.

**Ring.**   A synonym for *Pit.*

**Risk control.**   The use of trading rules to limit losses.

**Risk/reward ratio.** The ratio of the estimated potential loss of a trade to the estimated potential gain. Although, theoretically, the probability of a gain or loss should also be incorporated in any calculation, the ratio is frequently based naively on the magnitudes of the estimated gain or loss alone.

**Scalper.** A floor broker who trades for his own account and seeks to profit from very small price fluctuations. Typically, the scalper attempts to profit from the edge available in selling at the bid price and buying at the offered price—a trading approach that also provides liquidity to the market.

**Seat.** A membership on an exchange.

**Sentiment indicator.** A measure of the balance between bullish and bearish opinions. Sentiment indicators are used for contrary opinion trading. The put/call ratio is one example of a sentiment indicator.

**Short.** A position implemented with a sale, which profits from a declining price market. The term also refers to the trader or entity holding such a position.

**Slippage.** See *Skid.*

**Skid.** The difference between a theoretical execution price on a trade (for example, the midpoint of the opening range) and the actual fill price.

**Speculator.** A person who willingly accepts risk by buying and selling financial instruments or commodities in the hopes of profiting from anticipated price movements.

**Spike.** A price high (low) that is sharply above (below) the highs (lows) of the preceding and succeeding days. Spikes represent at least a temporary climax in buying (selling) pressure and may sometimes prove to be major tops or bottoms.

**Spread.** The combined purchase of a futures contract (or option) and sale of another contract (or option) in the same or a closely related market. Some examples of spreads include long June T-bonds/short September T-bonds, long Deutsche marks/short Swiss francs, and long IBM 130 call/short IBM 140 call.

**Stop order.** A buy order placed above the market (or sell order placed below the market) that becomes a market order when the specified price is reached. Although stop orders are sometimes used to implement new positions, they are most frequently used to limit losses. In this latter application, they are frequently called *stop-loss orders.*

**Support.** In technical analysis, a price area at which a falling market is expected to encounter increased buying support sufficient to stall or reverse the decline.

**System.** A specific set of rules used to generate buy and sell signals for a given market or set of markets.

**Systems trader.** A trader who utilizes systems to determine the timing of purchases and sales, rather than rely on a personal assessment of market conditions.

**Tape reader.** A trader who attempts to predict impending market direction by monitoring closely a stream of price quotes and accompanying volume figures.

**Technical analysis.** Price forecasting methods based on a study of price itself (and sometimes volume and open interest) as opposed to the underlying fundamental (i.e., economic) market factors. Technical analysis is often contrasted with fundamental analysis.

**Tick.** The minimum possible price movement, up or down, in a market.

**Trading range.** A sideways price band that encompasses all price activity during a specified period. A trading range implies a directionless market.

**Trend.** The tendency of prices to move in a given general direction (up or down).

**Trend-following system.** A system that generates buy and sell signals in the direction of a newly defined trend, based on the assumption that a trend, once established, will tend to continue.

**Uptick rule.** A stock market regulation that short sales can be implemented only at a price above the preceding transaction.

**Uptrend.** A general tendency for rising prices in a given market.

**Volatility.** A measure of price variability in a market. A volatile market is a market that is subject to wide price fluctuations.

**Volume.** The total number of shares or contracts traded during a given period.

**Whipsaw.** A price pattern characterized by repeated, abrupt reversals in trend. The term is often used to described losses resulting from the application of a trend-following system to a choppy or trendless market. In such markets, trend-following systems will tend to generate buy signals just before downside price reversals and sell signals just before upside price reversals.